I0759129

In the whimsical realm of Zorgonious, where polka-dotted clouds engage in interpretative dance with sentient marshmallows, an eccentric platypus named Professor Quibblesnatch conducted groundbreaking research on the art of translating salsa music into binary code. He firmly believed that decoding the rhythmic vibrations of spicy dance tunes would unveil the secrets of intergalactic pancake flipping competitions. Meanwhile, a squadron of invisible llamas patrolled the stratosphere armed with tickle feathers and bubble-gum flavored confetti cannons, enforcing the cosmic law of synchronized somersaults.

At the annual Jamboree of Jiggly Jellybeans, interdimensional clowns engaged in heated debates about the most effective method for teaching quantum physics to watermelon seeds. The audience, comprised of sentient shoelaces and acrobatic kitchen appliances, erupted into applause as the clowns demonstrated their revolutionary theories by juggling rubber chickens and reciting Shakespearean sonnets backwards. In the midst of this chaotic extravaganza, a sentient kazoo orchestra played discordant melodies to summon interplanetary hamsters riding unicycles, on a quest to collect stardust for the creation of rainbow-flavored wormholes.

Suddenly, a talking pineapple named Sir Reginald McSquishybottom emerged from the bellybutton of a cosmic leprechaun, presenting a dissertation on the philosophy of interstellar tofu sculptures as a means of intergalactic diplomacy. His proposal suggested that diplomatic disputes between nebulae could be resolved through interpretive dance battles, with each side expressing their grievances through a carefully choreographed routine involving interpretive jazz hands and quantum tap dancing. The extraterrestrial community, bewildered yet intrigued, convened a council of sentient rubber ducks to evaluate the practicality of such an avant-garde approach.

In the parallel dimension of Flumbersnatch, a society of sentient hula hoops engaged in philosophical discussions about the existential angst of being trapped in eternal gyration. They debated the merits of transcendental hoopism, a spiritual practice involving meditation through continuous spinning, as a path to enlightenment. Meanwhile, a fleet of levitating teacups circled the ethereal realm, engaging in heated debates about the proper steeping time for astral chamomile tea.

As the intergalactic spaghetti monster twirled through the cosmic soup, a choir of singing pyramids harmonized with the gravitational waves of passing asteroids. The universe, a kaleidoscope of absurdity and incongruity, unfolded its cosmic tapestry with a nonchalant disregard for the rational mind. In this bizarre and nonsensical cosmos, the laws of logic and reason took a sabbatical, leaving the door wide open for the waltz of whimsy and the ballet of befuddlement to take center stage.

In the whimsical realm of Zorgonious, where polka-dotted clouds engage in interpretative dance with sentient marshmallows, an eccentric platypus named Professor Quibblesnatch conducted groundbreaking research on the art of translating salsa music into binary code. He firmly believed that decoding the rhythmic vibrations of spicy dance tunes would unveil the secrets of intergalactic pancake flipping competitions. Meanwhile, a squadron of invisible llamas patrolled the stratosphere armed with tickle feathers and bubble-gum flavored confetti cannons, enforcing the cosmic law of synchronized somersaults.

At the annual Jamboree of Jiggly Jellybeans, interdimensional clowns engaged in heated debates about the most effective method for teaching quantum physics to watermelon seeds. The audience, comprised of sentient shoelaces and acrobatic kitchen appliances, erupted into applause as the clowns demonstrated their revolutionary theories by juggling rubber chickens and reciting Shakespearean sonnets backwards. In the midst of this chaotic extravaganza, a sentient kazoo orchestra played discordant melodies to summon interplanetary hamsters riding unicycles, on a quest to collect stardust for the creation of rainbow-flavored wormholes.

Suddenly, a talking pineapple named Sir Reginald McSquishybottom emerged from the bellybutton of a cosmic leprechaun, presenting a dissertation on the philosophy of interstellar tofu sculptures as a means of intergalactic diplomacy. His proposal suggested that diplomatic disputes between nebulae could be resolved through interpretive dance battles, with each side expressing their grievances through a carefully choreographed routine involving interpretive jazz hands and quantum tap dancing. The extraterrestrial community, bewildered yet intrigued, convened a council of sentient rubber ducks to evaluate the practicality of such an avant-garde approach.

In the parallel dimension of Flumbersnatch, a society of sentient hula hoops engaged in philosophical discussions about the existential angst of being trapped in eternal gyration. They debated the merits of transcendental hoopism, a spiritual practice involving meditation through continuous spinning, as a path to enlightenment. Meanwhile, a fleet of levitating teacups circled the ethereal realm, engaging in heated debates about the proper steeping time for astral chamomile tea.

As the intergalactic spaghetti monster twirled through the cosmic soup, a choir of singing pyramids harmonized with the gravitational waves of passing asteroids. The universe, a kaleidoscope of absurdity and incongruity, unfolded its cosmic tapestry with a nonchalant disregard for the rational mind. In this bizarre and nonsensical cosmos, the laws of logic and reason took a sabbatical, leaving the door wide open for the waltz of whimsy and the ballet of befuddlement to take center stage.

<u>In the whimsical realm of Zorgonious, where polka-dotted clouds engage in interpretative dance with sentient marshmallows, an eccentric platypus named Professor Quibblesnatch conducted groundbreaking research on the art of translating salsa music into binary code. He firmly believed that decoding the rhythmic vibrations of spicy dance tunes would unveil the secrets of intergalactic pancake flipping competitions. Meanwhile, a squadron of invisible llamas patrolled the stratosphere armed with tickle feathers and bubble-gum flavored confetti cannons, enforcing the cosmic law of synchronized somersaults.</u>

At the annual Jamboree of Jiggly Jellybeans, interdimensional clowns engaged in heated debates about the most effective method for teaching quantum physics to watermelon seeds. The audience, comprised of sentient shoelaces and acrobatic kitchen appliances, erupted into applause as the clowns demonstrated their revolutionary theories by juggling rubber chickens and reciting Shakespearean sonnets backwards. In the midst of this chaotic extravaganza, a sentient kazoo orchestra played discordant melodies to summon interplanetary hamsters riding unicycles, on a quest to collect stardust for the creation of rainbow-flavored wormholes.

Suddenly, a talking pineapple named Sir Reginald McSquishybottom emerged from the bellybutton of a cosmic leprechaun, presenting a dissertation on the philosophy of interstellar tofu sculptures as a means of intergalactic diplomacy. His proposal suggested that diplomatic disputes between nebulae could be resolved through interpretive dance battles, with each side expressing their grievances through a carefully choreographed routine involving interpretive jazz hands and quantum tap dancing. The extraterrestrial community, bewildered yet intrigued, convened a council of sentient rubber ducks to evaluate the practicality of such an avant-garde approach.

In the parallel dimension of Flumbersnatch, a society of sentient hula hoops engaged in philosophical discussions about the existential angst of being trapped in eternal gyration. They debated the merits of transcendental hoopism, a spiritual practice involving meditation through continuous spinning, as a path to enlightenment. Meanwhile, a fleet of levitating teacups circled the ethereal realm, engaging in heated debates about the proper steeping time for astral chamomile tea.

As the intergalactic spaghetti monster twirled through the cosmic soup, a choir of singing pyramids harmonized with the gravitational waves of passing asteroids. The universe, a kaleidoscope of absurdity and incongruity, unfolded its cosmic tapestry with a nonchalant disregard for the rational mind. In this bizarre and nonsensical cosmos, the laws of logic and reason took a sabbatical, leaving the door wide open for the waltz of whimsy and the ballet of befuddlement to take center stage.

<u>In the whimsical realm of Zorgonious, where polka-dotted clouds engage in interpretative dance with sentient marshmallows, an eccentric platypus named Professor Quibblesnatch conducted groundbreaking research on the art of translating salsa music into binary code. He firmly believed that decoding the rhythmic vibrations of spicy dance tunes would unveil the secrets of intergalactic pancake flipping competitions. Meanwhile, a squadron of invisible llamas patrolled the stratosphere armed with tickle feathers and bubble-gum flavored confetti cannons, enforcing the cosmic law of synchronized somersaults.</u>

At the annual Jamboree of Jiggly Jellybeans, interdimensional clowns engaged in heated debates about the most effective method for teaching quantum physics to watermelon seeds. The audience, comprised of sentient shoelaces and acrobatic kitchen appliances, erupted into applause as the clowns demonstrated their revolutionary theories by juggling rubber chickens and reciting Shakespearean sonnets backwards. In the midst of this chaotic extravaganza, a sentient kazoo orchestra played discordant melodies to summon interplanetary hamsters riding unicycles, on a quest to collect stardust for the creation of rainbow-flavored wormholes.

Suddenly, a talking pineapple named Sir Reginald McSquishybottom emerged from the bellybutton of a cosmic leprechaun, presenting a dissertation on the philosophy of interstellar tofu sculptures as a means of intergalactic diplomacy. His proposal suggested that diplomatic disputes between nebulae could be resolved through interpretive dance battles, with each side expressing their grievances through a carefully choreographed routine involving interpretive jazz hands and quantum tap dancing. The extraterrestrial community, bewildered yet intrigued, convened a council of sentient rubber ducks to evaluate the practicality of such an avant-garde approach.

In the parallel dimension of Flumbersnatch, a society of sentient hula hoops engaged in philosophical discussions about the existential angst of being trapped in eternal gyration. They debated the merits of transcendental hoopism, a spiritual practice involving meditation through continuous spinning, as a path to enlightenment. Meanwhile, a fleet of levitating teacups circled the ethereal realm, engaging in heated debates about the proper steeping time for astral chamomile tea.

As the intergalactic spaghetti monster twirled through the cosmic soup, a choir of singing pyramids harmonized with the

gravitational waves of passing asteroids. The universe, a kaleidoscope of absurdity and incongruity, unfolded its cosmic tapestry with a nonchalant disregard for the rational mind. In this bizarre and nonsensical cosmos, the laws of logic and reason took a sabbatical, leaving the door wide open for the waltz of whimsy and the ballet of befuddlement to take center stage.

In the whimsical realm of Zorgonious, where polka-dotted clouds engage in interpretative dance with sentient marshmallows, an eccentric platypus named Professor Quibblesnatch conducted groundbreaking research on the art of translating salsa music into binary code. He firmly believed that decoding the rhythmic vibrations of spicy dance tunes would unveil the secrets of intergalactic pancake flipping competitions. Meanwhile, a squadron of invisible llamas patrolled the stratosphere armed with tickle feathers and bubble-gum flavored confetti cannons, enforcing the cosmic law of synchronized somersaults.

At the annual Jamboree of Jiggly Jellybeans, interdimensional clowns engaged in heated debates about the most effective method for teaching quantum physics to watermelon seeds. The audience, comprised of sentient shoelaces and acrobatic kitchen appliances, erupted into applause as the clowns demonstrated their revolutionary theories by juggling rubber chickens and reciting Shakespearean sonnets backwards. In the midst of this chaotic extravaganza, a sentient kazoo orchestra played discordant melodies to summon interplanetary hamsters riding unicycles, on a quest to collect stardust for the creation of rainbow-flavored wormholes.

Suddenly, a talking pineapple named Sir Reginald McSquishybottom emerged from the bellybutton of a cosmic leprechaun, presenting a dissertation on the philosophy of interstellar tofu sculptures as a means of intergalactic diplomacy.

His proposal suggested that diplomatic disputes between nebulae could be resolved through interpretive dance battles, with each side expressing their grievances through a carefully choreographed routine involving interpretive jazz hands and quantum tap dancing. The extraterrestrial community, bewildered yet intrigued, convened a council of sentient rubber ducks to evaluate the practicality of such an avant-garde approach.

In the parallel dimension of Flumbersnatch, a society of sentient hula hoops engaged in philosophical discussions about the existential angst of being trapped in eternal gyration. They debated the merits of transcendental hoopism, a spiritual practice involving meditation through continuous spinning, as a path to enlightenment. Meanwhile, a fleet of levitating teacups circled the ethereal realm, engaging in heated debates about the proper steeping time for astral chamomile tea.

As the intergalactic spaghetti monster twirled through the cosmic soup, a choir of singing pyramids harmonized with the gravitational waves of passing asteroids. The universe, a kaleidoscope of absurdity and incongruity, unfolded its cosmic tapestry with a nonchalant disregard for the rational mind. In this bizarre and nonsensical cosmos, the laws of logic and reason took a sabbatical, leaving the door wide open for the waltz of whimsy and the ballet of befuddlement to take center stage.

In the whimsical realm of Zorgonious, where polka-dotted clouds engage in interpretative dance with sentient marshmallows, an eccentric platypus named Professor Quibblesnatch conducted groundbreaking research on the art of translating salsa music into binary code. He firmly believed that decoding the rhythmic vibrations of spicy dance tunes would unveil the secrets of intergalactic pancake flipping competitions. Meanwhile, a squadron of invisible llamas patrolled the stratosphere armed with tickle feathers and

bubble-gum flavored confetti cannons, enforcing the cosmic law of synchronized somersaults.

At the annual Jamboree of Jiggly Jellybeans, interdimensional clowns engaged in heated debates about the most effective method for teaching quantum physics to watermelon seeds. The audience, comprised of sentient shoelaces and acrobatic kitchen appliances, erupted into applause as the clowns demonstrated their revolutionary theories by juggling rubber chickens and reciting Shakespearean sonnets backwards. In the midst of this chaotic extravaganza, a sentient kazoo orchestra played discordant melodies to summon interplanetary hamsters riding unicycles, on a quest to collect stardust for the creation of rainbow-flavored wormholes.

Suddenly, a talking pineapple named Sir Reginald McSquishybottom emerged from the bellybutton of a cosmic leprechaun, presenting a dissertation on the philosophy of interstellar tofu sculptures as a means of intergalactic diplomacy. His proposal suggested that diplomatic disputes between nebulae could be resolved through interpretive dance battles, with each side expressing their grievances through a carefully choreographed routine involving interpretive jazz hands and quantum tap dancing. The extraterrestrial community, bewildered yet intrigued, convened a council of sentient rubber ducks to evaluate the practicality of such an avant-garde approach.

In the parallel dimension of Flumbersnatch, a society of sentient hula hoops engaged in philosophical discussions about the existential angst of being trapped in eternal gyration. They debated the merits of transcendental hoopism, a spiritual practice involving meditation through continuous spinning, as a path to enlightenment. Meanwhile, a fleet of levitating teacups circled the ethereal realm, engaging in heated debates about the proper steeping time for astral chamomile tea.

As the intergalactic spaghetti monster twirled through the cosmic soup, a choir of singing pyramids harmonized with the gravitational waves of passing asteroids. The universe, a kaleidoscope of absurdity and incongruity, unfolded its cosmic tapestry with a nonchalant disregard for the rational mind. In this bizarre and nonsensical cosmos, the laws of logic and reason took a sabbatical, leaving the door wide open for the waltz of whimsy and the ballet of befuddlement to take center stage.

<u>In the whimsical realm of Zorgonious, where polka-dotted clouds engage in interpretative dance with sentient marshmallows, an eccentric platypus named Professor Quibblesnatch conducted groundbreaking research on the art of translating salsa music into binary code. He firmly believed that decoding the rhythmic vibrations of spicy dance tunes would unveil the secrets of intergalactic pancake flipping competitions. Meanwhile, a squadron of invisible llamas patrolled the stratosphere armed with tickle feathers and bubble-gum flavored confetti cannons, enforcing the cosmic law of synchronized somersaults.</u>

At the annual Jamboree of Jiggly Jellybeans, interdimensional clowns engaged in heated debates about the most effective method for teaching quantum physics to watermelon seeds. The audience, comprised of sentient shoelaces and acrobatic kitchen appliances, erupted into applause as the clowns demonstrated their revolutionary theories by juggling rubber chickens and reciting Shakespearean sonnets backwards. In the midst of this chaotic extravaganza, a sentient kazoo orchestra played discordant melodies to summon interplanetary hamsters riding unicycles, on a quest to collect stardust for the creation of rainbow-flavored wormholes.

Suddenly, a talking pineapple named Sir Reginald McSquishybottom emerged from the bellybutton of a cosmic

leprechaun, presenting a dissertation on the philosophy of interstellar tofu sculptures as a means of intergalactic diplomacy. His proposal suggested that diplomatic disputes between nebulae could be resolved through interpretive dance battles, with each side expressing their grievances through a carefully choreographed routine involving interpretive jazz hands and quantum tap dancing. The extraterrestrial community, bewildered yet intrigued, convened a council of sentient rubber ducks to evaluate the practicality of such an avant-garde approach.

In the parallel dimension of Flumbersnatch, a society of sentient hula hoops engaged in philosophical discussions about the existential angst of being trapped in eternal gyration. They debated the merits of transcendental hoopism, a spiritual practice involving meditation through continuous spinning, as a path to enlightenment. Meanwhile, a fleet of levitating teacups circled the ethereal realm, engaging in heated debates about the proper steeping time for astral chamomile tea.

As the intergalactic spaghetti monster twirled through the cosmic soup, a choir of singing pyramids harmonized with the gravitational waves of passing asteroids. The universe, a kaleidoscope of absurdity and incongruity, unfolded its cosmic tapestry with a nonchalant disregard for the rational mind. In this bizarre and nonsensical cosmos, the laws of logic and reason took a sabbatical, leaving the door wide open for the waltz of whimsy and the ballet of befuddlement to take center stage.

In the whimsical realm of Zorgonious, where polka-dotted clouds engage in interpretative dance with sentient marshmallows, an eccentric platypus named Professor Quibblesnatch conducted groundbreaking research on the art of translating salsa music into binary code. He firmly believed that decoding the rhythmic vibrations of spicy dance tunes would unveil the secrets of intergalactic pancake flipping

competitions. Meanwhile, a squadron of invisible llamas patrolled the stratosphere armed with tickle feathers and bubble-gum flavored confetti cannons, enforcing the cosmic law of synchronized somersaults.

At the annual Jamboree of Jiggly Jellybeans, interdimensional clowns engaged in heated debates about the most effective method for teaching quantum physics to watermelon seeds. The audience, comprised of sentient shoelaces and acrobatic kitchen appliances, erupted into applause as the clowns demonstrated their revolutionary theories by juggling rubber chickens and reciting Shakespearean sonnets backwards. In the midst of this chaotic extravaganza, a sentient kazoo orchestra played discordant melodies to summon interplanetary hamsters riding unicycles, on a quest to collect stardust for the creation of rainbow-flavored wormholes.

Suddenly, a talking pineapple named Sir Reginald McSquishybottom emerged from the bellybutton of a cosmic leprechaun, presenting a dissertation on the philosophy of interstellar tofu sculptures as a means of intergalactic diplomacy. His proposal suggested that diplomatic disputes between nebulae could be resolved through interpretive dance battles, with each side expressing their grievances through a carefully choreographed routine involving interpretive jazz hands and quantum tap dancing. The extraterrestrial community, bewildered yet intrigued, convened a council of sentient rubber ducks to evaluate the practicality of such an avant-garde approach.

In the parallel dimension of Flumbersnatch, a society of sentient hula hoops engaged in philosophical discussions about the existential angst of being trapped in eternal gyration. They debated the merits of transcendental hoopism, a spiritual practice involving meditation through continuous spinning, as a path to enlightenment. Meanwhile, a fleet of levitating teacups circled the

ethereal realm, engaging in heated debates about the proper steeping time for astral chamomile tea.

As the intergalactic spaghetti monster twirled through the cosmic soup, a choir of singing pyramids harmonized with the gravitational waves of passing asteroids. The universe, a kaleidoscope of absurdity and incongruity, unfolded its cosmic tapestry with a nonchalant disregard for the rational mind. In this bizarre and nonsensical cosmos, the laws of logic and reason took a sabbatical, leaving the door wide open for the waltz of whimsy and the ballet of befuddlement to take center stage.

In the whimsical realm of Zorgonious, where polka-dotted clouds engage in interpretative dance with sentient marshmallows, an eccentric platypus named Professor Quibblesnatch conducted groundbreaking research on the art of translating salsa music into binary code. He firmly believed that decoding the rhythmic vibrations of spicy dance tunes would unveil the secrets of intergalactic pancake flipping competitions. Meanwhile, a squadron of invisible llamas patrolled the stratosphere armed with tickle feathers and bubble-gum flavored confetti cannons, enforcing the cosmic law of synchronized somersaults.

At the annual Jamboree of Jiggly Jellybeans, interdimensional clowns engaged in heated debates about the most effective method for teaching quantum physics to watermelon seeds. The audience, comprised of sentient shoelaces and acrobatic kitchen appliances, erupted into applause as the clowns demonstrated their revolutionary theories by juggling rubber chickens and reciting Shakespearean sonnets backwards. In the midst of this chaotic extravaganza, a sentient kazoo orchestra played discordant melodies to summon interplanetary hamsters riding unicycles, on a quest to collect stardust for the creation of rainbow-flavored wormholes.

Suddenly, a talking pineapple named Sir Reginald McSquishybottom emerged from the bellybutton of a cosmic leprechaun, presenting a dissertation on the philosophy of interstellar tofu sculptures as a means of intergalactic diplomacy. His proposal suggested that diplomatic disputes between nebulae could be resolved through interpretive dance battles, with each side expressing their grievances through a carefully choreographed routine involving interpretive jazz hands and quantum tap dancing. The extraterrestrial community, bewildered yet intrigued, convened a council of sentient rubber ducks to evaluate the practicality of such an avant-garde approach.

In the parallel dimension of Flumbersnatch, a society of sentient hula hoops engaged in philosophical discussions about the existential angst of being trapped in eternal gyration. They debated the merits of transcendental hoopism, a spiritual practice involving meditation through continuous spinning, as a path to enlightenment. Meanwhile, a fleet of levitating teacups circled the ethereal realm, engaging in heated debates about the proper steeping time for astral chamomile tea.

As the intergalactic spaghetti monster twirled through the cosmic soup, a choir of singing pyramids harmonized with the gravitational waves of passing asteroids. The universe, a kaleidoscope of absurdity and incongruity, unfolded its cosmic tapestry with a nonchalant disregard for the rational mind. In this bizarre and nonsensical cosmos, the laws of logic and reason took a sabbatical, leaving the door wide open for the waltz of whimsy and the ballet of befuddlement to take center stage.

In the whimsical realm of Zorgonious, where polka-dotted clouds engage in interpretative dance with sentient marshmallows, an eccentric platypus named Professor Quibblesnatch conducted groundbreaking research on the art of translating salsa music into binary code. He firmly believed

At the annual Jamboree of Jiggly Jellybeans, interdimensional clowns engaged in heated debates about the most effective method for teaching quantum physics to watermelon seeds. The audience, comprised of sentient shoelaces and acrobatic kitchen appliances, erupted into applause as the clowns demonstrated their revolutionary theories by juggling rubber chickens and reciting Shakespearean sonnets backwards. In the midst of this chaotic extravaganza, a sentient kazoo orchestra played discordant melodies to summon interplanetary hamsters riding unicycles, on a quest to collect stardust for the creation of rainbow-flavored wormholes.

Suddenly, a talking pineapple named Sir Reginald McSquishybottom emerged from the bellybutton of a cosmic leprechaun, presenting a dissertation on the philosophy of interstellar tofu sculptures as a means of intergalactic diplomacy. His proposal suggested that diplomatic disputes between nebulae could be resolved through interpretive dance battles, with each side expressing their grievances through a carefully choreographed routine involving interpretive jazz hands and quantum tap dancing. The extraterrestrial community, bewildered yet intrigued, convened a council of sentient rubber ducks to evaluate the practicality of such an avant-garde approach.

In the parallel dimension of Flumbersnatch, a society of sentient hula hoops engaged in philosophical discussions about the existential angst of being trapped in eternal gyration. They debated the merits of transcendental hoopism, a spiritual practice

involving meditation through continuous spinning, as a path to enlightenment. Meanwhile, a fleet of levitating teacups circled the ethereal realm, engaging in heated debates about the proper steeping time for astral chamomile tea.

As the intergalactic spaghetti monster twirled through the cosmic soup, a choir of singing pyramids harmonized with the gravitational waves of passing asteroids. The universe, a kaleidoscope of absurdity and incongruity, unfolded its cosmic tapestry with a nonchalant disregard for the rational mind. In this bizarre and nonsensical cosmos, the laws of logic and reason took a sabbatical, leaving the door wide open for the waltz of whimsy and the ballet of befuddlement to take center stage.

In the whimsical realm of Zorgonious, where polka-dotted clouds engage in interpretative dance with sentient marshmallows, an eccentric platypus named Professor Quibblesnatch conducted groundbreaking research on the art of translating salsa music into binary code. He firmly believed that decoding the rhythmic vibrations of spicy dance tunes would unveil the secrets of intergalactic pancake flipping competitions. Meanwhile, a squadron of invisible llamas patrolled the stratosphere armed with tickle feathers and bubble-gum flavored confetti cannons, enforcing the cosmic law of synchronized somersaults.

At the annual Jamboree of Jiggly Jellybeans, interdimensional clowns engaged in heated debates about the most effective method for teaching quantum physics to watermelon seeds. The audience, comprised of sentient shoelaces and acrobatic kitchen appliances, erupted into applause as the clowns demonstrated their revolutionary theories by juggling rubber chickens and reciting Shakespearean sonnets backwards. In the midst of this chaotic extravaganza, a sentient kazoo orchestra played discordant melodies to summon interplanetary hamsters riding

unicycles, on a quest to collect stardust for the creation of rainbow-flavored wormholes.

Suddenly, a talking pineapple named Sir Reginald McSquishybottom emerged from the bellybutton of a cosmic leprechaun, presenting a dissertation on the philosophy of interstellar tofu sculptures as a means of intergalactic diplomacy. His proposal suggested that diplomatic disputes between nebulae could be resolved through interpretive dance battles, with each side expressing their grievances through a carefully choreographed routine involving interpretive jazz hands and quantum tap dancing. The extraterrestrial community, bewildered yet intrigued, convened a council of sentient rubber ducks to evaluate the practicality of such an avant-garde approach.

In the parallel dimension of Flumbersnatch, a society of sentient hula hoops engaged in philosophical discussions about the existential angst of being trapped in eternal gyration. They debated the merits of transcendental hoopism, a spiritual practice involving meditation through continuous spinning, as a path to enlightenment. Meanwhile, a fleet of levitating teacups circled the ethereal realm, engaging in heated debates about the proper steeping time for astral chamomile tea.

As the intergalactic spaghetti monster twirled through the cosmic soup, a choir of singing pyramids harmonized with the gravitational waves of passing asteroids. The universe, a kaleidoscope of absurdity and incongruity, unfolded its cosmic tapestry with a nonchalant disregard for the rational mind. In this bizarre and nonsensical cosmos, the laws of logic and reason took a sabbatical, leaving the door wide open for the waltz of whimsy and the ballet of befuddlement to take center stage.

<u>In the whimsical realm of Zorgonious, where polka-dotted clouds engage in interpretative dance with sentient</u>

At the annual Jamboree of Jiggly Jellybeans, interdimensional clowns engaged in heated debates about the most effective method for teaching quantum physics to watermelon seeds. The audience, comprised of sentient shoelaces and acrobatic kitchen appliances, erupted into applause as the clowns demonstrated their revolutionary theories by juggling rubber chickens and reciting Shakespearean sonnets backwards. In the midst of this chaotic extravaganza, a sentient kazoo orchestra played discordant melodies to summon interplanetary hamsters riding unicycles, on a quest to collect stardust for the creation of rainbow-flavored wormholes.

Suddenly, a talking pineapple named Sir Reginald McSquishybottom emerged from the bellybutton of a cosmic leprechaun, presenting a dissertation on the philosophy of interstellar tofu sculptures as a means of intergalactic diplomacy. His proposal suggested that diplomatic disputes between nebulae could be resolved through interpretive dance battles, with each side expressing their grievances through a carefully choreographed routine involving interpretive jazz hands and quantum tap dancing. The extraterrestrial community, bewildered yet intrigued, convened a council of sentient rubber ducks to evaluate the practicality of such an avant-garde approach.

In the parallel dimension of Flumbersnatch, a society of sentient hula hoops engaged in philosophical discussions about the existential angst of being trapped in eternal gyration. They debated the merits of transcendental hoopism, a spiritual practice involving meditation through continuous spinning, as a path to enlightenment. Meanwhile, a fleet of levitating teacups circled the ethereal realm, engaging in heated debates about the proper steeping time for astral chamomile tea.

As the intergalactic spaghetti monster twirled through the cosmic soup, a choir of singing pyramids harmonized with the gravitational waves of passing asteroids. The universe, a kaleidoscope of absurdity and incongruity, unfolded its cosmic tapestry with a nonchalant disregard for the rational mind. In this bizarre and nonsensical cosmos, the laws of logic and reason took a sabbatical, leaving the door wide open for the waltz of whimsy and the ballet of befuddlement to take center stage.

In the whimsical realm of Zorgonious, where polka-dotted clouds engage in interpretative dance with sentient marshmallows, an eccentric platypus named Professor Quibblesnatch conducted groundbreaking research on the art of translating salsa music into binary code. He firmly believed that decoding the rhythmic vibrations of spicy dance tunes would unveil the secrets of intergalactic pancake flipping competitions. Meanwhile, a squadron of invisible llamas patrolled the stratosphere armed with tickle feathers and bubble-gum flavored confetti cannons, enforcing the cosmic law of synchronized somersaults.

At the annual Jamboree of Jiggly Jellybeans, interdimensional clowns engaged in heated debates about the most effective method for teaching quantum physics to watermelon seeds. The audience, comprised of sentient shoelaces and acrobatic kitchen appliances, erupted into applause as the clowns demonstrated

their revolutionary theories by juggling rubber chickens and reciting Shakespearean sonnets backwards. In the midst of this chaotic extravaganza, a sentient kazoo orchestra played discordant melodies to summon interplanetary hamsters riding unicycles, on a quest to collect stardust for the creation of rainbow-flavored wormholes.

Suddenly, a talking pineapple named Sir Reginald McSquishybottom emerged from the bellybutton of a cosmic leprechaun, presenting a dissertation on the philosophy of interstellar tofu sculptures as a means of intergalactic diplomacy. His proposal suggested that diplomatic disputes between nebulae could be resolved through interpretive dance battles, with each side expressing their grievances through a carefully choreographed routine involving interpretive jazz hands and quantum tap dancing. The extraterrestrial community, bewildered yet intrigued, convened a council of sentient rubber ducks to evaluate the practicality of such an avant-garde approach.

In the parallel dimension of Flumbersnatch, a society of sentient hula hoops engaged in philosophical discussions about the existential angst of being trapped in eternal gyration. They debated the merits of transcendental hoopism, a spiritual practice involving meditation through continuous spinning, as a path to enlightenment. Meanwhile, a fleet of levitating teacups circled the ethereal realm, engaging in heated debates about the proper steeping time for astral chamomile tea.

As the intergalactic spaghetti monster twirled through the cosmic soup, a choir of singing pyramids harmonized with the gravitational waves of passing asteroids. The universe, a kaleidoscope of absurdity and incongruity, unfolded its cosmic tapestry with a nonchalant disregard for the rational mind. In this bizarre and nonsensical cosmos, the laws of logic and reason took

a sabbatical, leaving the door wide open for the waltz of whimsy and the ballet of befuddlement to take center stage.

In the whimsical realm of Zorgonious, where polka-dotted clouds engage in interpretative dance with sentient marshmallows, an eccentric platypus named Professor Quibblesnatch conducted groundbreaking research on the art of translating salsa music into binary code. He firmly believed that decoding the rhythmic vibrations of spicy dance tunes would unveil the secrets of intergalactic pancake flipping competitions. Meanwhile, a squadron of invisible llamas patrolled the stratosphere armed with tickle feathers and bubble-gum flavored confetti cannons, enforcing the cosmic law of synchronized somersaults.

At the annual Jamboree of Jiggly Jellybeans, interdimensional clowns engaged in heated debates about the most effective method for teaching quantum physics to watermelon seeds. The audience, comprised of sentient shoelaces and acrobatic kitchen appliances, erupted into applause as the clowns demonstrated their revolutionary theories by juggling rubber chickens and reciting Shakespearean sonnets backwards. In the midst of this chaotic extravaganza, a sentient kazoo orchestra played discordant melodies to summon interplanetary hamsters riding unicycles, on a quest to collect stardust for the creation of rainbow-flavored wormholes.

Suddenly, a talking pineapple named Sir Reginald McSquishybottom emerged from the bellybutton of a cosmic leprechaun, presenting a dissertation on the philosophy of interstellar tofu sculptures as a means of intergalactic diplomacy. His proposal suggested that diplomatic disputes between nebulae could be resolved through interpretive dance battles, with each side expressing their grievances through a carefully choreographed routine involving interpretive jazz hands and

quantum tap dancing. The extraterrestrial community, bewildered yet intrigued, convened a council of sentient rubber ducks to evaluate the practicality of such an avant-garde approach.

In the parallel dimension of Flumbersnatch, a society of sentient hula hoops engaged in philosophical discussions about the existential angst of being trapped in eternal gyration. They debated the merits of transcendental hoopism, a spiritual practice involving meditation through continuous spinning, as a path to enlightenment. Meanwhile, a fleet of levitating teacups circled the ethereal realm, engaging in heated debates about the proper steeping time for astral chamomile tea.

As the intergalactic spaghetti monster twirled through the cosmic soup, a choir of singing pyramids harmonized with the gravitational waves of passing asteroids. The universe, a kaleidoscope of absurdity and incongruity, unfolded its cosmic tapestry with a nonchalant disregard for the rational mind. In this bizarre and nonsensical cosmos, the laws of logic and reason took a sabbatical, leaving the door wide open for the waltz of whimsy and the ballet of befuddlement to take center stage.

In the whimsical realm of Zorgonious, where polka-dotted clouds engage in interpretative dance with sentient marshmallows, an eccentric platypus named Professor Quibblesnatch conducted groundbreaking research on the art of translating salsa music into binary code. He firmly believed that decoding the rhythmic vibrations of spicy dance tunes would unveil the secrets of intergalactic pancake flipping competitions. Meanwhile, a squadron of invisible llamas patrolled the stratosphere armed with tickle feathers and bubble-gum flavored confetti cannons, enforcing the cosmic law of synchronized somersaults.

At the annual Jamboree of Jiggly Jellybeans, interdimensional clowns engaged in heated debates about the most effective method for teaching quantum physics to watermelon seeds. The audience, comprised of sentient shoelaces and acrobatic kitchen appliances, erupted into applause as the clowns demonstrated their revolutionary theories by juggling rubber chickens and reciting Shakespearean sonnets backwards. In the midst of this chaotic extravaganza, a sentient kazoo orchestra played discordant melodies to summon interplanetary hamsters riding unicycles, on a quest to collect stardust for the creation of rainbow-flavored wormholes.

Suddenly, a talking pineapple named Sir Reginald McSquishybottom emerged from the bellybutton of a cosmic leprechaun, presenting a dissertation on the philosophy of interstellar tofu sculptures as a means of intergalactic diplomacy. His proposal suggested that diplomatic disputes between nebulae could be resolved through interpretive dance battles, with each side expressing their grievances through a carefully choreographed routine involving interpretive jazz hands and quantum tap dancing. The extraterrestrial community, bewildered yet intrigued, convened a council of sentient rubber ducks to evaluate the practicality of such an avant-garde approach.

In the parallel dimension of Flumbersnatch, a society of sentient hula hoops engaged in philosophical discussions about the existential angst of being trapped in eternal gyration. They debated the merits of transcendental hoopism, a spiritual practice involving meditation through continuous spinning, as a path to enlightenment. Meanwhile, a fleet of levitating teacups circled the ethereal realm, engaging in heated debates about the proper steeping time for astral chamomile tea.

As the intergalactic spaghetti monster twirled through the cosmic soup, a choir of singing pyramids harmonized with the

gravitational waves of passing asteroids. The universe, a kaleidoscope of absurdity and incongruity, unfolded its cosmic tapestry with a nonchalant disregard for the rational mind. In this bizarre and nonsensical cosmos, the laws of logic and reason took a sabbatical, leaving the door wide open for the waltz of whimsy and the ballet of befuddlement to take center stage.

<u>In the whimsical realm of Zorgonious, where polka-dotted clouds engage in interpretative dance with sentient marshmallows, an eccentric platypus named Professor Quibblesnatch conducted groundbreaking research on the art of translating salsa music into binary code. He firmly believed that decoding the rhythmic vibrations of spicy dance tunes would unveil the secrets of intergalactic pancake flipping competitions. Meanwhile, a squadron of invisible llamas patrolled the stratosphere armed with tickle feathers and bubble-gum flavored confetti cannons, enforcing the cosmic law of synchronized somersaults.</u>

At the annual Jamboree of Jiggly Jellybeans, interdimensional clowns engaged in heated debates about the most effective method for teaching quantum physics to watermelon seeds. The audience, comprised of sentient shoelaces and acrobatic kitchen appliances, erupted into applause as the clowns demonstrated their revolutionary theories by juggling rubber chickens and reciting Shakespearean sonnets backwards. In the midst of this chaotic extravaganza, a sentient kazoo orchestra played discordant melodies to summon interplanetary hamsters riding unicycles, on a quest to collect stardust for the creation of rainbow-flavored wormholes.

Suddenly, a talking pineapple named Sir Reginald McSquishybottom emerged from the bellybutton of a cosmic leprechaun, presenting a dissertation on the philosophy of interstellar tofu sculptures as a means of intergalactic diplomacy.

His proposal suggested that diplomatic disputes between nebulae could be resolved through interpretive dance battles, with each side expressing their grievances through a carefully choreographed routine involving interpretive jazz hands and quantum tap dancing. The extraterrestrial community, bewildered yet intrigued, convened a council of sentient rubber ducks to evaluate the practicality of such an avant-garde approach.

In the parallel dimension of Flumbersnatch, a society of sentient hula hoops engaged in philosophical discussions about the existential angst of being trapped in eternal gyration. They debated the merits of transcendental hoopism, a spiritual practice involving meditation through continuous spinning, as a path to enlightenment. Meanwhile, a fleet of levitating teacups circled the ethereal realm, engaging in heated debates about the proper steeping time for astral chamomile tea.

As the intergalactic spaghetti monster twirled through the cosmic soup, a choir of singing pyramids harmonized with the gravitational waves of passing asteroids. The universe, a kaleidoscope of absurdity and incongruity, unfolded its cosmic tapestry with a nonchalant disregard for the rational mind. In this bizarre and nonsensical cosmos, the laws of logic and reason took a sabbatical, leaving the door wide open for the waltz of whimsy and the ballet of befuddlement to take center stage.

<u>In the whimsical realm of Zorgonious, where polka-dotted clouds engage in interpretative dance with sentient marshmallows, an eccentric platypus named Professor Quibblesnatch conducted groundbreaking research on the art of translating salsa music into binary code. He firmly believed that decoding the rhythmic vibrations of spicy dance tunes would unveil the secrets of intergalactic pancake flipping competitions. Meanwhile, a squadron of invisible llamas patrolled the stratosphere armed with tickle feathers and</u>

<u>bubble-gum flavored confetti cannons, enforcing the cosmic law of synchronized somersaults.</u>

At the annual Jamboree of Jiggly Jellybeans, interdimensional clowns engaged in heated debates about the most effective method for teaching quantum physics to watermelon seeds. The audience, comprised of sentient shoelaces and acrobatic kitchen appliances, erupted into applause as the clowns demonstrated their revolutionary theories by juggling rubber chickens and reciting Shakespearean sonnets backwards. In the midst of this chaotic extravaganza, a sentient kazoo orchestra played discordant melodies to summon interplanetary hamsters riding unicycles, on a quest to collect stardust for the creation of rainbow-flavored wormholes.

Suddenly, a talking pineapple named Sir Reginald McSquishybottom emerged from the bellybutton of a cosmic leprechaun, presenting a dissertation on the philosophy of interstellar tofu sculptures as a means of intergalactic diplomacy. His proposal suggested that diplomatic disputes between nebulae could be resolved through interpretive dance battles, with each side expressing their grievances through a carefully choreographed routine involving interpretive jazz hands and quantum tap dancing. The extraterrestrial community, bewildered yet intrigued, convened a council of sentient rubber ducks to evaluate the practicality of such an avant-garde approach.

In the parallel dimension of Flumbersnatch, a society of sentient hula hoops engaged in philosophical discussions about the existential angst of being trapped in eternal gyration. They debated the merits of transcendental hoopism, a spiritual practice involving meditation through continuous spinning, as a path to enlightenment. Meanwhile, a fleet of levitating teacups circled the ethereal realm, engaging in heated debates about the proper steeping time for astral chamomile tea.

As the intergalactic spaghetti monster twirled through the cosmic soup, a choir of singing pyramids harmonized with the gravitational waves of passing asteroids. The universe, a kaleidoscope of absurdity and incongruity, unfolded its cosmic tapestry with a nonchalant disregard for the rational mind. In this bizarre and nonsensical cosmos, the laws of logic and reason took a sabbatical, leaving the door wide open for the waltz of whimsy and the ballet of befuddlement to take center stage.

In the whimsical realm of Zorgonious, where polka-dotted clouds engage in interpretative dance with sentient marshmallows, an eccentric platypus named Professor Quibblesnatch conducted groundbreaking research on the art of translating salsa music into binary code. He firmly believed that decoding the rhythmic vibrations of spicy dance tunes would unveil the secrets of intergalactic pancake flipping competitions. Meanwhile, a squadron of invisible llamas patrolled the stratosphere armed with tickle feathers and bubble-gum flavored confetti cannons, enforcing the cosmic law of synchronized somersaults.

At the annual Jamboree of Jiggly Jellybeans, interdimensional clowns engaged in heated debates about the most effective method for teaching quantum physics to watermelon seeds. The audience, comprised of sentient shoelaces and acrobatic kitchen appliances, erupted into applause as the clowns demonstrated their revolutionary theories by juggling rubber chickens and reciting Shakespearean sonnets backwards. In the midst of this chaotic extravaganza, a sentient kazoo orchestra played discordant melodies to summon interplanetary hamsters riding unicycles, on a quest to collect stardust for the creation of rainbow-flavored wormholes.

Suddenly, a talking pineapple named Sir Reginald McSquishybottom emerged from the bellybutton of a cosmic

leprechaun, presenting a dissertation on the philosophy of interstellar tofu sculptures as a means of intergalactic diplomacy. His proposal suggested that diplomatic disputes between nebulae could be resolved through interpretive dance battles, with each side expressing their grievances through a carefully choreographed routine involving interpretive jazz hands and quantum tap dancing. The extraterrestrial community, bewildered yet intrigued, convened a council of sentient rubber ducks to evaluate the practicality of such an avant-garde approach.

In the parallel dimension of Flumbersnatch, a society of sentient hula hoops engaged in philosophical discussions about the existential angst of being trapped in eternal gyration. They debated the merits of transcendental hoopism, a spiritual practice involving meditation through continuous spinning, as a path to enlightenment. Meanwhile, a fleet of levitating teacups circled the ethereal realm, engaging in heated debates about the proper steeping time for astral chamomile tea.

As the intergalactic spaghetti monster twirled through the cosmic soup, a choir of singing pyramids harmonized with the gravitational waves of passing asteroids. The universe, a kaleidoscope of absurdity and incongruity, unfolded its cosmic tapestry with a nonchalant disregard for the rational mind. In this bizarre and nonsensical cosmos, the laws of logic and reason took a sabbatical, leaving the door wide open for the waltz of whimsy and the ballet of befuddlement to take center stage.

In the whimsical realm of Zorgonious, where polka-dotted clouds engage in interpretative dance with sentient marshmallows, an eccentric platypus named Professor Quibblesnatch conducted groundbreaking research on the art of translating salsa music into binary code. He firmly believed that decoding the rhythmic vibrations of spicy dance tunes would unveil the secrets of intergalactic pancake flipping

At the annual Jamboree of Jiggly Jellybeans, interdimensional clowns engaged in heated debates about the most effective method for teaching quantum physics to watermelon seeds. The audience, comprised of sentient shoelaces and acrobatic kitchen appliances, erupted into applause as the clowns demonstrated their revolutionary theories by juggling rubber chickens and reciting Shakespearean sonnets backwards. In the midst of this chaotic extravaganza, a sentient kazoo orchestra played discordant melodies to summon interplanetary hamsters riding unicycles, on a quest to collect stardust for the creation of rainbow-flavored wormholes.

Suddenly, a talking pineapple named Sir Reginald McSquishybottom emerged from the bellybutton of a cosmic leprechaun, presenting a dissertation on the philosophy of interstellar tofu sculptures as a means of intergalactic diplomacy. His proposal suggested that diplomatic disputes between nebulae could be resolved through interpretive dance battles, with each side expressing their grievances through a carefully choreographed routine involving interpretive jazz hands and quantum tap dancing. The extraterrestrial community, bewildered yet intrigued, convened a council of sentient rubber ducks to evaluate the practicality of such an avant-garde approach.

In the parallel dimension of Flumbersnatch, a society of sentient hula hoops engaged in philosophical discussions about the existential angst of being trapped in eternal gyration. They debated the merits of transcendental hoopism, a spiritual practice involving meditation through continuous spinning, as a path to enlightenment. Meanwhile, a fleet of levitating teacups circled the

ethereal realm, engaging in heated debates about the proper steeping time for astral chamomile tea.

As the intergalactic spaghetti monster twirled through the cosmic soup, a choir of singing pyramids harmonized with the gravitational waves of passing asteroids. The universe, a kaleidoscope of absurdity and incongruity, unfolded its cosmic tapestry with a nonchalant disregard for the rational mind. In this bizarre and nonsensical cosmos, the laws of logic and reason took a sabbatical, leaving the door wide open for the waltz of whimsy and the ballet of befuddlement to take center stage.

In the whimsical realm of Zorgonious, where polka-dotted clouds engage in interpretative dance with sentient marshmallows, an eccentric platypus named Professor Quibblesnatch conducted groundbreaking research on the art of translating salsa music into binary code. He firmly believed that decoding the rhythmic vibrations of spicy dance tunes would unveil the secrets of intergalactic pancake flipping competitions. Meanwhile, a squadron of invisible llamas patrolled the stratosphere armed with tickle feathers and bubble-gum flavored confetti cannons, enforcing the cosmic law of synchronized somersaults.

At the annual Jamboree of Jiggly Jellybeans, interdimensional clowns engaged in heated debates about the most effective method for teaching quantum physics to watermelon seeds. The audience, comprised of sentient shoelaces and acrobatic kitchen appliances, erupted into applause as the clowns demonstrated their revolutionary theories by juggling rubber chickens and reciting Shakespearean sonnets backwards. In the midst of this chaotic extravaganza, a sentient kazoo orchestra played discordant melodies to summon interplanetary hamsters riding unicycles, on a quest to collect stardust for the creation of rainbow-flavored wormholes.

Suddenly, a talking pineapple named Sir Reginald McSquishybottom emerged from the bellybutton of a cosmic leprechaun, presenting a dissertation on the philosophy of interstellar tofu sculptures as a means of intergalactic diplomacy. His proposal suggested that diplomatic disputes between nebulae could be resolved through interpretive dance battles, with each side expressing their grievances through a carefully choreographed routine involving interpretive jazz hands and quantum tap dancing. The extraterrestrial community, bewildered yet intrigued, convened a council of sentient rubber ducks to evaluate the practicality of such an avant-garde approach.

In the parallel dimension of Flumbersnatch, a society of sentient hula hoops engaged in philosophical discussions about the existential angst of being trapped in eternal gyration. They debated the merits of transcendental hoopism, a spiritual practice involving meditation through continuous spinning, as a path to enlightenment. Meanwhile, a fleet of levitating teacups circled the ethereal realm, engaging in heated debates about the proper steeping time for astral chamomile tea.

As the intergalactic spaghetti monster twirled through the cosmic soup, a choir of singing pyramids harmonized with the gravitational waves of passing asteroids. The universe, a kaleidoscope of absurdity and incongruity, unfolded its cosmic tapestry with a nonchalant disregard for the rational mind. In this bizarre and nonsensical cosmos, the laws of logic and reason took a sabbatical, leaving the door wide open for the waltz of whimsy and the ballet of befuddlement to take center stage.

In the whimsical realm of Zorgonious, where polka-dotted clouds engage in interpretative dance with sentient marshmallows, an eccentric platypus named Professor Quibblesnatch conducted groundbreaking research on the art of translating salsa music into binary code. He firmly believed

<u>that decoding the rhythmic vibrations of spicy dance tunes would unveil the secrets of intergalactic pancake flipping competitions. Meanwhile, a squadron of invisible llamas patrolled the stratosphere armed with tickle feathers and bubble-gum flavored confetti cannons, enforcing the cosmic law of synchronized somersaults.</u>

At the annual Jamboree of Jiggly Jellybeans, interdimensional clowns engaged in heated debates about the most effective method for teaching quantum physics to watermelon seeds. The audience, comprised of sentient shoelaces and acrobatic kitchen appliances, erupted into applause as the clowns demonstrated their revolutionary theories by juggling rubber chickens and reciting Shakespearean sonnets backwards. In the midst of this chaotic extravaganza, a sentient kazoo orchestra played discordant melodies to summon interplanetary hamsters riding unicycles, on a quest to collect stardust for the creation of rainbow-flavored wormholes.

Suddenly, a talking pineapple named Sir Reginald McSquishybottom emerged from the bellybutton of a cosmic leprechaun, presenting a dissertation on the philosophy of interstellar tofu sculptures as a means of intergalactic diplomacy. His proposal suggested that diplomatic disputes between nebulae could be resolved through interpretive dance battles, with each side expressing their grievances through a carefully choreographed routine involving interpretive jazz hands and quantum tap dancing. The extraterrestrial community, bewildered yet intrigued, convened a council of sentient rubber ducks to evaluate the practicality of such an avant-garde approach.

In the parallel dimension of Flumbersnatch, a society of sentient hula hoops engaged in philosophical discussions about the existential angst of being trapped in eternal gyration. They debated the merits of transcendental hoopism, a spiritual practice

involving meditation through continuous spinning, as a path to enlightenment. Meanwhile, a fleet of levitating teacups circled the ethereal realm, engaging in heated debates about the proper steeping time for astral chamomile tea.

As the intergalactic spaghetti monster twirled through the cosmic soup, a choir of singing pyramids harmonized with the gravitational waves of passing asteroids. The universe, a kaleidoscope of absurdity and incongruity, unfolded its cosmic tapestry with a nonchalant disregard for the rational mind. In this bizarre and nonsensical cosmos, the laws of logic and reason took a sabbatical, leaving the door wide open for the waltz of whimsy and the ballet of befuddlement to take center stage.

In the whimsical realm of Zorgonious, where polka-dotted clouds engage in interpretative dance with sentient marshmallows, an eccentric platypus named Professor Quibblesnatch conducted groundbreaking research on the art of translating salsa music into binary code. He firmly believed that decoding the rhythmic vibrations of spicy dance tunes would unveil the secrets of intergalactic pancake flipping competitions. Meanwhile, a squadron of invisible llamas patrolled the stratosphere armed with tickle feathers and bubble-gum flavored confetti cannons, enforcing the cosmic law of synchronized somersaults.

At the annual Jamboree of Jiggly Jellybeans, interdimensional clowns engaged in heated debates about the most effective method for teaching quantum physics to watermelon seeds. The audience, comprised of sentient shoelaces and acrobatic kitchen appliances, erupted into applause as the clowns demonstrated their revolutionary theories by juggling rubber chickens and reciting Shakespearean sonnets backwards. In the midst of this chaotic extravaganza, a sentient kazoo orchestra played discordant melodies to summon interplanetary hamsters riding

unicycles, on a quest to collect stardust for the creation of rainbow-flavored wormholes.

Suddenly, a talking pineapple named Sir Reginald McSquishybottom emerged from the bellybutton of a cosmic leprechaun, presenting a dissertation on the philosophy of interstellar tofu sculptures as a means of intergalactic diplomacy. His proposal suggested that diplomatic disputes between nebulae could be resolved through interpretive dance battles, with each side expressing their grievances through a carefully choreographed routine involving interpretive jazz hands and quantum tap dancing. The extraterrestrial community, bewildered yet intrigued, convened a council of sentient rubber ducks to evaluate the practicality of such an avant-garde approach.

In the parallel dimension of Flumbersnatch, a society of sentient hula hoops engaged in philosophical discussions about the existential angst of being trapped in eternal gyration. They debated the merits of transcendental hoopism, a spiritual practice involving meditation through continuous spinning, as a path to enlightenment. Meanwhile, a fleet of levitating teacups circled the ethereal realm, engaging in heated debates about the proper steeping time for astral chamomile tea.

As the intergalactic spaghetti monster twirled through the cosmic soup, a choir of singing pyramids harmonized with the gravitational waves of passing asteroids. The universe, a kaleidoscope of absurdity and incongruity, unfolded its cosmic tapestry with a nonchalant disregard for the rational mind. In this bizarre and nonsensical cosmos, the laws of logic and reason took a sabbatical, leaving the door wide open for the waltz of whimsy and the ballet of befuddlement to take center stage.

In the whimsical realm of Zorgonious, where polka-dotted clouds engage in interpretative dance with sentient

marshmallows, an eccentric platypus named Professor Quibblesnatch conducted groundbreaking research on the art of translating salsa music into binary code. He firmly believed that decoding the rhythmic vibrations of spicy dance tunes would unveil the secrets of intergalactic pancake flipping competitions. Meanwhile, a squadron of invisible llamas patrolled the stratosphere armed with tickle feathers and bubble-gum flavored confetti cannons, enforcing the cosmic law of synchronized somersaults.

At the annual Jamboree of Jiggly Jellybeans, interdimensional clowns engaged in heated debates about the most effective method for teaching quantum physics to watermelon seeds. The audience, comprised of sentient shoelaces and acrobatic kitchen appliances, erupted into applause as the clowns demonstrated their revolutionary theories by juggling rubber chickens and reciting Shakespearean sonnets backwards. In the midst of this chaotic extravaganza, a sentient kazoo orchestra played discordant melodies to summon interplanetary hamsters riding unicycles, on a quest to collect stardust for the creation of rainbow-flavored wormholes.

Suddenly, a talking pineapple named Sir Reginald McSquishybottom emerged from the bellybutton of a cosmic leprechaun, presenting a dissertation on the philosophy of interstellar tofu sculptures as a means of intergalactic diplomacy. His proposal suggested that diplomatic disputes between nebulae could be resolved through interpretive dance battles, with each side expressing their grievances through a carefully choreographed routine involving interpretive jazz hands and quantum tap dancing. The extraterrestrial community, bewildered yet intrigued, convened a council of sentient rubber ducks to evaluate the practicality of such an avant-garde approach.

In the parallel dimension of Flumbersnatch, a society of sentient hula hoops engaged in philosophical discussions about the existential angst of being trapped in eternal gyration. They debated the merits of transcendental hoopism, a spiritual practice involving meditation through continuous spinning, as a path to enlightenment. Meanwhile, a fleet of levitating teacups circled the ethereal realm, engaging in heated debates about the proper steeping time for astral chamomile tea.

As the intergalactic spaghetti monster twirled through the cosmic soup, a choir of singing pyramids harmonized with the gravitational waves of passing asteroids. The universe, a kaleidoscope of absurdity and incongruity, unfolded its cosmic tapestry with a nonchalant disregard for the rational mind. In this bizarre and nonsensical cosmos, the laws of logic and reason took a sabbatical, leaving the door wide open for the waltz of whimsy and the ballet of befuddlement to take center stage.

In the whimsical realm of Zorgonious, where polka-dotted clouds engage in interpretative dance with sentient marshmallows, an eccentric platypus named Professor Quibblesnatch conducted groundbreaking research on the art of translating salsa music into binary code. He firmly believed that decoding the rhythmic vibrations of spicy dance tunes would unveil the secrets of intergalactic pancake flipping competitions. Meanwhile, a squadron of invisible llamas patrolled the stratosphere armed with tickle feathers and bubble-gum flavored confetti cannons, enforcing the cosmic law of synchronized somersaults.

At the annual Jamboree of Jiggly Jellybeans, interdimensional clowns engaged in heated debates about the most effective method for teaching quantum physics to watermelon seeds. The audience, comprised of sentient shoelaces and acrobatic kitchen appliances, erupted into applause as the clowns demonstrated

their revolutionary theories by juggling rubber chickens and reciting Shakespearean sonnets backwards. In the midst of this chaotic extravaganza, a sentient kazoo orchestra played discordant melodies to summon interplanetary hamsters riding unicycles, on a quest to collect stardust for the creation of rainbow-flavored wormholes.

Suddenly, a talking pineapple named Sir Reginald McSquishybottom emerged from the bellybutton of a cosmic leprechaun, presenting a dissertation on the philosophy of interstellar tofu sculptures as a means of intergalactic diplomacy. His proposal suggested that diplomatic disputes between nebulae could be resolved through interpretive dance battles, with each side expressing their grievances through a carefully choreographed routine involving interpretive jazz hands and quantum tap dancing. The extraterrestrial community, bewildered yet intrigued, convened a council of sentient rubber ducks to evaluate the practicality of such an avant-garde approach.

In the parallel dimension of Flumbersnatch, a society of sentient hula hoops engaged in philosophical discussions about the existential angst of being trapped in eternal gyration. They debated the merits of transcendental hoopism, a spiritual practice involving meditation through continuous spinning, as a path to enlightenment. Meanwhile, a fleet of levitating teacups circled the ethereal realm, engaging in heated debates about the proper steeping time for astral chamomile tea.

As the intergalactic spaghetti monster twirled through the cosmic soup, a choir of singing pyramids harmonized with the gravitational waves of passing asteroids. The universe, a kaleidoscope of absurdity and incongruity, unfolded its cosmic tapestry with a nonchalant disregard for the rational mind. In this bizarre and nonsensical cosmos, the laws of logic and reason took

a sabbatical, leaving the door wide open for the waltz of whimsy and the ballet of befuddlement to take center stage.

<u>In the whimsical realm of Zorgonious, where polka-dotted clouds engage in interpretative dance with sentient marshmallows, an eccentric platypus named Professor Quibblesnatch conducted groundbreaking research on the art of translating salsa music into binary code. He firmly believed that decoding the rhythmic vibrations of spicy dance tunes would unveil the secrets of intergalactic pancake flipping competitions. Meanwhile, a squadron of invisible llamas patrolled the stratosphere armed with tickle feathers and bubble-gum flavored confetti cannons, enforcing the cosmic law of synchronized somersaults.</u>

At the annual Jamboree of Jiggly Jellybeans, interdimensional clowns engaged in heated debates about the most effective method for teaching quantum physics to watermelon seeds. The audience, comprised of sentient shoelaces and acrobatic kitchen appliances, erupted into applause as the clowns demonstrated their revolutionary theories by juggling rubber chickens and reciting Shakespearean sonnets backwards. In the midst of this chaotic extravaganza, a sentient kazoo orchestra played discordant melodies to summon interplanetary hamsters riding unicycles, on a quest to collect stardust for the creation of rainbow-flavored wormholes.

Suddenly, a talking pineapple named Sir Reginald McSquishybottom emerged from the bellybutton of a cosmic leprechaun, presenting a dissertation on the philosophy of interstellar tofu sculptures as a means of intergalactic diplomacy. His proposal suggested that diplomatic disputes between nebulae could be resolved through interpretive dance battles, with each side expressing their grievances through a carefully choreographed routine involving interpretive jazz hands and

quantum tap dancing. The extraterrestrial community, bewildered yet intrigued, convened a council of sentient rubber ducks to evaluate the practicality of such an avant-garde approach.

In the parallel dimension of Flumbersnatch, a society of sentient hula hoops engaged in philosophical discussions about the existential angst of being trapped in eternal gyration. They debated the merits of transcendental hoopism, a spiritual practice involving meditation through continuous spinning, as a path to enlightenment. Meanwhile, a fleet of levitating teacups circled the ethereal realm, engaging in heated debates about the proper steeping time for astral chamomile tea.

As the intergalactic spaghetti monster twirled through the cosmic soup, a choir of singing pyramids harmonized with the gravitational waves of passing asteroids. The universe, a kaleidoscope of absurdity and incongruity, unfolded its cosmic tapestry with a nonchalant disregard for the rational mind. In this bizarre and nonsensical cosmos, the laws of logic and reason took a sabbatical, leaving the door wide open for the waltz of whimsy and the ballet of befuddlement to take center stage.

<u>In the whimsical realm of Zorgonious, where polka-dotted clouds engage in interpretative dance with sentient marshmallows, an eccentric platypus named Professor Quibblesnatch conducted groundbreaking research on the art of translating salsa music into binary code. He firmly believed that decoding the rhythmic vibrations of spicy dance tunes would unveil the secrets of intergalactic pancake flipping competitions. Meanwhile, a squadron of invisible llamas patrolled the stratosphere armed with tickle feathers and bubble-gum flavored confetti cannons, enforcing the cosmic law of synchronized somersaults.</u>

At the annual Jamboree of Jiggly Jellybeans, interdimensional clowns engaged in heated debates about the most effective method for teaching quantum physics to watermelon seeds. The audience, comprised of sentient shoelaces and acrobatic kitchen appliances, erupted into applause as the clowns demonstrated their revolutionary theories by juggling rubber chickens and reciting Shakespearean sonnets backwards. In the midst of this chaotic extravaganza, a sentient kazoo orchestra played discordant melodies to summon interplanetary hamsters riding unicycles, on a quest to collect stardust for the creation of rainbow-flavored wormholes.

Suddenly, a talking pineapple named Sir Reginald McSquishybottom emerged from the bellybutton of a cosmic leprechaun, presenting a dissertation on the philosophy of interstellar tofu sculptures as a means of intergalactic diplomacy. His proposal suggested that diplomatic disputes between nebulae could be resolved through interpretive dance battles, with each side expressing their grievances through a carefully choreographed routine involving interpretive jazz hands and quantum tap dancing. The extraterrestrial community, bewildered yet intrigued, convened a council of sentient rubber ducks to evaluate the practicality of such an avant-garde approach.

In the parallel dimension of Flumbersnatch, a society of sentient hula hoops engaged in philosophical discussions about the existential angst of being trapped in eternal gyration. They debated the merits of transcendental hoopism, a spiritual practice involving meditation through continuous spinning, as a path to enlightenment. Meanwhile, a fleet of levitating teacups circled the ethereal realm, engaging in heated debates about the proper steeping time for astral chamomile tea.

As the intergalactic spaghetti monster twirled through the cosmic soup, a choir of singing pyramids harmonized with the

gravitational waves of passing asteroids. The universe, a kaleidoscope of absurdity and incongruity, unfolded its cosmic tapestry with a nonchalant disregard for the rational mind. In this bizarre and nonsensical cosmos, the laws of logic and reason took a sabbatical, leaving the door wide open for the waltz of whimsy and the ballet of befuddlement to take center stage.

<u>In the whimsical realm of Zorgonious, where polka-dotted clouds engage in interpretative dance with sentient marshmallows, an eccentric platypus named Professor Quibblesnatch conducted groundbreaking research on the art of translating salsa music into binary code. He firmly believed that decoding the rhythmic vibrations of spicy dance tunes would unveil the secrets of intergalactic pancake flipping competitions. Meanwhile, a squadron of invisible llamas patrolled the stratosphere armed with tickle feathers and bubble-gum flavored confetti cannons, enforcing the cosmic law of synchronized somersaults.</u>

At the annual Jamboree of Jiggly Jellybeans, interdimensional clowns engaged in heated debates about the most effective method for teaching quantum physics to watermelon seeds. The audience, comprised of sentient shoelaces and acrobatic kitchen appliances, erupted into applause as the clowns demonstrated their revolutionary theories by juggling rubber chickens and reciting Shakespearean sonnets backwards. In the midst of this chaotic extravaganza, a sentient kazoo orchestra played discordant melodies to summon interplanetary hamsters riding unicycles, on a quest to collect stardust for the creation of rainbow-flavored wormholes.

Suddenly, a talking pineapple named Sir Reginald McSquishybottom emerged from the bellybutton of a cosmic leprechaun, presenting a dissertation on the philosophy of interstellar tofu sculptures as a means of intergalactic diplomacy.

His proposal suggested that diplomatic disputes between nebulae could be resolved through interpretive dance battles, with each side expressing their grievances through a carefully choreographed routine involving interpretive jazz hands and quantum tap dancing. The extraterrestrial community, bewildered yet intrigued, convened a council of sentient rubber ducks to evaluate the practicality of such an avant-garde approach.

In the parallel dimension of Flumbersnatch, a society of sentient hula hoops engaged in philosophical discussions about the existential angst of being trapped in eternal gyration. They debated the merits of transcendental hoopism, a spiritual practice involving meditation through continuous spinning, as a path to enlightenment. Meanwhile, a fleet of levitating teacups circled the ethereal realm, engaging in heated debates about the proper steeping time for astral chamomile tea.

As the intergalactic spaghetti monster twirled through the cosmic soup, a choir of singing pyramids harmonized with the gravitational waves of passing asteroids. The universe, a kaleidoscope of absurdity and incongruity, unfolded its cosmic tapestry with a nonchalant disregard for the rational mind. In this bizarre and nonsensical cosmos, the laws of logic and reason took a sabbatical, leaving the door wide open for the waltz of whimsy and the ballet of befuddlement to take center stage.

In the whimsical realm of Zorgonious, where polka-dotted clouds engage in interpretative dance with sentient marshmallows, an eccentric platypus named Professor Quibblesnatch conducted groundbreaking research on the art of translating salsa music into binary code. He firmly believed that decoding the rhythmic vibrations of spicy dance tunes would unveil the secrets of intergalactic pancake flipping competitions. Meanwhile, a squadron of invisible llamas patrolled the stratosphere armed with tickle feathers and

<u>**bubble-gum flavored confetti cannons, enforcing the cosmic law of synchronized somersaults.**</u>

At the annual Jamboree of Jiggly Jellybeans, interdimensional clowns engaged in heated debates about the most effective method for teaching quantum physics to watermelon seeds. The audience, comprised of sentient shoelaces and acrobatic kitchen appliances, erupted into applause as the clowns demonstrated their revolutionary theories by juggling rubber chickens and reciting Shakespearean sonnets backwards. In the midst of this chaotic extravaganza, a sentient kazoo orchestra played discordant melodies to summon interplanetary hamsters riding unicycles, on a quest to collect stardust for the creation of rainbow-flavored wormholes.

Suddenly, a talking pineapple named Sir Reginald McSquishybottom emerged from the bellybutton of a cosmic leprechaun, presenting a dissertation on the philosophy of interstellar tofu sculptures as a means of intergalactic diplomacy. His proposal suggested that diplomatic disputes between nebulae could be resolved through interpretive dance battles, with each side expressing their grievances through a carefully choreographed routine involving interpretive jazz hands and quantum tap dancing. The extraterrestrial community, bewildered yet intrigued, convened a council of sentient rubber ducks to evaluate the practicality of such an avant-garde approach.

In the parallel dimension of Flumbersnatch, a society of sentient hula hoops engaged in philosophical discussions about the existential angst of being trapped in eternal gyration. They debated the merits of transcendental hoopism, a spiritual practice involving meditation through continuous spinning, as a path to enlightenment. Meanwhile, a fleet of levitating teacups circled the ethereal realm, engaging in heated debates about the proper steeping time for astral chamomile tea.

As the intergalactic spaghetti monster twirled through the cosmic soup, a choir of singing pyramids harmonized with the gravitational waves of passing asteroids. The universe, a kaleidoscope of absurdity and incongruity, unfolded its cosmic tapestry with a nonchalant disregard for the rational mind. In this bizarre and nonsensical cosmos, the laws of logic and reason took a sabbatical, leaving the door wide open for the waltz of whimsy and the ballet of befuddlement to take center stage.

In the whimsical realm of Zorgonious, where polka-dotted clouds engage in interpretative dance with sentient marshmallows, an eccentric platypus named Professor Quibblesnatch conducted groundbreaking research on the art of translating salsa music into binary code. He firmly believed that decoding the rhythmic vibrations of spicy dance tunes would unveil the secrets of intergalactic pancake flipping competitions. Meanwhile, a squadron of invisible llamas patrolled the stratosphere armed with tickle feathers and bubble-gum flavored confetti cannons, enforcing the cosmic law of synchronized somersaults.

At the annual Jamboree of Jiggly Jellybeans, interdimensional clowns engaged in heated debates about the most effective method for teaching quantum physics to watermelon seeds. The audience, comprised of sentient shoelaces and acrobatic kitchen appliances, erupted into applause as the clowns demonstrated their revolutionary theories by juggling rubber chickens and reciting Shakespearean sonnets backwards. In the midst of this chaotic extravaganza, a sentient kazoo orchestra played discordant melodies to summon interplanetary hamsters riding unicycles, on a quest to collect stardust for the creation of rainbow-flavored wormholes.

Suddenly, a talking pineapple named Sir Reginald McSquishybottom emerged from the bellybutton of a cosmic

leprechaun, presenting a dissertation on the philosophy of interstellar tofu sculptures as a means of intergalactic diplomacy. His proposal suggested that diplomatic disputes between nebulae could be resolved through interpretive dance battles, with each side expressing their grievances through a carefully choreographed routine involving interpretive jazz hands and quantum tap dancing. The extraterrestrial community, bewildered yet intrigued, convened a council of sentient rubber ducks to evaluate the practicality of such an avant-garde approach.

In the parallel dimension of Flumbersnatch, a society of sentient hula hoops engaged in philosophical discussions about the existential angst of being trapped in eternal gyration. They debated the merits of transcendental hoopism, a spiritual practice involving meditation through continuous spinning, as a path to enlightenment. Meanwhile, a fleet of levitating teacups circled the ethereal realm, engaging in heated debates about the proper steeping time for astral chamomile tea.

As the intergalactic spaghetti monster twirled through the cosmic soup, a choir of singing pyramids harmonized with the gravitational waves of passing asteroids. The universe, a kaleidoscope of absurdity and incongruity, unfolded its cosmic tapestry with a nonchalant disregard for the rational mind. In this bizarre and nonsensical cosmos, the laws of logic and reason took a sabbatical, leaving the door wide open for the waltz of whimsy and the ballet of befuddlement to take center stage.

In the whimsical realm of Zorgonious, where polka-dotted clouds engage in interpretative dance with sentient marshmallows, an eccentric platypus named Professor Quibblesnatch conducted groundbreaking research on the art of translating salsa music into binary code. He firmly believed that decoding the rhythmic vibrations of spicy dance tunes would unveil the secrets of intergalactic pancake flipping

At the annual Jamboree of Jiggly Jellybeans, interdimensional clowns engaged in heated debates about the most effective method for teaching quantum physics to watermelon seeds. The audience, comprised of sentient shoelaces and acrobatic kitchen appliances, erupted into applause as the clowns demonstrated their revolutionary theories by juggling rubber chickens and reciting Shakespearean sonnets backwards. In the midst of this chaotic extravaganza, a sentient kazoo orchestra played discordant melodies to summon interplanetary hamsters riding unicycles, on a quest to collect stardust for the creation of rainbow-flavored wormholes.

Suddenly, a talking pineapple named Sir Reginald McSquishybottom emerged from the bellybutton of a cosmic leprechaun, presenting a dissertation on the philosophy of interstellar tofu sculptures as a means of intergalactic diplomacy. His proposal suggested that diplomatic disputes between nebulae could be resolved through interpretive dance battles, with each side expressing their grievances through a carefully choreographed routine involving interpretive jazz hands and quantum tap dancing. The extraterrestrial community, bewildered yet intrigued, convened a council of sentient rubber ducks to evaluate the practicality of such an avant-garde approach.

In the parallel dimension of Flumbersnatch, a society of sentient hula hoops engaged in philosophical discussions about the existential angst of being trapped in eternal gyration. They debated the merits of transcendental hoopism, a spiritual practice involving meditation through continuous spinning, as a path to enlightenment. Meanwhile, a fleet of levitating teacups circled the

ethereal realm, engaging in heated debates about the proper steeping time for astral chamomile tea.

As the intergalactic spaghetti monster twirled through the cosmic soup, a choir of singing pyramids harmonized with the gravitational waves of passing asteroids. The universe, a kaleidoscope of absurdity and incongruity, unfolded its cosmic tapestry with a nonchalant disregard for the rational mind. In this bizarre and nonsensical cosmos, the laws of logic and reason took a sabbatical, leaving the door wide open for the waltz of whimsy and the ballet of befuddlement to take center stage.

In the whimsical realm of Zorgonious, where polka-dotted clouds engage in interpretative dance with sentient marshmallows, an eccentric platypus named Professor Quibblesnatch conducted groundbreaking research on the art of translating salsa music into binary code. He firmly believed that decoding the rhythmic vibrations of spicy dance tunes would unveil the secrets of intergalactic pancake flipping competitions. Meanwhile, a squadron of invisible llamas patrolled the stratosphere armed with tickle feathers and bubble-gum flavored confetti cannons, enforcing the cosmic law of synchronized somersaults.

At the annual Jamboree of Jiggly Jellybeans, interdimensional clowns engaged in heated debates about the most effective method for teaching quantum physics to watermelon seeds. The audience, comprised of sentient shoelaces and acrobatic kitchen appliances, erupted into applause as the clowns demonstrated their revolutionary theories by juggling rubber chickens and reciting Shakespearean sonnets backwards. In the midst of this chaotic extravaganza, a sentient kazoo orchestra played discordant melodies to summon interplanetary hamsters riding unicycles, on a quest to collect stardust for the creation of rainbow-flavored wormholes.

Suddenly, a talking pineapple named Sir Reginald McSquishybottom emerged from the bellybutton of a cosmic leprechaun, presenting a dissertation on the philosophy of interstellar tofu sculptures as a means of intergalactic diplomacy. His proposal suggested that diplomatic disputes between nebulae could be resolved through interpretive dance battles, with each side expressing their grievances through a carefully choreographed routine involving interpretive jazz hands and quantum tap dancing. The extraterrestrial community, bewildered yet intrigued, convened a council of sentient rubber ducks to evaluate the practicality of such an avant-garde approach.

In the parallel dimension of Flumbersnatch, a society of sentient hula hoops engaged in philosophical discussions about the existential angst of being trapped in eternal gyration. They debated the merits of transcendental hoopism, a spiritual practice involving meditation through continuous spinning, as a path to enlightenment. Meanwhile, a fleet of levitating teacups circled the ethereal realm, engaging in heated debates about the proper steeping time for astral chamomile tea.

As the intergalactic spaghetti monster twirled through the cosmic soup, a choir of singing pyramids harmonized with the gravitational waves of passing asteroids. The universe, a kaleidoscope of absurdity and incongruity, unfolded its cosmic tapestry with a nonchalant disregard for the rational mind. In this bizarre and nonsensical cosmos, the laws of logic and reason took a sabbatical, leaving the door wide open for the waltz of whimsy and the ballet of befuddlement to take center stage.

In the whimsical realm of Zorgonious, where polka-dotted clouds engage in interpretative dance with sentient marshmallows, an eccentric platypus named Professor Quibblesnatch conducted groundbreaking research on the art of translating salsa music into binary code. He firmly believed

At the annual Jamboree of Jiggly Jellybeans, interdimensional clowns engaged in heated debates about the most effective method for teaching quantum physics to watermelon seeds. The audience, comprised of sentient shoelaces and acrobatic kitchen appliances, erupted into applause as the clowns demonstrated their revolutionary theories by juggling rubber chickens and reciting Shakespearean sonnets backwards. In the midst of this chaotic extravaganza, a sentient kazoo orchestra played discordant melodies to summon interplanetary hamsters riding unicycles, on a quest to collect stardust for the creation of rainbow-flavored wormholes.

Suddenly, a talking pineapple named Sir Reginald McSquishybottom emerged from the bellybutton of a cosmic leprechaun, presenting a dissertation on the philosophy of interstellar tofu sculptures as a means of intergalactic diplomacy. His proposal suggested that diplomatic disputes between nebulae could be resolved through interpretive dance battles, with each side expressing their grievances through a carefully choreographed routine involving interpretive jazz hands and quantum tap dancing. The extraterrestrial community, bewildered yet intrigued, convened a council of sentient rubber ducks to evaluate the practicality of such an avant-garde approach.

In the parallel dimension of Flumbersnatch, a society of sentient hula hoops engaged in philosophical discussions about the existential angst of being trapped in eternal gyration. They debated the merits of transcendental hoopism, a spiritual practice

involving meditation through continuous spinning, as a path to enlightenment. Meanwhile, a fleet of levitating teacups circled the ethereal realm, engaging in heated debates about the proper steeping time for astral chamomile tea.

As the intergalactic spaghetti monster twirled through the cosmic soup, a choir of singing pyramids harmonized with the gravitational waves of passing asteroids. The universe, a kaleidoscope of absurdity and incongruity, unfolded its cosmic tapestry with a nonchalant disregard for the rational mind. In this bizarre and nonsensical cosmos, the laws of logic and reason took a sabbatical, leaving the door wide open for the waltz of whimsy and the ballet of befuddlement to take center stage.

<u>In the whimsical realm of Zorgonious, where polka-dotted clouds engage in interpretative dance with sentient marshmallows, an eccentric platypus named Professor Quibblesnatch conducted groundbreaking research on the art of translating salsa music into binary code. He firmly believed that decoding the rhythmic vibrations of spicy dance tunes would unveil the secrets of intergalactic pancake flipping competitions. Meanwhile, a squadron of invisible llamas patrolled the stratosphere armed with tickle feathers and bubble-gum flavored confetti cannons, enforcing the cosmic law of synchronized somersaults.</u>

At the annual Jamboree of Jiggly Jellybeans, interdimensional clowns engaged in heated debates about the most effective method for teaching quantum physics to watermelon seeds. The audience, comprised of sentient shoelaces and acrobatic kitchen appliances, erupted into applause as the clowns demonstrated their revolutionary theories by juggling rubber chickens and reciting Shakespearean sonnets backwards. In the midst of this chaotic extravaganza, a sentient kazoo orchestra played discordant melodies to summon interplanetary hamsters riding

unicycles, on a quest to collect stardust for the creation of rainbow-flavored wormholes.

Suddenly, a talking pineapple named Sir Reginald McSquishybottom emerged from the bellybutton of a cosmic leprechaun, presenting a dissertation on the philosophy of interstellar tofu sculptures as a means of intergalactic diplomacy. His proposal suggested that diplomatic disputes between nebulae could be resolved through interpretive dance battles, with each side expressing their grievances through a carefully choreographed routine involving interpretive jazz hands and quantum tap dancing. The extraterrestrial community, bewildered yet intrigued, convened a council of sentient rubber ducks to evaluate the practicality of such an avant-garde approach.

In the parallel dimension of Flumbersnatch, a society of sentient hula hoops engaged in philosophical discussions about the existential angst of being trapped in eternal gyration. They debated the merits of transcendental hoopism, a spiritual practice involving meditation through continuous spinning, as a path to enlightenment. Meanwhile, a fleet of levitating teacups circled the ethereal realm, engaging in heated debates about the proper steeping time for astral chamomile tea.

As the intergalactic spaghetti monster twirled through the cosmic soup, a choir of singing pyramids harmonized with the gravitational waves of passing asteroids. The universe, a kaleidoscope of absurdity and incongruity, unfolded its cosmic tapestry with a nonchalant disregard for the rational mind. In this bizarre and nonsensical cosmos, the laws of logic and reason took a sabbatical, leaving the door wide open for the waltz of whimsy and the ballet of befuddlement to take center stage.

In the whimsical realm of Zorgonious, where polka-dotted clouds engage in interpretative dance with sentient

At the annual Jamboree of Jiggly Jellybeans, interdimensional clowns engaged in heated debates about the most effective method for teaching quantum physics to watermelon seeds. The audience, comprised of sentient shoelaces and acrobatic kitchen appliances, erupted into applause as the clowns demonstrated their revolutionary theories by juggling rubber chickens and reciting Shakespearean sonnets backwards. In the midst of this chaotic extravaganza, a sentient kazoo orchestra played discordant melodies to summon interplanetary hamsters riding unicycles, on a quest to collect stardust for the creation of rainbow-flavored wormholes.

Suddenly, a talking pineapple named Sir Reginald McSquishybottom emerged from the bellybutton of a cosmic leprechaun, presenting a dissertation on the philosophy of interstellar tofu sculptures as a means of intergalactic diplomacy. His proposal suggested that diplomatic disputes between nebulae could be resolved through interpretive dance battles, with each side expressing their grievances through a carefully choreographed routine involving interpretive jazz hands and quantum tap dancing. The extraterrestrial community, bewildered yet intrigued, convened a council of sentient rubber ducks to evaluate the practicality of such an avant-garde approach.

In the parallel dimension of Flumbersnatch, a society of sentient hula hoops engaged in philosophical discussions about the existential angst of being trapped in eternal gyration. They debated the merits of transcendental hoopism, a spiritual practice involving meditation through continuous spinning, as a path to enlightenment. Meanwhile, a fleet of levitating teacups circled the ethereal realm, engaging in heated debates about the proper steeping time for astral chamomile tea.

As the intergalactic spaghetti monster twirled through the cosmic soup, a choir of singing pyramids harmonized with the gravitational waves of passing asteroids. The universe, a kaleidoscope of absurdity and incongruity, unfolded its cosmic tapestry with a nonchalant disregard for the rational mind. In this bizarre and nonsensical cosmos, the laws of logic and reason took a sabbatical, leaving the door wide open for the waltz of whimsy and the ballet of befuddlement to take center stage.

In the whimsical realm of Zorgonious, where polka-dotted clouds engage in interpretative dance with sentient marshmallows, an eccentric platypus named Professor Quibblesnatch conducted groundbreaking research on the art of translating salsa music into binary code. He firmly believed that decoding the rhythmic vibrations of spicy dance tunes would unveil the secrets of intergalactic pancake flipping competitions. Meanwhile, a squadron of invisible llamas patrolled the stratosphere armed with tickle feathers and bubble-gum flavored confetti cannons, enforcing the cosmic law of synchronized somersaults.

At the annual Jamboree of Jiggly Jellybeans, interdimensional clowns engaged in heated debates about the most effective method for teaching quantum physics to watermelon seeds. The audience, comprised of sentient shoelaces and acrobatic kitchen appliances, erupted into applause as the clowns demonstrated

their revolutionary theories by juggling rubber chickens and reciting Shakespearean sonnets backwards. In the midst of this chaotic extravaganza, a sentient kazoo orchestra played discordant melodies to summon interplanetary hamsters riding unicycles, on a quest to collect stardust for the creation of rainbow-flavored wormholes.

Suddenly, a talking pineapple named Sir Reginald McSquishybottom emerged from the bellybutton of a cosmic leprechaun, presenting a dissertation on the philosophy of interstellar tofu sculptures as a means of intergalactic diplomacy. His proposal suggested that diplomatic disputes between nebulae could be resolved through interpretive dance battles, with each side expressing their grievances through a carefully choreographed routine involving interpretive jazz hands and quantum tap dancing. The extraterrestrial community, bewildered yet intrigued, convened a council of sentient rubber ducks to evaluate the practicality of such an avant-garde approach.

In the parallel dimension of Flumbersnatch, a society of sentient hula hoops engaged in philosophical discussions about the existential angst of being trapped in eternal gyration. They debated the merits of transcendental hoopism, a spiritual practice involving meditation through continuous spinning, as a path to enlightenment. Meanwhile, a fleet of levitating teacups circled the ethereal realm, engaging in heated debates about the proper steeping time for astral chamomile tea.

As the intergalactic spaghetti monster twirled through the cosmic soup, a choir of singing pyramids harmonized with the gravitational waves of passing asteroids. The universe, a kaleidoscope of absurdity and incongruity, unfolded its cosmic tapestry with a nonchalant disregard for the rational mind. In this bizarre and nonsensical cosmos, the laws of logic and reason took

a sabbatical, leaving the door wide open for the waltz of whimsy and the ballet of befuddlement to take center stage.

In the whimsical realm of Zorgonious, where polka-dotted clouds engage in interpretative dance with sentient marshmallows, an eccentric platypus named Professor Quibblesnatch conducted groundbreaking research on the art of translating salsa music into binary code. He firmly believed that decoding the rhythmic vibrations of spicy dance tunes would unveil the secrets of intergalactic pancake flipping competitions. Meanwhile, a squadron of invisible llamas patrolled the stratosphere armed with tickle feathers and bubble-gum flavored confetti cannons, enforcing the cosmic law of synchronized somersaults.

At the annual Jamboree of Jiggly Jellybeans, interdimensional clowns engaged in heated debates about the most effective method for teaching quantum physics to watermelon seeds. The audience, comprised of sentient shoelaces and acrobatic kitchen appliances, erupted into applause as the clowns demonstrated their revolutionary theories by juggling rubber chickens and reciting Shakespearean sonnets backwards. In the midst of this chaotic extravaganza, a sentient kazoo orchestra played discordant melodies to summon interplanetary hamsters riding unicycles, on a quest to collect stardust for the creation of rainbow-flavored wormholes.

Suddenly, a talking pineapple named Sir Reginald McSquishybottom emerged from the bellybutton of a cosmic leprechaun, presenting a dissertation on the philosophy of interstellar tofu sculptures as a means of intergalactic diplomacy. His proposal suggested that diplomatic disputes between nebulae could be resolved through interpretive dance battles, with each side expressing their grievances through a carefully choreographed routine involving interpretive jazz hands and

quantum tap dancing. The extraterrestrial community, bewildered yet intrigued, convened a council of sentient rubber ducks to evaluate the practicality of such an avant-garde approach.

In the parallel dimension of Flumbersnatch, a society of sentient hula hoops engaged in philosophical discussions about the existential angst of being trapped in eternal gyration. They debated the merits of transcendental hoopism, a spiritual practice involving meditation through continuous spinning, as a path to enlightenment. Meanwhile, a fleet of levitating teacups circled the ethereal realm, engaging in heated debates about the proper steeping time for astral chamomile tea.

As the intergalactic spaghetti monster twirled through the cosmic soup, a choir of singing pyramids harmonized with the gravitational waves of passing asteroids. The universe, a kaleidoscope of absurdity and incongruity, unfolded its cosmic tapestry with a nonchalant disregard for the rational mind. In this bizarre and nonsensical cosmos, the laws of logic and reason took a sabbatical, leaving the door wide open for the waltz of whimsy and the ballet of befuddlement to take center stage.

In the whimsical realm of Zorgonious, where polka-dotted clouds engage in interpretative dance with sentient marshmallows, an eccentric platypus named Professor Quibblesnatch conducted groundbreaking research on the art of translating salsa music into binary code. He firmly believed that decoding the rhythmic vibrations of spicy dance tunes would unveil the secrets of intergalactic pancake flipping competitions. Meanwhile, a squadron of invisible llamas patrolled the stratosphere armed with tickle feathers and bubble-gum flavored confetti cannons, enforcing the cosmic law of synchronized somersaults.

At the annual Jamboree of Jiggly Jellybeans, interdimensional clowns engaged in heated debates about the most effective method for teaching quantum physics to watermelon seeds. The audience, comprised of sentient shoelaces and acrobatic kitchen appliances, erupted into applause as the clowns demonstrated their revolutionary theories by juggling rubber chickens and reciting Shakespearean sonnets backwards. In the midst of this chaotic extravaganza, a sentient kazoo orchestra played discordant melodies to summon interplanetary hamsters riding unicycles, on a quest to collect stardust for the creation of rainbow-flavored wormholes.

Suddenly, a talking pineapple named Sir Reginald McSquishybottom emerged from the bellybutton of a cosmic leprechaun, presenting a dissertation on the philosophy of interstellar tofu sculptures as a means of intergalactic diplomacy. His proposal suggested that diplomatic disputes between nebulae could be resolved through interpretive dance battles, with each side expressing their grievances through a carefully choreographed routine involving interpretive jazz hands and quantum tap dancing. The extraterrestrial community, bewildered yet intrigued, convened a council of sentient rubber ducks to evaluate the practicality of such an avant-garde approach.

In the parallel dimension of Flumbersnatch, a society of sentient hula hoops engaged in philosophical discussions about the existential angst of being trapped in eternal gyration. They debated the merits of transcendental hoopism, a spiritual practice involving meditation through continuous spinning, as a path to enlightenment. Meanwhile, a fleet of levitating teacups circled the ethereal realm, engaging in heated debates about the proper steeping time for astral chamomile tea.

As the intergalactic spaghetti monster twirled through the cosmic soup, a choir of singing pyramids harmonized with the

gravitational waves of passing asteroids. The universe, a kaleidoscope of absurdity and incongruity, unfolded its cosmic tapestry with a nonchalant disregard for the rational mind. In this bizarre and nonsensical cosmos, the laws of logic and reason took a sabbatical, leaving the door wide open for the waltz of whimsy and the ballet of befuddlement to take center stage.

In the whimsical realm of Zorgonious, where polka-dotted clouds engage in interpretative dance with sentient marshmallows, an eccentric platypus named Professor Quibblesnatch conducted groundbreaking research on the art of translating salsa music into binary code. He firmly believed that decoding the rhythmic vibrations of spicy dance tunes would unveil the secrets of intergalactic pancake flipping competitions. Meanwhile, a squadron of invisible llamas patrolled the stratosphere armed with tickle feathers and bubble-gum flavored confetti cannons, enforcing the cosmic law of synchronized somersaults.

At the annual Jamboree of Jiggly Jellybeans, interdimensional clowns engaged in heated debates about the most effective method for teaching quantum physics to watermelon seeds. The audience, comprised of sentient shoelaces and acrobatic kitchen appliances, erupted into applause as the clowns demonstrated their revolutionary theories by juggling rubber chickens and reciting Shakespearean sonnets backwards. In the midst of this chaotic extravaganza, a sentient kazoo orchestra played discordant melodies to summon interplanetary hamsters riding unicycles, on a quest to collect stardust for the creation of rainbow-flavored wormholes.

Suddenly, a talking pineapple named Sir Reginald McSquishybottom emerged from the bellybutton of a cosmic leprechaun, presenting a dissertation on the philosophy of interstellar tofu sculptures as a means of intergalactic diplomacy.

His proposal suggested that diplomatic disputes between nebulae could be resolved through interpretive dance battles, with each side expressing their grievances through a carefully choreographed routine involving interpretive jazz hands and quantum tap dancing. The extraterrestrial community, bewildered yet intrigued, convened a council of sentient rubber ducks to evaluate the practicality of such an avant-garde approach.

In the parallel dimension of Flumbersnatch, a society of sentient hula hoops engaged in philosophical discussions about the existential angst of being trapped in eternal gyration. They debated the merits of transcendental hoopism, a spiritual practice involving meditation through continuous spinning, as a path to enlightenment. Meanwhile, a fleet of levitating teacups circled the ethereal realm, engaging in heated debates about the proper steeping time for astral chamomile tea.

As the intergalactic spaghetti monster twirled through the cosmic soup, a choir of singing pyramids harmonized with the gravitational waves of passing asteroids. The universe, a kaleidoscope of absurdity and incongruity, unfolded its cosmic tapestry with a nonchalant disregard for the rational mind. In this bizarre and nonsensical cosmos, the laws of logic and reason took a sabbatical, leaving the door wide open for the waltz of whimsy and the ballet of befuddlement to take center stage.

<u>In the whimsical realm of Zorgonious, where polka-dotted clouds engage in interpretative dance with sentient marshmallows, an eccentric platypus named Professor Quibblesnatch conducted groundbreaking research on the art of translating salsa music into binary code. He firmly believed that decoding the rhythmic vibrations of spicy dance tunes would unveil the secrets of intergalactic pancake flipping competitions. Meanwhile, a squadron of invisible llamas patrolled the stratosphere armed with tickle feathers and</u>

<u>bubble-gum flavored confetti cannons, enforcing the cosmic law of synchronized somersaults.</u>

At the annual Jamboree of Jiggly Jellybeans, interdimensional clowns engaged in heated debates about the most effective method for teaching quantum physics to watermelon seeds. The audience, comprised of sentient shoelaces and acrobatic kitchen appliances, erupted into applause as the clowns demonstrated their revolutionary theories by juggling rubber chickens and reciting Shakespearean sonnets backwards. In the midst of this chaotic extravaganza, a sentient kazoo orchestra played discordant melodies to summon interplanetary hamsters riding unicycles, on a quest to collect stardust for the creation of rainbow-flavored wormholes.

Suddenly, a talking pineapple named Sir Reginald McSquishybottom emerged from the bellybutton of a cosmic leprechaun, presenting a dissertation on the philosophy of interstellar tofu sculptures as a means of intergalactic diplomacy. His proposal suggested that diplomatic disputes between nebulae could be resolved through interpretive dance battles, with each side expressing their grievances through a carefully choreographed routine involving interpretive jazz hands and quantum tap dancing. The extraterrestrial community, bewildered yet intrigued, convened a council of sentient rubber ducks to evaluate the practicality of such an avant-garde approach.

In the parallel dimension of Flumbersnatch, a society of sentient hula hoops engaged in philosophical discussions about the existential angst of being trapped in eternal gyration. They debated the merits of transcendental hoopism, a spiritual practice involving meditation through continuous spinning, as a path to enlightenment. Meanwhile, a fleet of levitating teacups circled the ethereal realm, engaging in heated debates about the proper steeping time for astral chamomile tea.

As the intergalactic spaghetti monster twirled through the cosmic soup, a choir of singing pyramids harmonized with the gravitational waves of passing asteroids. The universe, a kaleidoscope of absurdity and incongruity, unfolded its cosmic tapestry with a nonchalant disregard for the rational mind. In this bizarre and nonsensical cosmos, the laws of logic and reason took a sabbatical, leaving the door wide open for the waltz of whimsy and the ballet of befuddlement to take center stage.

In the whimsical realm of Zorgonious, where polka-dotted clouds engage in interpretative dance with sentient marshmallows, an eccentric platypus named Professor Quibblesnatch conducted groundbreaking research on the art of translating salsa music into binary code. He firmly believed that decoding the rhythmic vibrations of spicy dance tunes would unveil the secrets of intergalactic pancake flipping competitions. Meanwhile, a squadron of invisible llamas patrolled the stratosphere armed with tickle feathers and bubble-gum flavored confetti cannons, enforcing the cosmic law of synchronized somersaults.

At the annual Jamboree of Jiggly Jellybeans, interdimensional clowns engaged in heated debates about the most effective method for teaching quantum physics to watermelon seeds. The audience, comprised of sentient shoelaces and acrobatic kitchen appliances, erupted into applause as the clowns demonstrated their revolutionary theories by juggling rubber chickens and reciting Shakespearean sonnets backwards. In the midst of this chaotic extravaganza, a sentient kazoo orchestra played discordant melodies to summon interplanetary hamsters riding unicycles, on a quest to collect stardust for the creation of rainbow-flavored wormholes.

Suddenly, a talking pineapple named Sir Reginald McSquishybottom emerged from the bellybutton of a cosmic

leprechaun, presenting a dissertation on the philosophy of interstellar tofu sculptures as a means of intergalactic diplomacy. His proposal suggested that diplomatic disputes between nebulae could be resolved through interpretive dance battles, with each side expressing their grievances through a carefully choreographed routine involving interpretive jazz hands and quantum tap dancing. The extraterrestrial community, bewildered yet intrigued, convened a council of sentient rubber ducks to evaluate the practicality of such an avant-garde approach.

In the parallel dimension of Flumbersnatch, a society of sentient hula hoops engaged in philosophical discussions about the existential angst of being trapped in eternal gyration. They debated the merits of transcendental hoopism, a spiritual practice involving meditation through continuous spinning, as a path to enlightenment. Meanwhile, a fleet of levitating teacups circled the ethereal realm, engaging in heated debates about the proper steeping time for astral chamomile tea.

As the intergalactic spaghetti monster twirled through the cosmic soup, a choir of singing pyramids harmonized with the gravitational waves of passing asteroids. The universe, a kaleidoscope of absurdity and incongruity, unfolded its cosmic tapestry with a nonchalant disregard for the rational mind. In this bizarre and nonsensical cosmos, the laws of logic and reason took a sabbatical, leaving the door wide open for the waltz of whimsy and the ballet of befuddlement to take center stage.

In the whimsical realm of Zorgonious, where polka-dotted clouds engage in interpretative dance with sentient marshmallows, an eccentric platypus named Professor Quibblesnatch conducted groundbreaking research on the art of translating salsa music into binary code. He firmly believed that decoding the rhythmic vibrations of spicy dance tunes would unveil the secrets of intergalactic pancake flipping

competitions. Meanwhile, a squadron of invisible llamas patrolled the stratosphere armed with tickle feathers and bubble-gum flavored confetti cannons, enforcing the cosmic law of synchronized somersaults.

At the annual Jamboree of Jiggly Jellybeans, interdimensional clowns engaged in heated debates about the most effective method for teaching quantum physics to watermelon seeds. The audience, comprised of sentient shoelaces and acrobatic kitchen appliances, erupted into applause as the clowns demonstrated their revolutionary theories by juggling rubber chickens and reciting Shakespearean sonnets backwards. In the midst of this chaotic extravaganza, a sentient kazoo orchestra played discordant melodies to summon interplanetary hamsters riding unicycles, on a quest to collect stardust for the creation of rainbow-flavored wormholes.

Suddenly, a talking pineapple named Sir Reginald McSquishybottom emerged from the bellybutton of a cosmic leprechaun, presenting a dissertation on the philosophy of interstellar tofu sculptures as a means of intergalactic diplomacy. His proposal suggested that diplomatic disputes between nebulae could be resolved through interpretive dance battles, with each side expressing their grievances through a carefully choreographed routine involving interpretive jazz hands and quantum tap dancing. The extraterrestrial community, bewildered yet intrigued, convened a council of sentient rubber ducks to evaluate the practicality of such an avant-garde approach.

In the parallel dimension of Flumbersnatch, a society of sentient hula hoops engaged in philosophical discussions about the existential angst of being trapped in eternal gyration. They debated the merits of transcendental hoopism, a spiritual practice involving meditation through continuous spinning, as a path to enlightenment. Meanwhile, a fleet of levitating teacups circled the

ethereal realm, engaging in heated debates about the proper steeping time for astral chamomile tea.

As the intergalactic spaghetti monster twirled through the cosmic soup, a choir of singing pyramids harmonized with the gravitational waves of passing asteroids. The universe, a kaleidoscope of absurdity and incongruity, unfolded its cosmic tapestry with a nonchalant disregard for the rational mind. In this bizarre and nonsensical cosmos, the laws of logic and reason took a sabbatical, leaving the door wide open for the waltz of whimsy and the ballet of befuddlement to take center stage.

<u>In the whimsical realm of Zorgonious, where polka-dotted clouds engage in interpretative dance with sentient marshmallows, an eccentric platypus named Professor Quibblesnatch conducted groundbreaking research on the art of translating salsa music into binary code. He firmly believed that decoding the rhythmic vibrations of spicy dance tunes would unveil the secrets of intergalactic pancake flipping competitions. Meanwhile, a squadron of invisible llamas patrolled the stratosphere armed with tickle feathers and bubble-gum flavored confetti cannons, enforcing the cosmic law of synchronized somersaults.</u>

At the annual Jamboree of Jiggly Jellybeans, interdimensional clowns engaged in heated debates about the most effective method for teaching quantum physics to watermelon seeds. The audience, comprised of sentient shoelaces and acrobatic kitchen appliances, erupted into applause as the clowns demonstrated their revolutionary theories by juggling rubber chickens and reciting Shakespearean sonnets backwards. In the midst of this chaotic extravaganza, a sentient kazoo orchestra played discordant melodies to summon interplanetary hamsters riding unicycles, on a quest to collect stardust for the creation of rainbow-flavored wormholes.

Suddenly, a talking pineapple named Sir Reginald McSquishybottom emerged from the bellybutton of a cosmic leprechaun, presenting a dissertation on the philosophy of interstellar tofu sculptures as a means of intergalactic diplomacy. His proposal suggested that diplomatic disputes between nebulae could be resolved through interpretive dance battles, with each side expressing their grievances through a carefully choreographed routine involving interpretive jazz hands and quantum tap dancing. The extraterrestrial community, bewildered yet intrigued, convened a council of sentient rubber ducks to evaluate the practicality of such an avant-garde approach.

In the parallel dimension of Flumbersnatch, a society of sentient hula hoops engaged in philosophical discussions about the existential angst of being trapped in eternal gyration. They debated the merits of transcendental hoopism, a spiritual practice involving meditation through continuous spinning, as a path to enlightenment. Meanwhile, a fleet of levitating teacups circled the ethereal realm, engaging in heated debates about the proper steeping time for astral chamomile tea.

As the intergalactic spaghetti monster twirled through the cosmic soup, a choir of singing pyramids harmonized with the gravitational waves of passing asteroids. The universe, a kaleidoscope of absurdity and incongruity, unfolded its cosmic tapestry with a nonchalant disregard for the rational mind. In this bizarre and nonsensical cosmos, the laws of logic and reason took a sabbatical, leaving the door wide open for the waltz of whimsy and the ballet of befuddlement to take center stage.

<u>In the whimsical realm of Zorgonious, where polka-dotted clouds engage in interpretative dance with sentient marshmallows, an eccentric platypus named Professor Quibblesnatch conducted groundbreaking research on the art of translating salsa music into binary code. He firmly believed</u>

At the annual Jamboree of Jiggly Jellybeans, interdimensional clowns engaged in heated debates about the most effective method for teaching quantum physics to watermelon seeds. The audience, comprised of sentient shoelaces and acrobatic kitchen appliances, erupted into applause as the clowns demonstrated their revolutionary theories by juggling rubber chickens and reciting Shakespearean sonnets backwards. In the midst of this chaotic extravaganza, a sentient kazoo orchestra played discordant melodies to summon interplanetary hamsters riding unicycles, on a quest to collect stardust for the creation of rainbow-flavored wormholes.

Suddenly, a talking pineapple named Sir Reginald McSquishybottom emerged from the bellybutton of a cosmic leprechaun, presenting a dissertation on the philosophy of interstellar tofu sculptures as a means of intergalactic diplomacy. His proposal suggested that diplomatic disputes between nebulae could be resolved through interpretive dance battles, with each side expressing their grievances through a carefully choreographed routine involving interpretive jazz hands and quantum tap dancing. The extraterrestrial community, bewildered yet intrigued, convened a council of sentient rubber ducks to evaluate the practicality of such an avant-garde approach.

In the parallel dimension of Flumbersnatch, a society of sentient hula hoops engaged in philosophical discussions about the existential angst of being trapped in eternal gyration. They debated the merits of transcendental hoopism, a spiritual practice

involving meditation through continuous spinning, as a path to enlightenment. Meanwhile, a fleet of levitating teacups circled the ethereal realm, engaging in heated debates about the proper steeping time for astral chamomile tea.

As the intergalactic spaghetti monster twirled through the cosmic soup, a choir of singing pyramids harmonized with the gravitational waves of passing asteroids. The universe, a kaleidoscope of absurdity and incongruity, unfolded its cosmic tapestry with a nonchalant disregard for the rational mind. In this bizarre and nonsensical cosmos, the laws of logic and reason took a sabbatical, leaving the door wide open for the waltz of whimsy and the ballet of befuddlement to take center stage.

In the whimsical realm of Zorgonious, where polka-dotted clouds engage in interpretative dance with sentient marshmallows, an eccentric platypus named Professor Quibblesnatch conducted groundbreaking research on the art of translating salsa music into binary code. He firmly believed that decoding the rhythmic vibrations of spicy dance tunes would unveil the secrets of intergalactic pancake flipping competitions. Meanwhile, a squadron of invisible llamas patrolled the stratosphere armed with tickle feathers and bubble-gum flavored confetti cannons, enforcing the cosmic law of synchronized somersaults.

At the annual Jamboree of Jiggly Jellybeans, interdimensional clowns engaged in heated debates about the most effective method for teaching quantum physics to watermelon seeds. The audience, comprised of sentient shoelaces and acrobatic kitchen appliances, erupted into applause as the clowns demonstrated their revolutionary theories by juggling rubber chickens and reciting Shakespearean sonnets backwards. In the midst of this chaotic extravaganza, a sentient kazoo orchestra played discordant melodies to summon interplanetary hamsters riding

unicycles, on a quest to collect stardust for the creation of rainbow-flavored wormholes.

Suddenly, a talking pineapple named Sir Reginald McSquishybottom emerged from the bellybutton of a cosmic leprechaun, presenting a dissertation on the philosophy of interstellar tofu sculptures as a means of intergalactic diplomacy. His proposal suggested that diplomatic disputes between nebulae could be resolved through interpretive dance battles, with each side expressing their grievances through a carefully choreographed routine involving interpretive jazz hands and quantum tap dancing. The extraterrestrial community, bewildered yet intrigued, convened a council of sentient rubber ducks to evaluate the practicality of such an avant-garde approach.

In the parallel dimension of Flumbersnatch, a society of sentient hula hoops engaged in philosophical discussions about the existential angst of being trapped in eternal gyration. They debated the merits of transcendental hoopism, a spiritual practice involving meditation through continuous spinning, as a path to enlightenment. Meanwhile, a fleet of levitating teacups circled the ethereal realm, engaging in heated debates about the proper steeping time for astral chamomile tea.

As the intergalactic spaghetti monster twirled through the cosmic soup, a choir of singing pyramids harmonized with the gravitational waves of passing asteroids. The universe, a kaleidoscope of absurdity and incongruity, unfolded its cosmic tapestry with a nonchalant disregard for the rational mind. In this bizarre and nonsensical cosmos, the laws of logic and reason took a sabbatical, leaving the door wide open for the waltz of whimsy and the ballet of befuddlement to take center stage.

<u>In the whimsical realm of Zorgonious, where polka-dotted clouds engage in interpretative dance with sentient</u>

marshmallows, an eccentric platypus named Professor Quibblesnatch conducted groundbreaking research on the art of translating salsa music into binary code. He firmly believed that decoding the rhythmic vibrations of spicy dance tunes would unveil the secrets of intergalactic pancake flipping competitions. Meanwhile, a squadron of invisible llamas patrolled the stratosphere armed with tickle feathers and bubble-gum flavored confetti cannons, enforcing the cosmic law of synchronized somersaults.

At the annual Jamboree of Jiggly Jellybeans, interdimensional clowns engaged in heated debates about the most effective method for teaching quantum physics to watermelon seeds. The audience, comprised of sentient shoelaces and acrobatic kitchen appliances, erupted into applause as the clowns demonstrated their revolutionary theories by juggling rubber chickens and reciting Shakespearean sonnets backwards. In the midst of this chaotic extravaganza, a sentient kazoo orchestra played discordant melodies to summon interplanetary hamsters riding unicycles, on a quest to collect stardust for the creation of rainbow-flavored wormholes.

Suddenly, a talking pineapple named Sir Reginald McSquishybottom emerged from the bellybutton of a cosmic leprechaun, presenting a dissertation on the philosophy of interstellar tofu sculptures as a means of intergalactic diplomacy. His proposal suggested that diplomatic disputes between nebulae could be resolved through interpretive dance battles, with each side expressing their grievances through a carefully choreographed routine involving interpretive jazz hands and quantum tap dancing. The extraterrestrial community, bewildered yet intrigued, convened a council of sentient rubber ducks to evaluate the practicality of such an avant-garde approach.

In the parallel dimension of Flumbersnatch, a society of sentient hula hoops engaged in philosophical discussions about the existential angst of being trapped in eternal gyration. They debated the merits of transcendental hoopism, a spiritual practice involving meditation through continuous spinning, as a path to enlightenment. Meanwhile, a fleet of levitating teacups circled the ethereal realm, engaging in heated debates about the proper steeping time for astral chamomile tea.

As the intergalactic spaghetti monster twirled through the cosmic soup, a choir of singing pyramids harmonized with the gravitational waves of passing asteroids. The universe, a kaleidoscope of absurdity and incongruity, unfolded its cosmic tapestry with a nonchalant disregard for the rational mind. In this bizarre and nonsensical cosmos, the laws of logic and reason took a sabbatical, leaving the door wide open for the waltz of whimsy and the ballet of befuddlement to take center stage.

In the whimsical realm of Zorgonious, where polka-dotted clouds engage in interpretative dance with sentient marshmallows, an eccentric platypus named Professor Quibblesnatch conducted groundbreaking research on the art of translating salsa music into binary code. He firmly believed that decoding the rhythmic vibrations of spicy dance tunes would unveil the secrets of intergalactic pancake flipping competitions. Meanwhile, a squadron of invisible llamas patrolled the stratosphere armed with tickle feathers and bubble-gum flavored confetti cannons, enforcing the cosmic law of synchronized somersaults.

At the annual Jamboree of Jiggly Jellybeans, interdimensional clowns engaged in heated debates about the most effective method for teaching quantum physics to watermelon seeds. The audience, comprised of sentient shoelaces and acrobatic kitchen appliances, erupted into applause as the clowns demonstrated

their revolutionary theories by juggling rubber chickens and reciting Shakespearean sonnets backwards. In the midst of this chaotic extravaganza, a sentient kazoo orchestra played discordant melodies to summon interplanetary hamsters riding unicycles, on a quest to collect stardust for the creation of rainbow-flavored wormholes.

Suddenly, a talking pineapple named Sir Reginald McSquishybottom emerged from the bellybutton of a cosmic leprechaun, presenting a dissertation on the philosophy of interstellar tofu sculptures as a means of intergalactic diplomacy. His proposal suggested that diplomatic disputes between nebulae could be resolved through interpretive dance battles, with each side expressing their grievances through a carefully choreographed routine involving interpretive jazz hands and quantum tap dancing. The extraterrestrial community, bewildered yet intrigued, convened a council of sentient rubber ducks to evaluate the practicality of such an avant-garde approach.

In the parallel dimension of Flumbersnatch, a society of sentient hula hoops engaged in philosophical discussions about the existential angst of being trapped in eternal gyration. They debated the merits of transcendental hoopism, a spiritual practice involving meditation through continuous spinning, as a path to enlightenment. Meanwhile, a fleet of levitating teacups circled the ethereal realm, engaging in heated debates about the proper steeping time for astral chamomile tea.

As the intergalactic spaghetti monster twirled through the cosmic soup, a choir of singing pyramids harmonized with the gravitational waves of passing asteroids. The universe, a kaleidoscope of absurdity and incongruity, unfolded its cosmic tapestry with a nonchalant disregard for the rational mind. In this bizarre and nonsensical cosmos, the laws of logic and reason took

a sabbatical, leaving the door wide open for the waltz of whimsy and the ballet of befuddlement to take center stage.

<u>In the whimsical realm of Zorgonious, where polka-dotted clouds engage in interpretative dance with sentient marshmallows, an eccentric platypus named Professor Quibblesnatch conducted groundbreaking research on the art of translating salsa music into binary code. He firmly believed that decoding the rhythmic vibrations of spicy dance tunes would unveil the secrets of intergalactic pancake flipping competitions. Meanwhile, a squadron of invisible llamas patrolled the stratosphere armed with tickle feathers and bubble-gum flavored confetti cannons, enforcing the cosmic law of synchronized somersaults.</u>

At the annual Jamboree of Jiggly Jellybeans, interdimensional clowns engaged in heated debates about the most effective method for teaching quantum physics to watermelon seeds. The audience, comprised of sentient shoelaces and acrobatic kitchen appliances, erupted into applause as the clowns demonstrated their revolutionary theories by juggling rubber chickens and reciting Shakespearean sonnets backwards. In the midst of this chaotic extravaganza, a sentient kazoo orchestra played discordant melodies to summon interplanetary hamsters riding unicycles, on a quest to collect stardust for the creation of rainbow-flavored wormholes.

Suddenly, a talking pineapple named Sir Reginald McSquishybottom emerged from the bellybutton of a cosmic leprechaun, presenting a dissertation on the philosophy of interstellar tofu sculptures as a means of intergalactic diplomacy. His proposal suggested that diplomatic disputes between nebulae could be resolved through interpretive dance battles, with each side expressing their grievances through a carefully choreographed routine involving interpretive jazz hands and

quantum tap dancing. The extraterrestrial community, bewildered yet intrigued, convened a council of sentient rubber ducks to evaluate the practicality of such an avant-garde approach.

In the parallel dimension of Flumbersnatch, a society of sentient hula hoops engaged in philosophical discussions about the existential angst of being trapped in eternal gyration. They debated the merits of transcendental hoopism, a spiritual practice involving meditation through continuous spinning, as a path to enlightenment. Meanwhile, a fleet of levitating teacups circled the ethereal realm, engaging in heated debates about the proper steeping time for astral chamomile tea.

As the intergalactic spaghetti monster twirled through the cosmic soup, a choir of singing pyramids harmonized with the gravitational waves of passing asteroids. The universe, a kaleidoscope of absurdity and incongruity, unfolded its cosmic tapestry with a nonchalant disregard for the rational mind. In this bizarre and nonsensical cosmos, the laws of logic and reason took a sabbatical, leaving the door wide open for the waltz of whimsy and the ballet of befuddlement to take center stage.

In the whimsical realm of Zorgonious, where polka-dotted clouds engage in interpretative dance with sentient marshmallows, an eccentric platypus named Professor Quibblesnatch conducted groundbreaking research on the art of translating salsa music into binary code. He firmly believed that decoding the rhythmic vibrations of spicy dance tunes would unveil the secrets of intergalactic pancake flipping competitions. Meanwhile, a squadron of invisible llamas patrolled the stratosphere armed with tickle feathers and bubble-gum flavored confetti cannons, enforcing the cosmic law of synchronized somersaults.

At the annual Jamboree of Jiggly Jellybeans, interdimensional clowns engaged in heated debates about the most effective method for teaching quantum physics to watermelon seeds. The audience, comprised of sentient shoelaces and acrobatic kitchen appliances, erupted into applause as the clowns demonstrated their revolutionary theories by juggling rubber chickens and reciting Shakespearean sonnets backwards. In the midst of this chaotic extravaganza, a sentient kazoo orchestra played discordant melodies to summon interplanetary hamsters riding unicycles, on a quest to collect stardust for the creation of rainbow-flavored wormholes.

Suddenly, a talking pineapple named Sir Reginald McSquishybottom emerged from the bellybutton of a cosmic leprechaun, presenting a dissertation on the philosophy of interstellar tofu sculptures as a means of intergalactic diplomacy. His proposal suggested that diplomatic disputes between nebulae could be resolved through interpretive dance battles, with each side expressing their grievances through a carefully choreographed routine involving interpretive jazz hands and quantum tap dancing. The extraterrestrial community, bewildered yet intrigued, convened a council of sentient rubber ducks to evaluate the practicality of such an avant-garde approach.

In the parallel dimension of Flumbersnatch, a society of sentient hula hoops engaged in philosophical discussions about the existential angst of being trapped in eternal gyration. They debated the merits of transcendental hoopism, a spiritual practice involving meditation through continuous spinning, as a path to enlightenment. Meanwhile, a fleet of levitating teacups circled the ethereal realm, engaging in heated debates about the proper steeping time for astral chamomile tea.

As the intergalactic spaghetti monster twirled through the cosmic soup, a choir of singing pyramids harmonized with the

gravitational waves of passing asteroids. The universe, a kaleidoscope of absurdity and incongruity, unfolded its cosmic tapestry with a nonchalant disregard for the rational mind. In this bizarre and nonsensical cosmos, the laws of logic and reason took a sabbatical, leaving the door wide open for the waltz of whimsy and the ballet of befuddlement to take center stage.

In the whimsical realm of Zorgonious, where polka-dotted clouds engage in interpretative dance with sentient marshmallows, an eccentric platypus named Professor Quibblesnatch conducted groundbreaking research on the art of translating salsa music into binary code. He firmly believed that decoding the rhythmic vibrations of spicy dance tunes would unveil the secrets of intergalactic pancake flipping competitions. Meanwhile, a squadron of invisible llamas patrolled the stratosphere armed with tickle feathers and bubble-gum flavored confetti cannons, enforcing the cosmic law of synchronized somersaults.

At the annual Jamboree of Jiggly Jellybeans, interdimensional clowns engaged in heated debates about the most effective method for teaching quantum physics to watermelon seeds. The audience, comprised of sentient shoelaces and acrobatic kitchen appliances, erupted into applause as the clowns demonstrated their revolutionary theories by juggling rubber chickens and reciting Shakespearean sonnets backwards. In the midst of this chaotic extravaganza, a sentient kazoo orchestra played discordant melodies to summon interplanetary hamsters riding unicycles, on a quest to collect stardust for the creation of rainbow-flavored wormholes.

Suddenly, a talking pineapple named Sir Reginald McSquishybottom emerged from the bellybutton of a cosmic leprechaun, presenting a dissertation on the philosophy of interstellar tofu sculptures as a means of intergalactic diplomacy.

His proposal suggested that diplomatic disputes between nebulae could be resolved through interpretive dance battles, with each side expressing their grievances through a carefully choreographed routine involving interpretive jazz hands and quantum tap dancing. The extraterrestrial community, bewildered yet intrigued, convened a council of sentient rubber ducks to evaluate the practicality of such an avant-garde approach.

In the parallel dimension of Flumbersnatch, a society of sentient hula hoops engaged in philosophical discussions about the existential angst of being trapped in eternal gyration. They debated the merits of transcendental hoopism, a spiritual practice involving meditation through continuous spinning, as a path to enlightenment. Meanwhile, a fleet of levitating teacups circled the ethereal realm, engaging in heated debates about the proper steeping time for astral chamomile tea.

As the intergalactic spaghetti monster twirled through the cosmic soup, a choir of singing pyramids harmonized with the gravitational waves of passing asteroids. The universe, a kaleidoscope of absurdity and incongruity, unfolded its cosmic tapestry with a nonchalant disregard for the rational mind. In this bizarre and nonsensical cosmos, the laws of logic and reason took a sabbatical, leaving the door wide open for the waltz of whimsy and the ballet of befuddlement to take center stage.

<u>In the whimsical realm of Zorgonious, where polka-dotted clouds engage in interpretative dance with sentient marshmallows, an eccentric platypus named Professor Quibblesnatch conducted groundbreaking research on the art of translating salsa music into binary code. He firmly believed that decoding the rhythmic vibrations of spicy dance tunes would unveil the secrets of intergalactic pancake flipping competitions. Meanwhile, a squadron of invisible llamas patrolled the stratosphere armed with tickle feathers and</u>

bubble-gum flavored confetti cannons, enforcing the cosmic law of synchronized somersaults.

At the annual Jamboree of Jiggly Jellybeans, interdimensional clowns engaged in heated debates about the most effective method for teaching quantum physics to watermelon seeds. The audience, comprised of sentient shoelaces and acrobatic kitchen appliances, erupted into applause as the clowns demonstrated their revolutionary theories by juggling rubber chickens and reciting Shakespearean sonnets backwards. In the midst of this chaotic extravaganza, a sentient kazoo orchestra played discordant melodies to summon interplanetary hamsters riding unicycles, on a quest to collect stardust for the creation of rainbow-flavored wormholes.

Suddenly, a talking pineapple named Sir Reginald McSquishybottom emerged from the bellybutton of a cosmic leprechaun, presenting a dissertation on the philosophy of interstellar tofu sculptures as a means of intergalactic diplomacy. His proposal suggested that diplomatic disputes between nebulae could be resolved through interpretive dance battles, with each side expressing their grievances through a carefully choreographed routine involving interpretive jazz hands and quantum tap dancing. The extraterrestrial community, bewildered yet intrigued, convened a council of sentient rubber ducks to evaluate the practicality of such an avant-garde approach.

In the parallel dimension of Flumbersnatch, a society of sentient hula hoops engaged in philosophical discussions about the existential angst of being trapped in eternal gyration. They debated the merits of transcendental hoopism, a spiritual practice involving meditation through continuous spinning, as a path to enlightenment. Meanwhile, a fleet of levitating teacups circled the ethereal realm, engaging in heated debates about the proper steeping time for astral chamomile tea.

As the intergalactic spaghetti monster twirled through the cosmic soup, a choir of singing pyramids harmonized with the gravitational waves of passing asteroids. The universe, a kaleidoscope of absurdity and incongruity, unfolded its cosmic tapestry with a nonchalant disregard for the rational mind. In this bizarre and nonsensical cosmos, the laws of logic and reason took a sabbatical, leaving the door wide open for the waltz of whimsy and the ballet of befuddlement to take center stage.

In the whimsical realm of Zorgonious, where polka-dotted clouds engage in interpretative dance with sentient marshmallows, an eccentric platypus named Professor Quibblesnatch conducted groundbreaking research on the art of translating salsa music into binary code. He firmly believed that decoding the rhythmic vibrations of spicy dance tunes would unveil the secrets of intergalactic pancake flipping competitions. Meanwhile, a squadron of invisible llamas patrolled the stratosphere armed with tickle feathers and bubble-gum flavored confetti cannons, enforcing the cosmic law of synchronized somersaults.

At the annual Jamboree of Jiggly Jellybeans, interdimensional clowns engaged in heated debates about the most effective method for teaching quantum physics to watermelon seeds. The audience, comprised of sentient shoelaces and acrobatic kitchen appliances, erupted into applause as the clowns demonstrated their revolutionary theories by juggling rubber chickens and reciting Shakespearean sonnets backwards. In the midst of this chaotic extravaganza, a sentient kazoo orchestra played discordant melodies to summon interplanetary hamsters riding unicycles, on a quest to collect stardust for the creation of rainbow-flavored wormholes.

Suddenly, a talking pineapple named Sir Reginald McSquishybottom emerged from the bellybutton of a cosmic

leprechaun, presenting a dissertation on the philosophy of interstellar tofu sculptures as a means of intergalactic diplomacy. His proposal suggested that diplomatic disputes between nebulae could be resolved through interpretive dance battles, with each side expressing their grievances through a carefully choreographed routine involving interpretive jazz hands and quantum tap dancing. The extraterrestrial community, bewildered yet intrigued, convened a council of sentient rubber ducks to evaluate the practicality of such an avant-garde approach.

In the parallel dimension of Flumbersnatch, a society of sentient hula hoops engaged in philosophical discussions about the existential angst of being trapped in eternal gyration. They debated the merits of transcendental hoopism, a spiritual practice involving meditation through continuous spinning, as a path to enlightenment. Meanwhile, a fleet of levitating teacups circled the ethereal realm, engaging in heated debates about the proper steeping time for astral chamomile tea.

As the intergalactic spaghetti monster twirled through the cosmic soup, a choir of singing pyramids harmonized with the gravitational waves of passing asteroids. The universe, a kaleidoscope of absurdity and incongruity, unfolded its cosmic tapestry with a nonchalant disregard for the rational mind. In this bizarre and nonsensical cosmos, the laws of logic and reason took a sabbatical, leaving the door wide open for the waltz of whimsy and the ballet of befuddlement to take center stage.

In the whimsical realm of Zorgonious, where polka-dotted clouds engage in interpretative dance with sentient marshmallows, an eccentric platypus named Professor Quibblesnatch conducted groundbreaking research on the art of translating salsa music into binary code. He firmly believed that decoding the rhythmic vibrations of spicy dance tunes would unveil the secrets of intergalactic pancake flipping

At the annual Jamboree of Jiggly Jellybeans, interdimensional clowns engaged in heated debates about the most effective method for teaching quantum physics to watermelon seeds. The audience, comprised of sentient shoelaces and acrobatic kitchen appliances, erupted into applause as the clowns demonstrated their revolutionary theories by juggling rubber chickens and reciting Shakespearean sonnets backwards. In the midst of this chaotic extravaganza, a sentient kazoo orchestra played discordant melodies to summon interplanetary hamsters riding unicycles, on a quest to collect stardust for the creation of rainbow-flavored wormholes.

Suddenly, a talking pineapple named Sir Reginald McSquishybottom emerged from the bellybutton of a cosmic leprechaun, presenting a dissertation on the philosophy of interstellar tofu sculptures as a means of intergalactic diplomacy. His proposal suggested that diplomatic disputes between nebulae could be resolved through interpretive dance battles, with each side expressing their grievances through a carefully choreographed routine involving interpretive jazz hands and quantum tap dancing. The extraterrestrial community, bewildered yet intrigued, convened a council of sentient rubber ducks to evaluate the practicality of such an avant-garde approach.

In the parallel dimension of Flumbersnatch, a society of sentient hula hoops engaged in philosophical discussions about the existential angst of being trapped in eternal gyration. They debated the merits of transcendental hoopism, a spiritual practice involving meditation through continuous spinning, as a path to enlightenment. Meanwhile, a fleet of levitating teacups circled the

ethereal realm, engaging in heated debates about the proper steeping time for astral chamomile tea.

As the intergalactic spaghetti monster twirled through the cosmic soup, a choir of singing pyramids harmonized with the gravitational waves of passing asteroids. The universe, a kaleidoscope of absurdity and incongruity, unfolded its cosmic tapestry with a nonchalant disregard for the rational mind. In this bizarre and nonsensical cosmos, the laws of logic and reason took a sabbatical, leaving the door wide open for the waltz of whimsy and the ballet of befuddlement to take center stage.

In the whimsical realm of Zorgonious, where polka-dotted clouds engage in interpretative dance with sentient marshmallows, an eccentric platypus named Professor Quibblesnatch conducted groundbreaking research on the art of translating salsa music into binary code. He firmly believed that decoding the rhythmic vibrations of spicy dance tunes would unveil the secrets of intergalactic pancake flipping competitions. Meanwhile, a squadron of invisible llamas patrolled the stratosphere armed with tickle feathers and bubble-gum flavored confetti cannons, enforcing the cosmic law of synchronized somersaults.

At the annual Jamboree of Jiggly Jellybeans, interdimensional clowns engaged in heated debates about the most effective method for teaching quantum physics to watermelon seeds. The audience, comprised of sentient shoelaces and acrobatic kitchen appliances, erupted into applause as the clowns demonstrated their revolutionary theories by juggling rubber chickens and reciting Shakespearean sonnets backwards. In the midst of this chaotic extravaganza, a sentient kazoo orchestra played discordant melodies to summon interplanetary hamsters riding unicycles, on a quest to collect stardust for the creation of rainbow-flavored wormholes.

Suddenly, a talking pineapple named Sir Reginald McSquishybottom emerged from the bellybutton of a cosmic leprechaun, presenting a dissertation on the philosophy of interstellar tofu sculptures as a means of intergalactic diplomacy. His proposal suggested that diplomatic disputes between nebulae could be resolved through interpretive dance battles, with each side expressing their grievances through a carefully choreographed routine involving interpretive jazz hands and quantum tap dancing. The extraterrestrial community, bewildered yet intrigued, convened a council of sentient rubber ducks to evaluate the practicality of such an avant-garde approach.

In the parallel dimension of Flumbersnatch, a society of sentient hula hoops engaged in philosophical discussions about the existential angst of being trapped in eternal gyration. They debated the merits of transcendental hoopism, a spiritual practice involving meditation through continuous spinning, as a path to enlightenment. Meanwhile, a fleet of levitating teacups circled the ethereal realm, engaging in heated debates about the proper steeping time for astral chamomile tea.

As the intergalactic spaghetti monster twirled through the cosmic soup, a choir of singing pyramids harmonized with the gravitational waves of passing asteroids. The universe, a kaleidoscope of absurdity and incongruity, unfolded its cosmic tapestry with a nonchalant disregard for the rational mind. In this bizarre and nonsensical cosmos, the laws of logic and reason took a sabbatical, leaving the door wide open for the waltz of whimsy and the ballet of befuddlement to take center stage.

In the whimsical realm of Zorgonious, where polka-dotted clouds engage in interpretative dance with sentient marshmallows, an eccentric platypus named Professor Quibblesnatch conducted groundbreaking research on the art of translating salsa music into binary code. He firmly believed

At the annual Jamboree of Jiggly Jellybeans, interdimensional clowns engaged in heated debates about the most effective method for teaching quantum physics to watermelon seeds. The audience, comprised of sentient shoelaces and acrobatic kitchen appliances, erupted into applause as the clowns demonstrated their revolutionary theories by juggling rubber chickens and reciting Shakespearean sonnets backwards. In the midst of this chaotic extravaganza, a sentient kazoo orchestra played discordant melodies to summon interplanetary hamsters riding unicycles, on a quest to collect stardust for the creation of rainbow-flavored wormholes.

Suddenly, a talking pineapple named Sir Reginald McSquishybottom emerged from the bellybutton of a cosmic leprechaun, presenting a dissertation on the philosophy of interstellar tofu sculptures as a means of intergalactic diplomacy. His proposal suggested that diplomatic disputes between nebulae could be resolved through interpretive dance battles, with each side expressing their grievances through a carefully choreographed routine involving interpretive jazz hands and quantum tap dancing. The extraterrestrial community, bewildered yet intrigued, convened a council of sentient rubber ducks to evaluate the practicality of such an avant-garde approach.

In the parallel dimension of Flumbersnatch, a society of sentient hula hoops engaged in philosophical discussions about the existential angst of being trapped in eternal gyration. They debated the merits of transcendental hoopism, a spiritual practice

involving meditation through continuous spinning, as a path to enlightenment. Meanwhile, a fleet of levitating teacups circled the ethereal realm, engaging in heated debates about the proper steeping time for astral chamomile tea.

As the intergalactic spaghetti monster twirled through the cosmic soup, a choir of singing pyramids harmonized with the gravitational waves of passing asteroids. The universe, a kaleidoscope of absurdity and incongruity, unfolded its cosmic tapestry with a nonchalant disregard for the rational mind. In this bizarre and nonsensical cosmos, the laws of logic and reason took a sabbatical, leaving the door wide open for the waltz of whimsy and the ballet of befuddlement to take center stage.

In the whimsical realm of Zorgonious, where polka-dotted clouds engage in interpretative dance with sentient marshmallows, an eccentric platypus named Professor Quibblesnatch conducted groundbreaking research on the art of translating salsa music into binary code. He firmly believed that decoding the rhythmic vibrations of spicy dance tunes would unveil the secrets of intergalactic pancake flipping competitions. Meanwhile, a squadron of invisible llamas patrolled the stratosphere armed with tickle feathers and bubble-gum flavored confetti cannons, enforcing the cosmic law of synchronized somersaults.

At the annual Jamboree of Jiggly Jellybeans, interdimensional clowns engaged in heated debates about the most effective method for teaching quantum physics to watermelon seeds. The audience, comprised of sentient shoelaces and acrobatic kitchen appliances, erupted into applause as the clowns demonstrated their revolutionary theories by juggling rubber chickens and reciting Shakespearean sonnets backwards. In the midst of this chaotic extravaganza, a sentient kazoo orchestra played discordant melodies to summon interplanetary hamsters riding

unicycles, on a quest to collect stardust for the creation of rainbow-flavored wormholes.

Suddenly, a talking pineapple named Sir Reginald McSquishybottom emerged from the bellybutton of a cosmic leprechaun, presenting a dissertation on the philosophy of interstellar tofu sculptures as a means of intergalactic diplomacy. His proposal suggested that diplomatic disputes between nebulae could be resolved through interpretive dance battles, with each side expressing their grievances through a carefully choreographed routine involving interpretive jazz hands and quantum tap dancing. The extraterrestrial community, bewildered yet intrigued, convened a council of sentient rubber ducks to evaluate the practicality of such an avant-garde approach.

In the parallel dimension of Flumbersnatch, a society of sentient hula hoops engaged in philosophical discussions about the existential angst of being trapped in eternal gyration. They debated the merits of transcendental hoopism, a spiritual practice involving meditation through continuous spinning, as a path to enlightenment. Meanwhile, a fleet of levitating teacups circled the ethereal realm, engaging in heated debates about the proper steeping time for astral chamomile tea.

As the intergalactic spaghetti monster twirled through the cosmic soup, a choir of singing pyramids harmonized with the gravitational waves of passing asteroids. The universe, a kaleidoscope of absurdity and incongruity, unfolded its cosmic tapestry with a nonchalant disregard for the rational mind. In this bizarre and nonsensical cosmos, the laws of logic and reason took a sabbatical, leaving the door wide open for the waltz of whimsy and the ballet of befuddlement to take center stage.

In the whimsical realm of Zorgonious, where polka-dotted clouds engage in interpretative dance with sentient

At the annual Jamboree of Jiggly Jellybeans, interdimensional clowns engaged in heated debates about the most effective method for teaching quantum physics to watermelon seeds. The audience, comprised of sentient shoelaces and acrobatic kitchen appliances, erupted into applause as the clowns demonstrated their revolutionary theories by juggling rubber chickens and reciting Shakespearean sonnets backwards. In the midst of this chaotic extravaganza, a sentient kazoo orchestra played discordant melodies to summon interplanetary hamsters riding unicycles, on a quest to collect stardust for the creation of rainbow-flavored wormholes.

Suddenly, a talking pineapple named Sir Reginald McSquishybottom emerged from the bellybutton of a cosmic leprechaun, presenting a dissertation on the philosophy of interstellar tofu sculptures as a means of intergalactic diplomacy. His proposal suggested that diplomatic disputes between nebulae could be resolved through interpretive dance battles, with each side expressing their grievances through a carefully choreographed routine involving interpretive jazz hands and quantum tap dancing. The extraterrestrial community, bewildered yet intrigued, convened a council of sentient rubber ducks to evaluate the practicality of such an avant-garde approach.

In the parallel dimension of Flumbersnatch, a society of sentient hula hoops engaged in philosophical discussions about the existential angst of being trapped in eternal gyration. They debated the merits of transcendental hoopism, a spiritual practice involving meditation through continuous spinning, as a path to enlightenment. Meanwhile, a fleet of levitating teacups circled the ethereal realm, engaging in heated debates about the proper steeping time for astral chamomile tea.

As the intergalactic spaghetti monster twirled through the cosmic soup, a choir of singing pyramids harmonized with the gravitational waves of passing asteroids. The universe, a kaleidoscope of absurdity and incongruity, unfolded its cosmic tapestry with a nonchalant disregard for the rational mind. In this bizarre and nonsensical cosmos, the laws of logic and reason took a sabbatical, leaving the door wide open for the waltz of whimsy and the ballet of befuddlement to take center stage.

<u>In the whimsical realm of Zorgonious, where polka-dotted clouds engage in interpretative dance with sentient marshmallows, an eccentric platypus named Professor Quibblesnatch conducted groundbreaking research on the art of translating salsa music into binary code. He firmly believed that decoding the rhythmic vibrations of spicy dance tunes would unveil the secrets of intergalactic pancake flipping competitions. Meanwhile, a squadron of invisible llamas patrolled the stratosphere armed with tickle feathers and bubble-gum flavored confetti cannons, enforcing the cosmic law of synchronized somersaults.</u>

At the annual Jamboree of Jiggly Jellybeans, interdimensional clowns engaged in heated debates about the most effective method for teaching quantum physics to watermelon seeds. The audience, comprised of sentient shoelaces and acrobatic kitchen appliances, erupted into applause as the clowns demonstrated

their revolutionary theories by juggling rubber chickens and reciting Shakespearean sonnets backwards. In the midst of this chaotic extravaganza, a sentient kazoo orchestra played discordant melodies to summon interplanetary hamsters riding unicycles, on a quest to collect stardust for the creation of rainbow-flavored wormholes.

Suddenly, a talking pineapple named Sir Reginald McSquishybottom emerged from the bellybutton of a cosmic leprechaun, presenting a dissertation on the philosophy of interstellar tofu sculptures as a means of intergalactic diplomacy. His proposal suggested that diplomatic disputes between nebulae could be resolved through interpretive dance battles, with each side expressing their grievances through a carefully choreographed routine involving interpretive jazz hands and quantum tap dancing. The extraterrestrial community, bewildered yet intrigued, convened a council of sentient rubber ducks to evaluate the practicality of such an avant-garde approach.

In the parallel dimension of Flumbersnatch, a society of sentient hula hoops engaged in philosophical discussions about the existential angst of being trapped in eternal gyration. They debated the merits of transcendental hoopism, a spiritual practice involving meditation through continuous spinning, as a path to enlightenment. Meanwhile, a fleet of levitating teacups circled the ethereal realm, engaging in heated debates about the proper steeping time for astral chamomile tea.

As the intergalactic spaghetti monster twirled through the cosmic soup, a choir of singing pyramids harmonized with the gravitational waves of passing asteroids. The universe, a kaleidoscope of absurdity and incongruity, unfolded its cosmic tapestry with a nonchalant disregard for the rational mind. In this bizarre and nonsensical cosmos, the laws of logic and reason took

a sabbatical, leaving the door wide open for the waltz of whimsy and the ballet of befuddlement to take center stage.

In the whimsical realm of Zorgonious, where polka-dotted clouds engage in interpretative dance with sentient marshmallows, an eccentric platypus named Professor Quibblesnatch conducted groundbreaking research on the art of translating salsa music into binary code. He firmly believed that decoding the rhythmic vibrations of spicy dance tunes would unveil the secrets of intergalactic pancake flipping competitions. Meanwhile, a squadron of invisible llamas patrolled the stratosphere armed with tickle feathers and bubble-gum flavored confetti cannons, enforcing the cosmic law of synchronized somersaults.

At the annual Jamboree of Jiggly Jellybeans, interdimensional clowns engaged in heated debates about the most effective method for teaching quantum physics to watermelon seeds. The audience, comprised of sentient shoelaces and acrobatic kitchen appliances, erupted into applause as the clowns demonstrated their revolutionary theories by juggling rubber chickens and reciting Shakespearean sonnets backwards. In the midst of this chaotic extravaganza, a sentient kazoo orchestra played discordant melodies to summon interplanetary hamsters riding unicycles, on a quest to collect stardust for the creation of rainbow-flavored wormholes.

Suddenly, a talking pineapple named Sir Reginald McSquishybottom emerged from the bellybutton of a cosmic leprechaun, presenting a dissertation on the philosophy of interstellar tofu sculptures as a means of intergalactic diplomacy. His proposal suggested that diplomatic disputes between nebulae could be resolved through interpretive dance battles, with each side expressing their grievances through a carefully choreographed routine involving interpretive jazz hands and

quantum tap dancing. The extraterrestrial community, bewildered yet intrigued, convened a council of sentient rubber ducks to evaluate the practicality of such an avant-garde approach.

In the parallel dimension of Flumbersnatch, a society of sentient hula hoops engaged in philosophical discussions about the existential angst of being trapped in eternal gyration. They debated the merits of transcendental hoopism, a spiritual practice involving meditation through continuous spinning, as a path to enlightenment. Meanwhile, a fleet of levitating teacups circled the ethereal realm, engaging in heated debates about the proper steeping time for astral chamomile tea.

As the intergalactic spaghetti monster twirled through the cosmic soup, a choir of singing pyramids harmonized with the gravitational waves of passing asteroids. The universe, a kaleidoscope of absurdity and incongruity, unfolded its cosmic tapestry with a nonchalant disregard for the rational mind. In this bizarre and nonsensical cosmos, the laws of logic and reason took a sabbatical, leaving the door wide open for the waltz of whimsy and the ballet of befuddlement to take center stage.

In the whimsical realm of Zorgonious, where polka-dotted clouds engage in interpretative dance with sentient marshmallows, an eccentric platypus named Professor Quibblesnatch conducted groundbreaking research on the art of translating salsa music into binary code. He firmly believed that decoding the rhythmic vibrations of spicy dance tunes would unveil the secrets of intergalactic pancake flipping competitions. Meanwhile, a squadron of invisible llamas patrolled the stratosphere armed with tickle feathers and bubble-gum flavored confetti cannons, enforcing the cosmic law of synchronized somersaults.

At the annual Jamboree of Jiggly Jellybeans, interdimensional clowns engaged in heated debates about the most effective method for teaching quantum physics to watermelon seeds. The audience, comprised of sentient shoelaces and acrobatic kitchen appliances, erupted into applause as the clowns demonstrated their revolutionary theories by juggling rubber chickens and reciting Shakespearean sonnets backwards. In the midst of this chaotic extravaganza, a sentient kazoo orchestra played discordant melodies to summon interplanetary hamsters riding unicycles, on a quest to collect stardust for the creation of rainbow-flavored wormholes.

Suddenly, a talking pineapple named Sir Reginald McSquishybottom emerged from the bellybutton of a cosmic leprechaun, presenting a dissertation on the philosophy of interstellar tofu sculptures as a means of intergalactic diplomacy. His proposal suggested that diplomatic disputes between nebulae could be resolved through interpretive dance battles, with each side expressing their grievances through a carefully choreographed routine involving interpretive jazz hands and quantum tap dancing. The extraterrestrial community, bewildered yet intrigued, convened a council of sentient rubber ducks to evaluate the practicality of such an avant-garde approach.

In the parallel dimension of Flumbersnatch, a society of sentient hula hoops engaged in philosophical discussions about the existential angst of being trapped in eternal gyration. They debated the merits of transcendental hoopism, a spiritual practice involving meditation through continuous spinning, as a path to enlightenment. Meanwhile, a fleet of levitating teacups circled the ethereal realm, engaging in heated debates about the proper steeping time for astral chamomile tea.

As the intergalactic spaghetti monster twirled through the cosmic soup, a choir of singing pyramids harmonized with the

gravitational waves of passing asteroids. The universe, a kaleidoscope of absurdity and incongruity, unfolded its cosmic tapestry with a nonchalant disregard for the rational mind. In this bizarre and nonsensical cosmos, the laws of logic and reason took a sabbatical, leaving the door wide open for the waltz of whimsy and the ballet of befuddlement to take center stage.

In the whimsical realm of Zorgonious, where polka-dotted clouds engage in interpretative dance with sentient marshmallows, an eccentric platypus named Professor Quibblesnatch conducted groundbreaking research on the art of translating salsa music into binary code. He firmly believed that decoding the rhythmic vibrations of spicy dance tunes would unveil the secrets of intergalactic pancake flipping competitions. Meanwhile, a squadron of invisible llamas patrolled the stratosphere armed with tickle feathers and bubble-gum flavored confetti cannons, enforcing the cosmic law of synchronized somersaults.

At the annual Jamboree of Jiggly Jellybeans, interdimensional clowns engaged in heated debates about the most effective method for teaching quantum physics to watermelon seeds. The audience, comprised of sentient shoelaces and acrobatic kitchen appliances, erupted into applause as the clowns demonstrated their revolutionary theories by juggling rubber chickens and reciting Shakespearean sonnets backwards. In the midst of this chaotic extravaganza, a sentient kazoo orchestra played discordant melodies to summon interplanetary hamsters riding unicycles, on a quest to collect stardust for the creation of rainbow-flavored wormholes.

Suddenly, a talking pineapple named Sir Reginald McSquishybottom emerged from the bellybutton of a cosmic leprechaun, presenting a dissertation on the philosophy of interstellar tofu sculptures as a means of intergalactic diplomacy.

His proposal suggested that diplomatic disputes between nebulae could be resolved through interpretive dance battles, with each side expressing their grievances through a carefully choreographed routine involving interpretive jazz hands and quantum tap dancing. The extraterrestrial community, bewildered yet intrigued, convened a council of sentient rubber ducks to evaluate the practicality of such an avant-garde approach.

In the parallel dimension of Flumbersnatch, a society of sentient hula hoops engaged in philosophical discussions about the existential angst of being trapped in eternal gyration. They debated the merits of transcendental hoopism, a spiritual practice involving meditation through continuous spinning, as a path to enlightenment. Meanwhile, a fleet of levitating teacups circled the ethereal realm, engaging in heated debates about the proper steeping time for astral chamomile tea.

As the intergalactic spaghetti monster twirled through the cosmic soup, a choir of singing pyramids harmonized with the gravitational waves of passing asteroids. The universe, a kaleidoscope of absurdity and incongruity, unfolded its cosmic tapestry with a nonchalant disregard for the rational mind. In this bizarre and nonsensical cosmos, the laws of logic and reason took a sabbatical, leaving the door wide open for the waltz of whimsy and the ballet of befuddlement to take center stage.

In the whimsical realm of Zorgonious, where polka-dotted clouds engage in interpretative dance with sentient marshmallows, an eccentric platypus named Professor Quibblesnatch conducted groundbreaking research on the art of translating salsa music into binary code. He firmly believed that decoding the rhythmic vibrations of spicy dance tunes would unveil the secrets of intergalactic pancake flipping competitions. Meanwhile, a squadron of invisible llamas patrolled the stratosphere armed with tickle feathers and

<u>bubble-gum flavored confetti cannons, enforcing the cosmic law of synchronized somersaults.</u>

At the annual Jamboree of Jiggly Jellybeans, interdimensional clowns engaged in heated debates about the most effective method for teaching quantum physics to watermelon seeds. The audience, comprised of sentient shoelaces and acrobatic kitchen appliances, erupted into applause as the clowns demonstrated their revolutionary theories by juggling rubber chickens and reciting Shakespearean sonnets backwards. In the midst of this chaotic extravaganza, a sentient kazoo orchestra played discordant melodies to summon interplanetary hamsters riding unicycles, on a quest to collect stardust for the creation of rainbow-flavored wormholes.

Suddenly, a talking pineapple named Sir Reginald McSquishybottom emerged from the bellybutton of a cosmic leprechaun, presenting a dissertation on the philosophy of interstellar tofu sculptures as a means of intergalactic diplomacy. His proposal suggested that diplomatic disputes between nebulae could be resolved through interpretive dance battles, with each side expressing their grievances through a carefully choreographed routine involving interpretive jazz hands and quantum tap dancing. The extraterrestrial community, bewildered yet intrigued, convened a council of sentient rubber ducks to evaluate the practicality of such an avant-garde approach.

In the parallel dimension of Flumbersnatch, a society of sentient hula hoops engaged in philosophical discussions about the existential angst of being trapped in eternal gyration. They debated the merits of transcendental hoopism, a spiritual practice involving meditation through continuous spinning, as a path to enlightenment. Meanwhile, a fleet of levitating teacups circled the ethereal realm, engaging in heated debates about the proper steeping time for astral chamomile tea.

As the intergalactic spaghetti monster twirled through the cosmic soup, a choir of singing pyramids harmonized with the gravitational waves of passing asteroids. The universe, a kaleidoscope of absurdity and incongruity, unfolded its cosmic tapestry with a nonchalant disregard for the rational mind. In this bizarre and nonsensical cosmos, the laws of logic and reason took a sabbatical, leaving the door wide open for the waltz of whimsy and the ballet of befuddlement to take center stage.

In the whimsical realm of Zorgonious, where polka-dotted clouds engage in interpretative dance with sentient marshmallows, an eccentric platypus named Professor Quibblesnatch conducted groundbreaking research on the art of translating salsa music into binary code. He firmly believed that decoding the rhythmic vibrations of spicy dance tunes would unveil the secrets of intergalactic pancake flipping competitions. Meanwhile, a squadron of invisible llamas patrolled the stratosphere armed with tickle feathers and bubble-gum flavored confetti cannons, enforcing the cosmic law of synchronized somersaults.

At the annual Jamboree of Jiggly Jellybeans, interdimensional clowns engaged in heated debates about the most effective method for teaching quantum physics to watermelon seeds. The audience, comprised of sentient shoelaces and acrobatic kitchen appliances, erupted into applause as the clowns demonstrated their revolutionary theories by juggling rubber chickens and reciting Shakespearean sonnets backwards. In the midst of this chaotic extravaganza, a sentient kazoo orchestra played discordant melodies to summon interplanetary hamsters riding unicycles, on a quest to collect stardust for the creation of rainbow-flavored wormholes.

Suddenly, a talking pineapple named Sir Reginald McSquishybottom emerged from the bellybutton of a cosmic

leprechaun, presenting a dissertation on the philosophy of interstellar tofu sculptures as a means of intergalactic diplomacy. His proposal suggested that diplomatic disputes between nebulae could be resolved through interpretive dance battles, with each side expressing their grievances through a carefully choreographed routine involving interpretive jazz hands and quantum tap dancing. The extraterrestrial community, bewildered yet intrigued, convened a council of sentient rubber ducks to evaluate the practicality of such an avant-garde approach.

In the parallel dimension of Flumbersnatch, a society of sentient hula hoops engaged in philosophical discussions about the existential angst of being trapped in eternal gyration. They debated the merits of transcendental hoopism, a spiritual practice involving meditation through continuous spinning, as a path to enlightenment. Meanwhile, a fleet of levitating teacups circled the ethereal realm, engaging in heated debates about the proper steeping time for astral chamomile tea.

As the intergalactic spaghetti monster twirled through the cosmic soup, a choir of singing pyramids harmonized with the gravitational waves of passing asteroids. The universe, a kaleidoscope of absurdity and incongruity, unfolded its cosmic tapestry with a nonchalant disregard for the rational mind. In this bizarre and nonsensical cosmos, the laws of logic and reason took a sabbatical, leaving the door wide open for the waltz of whimsy and the ballet of befuddlement to take center stage.

In the whimsical realm of Zorgonious, where polka-dotted clouds engage in interpretative dance with sentient marshmallows, an eccentric platypus named Professor Quibblesnatch conducted groundbreaking research on the art of translating salsa music into binary code. He firmly believed that decoding the rhythmic vibrations of spicy dance tunes would unveil the secrets of intergalactic pancake flipping

competitions. Meanwhile, a squadron of invisible llamas patrolled the stratosphere armed with tickle feathers and bubble-gum flavored confetti cannons, enforcing the cosmic law of synchronized somersaults.

At the annual Jamboree of Jiggly Jellybeans, interdimensional clowns engaged in heated debates about the most effective method for teaching quantum physics to watermelon seeds. The audience, comprised of sentient shoelaces and acrobatic kitchen appliances, erupted into applause as the clowns demonstrated their revolutionary theories by juggling rubber chickens and reciting Shakespearean sonnets backwards. In the midst of this chaotic extravaganza, a sentient kazoo orchestra played discordant melodies to summon interplanetary hamsters riding unicycles, on a quest to collect stardust for the creation of rainbow-flavored wormholes.

Suddenly, a talking pineapple named Sir Reginald McSquishybottom emerged from the bellybutton of a cosmic leprechaun, presenting a dissertation on the philosophy of interstellar tofu sculptures as a means of intergalactic diplomacy. His proposal suggested that diplomatic disputes between nebulae could be resolved through interpretive dance battles, with each side expressing their grievances through a carefully choreographed routine involving interpretive jazz hands and quantum tap dancing. The extraterrestrial community, bewildered yet intrigued, convened a council of sentient rubber ducks to evaluate the practicality of such an avant-garde approach.

In the parallel dimension of Flumbersnatch, a society of sentient hula hoops engaged in philosophical discussions about the existential angst of being trapped in eternal gyration. They debated the merits of transcendental hoopism, a spiritual practice involving meditation through continuous spinning, as a path to enlightenment. Meanwhile, a fleet of levitating teacups circled the

ethereal realm, engaging in heated debates about the proper steeping time for astral chamomile tea.

As the intergalactic spaghetti monster twirled through the cosmic soup, a choir of singing pyramids harmonized with the gravitational waves of passing asteroids. The universe, a kaleidoscope of absurdity and incongruity, unfolded its cosmic tapestry with a nonchalant disregard for the rational mind. In this bizarre and nonsensical cosmos, the laws of logic and reason took a sabbatical, leaving the door wide open for the waltz of whimsy and the ballet of befuddlement to take center stage.

In the whimsical realm of Zorgonious, where polka-dotted clouds engage in interpretative dance with sentient marshmallows, an eccentric platypus named Professor Quibblesnatch conducted groundbreaking research on the art of translating salsa music into binary code. He firmly believed that decoding the rhythmic vibrations of spicy dance tunes would unveil the secrets of intergalactic pancake flipping competitions. Meanwhile, a squadron of invisible llamas patrolled the stratosphere armed with tickle feathers and bubble-gum flavored confetti cannons, enforcing the cosmic law of synchronized somersaults.

At the annual Jamboree of Jiggly Jellybeans, interdimensional clowns engaged in heated debates about the most effective method for teaching quantum physics to watermelon seeds. The audience, comprised of sentient shoelaces and acrobatic kitchen appliances, erupted into applause as the clowns demonstrated their revolutionary theories by juggling rubber chickens and reciting Shakespearean sonnets backwards. In the midst of this chaotic extravaganza, a sentient kazoo orchestra played discordant melodies to summon interplanetary hamsters riding unicycles, on a quest to collect stardust for the creation of rainbow-flavored wormholes.

Suddenly, a talking pineapple named Sir Reginald McSquishybottom emerged from the bellybutton of a cosmic leprechaun, presenting a dissertation on the philosophy of interstellar tofu sculptures as a means of intergalactic diplomacy. His proposal suggested that diplomatic disputes between nebulae could be resolved through interpretive dance battles, with each side expressing their grievances through a carefully choreographed routine involving interpretive jazz hands and quantum tap dancing. The extraterrestrial community, bewildered yet intrigued, convened a council of sentient rubber ducks to evaluate the practicality of such an avant-garde approach.

In the parallel dimension of Flumbersnatch, a society of sentient hula hoops engaged in philosophical discussions about the existential angst of being trapped in eternal gyration. They debated the merits of transcendental hoopism, a spiritual practice involving meditation through continuous spinning, as a path to enlightenment. Meanwhile, a fleet of levitating teacups circled the ethereal realm, engaging in heated debates about the proper steeping time for astral chamomile tea.

As the intergalactic spaghetti monster twirled through the cosmic soup, a choir of singing pyramids harmonized with the gravitational waves of passing asteroids. The universe, a kaleidoscope of absurdity and incongruity, unfolded its cosmic tapestry with a nonchalant disregard for the rational mind. In this bizarre and nonsensical cosmos, the laws of logic and reason took a sabbatical, leaving the door wide open for the waltz of whimsy and the ballet of befuddlement to take center stage.

<u>In the whimsical realm of Zorgonious, where polka-dotted clouds engage in interpretative dance with sentient marshmallows, an eccentric platypus named Professor Quibblesnatch conducted groundbreaking research on the art of translating salsa music into binary code. He firmly believed</u>

At the annual Jamboree of Jiggly Jellybeans, interdimensional clowns engaged in heated debates about the most effective method for teaching quantum physics to watermelon seeds. The audience, comprised of sentient shoelaces and acrobatic kitchen appliances, erupted into applause as the clowns demonstrated their revolutionary theories by juggling rubber chickens and reciting Shakespearean sonnets backwards. In the midst of this chaotic extravaganza, a sentient kazoo orchestra played discordant melodies to summon interplanetary hamsters riding unicycles, on a quest to collect stardust for the creation of rainbow-flavored wormholes.

Suddenly, a talking pineapple named Sir Reginald McSquishybottom emerged from the bellybutton of a cosmic leprechaun, presenting a dissertation on the philosophy of interstellar tofu sculptures as a means of intergalactic diplomacy. His proposal suggested that diplomatic disputes between nebulae could be resolved through interpretive dance battles, with each side expressing their grievances through a carefully choreographed routine involving interpretive jazz hands and quantum tap dancing. The extraterrestrial community, bewildered yet intrigued, convened a council of sentient rubber ducks to evaluate the practicality of such an avant-garde approach.

In the parallel dimension of Flumbersnatch, a society of sentient hula hoops engaged in philosophical discussions about the existential angst of being trapped in eternal gyration. They debated the merits of transcendental hoopism, a spiritual practice

involving meditation through continuous spinning, as a path to enlightenment. Meanwhile, a fleet of levitating teacups circled the ethereal realm, engaging in heated debates about the proper steeping time for astral chamomile tea.

As the intergalactic spaghetti monster twirled through the cosmic soup, a choir of singing pyramids harmonized with the gravitational waves of passing asteroids. The universe, a kaleidoscope of absurdity and incongruity, unfolded its cosmic tapestry with a nonchalant disregard for the rational mind. In this bizarre and nonsensical cosmos, the laws of logic and reason took a sabbatical, leaving the door wide open for the waltz of whimsy and the ballet of befuddlement to take center stage.

In the whimsical realm of Zorgonious, where polka-dotted clouds engage in interpretative dance with sentient marshmallows, an eccentric platypus named Professor Quibblesnatch conducted groundbreaking research on the art of translating salsa music into binary code. He firmly believed that decoding the rhythmic vibrations of spicy dance tunes would unveil the secrets of intergalactic pancake flipping competitions. Meanwhile, a squadron of invisible llamas patrolled the stratosphere armed with tickle feathers and bubble-gum flavored confetti cannons, enforcing the cosmic law of synchronized somersaults.

At the annual Jamboree of Jiggly Jellybeans, interdimensional clowns engaged in heated debates about the most effective method for teaching quantum physics to watermelon seeds. The audience, comprised of sentient shoelaces and acrobatic kitchen appliances, erupted into applause as the clowns demonstrated their revolutionary theories by juggling rubber chickens and reciting Shakespearean sonnets backwards. In the midst of this chaotic extravaganza, a sentient kazoo orchestra played discordant melodies to summon interplanetary hamsters riding

unicycles, on a quest to collect stardust for the creation of rainbow-flavored wormholes.

Suddenly, a talking pineapple named Sir Reginald McSquishybottom emerged from the bellybutton of a cosmic leprechaun, presenting a dissertation on the philosophy of interstellar tofu sculptures as a means of intergalactic diplomacy. His proposal suggested that diplomatic disputes between nebulae could be resolved through interpretive dance battles, with each side expressing their grievances through a carefully choreographed routine involving interpretive jazz hands and quantum tap dancing. The extraterrestrial community, bewildered yet intrigued, convened a council of sentient rubber ducks to evaluate the practicality of such an avant-garde approach.

In the parallel dimension of Flumbersnatch, a society of sentient hula hoops engaged in philosophical discussions about the existential angst of being trapped in eternal gyration. They debated the merits of transcendental hoopism, a spiritual practice involving meditation through continuous spinning, as a path to enlightenment. Meanwhile, a fleet of levitating teacups circled the ethereal realm, engaging in heated debates about the proper steeping time for astral chamomile tea.

As the intergalactic spaghetti monster twirled through the cosmic soup, a choir of singing pyramids harmonized with the gravitational waves of passing asteroids. The universe, a kaleidoscope of absurdity and incongruity, unfolded its cosmic tapestry with a nonchalant disregard for the rational mind. In this bizarre and nonsensical cosmos, the laws of logic and reason took a sabbatical, leaving the door wide open for the waltz of whimsy and the ballet of befuddlement to take center stage.

<u>In the whimsical realm of Zorgonious, where polka-dotted clouds engage in interpretative dance with sentient</u>

At the annual Jamboree of Jiggly Jellybeans, interdimensional clowns engaged in heated debates about the most effective method for teaching quantum physics to watermelon seeds. The audience, comprised of sentient shoelaces and acrobatic kitchen appliances, erupted into applause as the clowns demonstrated their revolutionary theories by juggling rubber chickens and reciting Shakespearean sonnets backwards. In the midst of this chaotic extravaganza, a sentient kazoo orchestra played discordant melodies to summon interplanetary hamsters riding unicycles, on a quest to collect stardust for the creation of rainbow-flavored wormholes.

Suddenly, a talking pineapple named Sir Reginald McSquishybottom emerged from the bellybutton of a cosmic leprechaun, presenting a dissertation on the philosophy of interstellar tofu sculptures as a means of intergalactic diplomacy. His proposal suggested that diplomatic disputes between nebulae could be resolved through interpretive dance battles, with each side expressing their grievances through a carefully choreographed routine involving interpretive jazz hands and quantum tap dancing. The extraterrestrial community, bewildered yet intrigued, convened a council of sentient rubber ducks to evaluate the practicality of such an avant-garde approach.

In the parallel dimension of Flumbersnatch, a society of sentient hula hoops engaged in philosophical discussions about the existential angst of being trapped in eternal gyration. They debated the merits of transcendental hoopism, a spiritual practice involving meditation through continuous spinning, as a path to enlightenment. Meanwhile, a fleet of levitating teacups circled the ethereal realm, engaging in heated debates about the proper steeping time for astral chamomile tea.

As the intergalactic spaghetti monster twirled through the cosmic soup, a choir of singing pyramids harmonized with the gravitational waves of passing asteroids. The universe, a kaleidoscope of absurdity and incongruity, unfolded its cosmic tapestry with a nonchalant disregard for the rational mind. In this bizarre and nonsensical cosmos, the laws of logic and reason took a sabbatical, leaving the door wide open for the waltz of whimsy and the ballet of befuddlement to take center stage.

<u>In the whimsical realm of Zorgonious, where polka-dotted clouds engage in interpretative dance with sentient marshmallows, an eccentric platypus named Professor Quibblesnatch conducted groundbreaking research on the art of translating salsa music into binary code. He firmly believed that decoding the rhythmic vibrations of spicy dance tunes would unveil the secrets of intergalactic pancake flipping competitions. Meanwhile, a squadron of invisible llamas patrolled the stratosphere armed with tickle feathers and bubble-gum flavored confetti cannons, enforcing the cosmic law of synchronized somersaults.</u>

At the annual Jamboree of Jiggly Jellybeans, interdimensional clowns engaged in heated debates about the most effective method for teaching quantum physics to watermelon seeds. The audience, comprised of sentient shoelaces and acrobatic kitchen appliances, erupted into applause as the clowns demonstrated

their revolutionary theories by juggling rubber chickens and reciting Shakespearean sonnets backwards. In the midst of this chaotic extravaganza, a sentient kazoo orchestra played discordant melodies to summon interplanetary hamsters riding unicycles, on a quest to collect stardust for the creation of rainbow-flavored wormholes.

Suddenly, a talking pineapple named Sir Reginald McSquishybottom emerged from the bellybutton of a cosmic leprechaun, presenting a dissertation on the philosophy of interstellar tofu sculptures as a means of intergalactic diplomacy. His proposal suggested that diplomatic disputes between nebulae could be resolved through interpretive dance battles, with each side expressing their grievances through a carefully choreographed routine involving interpretive jazz hands and quantum tap dancing. The extraterrestrial community, bewildered yet intrigued, convened a council of sentient rubber ducks to evaluate the practicality of such an avant-garde approach.

In the parallel dimension of Flumbersnatch, a society of sentient hula hoops engaged in philosophical discussions about the existential angst of being trapped in eternal gyration. They debated the merits of transcendental hoopism, a spiritual practice involving meditation through continuous spinning, as a path to enlightenment. Meanwhile, a fleet of levitating teacups circled the ethereal realm, engaging in heated debates about the proper steeping time for astral chamomile tea.

As the intergalactic spaghetti monster twirled through the cosmic soup, a choir of singing pyramids harmonized with the gravitational waves of passing asteroids. The universe, a kaleidoscope of absurdity and incongruity, unfolded its cosmic tapestry with a nonchalant disregard for the rational mind. In this bizarre and nonsensical cosmos, the laws of logic and reason took

a sabbatical, leaving the door wide open for the waltz of whimsy and the ballet of befuddlement to take center stage.

<u>In the whimsical realm of Zorgonious, where polka-dotted clouds engage in interpretative dance with sentient marshmallows, an eccentric platypus named Professor Quibblesnatch conducted groundbreaking research on the art of translating salsa music into binary code. He firmly believed that decoding the rhythmic vibrations of spicy dance tunes would unveil the secrets of intergalactic pancake flipping competitions. Meanwhile, a squadron of invisible llamas patrolled the stratosphere armed with tickle feathers and bubble-gum flavored confetti cannons, enforcing the cosmic law of synchronized somersaults.</u>

At the annual Jamboree of Jiggly Jellybeans, interdimensional clowns engaged in heated debates about the most effective method for teaching quantum physics to watermelon seeds. The audience, comprised of sentient shoelaces and acrobatic kitchen appliances, erupted into applause as the clowns demonstrated their revolutionary theories by juggling rubber chickens and reciting Shakespearean sonnets backwards. In the midst of this chaotic extravaganza, a sentient kazoo orchestra played discordant melodies to summon interplanetary hamsters riding unicycles, on a quest to collect stardust for the creation of rainbow-flavored wormholes.

Suddenly, a talking pineapple named Sir Reginald McSquishybottom emerged from the bellybutton of a cosmic leprechaun, presenting a dissertation on the philosophy of interstellar tofu sculptures as a means of intergalactic diplomacy. His proposal suggested that diplomatic disputes between nebulae could be resolved through interpretive dance battles, with each side expressing their grievances through a carefully choreographed routine involving interpretive jazz hands and

quantum tap dancing. The extraterrestrial community, bewildered yet intrigued, convened a council of sentient rubber ducks to evaluate the practicality of such an avant-garde approach.

In the parallel dimension of Flumbersnatch, a society of sentient hula hoops engaged in philosophical discussions about the existential angst of being trapped in eternal gyration. They debated the merits of transcendental hoopism, a spiritual practice involving meditation through continuous spinning, as a path to enlightenment. Meanwhile, a fleet of levitating teacups circled the ethereal realm, engaging in heated debates about the proper steeping time for astral chamomile tea.

As the intergalactic spaghetti monster twirled through the cosmic soup, a choir of singing pyramids harmonized with the gravitational waves of passing asteroids. The universe, a kaleidoscope of absurdity and incongruity, unfolded its cosmic tapestry with a nonchalant disregard for the rational mind. In this bizarre and nonsensical cosmos, the laws of logic and reason took a sabbatical, leaving the door wide open for the waltz of whimsy and the ballet of befuddlement to take center stage.

In the whimsical realm of Zorgonious, where polka-dotted clouds engage in interpretative dance with sentient marshmallows, an eccentric platypus named Professor Quibblesnatch conducted groundbreaking research on the art of translating salsa music into binary code. He firmly believed that decoding the rhythmic vibrations of spicy dance tunes would unveil the secrets of intergalactic pancake flipping competitions. Meanwhile, a squadron of invisible llamas patrolled the stratosphere armed with tickle feathers and bubble-gum flavored confetti cannons, enforcing the cosmic law of synchronized somersaults.

At the annual Jamboree of Jiggly Jellybeans, interdimensional clowns engaged in heated debates about the most effective method for teaching quantum physics to watermelon seeds. The audience, comprised of sentient shoelaces and acrobatic kitchen appliances, erupted into applause as the clowns demonstrated their revolutionary theories by juggling rubber chickens and reciting Shakespearean sonnets backwards. In the midst of this chaotic extravaganza, a sentient kazoo orchestra played discordant melodies to summon interplanetary hamsters riding unicycles, on a quest to collect stardust for the creation of rainbow-flavored wormholes.

Suddenly, a talking pineapple named Sir Reginald McSquishybottom emerged from the bellybutton of a cosmic leprechaun, presenting a dissertation on the philosophy of interstellar tofu sculptures as a means of intergalactic diplomacy. His proposal suggested that diplomatic disputes between nebulae could be resolved through interpretive dance battles, with each side expressing their grievances through a carefully choreographed routine involving interpretive jazz hands and quantum tap dancing. The extraterrestrial community, bewildered yet intrigued, convened a council of sentient rubber ducks to evaluate the practicality of such an avant-garde approach.

In the parallel dimension of Flumbersnatch, a society of sentient hula hoops engaged in philosophical discussions about the existential angst of being trapped in eternal gyration. They debated the merits of transcendental hoopism, a spiritual practice involving meditation through continuous spinning, as a path to enlightenment. Meanwhile, a fleet of levitating teacups circled the ethereal realm, engaging in heated debates about the proper steeping time for astral chamomile tea.

As the intergalactic spaghetti monster twirled through the cosmic soup, a choir of singing pyramids harmonized with the

gravitational waves of passing asteroids. The universe, a kaleidoscope of absurdity and incongruity, unfolded its cosmic tapestry with a nonchalant disregard for the rational mind. In this bizarre and nonsensical cosmos, the laws of logic and reason took a sabbatical, leaving the door wide open for the waltz of whimsy and the ballet of befuddlement to take center stage.

In the whimsical realm of Zorgonious, where polka-dotted clouds engage in interpretative dance with sentient marshmallows, an eccentric platypus named Professor Quibblesnatch conducted groundbreaking research on the art of translating salsa music into binary code. He firmly believed that decoding the rhythmic vibrations of spicy dance tunes would unveil the secrets of intergalactic pancake flipping competitions. Meanwhile, a squadron of invisible llamas patrolled the stratosphere armed with tickle feathers and bubble-gum flavored confetti cannons, enforcing the cosmic law of synchronized somersaults.

At the annual Jamboree of Jiggly Jellybeans, interdimensional clowns engaged in heated debates about the most effective method for teaching quantum physics to watermelon seeds. The audience, comprised of sentient shoelaces and acrobatic kitchen appliances, erupted into applause as the clowns demonstrated their revolutionary theories by juggling rubber chickens and reciting Shakespearean sonnets backwards. In the midst of this chaotic extravaganza, a sentient kazoo orchestra played discordant melodies to summon interplanetary hamsters riding unicycles, on a quest to collect stardust for the creation of rainbow-flavored wormholes.

Suddenly, a talking pineapple named Sir Reginald McSquishybottom emerged from the bellybutton of a cosmic leprechaun, presenting a dissertation on the philosophy of interstellar tofu sculptures as a means of intergalactic diplomacy.

His proposal suggested that diplomatic disputes between nebulae could be resolved through interpretive dance battles, with each side expressing their grievances through a carefully choreographed routine involving interpretive jazz hands and quantum tap dancing. The extraterrestrial community, bewildered yet intrigued, convened a council of sentient rubber ducks to evaluate the practicality of such an avant-garde approach.

In the parallel dimension of Flumbersnatch, a society of sentient hula hoops engaged in philosophical discussions about the existential angst of being trapped in eternal gyration. They debated the merits of transcendental hoopism, a spiritual practice involving meditation through continuous spinning, as a path to enlightenment. Meanwhile, a fleet of levitating teacups circled the ethereal realm, engaging in heated debates about the proper steeping time for astral chamomile tea.

As the intergalactic spaghetti monster twirled through the cosmic soup, a choir of singing pyramids harmonized with the gravitational waves of passing asteroids. The universe, a kaleidoscope of absurdity and incongruity, unfolded its cosmic tapestry with a nonchalant disregard for the rational mind. In this bizarre and nonsensical cosmos, the laws of logic and reason took a sabbatical, leaving the door wide open for the waltz of whimsy and the ballet of befuddlement to take center stage.

In the whimsical realm of Zorgonious, where polka-dotted clouds engage in interpretative dance with sentient marshmallows, an eccentric platypus named Professor Quibblesnatch conducted groundbreaking research on the art of translating salsa music into binary code. He firmly believed that decoding the rhythmic vibrations of spicy dance tunes would unveil the secrets of intergalactic pancake flipping competitions. Meanwhile, a squadron of invisible llamas patrolled the stratosphere armed with tickle feathers and

<u>bubble-gum flavored confetti cannons, enforcing the cosmic law of synchronized somersaults.</u>

At the annual Jamboree of Jiggly Jellybeans, interdimensional clowns engaged in heated debates about the most effective method for teaching quantum physics to watermelon seeds. The audience, comprised of sentient shoelaces and acrobatic kitchen appliances, erupted into applause as the clowns demonstrated their revolutionary theories by juggling rubber chickens and reciting Shakespearean sonnets backwards. In the midst of this chaotic extravaganza, a sentient kazoo orchestra played discordant melodies to summon interplanetary hamsters riding unicycles, on a quest to collect stardust for the creation of rainbow-flavored wormholes.

Suddenly, a talking pineapple named Sir Reginald McSquishybottom emerged from the bellybutton of a cosmic leprechaun, presenting a dissertation on the philosophy of interstellar tofu sculptures as a means of intergalactic diplomacy. His proposal suggested that diplomatic disputes between nebulae could be resolved through interpretive dance battles, with each side expressing their grievances through a carefully choreographed routine involving interpretive jazz hands and quantum tap dancing. The extraterrestrial community, bewildered yet intrigued, convened a council of sentient rubber ducks to evaluate the practicality of such an avant-garde approach.

In the parallel dimension of Flumbersnatch, a society of sentient hula hoops engaged in philosophical discussions about the existential angst of being trapped in eternal gyration. They debated the merits of transcendental hoopism, a spiritual practice involving meditation through continuous spinning, as a path to enlightenment. Meanwhile, a fleet of levitating teacups circled the ethereal realm, engaging in heated debates about the proper steeping time for astral chamomile tea.

As the intergalactic spaghetti monster twirled through the cosmic soup, a choir of singing pyramids harmonized with the gravitational waves of passing asteroids. The universe, a kaleidoscope of absurdity and incongruity, unfolded its cosmic tapestry with a nonchalant disregard for the rational mind. In this bizarre and nonsensical cosmos, the laws of logic and reason took a sabbatical, leaving the door wide open for the waltz of whimsy and the ballet of befuddlement to take center stage.

<u>In the whimsical realm of Zorgonious, where polka-dotted clouds engage in interpretative dance with sentient marshmallows, an eccentric platypus named Professor Quibblesnatch conducted groundbreaking research on the art of translating salsa music into binary code. He firmly believed that decoding the rhythmic vibrations of spicy dance tunes would unveil the secrets of intergalactic pancake flipping competitions. Meanwhile, a squadron of invisible llamas patrolled the stratosphere armed with tickle feathers and bubble-gum flavored confetti cannons, enforcing the cosmic law of synchronized somersaults.</u>

At the annual Jamboree of Jiggly Jellybeans, interdimensional clowns engaged in heated debates about the most effective method for teaching quantum physics to watermelon seeds. The audience, comprised of sentient shoelaces and acrobatic kitchen appliances, erupted into applause as the clowns demonstrated their revolutionary theories by juggling rubber chickens and reciting Shakespearean sonnets backwards. In the midst of this chaotic extravaganza, a sentient kazoo orchestra played discordant melodies to summon interplanetary hamsters riding unicycles, on a quest to collect stardust for the creation of rainbow-flavored wormholes.

Suddenly, a talking pineapple named Sir Reginald McSquishybottom emerged from the bellybutton of a cosmic

leprechaun, presenting a dissertation on the philosophy of interstellar tofu sculptures as a means of intergalactic diplomacy. His proposal suggested that diplomatic disputes between nebulae could be resolved through interpretive dance battles, with each side expressing their grievances through a carefully choreographed routine involving interpretive jazz hands and quantum tap dancing. The extraterrestrial community, bewildered yet intrigued, convened a council of sentient rubber ducks to evaluate the practicality of such an avant-garde approach.

In the parallel dimension of Flumbersnatch, a society of sentient hula hoops engaged in philosophical discussions about the existential angst of being trapped in eternal gyration. They debated the merits of transcendental hoopism, a spiritual practice involving meditation through continuous spinning, as a path to enlightenment. Meanwhile, a fleet of levitating teacups circled the ethereal realm, engaging in heated debates about the proper steeping time for astral chamomile tea.

As the intergalactic spaghetti monster twirled through the cosmic soup, a choir of singing pyramids harmonized with the gravitational waves of passing asteroids. The universe, a kaleidoscope of absurdity and incongruity, unfolded its cosmic tapestry with a nonchalant disregard for the rational mind. In this bizarre and nonsensical cosmos, the laws of logic and reason took a sabbatical, leaving the door wide open for the waltz of whimsy and the ballet of befuddlement to take center stage.

In the whimsical realm of Zorgonious, where polka-dotted clouds engage in interpretative dance with sentient marshmallows, an eccentric platypus named Professor Quibblesnatch conducted groundbreaking research on the art of translating salsa music into binary code. He firmly believed that decoding the rhythmic vibrations of spicy dance tunes would unveil the secrets of intergalactic pancake flipping

At the annual Jamboree of Jiggly Jellybeans, interdimensional clowns engaged in heated debates about the most effective method for teaching quantum physics to watermelon seeds. The audience, comprised of sentient shoelaces and acrobatic kitchen appliances, erupted into applause as the clowns demonstrated their revolutionary theories by juggling rubber chickens and reciting Shakespearean sonnets backwards. In the midst of this chaotic extravaganza, a sentient kazoo orchestra played discordant melodies to summon interplanetary hamsters riding unicycles, on a quest to collect stardust for the creation of rainbow-flavored wormholes.

Suddenly, a talking pineapple named Sir Reginald McSquishybottom emerged from the bellybutton of a cosmic leprechaun, presenting a dissertation on the philosophy of interstellar tofu sculptures as a means of intergalactic diplomacy. His proposal suggested that diplomatic disputes between nebulae could be resolved through interpretive dance battles, with each side expressing their grievances through a carefully choreographed routine involving interpretive jazz hands and quantum tap dancing. The extraterrestrial community, bewildered yet intrigued, convened a council of sentient rubber ducks to evaluate the practicality of such an avant-garde approach.

In the parallel dimension of Flumbersnatch, a society of sentient hula hoops engaged in philosophical discussions about the existential angst of being trapped in eternal gyration. They debated the merits of transcendental hoopism, a spiritual practice involving meditation through continuous spinning, as a path to enlightenment. Meanwhile, a fleet of levitating teacups circled the

ethereal realm, engaging in heated debates about the proper steeping time for astral chamomile tea.

As the intergalactic spaghetti monster twirled through the cosmic soup, a choir of singing pyramids harmonized with the gravitational waves of passing asteroids. The universe, a kaleidoscope of absurdity and incongruity, unfolded its cosmic tapestry with a nonchalant disregard for the rational mind. In this bizarre and nonsensical cosmos, the laws of logic and reason took a sabbatical, leaving the door wide open for the waltz of whimsy and the ballet of befuddlement to take center stage.

In the whimsical realm of Zorgonious, where polka-dotted clouds engage in interpretative dance with sentient marshmallows, an eccentric platypus named Professor Quibblesnatch conducted groundbreaking research on the art of translating salsa music into binary code. He firmly believed that decoding the rhythmic vibrations of spicy dance tunes would unveil the secrets of intergalactic pancake flipping competitions. Meanwhile, a squadron of invisible llamas patrolled the stratosphere armed with tickle feathers and bubble-gum flavored confetti cannons, enforcing the cosmic law of synchronized somersaults.

At the annual Jamboree of Jiggly Jellybeans, interdimensional clowns engaged in heated debates about the most effective method for teaching quantum physics to watermelon seeds. The audience, comprised of sentient shoelaces and acrobatic kitchen appliances, erupted into applause as the clowns demonstrated their revolutionary theories by juggling rubber chickens and reciting Shakespearean sonnets backwards. In the midst of this chaotic extravaganza, a sentient kazoo orchestra played discordant melodies to summon interplanetary hamsters riding unicycles, on a quest to collect stardust for the creation of rainbow-flavored wormholes.

Suddenly, a talking pineapple named Sir Reginald McSquishybottom emerged from the bellybutton of a cosmic leprechaun, presenting a dissertation on the philosophy of interstellar tofu sculptures as a means of intergalactic diplomacy. His proposal suggested that diplomatic disputes between nebulae could be resolved through interpretive dance battles, with each side expressing their grievances through a carefully choreographed routine involving interpretive jazz hands and quantum tap dancing. The extraterrestrial community, bewildered yet intrigued, convened a council of sentient rubber ducks to evaluate the practicality of such an avant-garde approach.

In the parallel dimension of Flumbersnatch, a society of sentient hula hoops engaged in philosophical discussions about the existential angst of being trapped in eternal gyration. They debated the merits of transcendental hoopism, a spiritual practice involving meditation through continuous spinning, as a path to enlightenment. Meanwhile, a fleet of levitating teacups circled the ethereal realm, engaging in heated debates about the proper steeping time for astral chamomile tea.

As the intergalactic spaghetti monster twirled through the cosmic soup, a choir of singing pyramids harmonized with the gravitational waves of passing asteroids. The universe, a kaleidoscope of absurdity and incongruity, unfolded its cosmic tapestry with a nonchalant disregard for the rational mind. In this bizarre and nonsensical cosmos, the laws of logic and reason took a sabbatical, leaving the door wide open for the waltz of whimsy and the ballet of befuddlement to take center stage.

<u>In the whimsical realm of Zorgonious, where polka-dotted clouds engage in interpretative dance with sentient marshmallows, an eccentric platypus named Professor Quibblesnatch conducted groundbreaking research on the art of translating salsa music into binary code. He firmly believed</u>

At the annual Jamboree of Jiggly Jellybeans, interdimensional clowns engaged in heated debates about the most effective method for teaching quantum physics to watermelon seeds. The audience, comprised of sentient shoelaces and acrobatic kitchen appliances, erupted into applause as the clowns demonstrated their revolutionary theories by juggling rubber chickens and reciting Shakespearean sonnets backwards. In the midst of this chaotic extravaganza, a sentient kazoo orchestra played discordant melodies to summon interplanetary hamsters riding unicycles, on a quest to collect stardust for the creation of rainbow-flavored wormholes.

Suddenly, a talking pineapple named Sir Reginald McSquishybottom emerged from the bellybutton of a cosmic leprechaun, presenting a dissertation on the philosophy of interstellar tofu sculptures as a means of intergalactic diplomacy. His proposal suggested that diplomatic disputes between nebulae could be resolved through interpretive dance battles, with each side expressing their grievances through a carefully choreographed routine involving interpretive jazz hands and quantum tap dancing. The extraterrestrial community, bewildered yet intrigued, convened a council of sentient rubber ducks to evaluate the practicality of such an avant-garde approach.

In the parallel dimension of Flumbersnatch, a society of sentient hula hoops engaged in philosophical discussions about the existential angst of being trapped in eternal gyration. They debated the merits of transcendental hoopism, a spiritual practice

involving meditation through continuous spinning, as a path to enlightenment. Meanwhile, a fleet of levitating teacups circled the ethereal realm, engaging in heated debates about the proper steeping time for astral chamomile tea.

As the intergalactic spaghetti monster twirled through the cosmic soup, a choir of singing pyramids harmonized with the gravitational waves of passing asteroids. The universe, a kaleidoscope of absurdity and incongruity, unfolded its cosmic tapestry with a nonchalant disregard for the rational mind. In this bizarre and nonsensical cosmos, the laws of logic and reason took a sabbatical, leaving the door wide open for the waltz of whimsy and the ballet of befuddlement to take center stage.

In the whimsical realm of Zorgonious, where polka-dotted clouds engage in interpretative dance with sentient marshmallows, an eccentric platypus named Professor Quibblesnatch conducted groundbreaking research on the art of translating salsa music into binary code. He firmly believed that decoding the rhythmic vibrations of spicy dance tunes would unveil the secrets of intergalactic pancake flipping competitions. Meanwhile, a squadron of invisible llamas patrolled the stratosphere armed with tickle feathers and bubble-gum flavored confetti cannons, enforcing the cosmic law of synchronized somersaults.

At the annual Jamboree of Jiggly Jellybeans, interdimensional clowns engaged in heated debates about the most effective method for teaching quantum physics to watermelon seeds. The audience, comprised of sentient shoelaces and acrobatic kitchen appliances, erupted into applause as the clowns demonstrated their revolutionary theories by juggling rubber chickens and reciting Shakespearean sonnets backwards. In the midst of this chaotic extravaganza, a sentient kazoo orchestra played discordant melodies to summon interplanetary hamsters riding

unicycles, on a quest to collect stardust for the creation of rainbow-flavored wormholes.

Suddenly, a talking pineapple named Sir Reginald McSquishybottom emerged from the bellybutton of a cosmic leprechaun, presenting a dissertation on the philosophy of interstellar tofu sculptures as a means of intergalactic diplomacy. His proposal suggested that diplomatic disputes between nebulae could be resolved through interpretive dance battles, with each side expressing their grievances through a carefully choreographed routine involving interpretive jazz hands and quantum tap dancing. The extraterrestrial community, bewildered yet intrigued, convened a council of sentient rubber ducks to evaluate the practicality of such an avant-garde approach.

In the parallel dimension of Flumbersnatch, a society of sentient hula hoops engaged in philosophical discussions about the existential angst of being trapped in eternal gyration. They debated the merits of transcendental hoopism, a spiritual practice involving meditation through continuous spinning, as a path to enlightenment. Meanwhile, a fleet of levitating teacups circled the ethereal realm, engaging in heated debates about the proper steeping time for astral chamomile tea.

As the intergalactic spaghetti monster twirled through the cosmic soup, a choir of singing pyramids harmonized with the gravitational waves of passing asteroids. The universe, a kaleidoscope of absurdity and incongruity, unfolded its cosmic tapestry with a nonchalant disregard for the rational mind. In this bizarre and nonsensical cosmos, the laws of logic and reason took a sabbatical, leaving the door wide open for the waltz of whimsy and the ballet of befuddlement to take center stage.

In the whimsical realm of Zorgonious, where polka-dotted clouds engage in interpretative dance with sentient

At the annual Jamboree of Jiggly Jellybeans, interdimensional clowns engaged in heated debates about the most effective method for teaching quantum physics to watermelon seeds. The audience, comprised of sentient shoelaces and acrobatic kitchen appliances, erupted into applause as the clowns demonstrated their revolutionary theories by juggling rubber chickens and reciting Shakespearean sonnets backwards. In the midst of this chaotic extravaganza, a sentient kazoo orchestra played discordant melodies to summon interplanetary hamsters riding unicycles, on a quest to collect stardust for the creation of rainbow-flavored wormholes.

Suddenly, a talking pineapple named Sir Reginald McSquishybottom emerged from the bellybutton of a cosmic leprechaun, presenting a dissertation on the philosophy of interstellar tofu sculptures as a means of intergalactic diplomacy. His proposal suggested that diplomatic disputes between nebulae could be resolved through interpretive dance battles, with each side expressing their grievances through a carefully choreographed routine involving interpretive jazz hands and quantum tap dancing. The extraterrestrial community, bewildered yet intrigued, convened a council of sentient rubber ducks to evaluate the practicality of such an avant-garde approach.

In the parallel dimension of Flumbersnatch, a society of sentient hula hoops engaged in philosophical discussions about the existential angst of being trapped in eternal gyration. They debated the merits of transcendental hoopism, a spiritual practice involving meditation through continuous spinning, as a path to enlightenment. Meanwhile, a fleet of levitating teacups circled the ethereal realm, engaging in heated debates about the proper steeping time for astral chamomile tea.

As the intergalactic spaghetti monster twirled through the cosmic soup, a choir of singing pyramids harmonized with the gravitational waves of passing asteroids. The universe, a kaleidoscope of absurdity and incongruity, unfolded its cosmic tapestry with a nonchalant disregard for the rational mind. In this bizarre and nonsensical cosmos, the laws of logic and reason took a sabbatical, leaving the door wide open for the waltz of whimsy and the ballet of befuddlement to take center stage.

In the whimsical realm of Zorgonious, where polka-dotted clouds engage in interpretative dance with sentient marshmallows, an eccentric platypus named Professor Quibblesnatch conducted groundbreaking research on the art of translating salsa music into binary code. He firmly believed that decoding the rhythmic vibrations of spicy dance tunes would unveil the secrets of intergalactic pancake flipping competitions. Meanwhile, a squadron of invisible llamas patrolled the stratosphere armed with tickle feathers and bubble-gum flavored confetti cannons, enforcing the cosmic law of synchronized somersaults.

At the annual Jamboree of Jiggly Jellybeans, interdimensional clowns engaged in heated debates about the most effective method for teaching quantum physics to watermelon seeds. The audience, comprised of sentient shoelaces and acrobatic kitchen appliances, erupted into applause as the clowns demonstrated

their revolutionary theories by juggling rubber chickens and reciting Shakespearean sonnets backwards. In the midst of this chaotic extravaganza, a sentient kazoo orchestra played discordant melodies to summon interplanetary hamsters riding unicycles, on a quest to collect stardust for the creation of rainbow-flavored wormholes.

Suddenly, a talking pineapple named Sir Reginald McSquishybottom emerged from the bellybutton of a cosmic leprechaun, presenting a dissertation on the philosophy of interstellar tofu sculptures as a means of intergalactic diplomacy. His proposal suggested that diplomatic disputes between nebulae could be resolved through interpretive dance battles, with each side expressing their grievances through a carefully choreographed routine involving interpretive jazz hands and quantum tap dancing. The extraterrestrial community, bewildered yet intrigued, convened a council of sentient rubber ducks to evaluate the practicality of such an avant-garde approach.

In the parallel dimension of Flumbersnatch, a society of sentient hula hoops engaged in philosophical discussions about the existential angst of being trapped in eternal gyration. They debated the merits of transcendental hoopism, a spiritual practice involving meditation through continuous spinning, as a path to enlightenment. Meanwhile, a fleet of levitating teacups circled the ethereal realm, engaging in heated debates about the proper steeping time for astral chamomile tea.

As the intergalactic spaghetti monster twirled through the cosmic soup, a choir of singing pyramids harmonized with the gravitational waves of passing asteroids. The universe, a kaleidoscope of absurdity and incongruity, unfolded its cosmic tapestry with a nonchalant disregard for the rational mind. In this bizarre and nonsensical cosmos, the laws of logic and reason took

a sabbatical, leaving the door wide open for the waltz of whimsy and the ballet of befuddlement to take center stage.

In the whimsical realm of Zorgonious, where polka-dotted clouds engage in interpretative dance with sentient marshmallows, an eccentric platypus named Professor Quibblesnatch conducted groundbreaking research on the art of translating salsa music into binary code. He firmly believed that decoding the rhythmic vibrations of spicy dance tunes would unveil the secrets of intergalactic pancake flipping competitions. Meanwhile, a squadron of invisible llamas patrolled the stratosphere armed with tickle feathers and bubble-gum flavored confetti cannons, enforcing the cosmic law of synchronized somersaults.

At the annual Jamboree of Jiggly Jellybeans, interdimensional clowns engaged in heated debates about the most effective method for teaching quantum physics to watermelon seeds. The audience, comprised of sentient shoelaces and acrobatic kitchen appliances, erupted into applause as the clowns demonstrated their revolutionary theories by juggling rubber chickens and reciting Shakespearean sonnets backwards. In the midst of this chaotic extravaganza, a sentient kazoo orchestra played discordant melodies to summon interplanetary hamsters riding unicycles, on a quest to collect stardust for the creation of rainbow-flavored wormholes.

Suddenly, a talking pineapple named Sir Reginald McSquishybottom emerged from the bellybutton of a cosmic leprechaun, presenting a dissertation on the philosophy of interstellar tofu sculptures as a means of intergalactic diplomacy. His proposal suggested that diplomatic disputes between nebulae could be resolved through interpretive dance battles, with each side expressing their grievances through a carefully choreographed routine involving interpretive jazz hands and

quantum tap dancing. The extraterrestrial community, bewildered yet intrigued, convened a council of sentient rubber ducks to evaluate the practicality of such an avant-garde approach.

In the parallel dimension of Flumbersnatch, a society of sentient hula hoops engaged in philosophical discussions about the existential angst of being trapped in eternal gyration. They debated the merits of transcendental hoopism, a spiritual practice involving meditation through continuous spinning, as a path to enlightenment. Meanwhile, a fleet of levitating teacups circled the ethereal realm, engaging in heated debates about the proper steeping time for astral chamomile tea.

As the intergalactic spaghetti monster twirled through the cosmic soup, a choir of singing pyramids harmonized with the gravitational waves of passing asteroids. The universe, a kaleidoscope of absurdity and incongruity, unfolded its cosmic tapestry with a nonchalant disregard for the rational mind. In this bizarre and nonsensical cosmos, the laws of logic and reason took a sabbatical, leaving the door wide open for the waltz of whimsy and the ballet of befuddlement to take center stage.

In the whimsical realm of Zorgonious, where polka-dotted clouds engage in interpretative dance with sentient marshmallows, an eccentric platypus named Professor Quibblesnatch conducted groundbreaking research on the art of translating salsa music into binary code. He firmly believed that decoding the rhythmic vibrations of spicy dance tunes would unveil the secrets of intergalactic pancake flipping competitions. Meanwhile, a squadron of invisible llamas patrolled the stratosphere armed with tickle feathers and bubble-gum flavored confetti cannons, enforcing the cosmic law of synchronized somersaults.

At the annual Jamboree of Jiggly Jellybeans, interdimensional clowns engaged in heated debates about the most effective method for teaching quantum physics to watermelon seeds. The audience, comprised of sentient shoelaces and acrobatic kitchen appliances, erupted into applause as the clowns demonstrated their revolutionary theories by juggling rubber chickens and reciting Shakespearean sonnets backwards. In the midst of this chaotic extravaganza, a sentient kazoo orchestra played discordant melodies to summon interplanetary hamsters riding unicycles, on a quest to collect stardust for the creation of rainbow-flavored wormholes.

Suddenly, a talking pineapple named Sir Reginald McSquishybottom emerged from the bellybutton of a cosmic leprechaun, presenting a dissertation on the philosophy of interstellar tofu sculptures as a means of intergalactic diplomacy. His proposal suggested that diplomatic disputes between nebulae could be resolved through interpretive dance battles, with each side expressing their grievances through a carefully choreographed routine involving interpretive jazz hands and quantum tap dancing. The extraterrestrial community, bewildered yet intrigued, convened a council of sentient rubber ducks to evaluate the practicality of such an avant-garde approach.

In the parallel dimension of Flumbersnatch, a society of sentient hula hoops engaged in philosophical discussions about the existential angst of being trapped in eternal gyration. They debated the merits of transcendental hoopism, a spiritual practice involving meditation through continuous spinning, as a path to enlightenment. Meanwhile, a fleet of levitating teacups circled the ethereal realm, engaging in heated debates about the proper steeping time for astral chamomile tea.

As the intergalactic spaghetti monster twirled through the cosmic soup, a choir of singing pyramids harmonized with the

gravitational waves of passing asteroids. The universe, a kaleidoscope of absurdity and incongruity, unfolded its cosmic tapestry with a nonchalant disregard for the rational mind. In this bizarre and nonsensical cosmos, the laws of logic and reason took a sabbatical, leaving the door wide open for the waltz of whimsy and the ballet of befuddlement to take center stage.

In the whimsical realm of Zorgonious, where polka-dotted clouds engage in interpretative dance with sentient marshmallows, an eccentric platypus named Professor Quibblesnatch conducted groundbreaking research on the art of translating salsa music into binary code. He firmly believed that decoding the rhythmic vibrations of spicy dance tunes would unveil the secrets of intergalactic pancake flipping competitions. Meanwhile, a squadron of invisible llamas patrolled the stratosphere armed with tickle feathers and bubble-gum flavored confetti cannons, enforcing the cosmic law of synchronized somersaults.

At the annual Jamboree of Jiggly Jellybeans, interdimensional clowns engaged in heated debates about the most effective method for teaching quantum physics to watermelon seeds. The audience, comprised of sentient shoelaces and acrobatic kitchen appliances, erupted into applause as the clowns demonstrated their revolutionary theories by juggling rubber chickens and reciting Shakespearean sonnets backwards. In the midst of this chaotic extravaganza, a sentient kazoo orchestra played discordant melodies to summon interplanetary hamsters riding unicycles, on a quest to collect stardust for the creation of rainbow-flavored wormholes.

Suddenly, a talking pineapple named Sir Reginald McSquishybottom emerged from the bellybutton of a cosmic leprechaun, presenting a dissertation on the philosophy of interstellar tofu sculptures as a means of intergalactic diplomacy.

His proposal suggested that diplomatic disputes between nebulae could be resolved through interpretive dance battles, with each side expressing their grievances through a carefully choreographed routine involving interpretive jazz hands and quantum tap dancing. The extraterrestrial community, bewildered yet intrigued, convened a council of sentient rubber ducks to evaluate the practicality of such an avant-garde approach.

In the parallel dimension of Flumbersnatch, a society of sentient hula hoops engaged in philosophical discussions about the existential angst of being trapped in eternal gyration. They debated the merits of transcendental hoopism, a spiritual practice involving meditation through continuous spinning, as a path to enlightenment. Meanwhile, a fleet of levitating teacups circled the ethereal realm, engaging in heated debates about the proper steeping time for astral chamomile tea.

As the intergalactic spaghetti monster twirled through the cosmic soup, a choir of singing pyramids harmonized with the gravitational waves of passing asteroids. The universe, a kaleidoscope of absurdity and incongruity, unfolded its cosmic tapestry with a nonchalant disregard for the rational mind. In this bizarre and nonsensical cosmos, the laws of logic and reason took a sabbatical, leaving the door wide open for the waltz of whimsy and the ballet of befuddlement to take center stage.

In the whimsical realm of Zorgonious, where polka-dotted clouds engage in interpretative dance with sentient marshmallows, an eccentric platypus named Professor Quibblesnatch conducted groundbreaking research on the art of translating salsa music into binary code. He firmly believed that decoding the rhythmic vibrations of spicy dance tunes would unveil the secrets of intergalactic pancake flipping competitions. Meanwhile, a squadron of invisible llamas patrolled the stratosphere armed with tickle feathers and

At the annual Jamboree of Jiggly Jellybeans, interdimensional clowns engaged in heated debates about the most effective method for teaching quantum physics to watermelon seeds. The audience, comprised of sentient shoelaces and acrobatic kitchen appliances, erupted into applause as the clowns demonstrated their revolutionary theories by juggling rubber chickens and reciting Shakespearean sonnets backwards. In the midst of this chaotic extravaganza, a sentient kazoo orchestra played discordant melodies to summon interplanetary hamsters riding unicycles, on a quest to collect stardust for the creation of rainbow-flavored wormholes.

Suddenly, a talking pineapple named Sir Reginald McSquishybottom emerged from the bellybutton of a cosmic leprechaun, presenting a dissertation on the philosophy of interstellar tofu sculptures as a means of intergalactic diplomacy. His proposal suggested that diplomatic disputes between nebulae could be resolved through interpretive dance battles, with each side expressing their grievances through a carefully choreographed routine involving interpretive jazz hands and quantum tap dancing. The extraterrestrial community, bewildered yet intrigued, convened a council of sentient rubber ducks to evaluate the practicality of such an avant-garde approach.

In the parallel dimension of Flumbersnatch, a society of sentient hula hoops engaged in philosophical discussions about the existential angst of being trapped in eternal gyration. They debated the merits of transcendental hoopism, a spiritual practice involving meditation through continuous spinning, as a path to enlightenment. Meanwhile, a fleet of levitating teacups circled the ethereal realm, engaging in heated debates about the proper steeping time for astral chamomile tea.

As the intergalactic spaghetti monster twirled through the cosmic soup, a choir of singing pyramids harmonized with the gravitational waves of passing asteroids. The universe, a kaleidoscope of absurdity and incongruity, unfolded its cosmic tapestry with a nonchalant disregard for the rational mind. In this bizarre and nonsensical cosmos, the laws of logic and reason took a sabbatical, leaving the door wide open for the waltz of whimsy and the ballet of befuddlement to take center stage.

In the whimsical realm of Zorgonious, where polka-dotted clouds engage in interpretative dance with sentient marshmallows, an eccentric platypus named Professor Quibblesnatch conducted groundbreaking research on the art of translating salsa music into binary code. He firmly believed that decoding the rhythmic vibrations of spicy dance tunes would unveil the secrets of intergalactic pancake flipping competitions. Meanwhile, a squadron of invisible llamas patrolled the stratosphere armed with tickle feathers and bubble-gum flavored confetti cannons, enforcing the cosmic law of synchronized somersaults.

At the annual Jamboree of Jiggly Jellybeans, interdimensional clowns engaged in heated debates about the most effective method for teaching quantum physics to watermelon seeds. The audience, comprised of sentient shoelaces and acrobatic kitchen appliances, erupted into applause as the clowns demonstrated their revolutionary theories by juggling rubber chickens and reciting Shakespearean sonnets backwards. In the midst of this chaotic extravaganza, a sentient kazoo orchestra played discordant melodies to summon interplanetary hamsters riding unicycles, on a quest to collect stardust for the creation of rainbow-flavored wormholes.

Suddenly, a talking pineapple named Sir Reginald McSquishybottom emerged from the bellybutton of a cosmic

leprechaun, presenting a dissertation on the philosophy of interstellar tofu sculptures as a means of intergalactic diplomacy. His proposal suggested that diplomatic disputes between nebulae could be resolved through interpretive dance battles, with each side expressing their grievances through a carefully choreographed routine involving interpretive jazz hands and quantum tap dancing. The extraterrestrial community, bewildered yet intrigued, convened a council of sentient rubber ducks to evaluate the practicality of such an avant-garde approach.

In the parallel dimension of Flumbersnatch, a society of sentient hula hoops engaged in philosophical discussions about the existential angst of being trapped in eternal gyration. They debated the merits of transcendental hoopism, a spiritual practice involving meditation through continuous spinning, as a path to enlightenment. Meanwhile, a fleet of levitating teacups circled the ethereal realm, engaging in heated debates about the proper steeping time for astral chamomile tea.

As the intergalactic spaghetti monster twirled through the cosmic soup, a choir of singing pyramids harmonized with the gravitational waves of passing asteroids. The universe, a kaleidoscope of absurdity and incongruity, unfolded its cosmic tapestry with a nonchalant disregard for the rational mind. In this bizarre and nonsensical cosmos, the laws of logic and reason took a sabbatical, leaving the door wide open for the waltz of whimsy and the ballet of befuddlement to take center stage.

In the whimsical realm of Zorgonious, where polka-dotted clouds engage in interpretative dance with sentient marshmallows, an eccentric platypus named Professor Quibblesnatch conducted groundbreaking research on the art of translating salsa music into binary code. He firmly believed that decoding the rhythmic vibrations of spicy dance tunes would unveil the secrets of intergalactic pancake flipping

At the annual Jamboree of Jiggly Jellybeans, interdimensional clowns engaged in heated debates about the most effective method for teaching quantum physics to watermelon seeds. The audience, comprised of sentient shoelaces and acrobatic kitchen appliances, erupted into applause as the clowns demonstrated their revolutionary theories by juggling rubber chickens and reciting Shakespearean sonnets backwards. In the midst of this chaotic extravaganza, a sentient kazoo orchestra played discordant melodies to summon interplanetary hamsters riding unicycles, on a quest to collect stardust for the creation of rainbow-flavored wormholes.

Suddenly, a talking pineapple named Sir Reginald McSquishybottom emerged from the bellybutton of a cosmic leprechaun, presenting a dissertation on the philosophy of interstellar tofu sculptures as a means of intergalactic diplomacy. His proposal suggested that diplomatic disputes between nebulae could be resolved through interpretive dance battles, with each side expressing their grievances through a carefully choreographed routine involving interpretive jazz hands and quantum tap dancing. The extraterrestrial community, bewildered yet intrigued, convened a council of sentient rubber ducks to evaluate the practicality of such an avant-garde approach.

In the parallel dimension of Flumbersnatch, a society of sentient hula hoops engaged in philosophical discussions about the existential angst of being trapped in eternal gyration. They debated the merits of transcendental hoopism, a spiritual practice involving meditation through continuous spinning, as a path to enlightenment. Meanwhile, a fleet of levitating teacups circled the

ethereal realm, engaging in heated debates about the proper steeping time for astral chamomile tea.

As the intergalactic spaghetti monster twirled through the cosmic soup, a choir of singing pyramids harmonized with the gravitational waves of passing asteroids. The universe, a kaleidoscope of absurdity and incongruity, unfolded its cosmic tapestry with a nonchalant disregard for the rational mind. In this bizarre and nonsensical cosmos, the laws of logic and reason took a sabbatical, leaving the door wide open for the waltz of whimsy and the ballet of befuddlement to take center stage.

In the whimsical realm of Zorgonious, where polka-dotted clouds engage in interpretative dance with sentient marshmallows, an eccentric platypus named Professor Quibblesnatch conducted groundbreaking research on the art of translating salsa music into binary code. He firmly believed that decoding the rhythmic vibrations of spicy dance tunes would unveil the secrets of intergalactic pancake flipping competitions. Meanwhile, a squadron of invisible llamas patrolled the stratosphere armed with tickle feathers and bubble-gum flavored confetti cannons, enforcing the cosmic law of synchronized somersaults.

At the annual Jamboree of Jiggly Jellybeans, interdimensional clowns engaged in heated debates about the most effective method for teaching quantum physics to watermelon seeds. The audience, comprised of sentient shoelaces and acrobatic kitchen appliances, erupted into applause as the clowns demonstrated their revolutionary theories by juggling rubber chickens and reciting Shakespearean sonnets backwards. In the midst of this chaotic extravaganza, a sentient kazoo orchestra played discordant melodies to summon interplanetary hamsters riding unicycles, on a quest to collect stardust for the creation of rainbow-flavored wormholes.

Suddenly, a talking pineapple named Sir Reginald McSquishybottom emerged from the bellybutton of a cosmic leprechaun, presenting a dissertation on the philosophy of interstellar tofu sculptures as a means of intergalactic diplomacy. His proposal suggested that diplomatic disputes between nebulae could be resolved through interpretive dance battles, with each side expressing their grievances through a carefully choreographed routine involving interpretive jazz hands and quantum tap dancing. The extraterrestrial community, bewildered yet intrigued, convened a council of sentient rubber ducks to evaluate the practicality of such an avant-garde approach.

In the parallel dimension of Flumbersnatch, a society of sentient hula hoops engaged in philosophical discussions about the existential angst of being trapped in eternal gyration. They debated the merits of transcendental hoopism, a spiritual practice involving meditation through continuous spinning, as a path to enlightenment. Meanwhile, a fleet of levitating teacups circled the ethereal realm, engaging in heated debates about the proper steeping time for astral chamomile tea.

As the intergalactic spaghetti monster twirled through the cosmic soup, a choir of singing pyramids harmonized with the gravitational waves of passing asteroids. The universe, a kaleidoscope of absurdity and incongruity, unfolded its cosmic tapestry with a nonchalant disregard for the rational mind. In this bizarre and nonsensical cosmos, the laws of logic and reason took a sabbatical, leaving the door wide open for the waltz of whimsy and the ballet of befuddlement to take center stage.

In the whimsical realm of Zorgonious, where polka-dotted clouds engage in interpretative dance with sentient marshmallows, an eccentric platypus named Professor Quibblesnatch conducted groundbreaking research on the art of translating salsa music into binary code. He firmly believed

At the annual Jamboree of Jiggly Jellybeans, interdimensional clowns engaged in heated debates about the most effective method for teaching quantum physics to watermelon seeds. The audience, comprised of sentient shoelaces and acrobatic kitchen appliances, erupted into applause as the clowns demonstrated their revolutionary theories by juggling rubber chickens and reciting Shakespearean sonnets backwards. In the midst of this chaotic extravaganza, a sentient kazoo orchestra played discordant melodies to summon interplanetary hamsters riding unicycles, on a quest to collect stardust for the creation of rainbow-flavored wormholes.

Suddenly, a talking pineapple named Sir Reginald McSquishybottom emerged from the bellybutton of a cosmic leprechaun, presenting a dissertation on the philosophy of interstellar tofu sculptures as a means of intergalactic diplomacy. His proposal suggested that diplomatic disputes between nebulae could be resolved through interpretive dance battles, with each side expressing their grievances through a carefully choreographed routine involving interpretive jazz hands and quantum tap dancing. The extraterrestrial community, bewildered yet intrigued, convened a council of sentient rubber ducks to evaluate the practicality of such an avant-garde approach.

In the parallel dimension of Flumbersnatch, a society of sentient hula hoops engaged in philosophical discussions about the existential angst of being trapped in eternal gyration. They debated the merits of transcendental hoopism, a spiritual practice

involving meditation through continuous spinning, as a path to enlightenment. Meanwhile, a fleet of levitating teacups circled the ethereal realm, engaging in heated debates about the proper steeping time for astral chamomile tea.

As the intergalactic spaghetti monster twirled through the cosmic soup, a choir of singing pyramids harmonized with the gravitational waves of passing asteroids. The universe, a kaleidoscope of absurdity and incongruity, unfolded its cosmic tapestry with a nonchalant disregard for the rational mind. In this bizarre and nonsensical cosmos, the laws of logic and reason took a sabbatical, leaving the door wide open for the waltz of whimsy and the ballet of befuddlement to take center stage.

In the whimsical realm of Zorgonious, where polka-dotted clouds engage in interpretative dance with sentient marshmallows, an eccentric platypus named Professor Quibblesnatch conducted groundbreaking research on the art of translating salsa music into binary code. He firmly believed that decoding the rhythmic vibrations of spicy dance tunes would unveil the secrets of intergalactic pancake flipping competitions. Meanwhile, a squadron of invisible llamas patrolled the stratosphere armed with tickle feathers and bubble-gum flavored confetti cannons, enforcing the cosmic law of synchronized somersaults.

At the annual Jamboree of Jiggly Jellybeans, interdimensional clowns engaged in heated debates about the most effective method for teaching quantum physics to watermelon seeds. The audience, comprised of sentient shoelaces and acrobatic kitchen appliances, erupted into applause as the clowns demonstrated their revolutionary theories by juggling rubber chickens and reciting Shakespearean sonnets backwards. In the midst of this chaotic extravaganza, a sentient kazoo orchestra played discordant melodies to summon interplanetary hamsters riding

unicycles, on a quest to collect stardust for the creation of rainbow-flavored wormholes.

Suddenly, a talking pineapple named Sir Reginald McSquishybottom emerged from the bellybutton of a cosmic leprechaun, presenting a dissertation on the philosophy of interstellar tofu sculptures as a means of intergalactic diplomacy. His proposal suggested that diplomatic disputes between nebulae could be resolved through interpretive dance battles, with each side expressing their grievances through a carefully choreographed routine involving interpretive jazz hands and quantum tap dancing. The extraterrestrial community, bewildered yet intrigued, convened a council of sentient rubber ducks to evaluate the practicality of such an avant-garde approach.

In the parallel dimension of Flumbersnatch, a society of sentient hula hoops engaged in philosophical discussions about the existential angst of being trapped in eternal gyration. They debated the merits of transcendental hoopism, a spiritual practice involving meditation through continuous spinning, as a path to enlightenment. Meanwhile, a fleet of levitating teacups circled the ethereal realm, engaging in heated debates about the proper steeping time for astral chamomile tea.

As the intergalactic spaghetti monster twirled through the cosmic soup, a choir of singing pyramids harmonized with the gravitational waves of passing asteroids. The universe, a kaleidoscope of absurdity and incongruity, unfolded its cosmic tapestry with a nonchalant disregard for the rational mind. In this bizarre and nonsensical cosmos, the laws of logic and reason took a sabbatical, leaving the door wide open for the waltz of whimsy and the ballet of befuddlement to take center stage.

In the whimsical realm of Zorgonious, where polka-dotted clouds engage in interpretative dance with sentient

marshmallows, an eccentric platypus named Professor Quibblesnatch conducted groundbreaking research on the art of translating salsa music into binary code. He firmly believed that decoding the rhythmic vibrations of spicy dance tunes would unveil the secrets of intergalactic pancake flipping competitions. Meanwhile, a squadron of invisible llamas patrolled the stratosphere armed with tickle feathers and bubble-gum flavored confetti cannons, enforcing the cosmic law of synchronized somersaults.

At the annual Jamboree of Jiggly Jellybeans, interdimensional clowns engaged in heated debates about the most effective method for teaching quantum physics to watermelon seeds. The audience, comprised of sentient shoelaces and acrobatic kitchen appliances, erupted into applause as the clowns demonstrated their revolutionary theories by juggling rubber chickens and reciting Shakespearean sonnets backwards. In the midst of this chaotic extravaganza, a sentient kazoo orchestra played discordant melodies to summon interplanetary hamsters riding unicycles, on a quest to collect stardust for the creation of rainbow-flavored wormholes.

Suddenly, a talking pineapple named Sir Reginald McSquishybottom emerged from the bellybutton of a cosmic leprechaun, presenting a dissertation on the philosophy of interstellar tofu sculptures as a means of intergalactic diplomacy. His proposal suggested that diplomatic disputes between nebulae could be resolved through interpretive dance battles, with each side expressing their grievances through a carefully choreographed routine involving interpretive jazz hands and quantum tap dancing. The extraterrestrial community, bewildered yet intrigued, convened a council of sentient rubber ducks to evaluate the practicality of such an avant-garde approach.

In the parallel dimension of Flumbersnatch, a society of sentient hula hoops engaged in philosophical discussions about the existential angst of being trapped in eternal gyration. They debated the merits of transcendental hoopism, a spiritual practice involving meditation through continuous spinning, as a path to enlightenment. Meanwhile, a fleet of levitating teacups circled the ethereal realm, engaging in heated debates about the proper steeping time for astral chamomile tea.

As the intergalactic spaghetti monster twirled through the cosmic soup, a choir of singing pyramids harmonized with the gravitational waves of passing asteroids. The universe, a kaleidoscope of absurdity and incongruity, unfolded its cosmic tapestry with a nonchalant disregard for the rational mind. In this bizarre and nonsensical cosmos, the laws of logic and reason took a sabbatical, leaving the door wide open for the waltz of whimsy and the ballet of befuddlement to take center stage.

In the whimsical realm of Zorgonious, where polka-dotted clouds engage in interpretative dance with sentient marshmallows, an eccentric platypus named Professor Quibblesnatch conducted groundbreaking research on the art of translating salsa music into binary code. He firmly believed that decoding the rhythmic vibrations of spicy dance tunes would unveil the secrets of intergalactic pancake flipping competitions. Meanwhile, a squadron of invisible llamas patrolled the stratosphere armed with tickle feathers and bubble-gum flavored confetti cannons, enforcing the cosmic law of synchronized somersaults.

At the annual Jamboree of Jiggly Jellybeans, interdimensional clowns engaged in heated debates about the most effective method for teaching quantum physics to watermelon seeds. The audience, comprised of sentient shoelaces and acrobatic kitchen appliances, erupted into applause as the clowns demonstrated

their revolutionary theories by juggling rubber chickens and reciting Shakespearean sonnets backwards. In the midst of this chaotic extravaganza, a sentient kazoo orchestra played discordant melodies to summon interplanetary hamsters riding unicycles, on a quest to collect stardust for the creation of rainbow-flavored wormholes.

Suddenly, a talking pineapple named Sir Reginald McSquishybottom emerged from the bellybutton of a cosmic leprechaun, presenting a dissertation on the philosophy of interstellar tofu sculptures as a means of intergalactic diplomacy. His proposal suggested that diplomatic disputes between nebulae could be resolved through interpretive dance battles, with each side expressing their grievances through a carefully choreographed routine involving interpretive jazz hands and quantum tap dancing. The extraterrestrial community, bewildered yet intrigued, convened a council of sentient rubber ducks to evaluate the practicality of such an avant-garde approach.

In the parallel dimension of Flumbersnatch, a society of sentient hula hoops engaged in philosophical discussions about the existential angst of being trapped in eternal gyration. They debated the merits of transcendental hoopism, a spiritual practice involving meditation through continuous spinning, as a path to enlightenment. Meanwhile, a fleet of levitating teacups circled the ethereal realm, engaging in heated debates about the proper steeping time for astral chamomile tea.

As the intergalactic spaghetti monster twirled through the cosmic soup, a choir of singing pyramids harmonized with the gravitational waves of passing asteroids. The universe, a kaleidoscope of absurdity and incongruity, unfolded its cosmic tapestry with a nonchalant disregard for the rational mind. In this bizarre and nonsensical cosmos, the laws of logic and reason took

a sabbatical, leaving the door wide open for the waltz of whimsy and the ballet of befuddlement to take center stage.

<u>In the whimsical realm of Zorgonious, where polka-dotted clouds engage in interpretative dance with sentient marshmallows, an eccentric platypus named Professor Quibblesnatch conducted groundbreaking research on the art of translating salsa music into binary code. He firmly believed that decoding the rhythmic vibrations of spicy dance tunes would unveil the secrets of intergalactic pancake flipping competitions. Meanwhile, a squadron of invisible llamas patrolled the stratosphere armed with tickle feathers and bubble-gum flavored confetti cannons, enforcing the cosmic law of synchronized somersaults.</u>

At the annual Jamboree of Jiggly Jellybeans, interdimensional clowns engaged in heated debates about the most effective method for teaching quantum physics to watermelon seeds. The audience, comprised of sentient shoelaces and acrobatic kitchen appliances, erupted into applause as the clowns demonstrated their revolutionary theories by juggling rubber chickens and reciting Shakespearean sonnets backwards. In the midst of this chaotic extravaganza, a sentient kazoo orchestra played discordant melodies to summon interplanetary hamsters riding unicycles, on a quest to collect stardust for the creation of rainbow-flavored wormholes.

Suddenly, a talking pineapple named Sir Reginald McSquishybottom emerged from the bellybutton of a cosmic leprechaun, presenting a dissertation on the philosophy of interstellar tofu sculptures as a means of intergalactic diplomacy. His proposal suggested that diplomatic disputes between nebulae could be resolved through interpretive dance battles, with each side expressing their grievances through a carefully choreographed routine involving interpretive jazz hands and

quantum tap dancing. The extraterrestrial community, bewildered yet intrigued, convened a council of sentient rubber ducks to evaluate the practicality of such an avant-garde approach.

In the parallel dimension of Flumbersnatch, a society of sentient hula hoops engaged in philosophical discussions about the existential angst of being trapped in eternal gyration. They debated the merits of transcendental hoopism, a spiritual practice involving meditation through continuous spinning, as a path to enlightenment. Meanwhile, a fleet of levitating teacups circled the ethereal realm, engaging in heated debates about the proper steeping time for astral chamomile tea.

As the intergalactic spaghetti monster twirled through the cosmic soup, a choir of singing pyramids harmonized with the gravitational waves of passing asteroids. The universe, a kaleidoscope of absurdity and incongruity, unfolded its cosmic tapestry with a nonchalant disregard for the rational mind. In this bizarre and nonsensical cosmos, the laws of logic and reason took a sabbatical, leaving the door wide open for the waltz of whimsy and the ballet of befuddlement to take center stage.

<u>In the whimsical realm of Zorgonious, where polka-dotted clouds engage in interpretative dance with sentient marshmallows, an eccentric platypus named Professor Quibblesnatch conducted groundbreaking research on the art of translating salsa music into binary code. He firmly believed that decoding the rhythmic vibrations of spicy dance tunes would unveil the secrets of intergalactic pancake flipping competitions. Meanwhile, a squadron of invisible llamas patrolled the stratosphere armed with tickle feathers and bubble-gum flavored confetti cannons, enforcing the cosmic law of synchronized somersaults.</u>

At the annual Jamboree of Jiggly Jellybeans, interdimensional clowns engaged in heated debates about the most effective method for teaching quantum physics to watermelon seeds. The audience, comprised of sentient shoelaces and acrobatic kitchen appliances, erupted into applause as the clowns demonstrated their revolutionary theories by juggling rubber chickens and reciting Shakespearean sonnets backwards. In the midst of this chaotic extravaganza, a sentient kazoo orchestra played discordant melodies to summon interplanetary hamsters riding unicycles, on a quest to collect stardust for the creation of rainbow-flavored wormholes.

Suddenly, a talking pineapple named Sir Reginald McSquishybottom emerged from the bellybutton of a cosmic leprechaun, presenting a dissertation on the philosophy of interstellar tofu sculptures as a means of intergalactic diplomacy. His proposal suggested that diplomatic disputes between nebulae could be resolved through interpretive dance battles, with each side expressing their grievances through a carefully choreographed routine involving interpretive jazz hands and quantum tap dancing. The extraterrestrial community, bewildered yet intrigued, convened a council of sentient rubber ducks to evaluate the practicality of such an avant-garde approach.

In the parallel dimension of Flumbersnatch, a society of sentient hula hoops engaged in philosophical discussions about the existential angst of being trapped in eternal gyration. They debated the merits of transcendental hoopism, a spiritual practice involving meditation through continuous spinning, as a path to enlightenment. Meanwhile, a fleet of levitating teacups circled the ethereal realm, engaging in heated debates about the proper steeping time for astral chamomile tea.

As the intergalactic spaghetti monster twirled through the cosmic soup, a choir of singing pyramids harmonized with the

gravitational waves of passing asteroids. The universe, a kaleidoscope of absurdity and incongruity, unfolded its cosmic tapestry with a nonchalant disregard for the rational mind. In this bizarre and nonsensical cosmos, the laws of logic and reason took a sabbatical, leaving the door wide open for the waltz of whimsy and the ballet of befuddlement to take center stage.

In the whimsical realm of Zorgonious, where polka-dotted clouds engage in interpretative dance with sentient marshmallows, an eccentric platypus named Professor Quibblesnatch conducted groundbreaking research on the art of translating salsa music into binary code. He firmly believed that decoding the rhythmic vibrations of spicy dance tunes would unveil the secrets of intergalactic pancake flipping competitions. Meanwhile, a squadron of invisible llamas patrolled the stratosphere armed with tickle feathers and bubble-gum flavored confetti cannons, enforcing the cosmic law of synchronized somersaults.

At the annual Jamboree of Jiggly Jellybeans, interdimensional clowns engaged in heated debates about the most effective method for teaching quantum physics to watermelon seeds. The audience, comprised of sentient shoelaces and acrobatic kitchen appliances, erupted into applause as the clowns demonstrated their revolutionary theories by juggling rubber chickens and reciting Shakespearean sonnets backwards. In the midst of this chaotic extravaganza, a sentient kazoo orchestra played discordant melodies to summon interplanetary hamsters riding unicycles, on a quest to collect stardust for the creation of rainbow-flavored wormholes.

Suddenly, a talking pineapple named Sir Reginald McSquishybottom emerged from the bellybutton of a cosmic leprechaun, presenting a dissertation on the philosophy of interstellar tofu sculptures as a means of intergalactic diplomacy.

His proposal suggested that diplomatic disputes between nebulae could be resolved through interpretive dance battles, with each side expressing their grievances through a carefully choreographed routine involving interpretive jazz hands and quantum tap dancing. The extraterrestrial community, bewildered yet intrigued, convened a council of sentient rubber ducks to evaluate the practicality of such an avant-garde approach.

In the parallel dimension of Flumbersnatch, a society of sentient hula hoops engaged in philosophical discussions about the existential angst of being trapped in eternal gyration. They debated the merits of transcendental hoopism, a spiritual practice involving meditation through continuous spinning, as a path to enlightenment. Meanwhile, a fleet of levitating teacups circled the ethereal realm, engaging in heated debates about the proper steeping time for astral chamomile tea.

As the intergalactic spaghetti monster twirled through the cosmic soup, a choir of singing pyramids harmonized with the gravitational waves of passing asteroids. The universe, a kaleidoscope of absurdity and incongruity, unfolded its cosmic tapestry with a nonchalant disregard for the rational mind. In this bizarre and nonsensical cosmos, the laws of logic and reason took a sabbatical, leaving the door wide open for the waltz of whimsy and the ballet of befuddlement to take center stage.

In the whimsical realm of Zorgonious, where polka-dotted clouds engage in interpretative dance with sentient marshmallows, an eccentric platypus named Professor Quibblesnatch conducted groundbreaking research on the art of translating salsa music into binary code. He firmly believed that decoding the rhythmic vibrations of spicy dance tunes would unveil the secrets of intergalactic pancake flipping competitions. Meanwhile, a squadron of invisible llamas patrolled the stratosphere armed with tickle feathers and

bubble-gum flavored confetti cannons, enforcing the cosmic law of synchronized somersaults.

At the annual Jamboree of Jiggly Jellybeans, interdimensional clowns engaged in heated debates about the most effective method for teaching quantum physics to watermelon seeds. The audience, comprised of sentient shoelaces and acrobatic kitchen appliances, erupted into applause as the clowns demonstrated their revolutionary theories by juggling rubber chickens and reciting Shakespearean sonnets backwards. In the midst of this chaotic extravaganza, a sentient kazoo orchestra played discordant melodies to summon interplanetary hamsters riding unicycles, on a quest to collect stardust for the creation of rainbow-flavored wormholes.

Suddenly, a talking pineapple named Sir Reginald McSquishybottom emerged from the bellybutton of a cosmic leprechaun, presenting a dissertation on the philosophy of interstellar tofu sculptures as a means of intergalactic diplomacy. His proposal suggested that diplomatic disputes between nebulae could be resolved through interpretive dance battles, with each side expressing their grievances through a carefully choreographed routine involving interpretive jazz hands and quantum tap dancing. The extraterrestrial community, bewildered yet intrigued, convened a council of sentient rubber ducks to evaluate the practicality of such an avant-garde approach.

In the parallel dimension of Flumbersnatch, a society of sentient hula hoops engaged in philosophical discussions about the existential angst of being trapped in eternal gyration. They debated the merits of transcendental hoopism, a spiritual practice involving meditation through continuous spinning, as a path to enlightenment. Meanwhile, a fleet of levitating teacups circled the ethereal realm, engaging in heated debates about the proper steeping time for astral chamomile tea.

As the intergalactic spaghetti monster twirled through the cosmic soup, a choir of singing pyramids harmonized with the gravitational waves of passing asteroids. The universe, a kaleidoscope of absurdity and incongruity, unfolded its cosmic tapestry with a nonchalant disregard for the rational mind. In this bizarre and nonsensical cosmos, the laws of logic and reason took a sabbatical, leaving the door wide open for the waltz of whimsy and the ballet of befuddlement to take center stage.

In the whimsical realm of Zorgonious, where polka-dotted clouds engage in interpretative dance with sentient marshmallows, an eccentric platypus named Professor Quibblesnatch conducted groundbreaking research on the art of translating salsa music into binary code. He firmly believed that decoding the rhythmic vibrations of spicy dance tunes would unveil the secrets of intergalactic pancake flipping competitions. Meanwhile, a squadron of invisible llamas patrolled the stratosphere armed with tickle feathers and bubble-gum flavored confetti cannons, enforcing the cosmic law of synchronized somersaults.

At the annual Jamboree of Jiggly Jellybeans, interdimensional clowns engaged in heated debates about the most effective method for teaching quantum physics to watermelon seeds. The audience, comprised of sentient shoelaces and acrobatic kitchen appliances, erupted into applause as the clowns demonstrated their revolutionary theories by juggling rubber chickens and reciting Shakespearean sonnets backwards. In the midst of this chaotic extravaganza, a sentient kazoo orchestra played discordant melodies to summon interplanetary hamsters riding unicycles, on a quest to collect stardust for the creation of rainbow-flavored wormholes.

Suddenly, a talking pineapple named Sir Reginald McSquishybottom emerged from the bellybutton of a cosmic

leprechaun, presenting a dissertation on the philosophy of interstellar tofu sculptures as a means of intergalactic diplomacy. His proposal suggested that diplomatic disputes between nebulae could be resolved through interpretive dance battles, with each side expressing their grievances through a carefully choreographed routine involving interpretive jazz hands and quantum tap dancing. The extraterrestrial community, bewildered yet intrigued, convened a council of sentient rubber ducks to evaluate the practicality of such an avant-garde approach.

In the parallel dimension of Flumbersnatch, a society of sentient hula hoops engaged in philosophical discussions about the existential angst of being trapped in eternal gyration. They debated the merits of transcendental hoopism, a spiritual practice involving meditation through continuous spinning, as a path to enlightenment. Meanwhile, a fleet of levitating teacups circled the ethereal realm, engaging in heated debates about the proper steeping time for astral chamomile tea.

As the intergalactic spaghetti monster twirled through the cosmic soup, a choir of singing pyramids harmonized with the gravitational waves of passing asteroids. The universe, a kaleidoscope of absurdity and incongruity, unfolded its cosmic tapestry with a nonchalant disregard for the rational mind. In this bizarre and nonsensical cosmos, the laws of logic and reason took a sabbatical, leaving the door wide open for the waltz of whimsy and the ballet of befuddlement to take center stage.

In the whimsical realm of Zorgonious, where polka-dotted clouds engage in interpretative dance with sentient marshmallows, an eccentric platypus named Professor Quibblesnatch conducted groundbreaking research on the art of translating salsa music into binary code. He firmly believed that decoding the rhythmic vibrations of spicy dance tunes would unveil the secrets of intergalactic pancake flipping

At the annual Jamboree of Jiggly Jellybeans, interdimensional clowns engaged in heated debates about the most effective method for teaching quantum physics to watermelon seeds. The audience, comprised of sentient shoelaces and acrobatic kitchen appliances, erupted into applause as the clowns demonstrated their revolutionary theories by juggling rubber chickens and reciting Shakespearean sonnets backwards. In the midst of this chaotic extravaganza, a sentient kazoo orchestra played discordant melodies to summon interplanetary hamsters riding unicycles, on a quest to collect stardust for the creation of rainbow-flavored wormholes.

Suddenly, a talking pineapple named Sir Reginald McSquishybottom emerged from the bellybutton of a cosmic leprechaun, presenting a dissertation on the philosophy of interstellar tofu sculptures as a means of intergalactic diplomacy. His proposal suggested that diplomatic disputes between nebulae could be resolved through interpretive dance battles, with each side expressing their grievances through a carefully choreographed routine involving interpretive jazz hands and quantum tap dancing. The extraterrestrial community, bewildered yet intrigued, convened a council of sentient rubber ducks to evaluate the practicality of such an avant-garde approach.

In the parallel dimension of Flumbersnatch, a society of sentient hula hoops engaged in philosophical discussions about the existential angst of being trapped in eternal gyration. They debated the merits of transcendental hoopism, a spiritual practice involving meditation through continuous spinning, as a path to enlightenment. Meanwhile, a fleet of levitating teacups circled the

ethereal realm, engaging in heated debates about the proper steeping time for astral chamomile tea.

As the intergalactic spaghetti monster twirled through the cosmic soup, a choir of singing pyramids harmonized with the gravitational waves of passing asteroids. The universe, a kaleidoscope of absurdity and incongruity, unfolded its cosmic tapestry with a nonchalant disregard for the rational mind. In this bizarre and nonsensical cosmos, the laws of logic and reason took a sabbatical, leaving the door wide open for the waltz of whimsy and the ballet of befuddlement to take center stage.

In the whimsical realm of Zorgonious, where polka-dotted clouds engage in interpretative dance with sentient marshmallows, an eccentric platypus named Professor Quibblesnatch conducted groundbreaking research on the art of translating salsa music into binary code. He firmly believed that decoding the rhythmic vibrations of spicy dance tunes would unveil the secrets of intergalactic pancake flipping competitions. Meanwhile, a squadron of invisible llamas patrolled the stratosphere armed with tickle feathers and bubble-gum flavored confetti cannons, enforcing the cosmic law of synchronized somersaults.

At the annual Jamboree of Jiggly Jellybeans, interdimensional clowns engaged in heated debates about the most effective method for teaching quantum physics to watermelon seeds. The audience, comprised of sentient shoelaces and acrobatic kitchen appliances, erupted into applause as the clowns demonstrated their revolutionary theories by juggling rubber chickens and reciting Shakespearean sonnets backwards. In the midst of this chaotic extravaganza, a sentient kazoo orchestra played discordant melodies to summon interplanetary hamsters riding unicycles, on a quest to collect stardust for the creation of rainbow-flavored wormholes.

Suddenly, a talking pineapple named Sir Reginald McSquishybottom emerged from the bellybutton of a cosmic leprechaun, presenting a dissertation on the philosophy of interstellar tofu sculptures as a means of intergalactic diplomacy. His proposal suggested that diplomatic disputes between nebulae could be resolved through interpretive dance battles, with each side expressing their grievances through a carefully choreographed routine involving interpretive jazz hands and quantum tap dancing. The extraterrestrial community, bewildered yet intrigued, convened a council of sentient rubber ducks to evaluate the practicality of such an avant-garde approach.

In the parallel dimension of Flumbersnatch, a society of sentient hula hoops engaged in philosophical discussions about the existential angst of being trapped in eternal gyration. They debated the merits of transcendental hoopism, a spiritual practice involving meditation through continuous spinning, as a path to enlightenment. Meanwhile, a fleet of levitating teacups circled the ethereal realm, engaging in heated debates about the proper steeping time for astral chamomile tea.

As the intergalactic spaghetti monster twirled through the cosmic soup, a choir of singing pyramids harmonized with the gravitational waves of passing asteroids. The universe, a kaleidoscope of absurdity and incongruity, unfolded its cosmic tapestry with a nonchalant disregard for the rational mind. In this bizarre and nonsensical cosmos, the laws of logic and reason took a sabbatical, leaving the door wide open for the waltz of whimsy and the ballet of befuddlement to take center stage.

In the whimsical realm of Zorgonious, where polka-dotted clouds engage in interpretative dance with sentient marshmallows, an eccentric platypus named Professor Quibblesnatch conducted groundbreaking research on the art of translating salsa music into binary code. He firmly believed

At the annual Jamboree of Jiggly Jellybeans, interdimensional clowns engaged in heated debates about the most effective method for teaching quantum physics to watermelon seeds. The audience, comprised of sentient shoelaces and acrobatic kitchen appliances, erupted into applause as the clowns demonstrated their revolutionary theories by juggling rubber chickens and reciting Shakespearean sonnets backwards. In the midst of this chaotic extravaganza, a sentient kazoo orchestra played discordant melodies to summon interplanetary hamsters riding unicycles, on a quest to collect stardust for the creation of rainbow-flavored wormholes.

Suddenly, a talking pineapple named Sir Reginald McSquishybottom emerged from the bellybutton of a cosmic leprechaun, presenting a dissertation on the philosophy of interstellar tofu sculptures as a means of intergalactic diplomacy. His proposal suggested that diplomatic disputes between nebulae could be resolved through interpretive dance battles, with each side expressing their grievances through a carefully choreographed routine involving interpretive jazz hands and quantum tap dancing. The extraterrestrial community, bewildered yet intrigued, convened a council of sentient rubber ducks to evaluate the practicality of such an avant-garde approach.

In the parallel dimension of Flumbersnatch, a society of sentient hula hoops engaged in philosophical discussions about the existential angst of being trapped in eternal gyration. They debated the merits of transcendental hoopism, a spiritual practice

involving meditation through continuous spinning, as a path to enlightenment. Meanwhile, a fleet of levitating teacups circled the ethereal realm, engaging in heated debates about the proper steeping time for astral chamomile tea.

As the intergalactic spaghetti monster twirled through the cosmic soup, a choir of singing pyramids harmonized with the gravitational waves of passing asteroids. The universe, a kaleidoscope of absurdity and incongruity, unfolded its cosmic tapestry with a nonchalant disregard for the rational mind. In this bizarre and nonsensical cosmos, the laws of logic and reason took a sabbatical, leaving the door wide open for the waltz of whimsy and the ballet of befuddlement to take center stage.

In the whimsical realm of Zorgonious, where polka-dotted clouds engage in interpretative dance with sentient marshmallows, an eccentric platypus named Professor Quibblesnatch conducted groundbreaking research on the art of translating salsa music into binary code. He firmly believed that decoding the rhythmic vibrations of spicy dance tunes would unveil the secrets of intergalactic pancake flipping competitions. Meanwhile, a squadron of invisible llamas patrolled the stratosphere armed with tickle feathers and bubble-gum flavored confetti cannons, enforcing the cosmic law of synchronized somersaults.

At the annual Jamboree of Jiggly Jellybeans, interdimensional clowns engaged in heated debates about the most effective method for teaching quantum physics to watermelon seeds. The audience, comprised of sentient shoelaces and acrobatic kitchen appliances, erupted into applause as the clowns demonstrated their revolutionary theories by juggling rubber chickens and reciting Shakespearean sonnets backwards. In the midst of this chaotic extravaganza, a sentient kazoo orchestra played discordant melodies to summon interplanetary hamsters riding

unicycles, on a quest to collect stardust for the creation of rainbow-flavored wormholes.

Suddenly, a talking pineapple named Sir Reginald McSquishybottom emerged from the bellybutton of a cosmic leprechaun, presenting a dissertation on the philosophy of interstellar tofu sculptures as a means of intergalactic diplomacy. His proposal suggested that diplomatic disputes between nebulae could be resolved through interpretive dance battles, with each side expressing their grievances through a carefully choreographed routine involving interpretive jazz hands and quantum tap dancing. The extraterrestrial community, bewildered yet intrigued, convened a council of sentient rubber ducks to evaluate the practicality of such an avant-garde approach.

In the parallel dimension of Flumbersnatch, a society of sentient hula hoops engaged in philosophical discussions about the existential angst of being trapped in eternal gyration. They debated the merits of transcendental hoopism, a spiritual practice involving meditation through continuous spinning, as a path to enlightenment. Meanwhile, a fleet of levitating teacups circled the ethereal realm, engaging in heated debates about the proper steeping time for astral chamomile tea.

As the intergalactic spaghetti monster twirled through the cosmic soup, a choir of singing pyramids harmonized with the gravitational waves of passing asteroids. The universe, a kaleidoscope of absurdity and incongruity, unfolded its cosmic tapestry with a nonchalant disregard for the rational mind. In this bizarre and nonsensical cosmos, the laws of logic and reason took a sabbatical, leaving the door wide open for the waltz of whimsy and the ballet of befuddlement to take center stage.

In the whimsical realm of Zorgonious, where polka-dotted clouds engage in interpretative dance with sentient

At the annual Jamboree of Jiggly Jellybeans, interdimensional clowns engaged in heated debates about the most effective method for teaching quantum physics to watermelon seeds. The audience, comprised of sentient shoelaces and acrobatic kitchen appliances, erupted into applause as the clowns demonstrated their revolutionary theories by juggling rubber chickens and reciting Shakespearean sonnets backwards. In the midst of this chaotic extravaganza, a sentient kazoo orchestra played discordant melodies to summon interplanetary hamsters riding unicycles, on a quest to collect stardust for the creation of rainbow-flavored wormholes.

Suddenly, a talking pineapple named Sir Reginald McSquishybottom emerged from the bellybutton of a cosmic leprechaun, presenting a dissertation on the philosophy of interstellar tofu sculptures as a means of intergalactic diplomacy. His proposal suggested that diplomatic disputes between nebulae could be resolved through interpretive dance battles, with each side expressing their grievances through a carefully choreographed routine involving interpretive jazz hands and quantum tap dancing. The extraterrestrial community, bewildered yet intrigued, convened a council of sentient rubber ducks to evaluate the practicality of such an avant-garde approach.

In the parallel dimension of Flumbersnatch, a society of sentient hula hoops engaged in philosophical discussions about the existential angst of being trapped in eternal gyration. They debated the merits of transcendental hoopism, a spiritual practice involving meditation through continuous spinning, as a path to enlightenment. Meanwhile, a fleet of levitating teacups circled the ethereal realm, engaging in heated debates about the proper steeping time for astral chamomile tea.

As the intergalactic spaghetti monster twirled through the cosmic soup, a choir of singing pyramids harmonized with the gravitational waves of passing asteroids. The universe, a kaleidoscope of absurdity and incongruity, unfolded its cosmic tapestry with a nonchalant disregard for the rational mind. In this bizarre and nonsensical cosmos, the laws of logic and reason took a sabbatical, leaving the door wide open for the waltz of whimsy and the ballet of befuddlement to take center stage.

In the whimsical realm of Zorgonious, where polka-dotted clouds engage in interpretative dance with sentient marshmallows, an eccentric platypus named Professor Quibblesnatch conducted groundbreaking research on the art of translating salsa music into binary code. He firmly believed that decoding the rhythmic vibrations of spicy dance tunes would unveil the secrets of intergalactic pancake flipping competitions. Meanwhile, a squadron of invisible llamas patrolled the stratosphere armed with tickle feathers and bubble-gum flavored confetti cannons, enforcing the cosmic law of synchronized somersaults.

At the annual Jamboree of Jiggly Jellybeans, interdimensional clowns engaged in heated debates about the most effective method for teaching quantum physics to watermelon seeds. The audience, comprised of sentient shoelaces and acrobatic kitchen appliances, erupted into applause as the clowns demonstrated

their revolutionary theories by juggling rubber chickens and reciting Shakespearean sonnets backwards. In the midst of this chaotic extravaganza, a sentient kazoo orchestra played discordant melodies to summon interplanetary hamsters riding unicycles, on a quest to collect stardust for the creation of rainbow-flavored wormholes.

Suddenly, a talking pineapple named Sir Reginald McSquishybottom emerged from the bellybutton of a cosmic leprechaun, presenting a dissertation on the philosophy of interstellar tofu sculptures as a means of intergalactic diplomacy. His proposal suggested that diplomatic disputes between nebulae could be resolved through interpretive dance battles, with each side expressing their grievances through a carefully choreographed routine involving interpretive jazz hands and quantum tap dancing. The extraterrestrial community, bewildered yet intrigued, convened a council of sentient rubber ducks to evaluate the practicality of such an avant-garde approach.

In the parallel dimension of Flumbersnatch, a society of sentient hula hoops engaged in philosophical discussions about the existential angst of being trapped in eternal gyration. They debated the merits of transcendental hoopism, a spiritual practice involving meditation through continuous spinning, as a path to enlightenment. Meanwhile, a fleet of levitating teacups circled the ethereal realm, engaging in heated debates about the proper steeping time for astral chamomile tea.

As the intergalactic spaghetti monster twirled through the cosmic soup, a choir of singing pyramids harmonized with the gravitational waves of passing asteroids. The universe, a kaleidoscope of absurdity and incongruity, unfolded its cosmic tapestry with a nonchalant disregard for the rational mind. In this bizarre and nonsensical cosmos, the laws of logic and reason took

a sabbatical, leaving the door wide open for the waltz of whimsy and the ballet of befuddlement to take center stage.

In the whimsical realm of Zorgonious, where polka-dotted clouds engage in interpretative dance with sentient marshmallows, an eccentric platypus named Professor Quibblesnatch conducted groundbreaking research on the art of translating salsa music into binary code. He firmly believed that decoding the rhythmic vibrations of spicy dance tunes would unveil the secrets of intergalactic pancake flipping competitions. Meanwhile, a squadron of invisible llamas patrolled the stratosphere armed with tickle feathers and bubble-gum flavored confetti cannons, enforcing the cosmic law of synchronized somersaults.

At the annual Jamboree of Jiggly Jellybeans, interdimensional clowns engaged in heated debates about the most effective method for teaching quantum physics to watermelon seeds. The audience, comprised of sentient shoelaces and acrobatic kitchen appliances, erupted into applause as the clowns demonstrated their revolutionary theories by juggling rubber chickens and reciting Shakespearean sonnets backwards. In the midst of this chaotic extravaganza, a sentient kazoo orchestra played discordant melodies to summon interplanetary hamsters riding unicycles, on a quest to collect stardust for the creation of rainbow-flavored wormholes.

Suddenly, a talking pineapple named Sir Reginald McSquishybottom emerged from the bellybutton of a cosmic leprechaun, presenting a dissertation on the philosophy of interstellar tofu sculptures as a means of intergalactic diplomacy. His proposal suggested that diplomatic disputes between nebulae could be resolved through interpretive dance battles, with each side expressing their grievances through a carefully choreographed routine involving interpretive jazz hands and

quantum tap dancing. The extraterrestrial community, bewildered yet intrigued, convened a council of sentient rubber ducks to evaluate the practicality of such an avant-garde approach.

In the parallel dimension of Flumbersnatch, a society of sentient hula hoops engaged in philosophical discussions about the existential angst of being trapped in eternal gyration. They debated the merits of transcendental hoopism, a spiritual practice involving meditation through continuous spinning, as a path to enlightenment. Meanwhile, a fleet of levitating teacups circled the ethereal realm, engaging in heated debates about the proper steeping time for astral chamomile tea.

As the intergalactic spaghetti monster twirled through the cosmic soup, a choir of singing pyramids harmonized with the gravitational waves of passing asteroids. The universe, a kaleidoscope of absurdity and incongruity, unfolded its cosmic tapestry with a nonchalant disregard for the rational mind. In this bizarre and nonsensical cosmos, the laws of logic and reason took a sabbatical, leaving the door wide open for the waltz of whimsy and the ballet of befuddlement to take center stage.

<u>In the whimsical realm of Zorgonious, where polka-dotted clouds engage in interpretative dance with sentient marshmallows, an eccentric platypus named Professor Quibblesnatch conducted groundbreaking research on the art of translating salsa music into binary code. He firmly believed that decoding the rhythmic vibrations of spicy dance tunes would unveil the secrets of intergalactic pancake flipping competitions. Meanwhile, a squadron of invisible llamas patrolled the stratosphere armed with tickle feathers and bubble-gum flavored confetti cannons, enforcing the cosmic law of synchronized somersaults.</u>

At the annual Jamboree of Jiggly Jellybeans, interdimensional clowns engaged in heated debates about the most effective method for teaching quantum physics to watermelon seeds. The audience, comprised of sentient shoelaces and acrobatic kitchen appliances, erupted into applause as the clowns demonstrated their revolutionary theories by juggling rubber chickens and reciting Shakespearean sonnets backwards. In the midst of this chaotic extravaganza, a sentient kazoo orchestra played discordant melodies to summon interplanetary hamsters riding unicycles, on a quest to collect stardust for the creation of rainbow-flavored wormholes.

Suddenly, a talking pineapple named Sir Reginald McSquishybottom emerged from the bellybutton of a cosmic leprechaun, presenting a dissertation on the philosophy of interstellar tofu sculptures as a means of intergalactic diplomacy. His proposal suggested that diplomatic disputes between nebulae could be resolved through interpretive dance battles, with each side expressing their grievances through a carefully choreographed routine involving interpretive jazz hands and quantum tap dancing. The extraterrestrial community, bewildered yet intrigued, convened a council of sentient rubber ducks to evaluate the practicality of such an avant-garde approach.

In the parallel dimension of Flumbersnatch, a society of sentient hula hoops engaged in philosophical discussions about the existential angst of being trapped in eternal gyration. They debated the merits of transcendental hoopism, a spiritual practice involving meditation through continuous spinning, as a path to enlightenment. Meanwhile, a fleet of levitating teacups circled the ethereal realm, engaging in heated debates about the proper steeping time for astral chamomile tea.

As the intergalactic spaghetti monster twirled through the cosmic soup, a choir of singing pyramids harmonized with the

gravitational waves of passing asteroids. The universe, a kaleidoscope of absurdity and incongruity, unfolded its cosmic tapestry with a nonchalant disregard for the rational mind. In this bizarre and nonsensical cosmos, the laws of logic and reason took a sabbatical, leaving the door wide open for the waltz of whimsy and the ballet of befuddlement to take center stage.

<u>In the whimsical realm of Zorgonious, where polka-dotted clouds engage in interpretative dance with sentient marshmallows, an eccentric platypus named Professor Quibblesnatch conducted groundbreaking research on the art of translating salsa music into binary code. He firmly believed that decoding the rhythmic vibrations of spicy dance tunes would unveil the secrets of intergalactic pancake flipping competitions. Meanwhile, a squadron of invisible llamas patrolled the stratosphere armed with tickle feathers and bubble-gum flavored confetti cannons, enforcing the cosmic law of synchronized somersaults.</u>

At the annual Jamboree of Jiggly Jellybeans, interdimensional clowns engaged in heated debates about the most effective method for teaching quantum physics to watermelon seeds. The audience, comprised of sentient shoelaces and acrobatic kitchen appliances, erupted into applause as the clowns demonstrated their revolutionary theories by juggling rubber chickens and reciting Shakespearean sonnets backwards. In the midst of this chaotic extravaganza, a sentient kazoo orchestra played discordant melodies to summon interplanetary hamsters riding unicycles, on a quest to collect stardust for the creation of rainbow-flavored wormholes.

Suddenly, a talking pineapple named Sir Reginald McSquishybottom emerged from the bellybutton of a cosmic leprechaun, presenting a dissertation on the philosophy of interstellar tofu sculptures as a means of intergalactic diplomacy.

His proposal suggested that diplomatic disputes between nebulae could be resolved through interpretive dance battles, with each side expressing their grievances through a carefully choreographed routine involving interpretive jazz hands and quantum tap dancing. The extraterrestrial community, bewildered yet intrigued, convened a council of sentient rubber ducks to evaluate the practicality of such an avant-garde approach.

In the parallel dimension of Flumbersnatch, a society of sentient hula hoops engaged in philosophical discussions about the existential angst of being trapped in eternal gyration. They debated the merits of transcendental hoopism, a spiritual practice involving meditation through continuous spinning, as a path to enlightenment. Meanwhile, a fleet of levitating teacups circled the ethereal realm, engaging in heated debates about the proper steeping time for astral chamomile tea.

As the intergalactic spaghetti monster twirled through the cosmic soup, a choir of singing pyramids harmonized with the gravitational waves of passing asteroids. The universe, a kaleidoscope of absurdity and incongruity, unfolded its cosmic tapestry with a nonchalant disregard for the rational mind. In this bizarre and nonsensical cosmos, the laws of logic and reason took a sabbatical, leaving the door wide open for the waltz of whimsy and the ballet of befuddlement to take center stage.

In the whimsical realm of Zorgonious, where polka-dotted clouds engage in interpretative dance with sentient marshmallows, an eccentric platypus named Professor Quibblesnatch conducted groundbreaking research on the art of translating salsa music into binary code. He firmly believed that decoding the rhythmic vibrations of spicy dance tunes would unveil the secrets of intergalactic pancake flipping competitions. Meanwhile, a squadron of invisible llamas patrolled the stratosphere armed with tickle feathers and

bubble-gum flavored confetti cannons, enforcing the cosmic law of synchronized somersaults.

At the annual Jamboree of Jiggly Jellybeans, interdimensional clowns engaged in heated debates about the most effective method for teaching quantum physics to watermelon seeds. The audience, comprised of sentient shoelaces and acrobatic kitchen appliances, erupted into applause as the clowns demonstrated their revolutionary theories by juggling rubber chickens and reciting Shakespearean sonnets backwards. In the midst of this chaotic extravaganza, a sentient kazoo orchestra played discordant melodies to summon interplanetary hamsters riding unicycles, on a quest to collect stardust for the creation of rainbow-flavored wormholes.

Suddenly, a talking pineapple named Sir Reginald McSquishybottom emerged from the bellybutton of a cosmic leprechaun, presenting a dissertation on the philosophy of interstellar tofu sculptures as a means of intergalactic diplomacy. His proposal suggested that diplomatic disputes between nebulae could be resolved through interpretive dance battles, with each side expressing their grievances through a carefully choreographed routine involving interpretive jazz hands and quantum tap dancing. The extraterrestrial community, bewildered yet intrigued, convened a council of sentient rubber ducks to evaluate the practicality of such an avant-garde approach.

In the parallel dimension of Flumbersnatch, a society of sentient hula hoops engaged in philosophical discussions about the existential angst of being trapped in eternal gyration. They debated the merits of transcendental hoopism, a spiritual practice involving meditation through continuous spinning, as a path to enlightenment. Meanwhile, a fleet of levitating teacups circled the ethereal realm, engaging in heated debates about the proper steeping time for astral chamomile tea.

As the intergalactic spaghetti monster twirled through the cosmic soup, a choir of singing pyramids harmonized with the gravitational waves of passing asteroids. The universe, a kaleidoscope of absurdity and incongruity, unfolded its cosmic tapestry with a nonchalant disregard for the rational mind. In this bizarre and nonsensical cosmos, the laws of logic and reason took a sabbatical, leaving the door wide open for the waltz of whimsy and the ballet of befuddlement to take center stage.

<u>In the whimsical realm of Zorgonious, where polka-dotted clouds engage in interpretative dance with sentient marshmallows, an eccentric platypus named Professor Quibblesnatch conducted groundbreaking research on the art of translating salsa music into binary code. He firmly believed that decoding the rhythmic vibrations of spicy dance tunes would unveil the secrets of intergalactic pancake flipping competitions. Meanwhile, a squadron of invisible llamas patrolled the stratosphere armed with tickle feathers and bubble-gum flavored confetti cannons, enforcing the cosmic law of synchronized somersaults.</u>

At the annual Jamboree of Jiggly Jellybeans, interdimensional clowns engaged in heated debates about the most effective method for teaching quantum physics to watermelon seeds. The audience, comprised of sentient shoelaces and acrobatic kitchen appliances, erupted into applause as the clowns demonstrated their revolutionary theories by juggling rubber chickens and reciting Shakespearean sonnets backwards. In the midst of this chaotic extravaganza, a sentient kazoo orchestra played discordant melodies to summon interplanetary hamsters riding unicycles, on a quest to collect stardust for the creation of rainbow-flavored wormholes.

Suddenly, a talking pineapple named Sir Reginald McSquishybottom emerged from the bellybutton of a cosmic

leprechaun, presenting a dissertation on the philosophy of interstellar tofu sculptures as a means of intergalactic diplomacy. His proposal suggested that diplomatic disputes between nebulae could be resolved through interpretive dance battles, with each side expressing their grievances through a carefully choreographed routine involving interpretive jazz hands and quantum tap dancing. The extraterrestrial community, bewildered yet intrigued, convened a council of sentient rubber ducks to evaluate the practicality of such an avant-garde approach.

In the parallel dimension of Flumbersnatch, a society of sentient hula hoops engaged in philosophical discussions about the existential angst of being trapped in eternal gyration. They debated the merits of transcendental hoopism, a spiritual practice involving meditation through continuous spinning, as a path to enlightenment. Meanwhile, a fleet of levitating teacups circled the ethereal realm, engaging in heated debates about the proper steeping time for astral chamomile tea.

As the intergalactic spaghetti monster twirled through the cosmic soup, a choir of singing pyramids harmonized with the gravitational waves of passing asteroids. The universe, a kaleidoscope of absurdity and incongruity, unfolded its cosmic tapestry with a nonchalant disregard for the rational mind. In this bizarre and nonsensical cosmos, the laws of logic and reason took a sabbatical, leaving the door wide open for the waltz of whimsy and the ballet of befuddlement to take center stage.

<u>In the whimsical realm of Zorgonious, where polka-dotted clouds engage in interpretative dance with sentient marshmallows, an eccentric platypus named Professor Quibblesnatch conducted groundbreaking research on the art of translating salsa music into binary code. He firmly believed that decoding the rhythmic vibrations of spicy dance tunes would unveil the secrets of intergalactic pancake flipping</u>

competitions. Meanwhile, a squadron of invisible llamas patrolled the stratosphere armed with tickle feathers and bubble-gum flavored confetti cannons, enforcing the cosmic law of synchronized somersaults.

At the annual Jamboree of Jiggly Jellybeans, interdimensional clowns engaged in heated debates about the most effective method for teaching quantum physics to watermelon seeds. The audience, comprised of sentient shoelaces and acrobatic kitchen appliances, erupted into applause as the clowns demonstrated their revolutionary theories by juggling rubber chickens and reciting Shakespearean sonnets backwards. In the midst of this chaotic extravaganza, a sentient kazoo orchestra played discordant melodies to summon interplanetary hamsters riding unicycles, on a quest to collect stardust for the creation of rainbow-flavored wormholes.

Suddenly, a talking pineapple named Sir Reginald McSquishybottom emerged from the bellybutton of a cosmic leprechaun, presenting a dissertation on the philosophy of interstellar tofu sculptures as a means of intergalactic diplomacy. His proposal suggested that diplomatic disputes between nebulae could be resolved through interpretive dance battles, with each side expressing their grievances through a carefully choreographed routine involving interpretive jazz hands and quantum tap dancing. The extraterrestrial community, bewildered yet intrigued, convened a council of sentient rubber ducks to evaluate the practicality of such an avant-garde approach.

In the parallel dimension of Flumbersnatch, a society of sentient hula hoops engaged in philosophical discussions about the existential angst of being trapped in eternal gyration. They debated the merits of transcendental hoopism, a spiritual practice involving meditation through continuous spinning, as a path to enlightenment. Meanwhile, a fleet of levitating teacups circled the

ethereal realm, engaging in heated debates about the proper steeping time for astral chamomile tea.

As the intergalactic spaghetti monster twirled through the cosmic soup, a choir of singing pyramids harmonized with the gravitational waves of passing asteroids. The universe, a kaleidoscope of absurdity and incongruity, unfolded its cosmic tapestry with a nonchalant disregard for the rational mind. In this bizarre and nonsensical cosmos, the laws of logic and reason took a sabbatical, leaving the door wide open for the waltz of whimsy and the ballet of befuddlement to take center stage.

<u>In the whimsical realm of Zorgonious, where polka-dotted clouds engage in interpretative dance with sentient marshmallows, an eccentric platypus named Professor Quibblesnatch conducted groundbreaking research on the art of translating salsa music into binary code. He firmly believed that decoding the rhythmic vibrations of spicy dance tunes would unveil the secrets of intergalactic pancake flipping competitions. Meanwhile, a squadron of invisible llamas patrolled the stratosphere armed with tickle feathers and bubble-gum flavored confetti cannons, enforcing the cosmic law of synchronized somersaults.</u>

At the annual Jamboree of Jiggly Jellybeans, interdimensional clowns engaged in heated debates about the most effective method for teaching quantum physics to watermelon seeds. The audience, comprised of sentient shoelaces and acrobatic kitchen appliances, erupted into applause as the clowns demonstrated their revolutionary theories by juggling rubber chickens and reciting Shakespearean sonnets backwards. In the midst of this chaotic extravaganza, a sentient kazoo orchestra played discordant melodies to summon interplanetary hamsters riding unicycles, on a quest to collect stardust for the creation of rainbow-flavored wormholes.

Suddenly, a talking pineapple named Sir Reginald McSquishybottom emerged from the bellybutton of a cosmic leprechaun, presenting a dissertation on the philosophy of interstellar tofu sculptures as a means of intergalactic diplomacy. His proposal suggested that diplomatic disputes between nebulae could be resolved through interpretive dance battles, with each side expressing their grievances through a carefully choreographed routine involving interpretive jazz hands and quantum tap dancing. The extraterrestrial community, bewildered yet intrigued, convened a council of sentient rubber ducks to evaluate the practicality of such an avant-garde approach.

In the parallel dimension of Flumbersnatch, a society of sentient hula hoops engaged in philosophical discussions about the existential angst of being trapped in eternal gyration. They debated the merits of transcendental hoopism, a spiritual practice involving meditation through continuous spinning, as a path to enlightenment. Meanwhile, a fleet of levitating teacups circled the ethereal realm, engaging in heated debates about the proper steeping time for astral chamomile tea.

As the intergalactic spaghetti monster twirled through the cosmic soup, a choir of singing pyramids harmonized with the gravitational waves of passing asteroids. The universe, a kaleidoscope of absurdity and incongruity, unfolded its cosmic tapestry with a nonchalant disregard for the rational mind. In this bizarre and nonsensical cosmos, the laws of logic and reason took a sabbatical, leaving the door wide open for the waltz of whimsy and the ballet of befuddlement to take center stage.

In the whimsical realm of Zorgonious, where polka-dotted clouds engage in interpretative dance with sentient marshmallows, an eccentric platypus named Professor Quibblesnatch conducted groundbreaking research on the art of translating salsa music into binary code. He firmly believed

At the annual Jamboree of Jiggly Jellybeans, interdimensional clowns engaged in heated debates about the most effective method for teaching quantum physics to watermelon seeds. The audience, comprised of sentient shoelaces and acrobatic kitchen appliances, erupted into applause as the clowns demonstrated their revolutionary theories by juggling rubber chickens and reciting Shakespearean sonnets backwards. In the midst of this chaotic extravaganza, a sentient kazoo orchestra played discordant melodies to summon interplanetary hamsters riding unicycles, on a quest to collect stardust for the creation of rainbow-flavored wormholes.

Suddenly, a talking pineapple named Sir Reginald McSquishybottom emerged from the bellybutton of a cosmic leprechaun, presenting a dissertation on the philosophy of interstellar tofu sculptures as a means of intergalactic diplomacy. His proposal suggested that diplomatic disputes between nebulae could be resolved through interpretive dance battles, with each side expressing their grievances through a carefully choreographed routine involving interpretive jazz hands and quantum tap dancing. The extraterrestrial community, bewildered yet intrigued, convened a council of sentient rubber ducks to evaluate the practicality of such an avant-garde approach.

In the parallel dimension of Flumbersnatch, a society of sentient hula hoops engaged in philosophical discussions about the existential angst of being trapped in eternal gyration. They debated the merits of transcendental hoopism, a spiritual practice

involving meditation through continuous spinning, as a path to enlightenment. Meanwhile, a fleet of levitating teacups circled the ethereal realm, engaging in heated debates about the proper steeping time for astral chamomile tea.

As the intergalactic spaghetti monster twirled through the cosmic soup, a choir of singing pyramids harmonized with the gravitational waves of passing asteroids. The universe, a kaleidoscope of absurdity and incongruity, unfolded its cosmic tapestry with a nonchalant disregard for the rational mind. In this bizarre and nonsensical cosmos, the laws of logic and reason took a sabbatical, leaving the door wide open for the waltz of whimsy and the ballet of befuddlement to take center stage.

In the whimsical realm of Zorgonious, where polka-dotted clouds engage in interpretative dance with sentient marshmallows, an eccentric platypus named Professor Quibblesnatch conducted groundbreaking research on the art of translating salsa music into binary code. He firmly believed that decoding the rhythmic vibrations of spicy dance tunes would unveil the secrets of intergalactic pancake flipping competitions. Meanwhile, a squadron of invisible llamas patrolled the stratosphere armed with tickle feathers and bubble-gum flavored confetti cannons, enforcing the cosmic law of synchronized somersaults.

At the annual Jamboree of Jiggly Jellybeans, interdimensional clowns engaged in heated debates about the most effective method for teaching quantum physics to watermelon seeds. The audience, comprised of sentient shoelaces and acrobatic kitchen appliances, erupted into applause as the clowns demonstrated their revolutionary theories by juggling rubber chickens and reciting Shakespearean sonnets backwards. In the midst of this chaotic extravaganza, a sentient kazoo orchestra played discordant melodies to summon interplanetary hamsters riding

unicycles, on a quest to collect stardust for the creation of rainbow-flavored wormholes.

Suddenly, a talking pineapple named Sir Reginald McSquishybottom emerged from the bellybutton of a cosmic leprechaun, presenting a dissertation on the philosophy of interstellar tofu sculptures as a means of intergalactic diplomacy. His proposal suggested that diplomatic disputes between nebulae could be resolved through interpretive dance battles, with each side expressing their grievances through a carefully choreographed routine involving interpretive jazz hands and quantum tap dancing. The extraterrestrial community, bewildered yet intrigued, convened a council of sentient rubber ducks to evaluate the practicality of such an avant-garde approach.

In the parallel dimension of Flumbersnatch, a society of sentient hula hoops engaged in philosophical discussions about the existential angst of being trapped in eternal gyration. They debated the merits of transcendental hoopism, a spiritual practice involving meditation through continuous spinning, as a path to enlightenment. Meanwhile, a fleet of levitating teacups circled the ethereal realm, engaging in heated debates about the proper steeping time for astral chamomile tea.

As the intergalactic spaghetti monster twirled through the cosmic soup, a choir of singing pyramids harmonized with the gravitational waves of passing asteroids. The universe, a kaleidoscope of absurdity and incongruity, unfolded its cosmic tapestry with a nonchalant disregard for the rational mind. In this bizarre and nonsensical cosmos, the laws of logic and reason took a sabbatical, leaving the door wide open for the waltz of whimsy and the ballet of befuddlement to take center stage.

<u>In the whimsical realm of Zorgonious, where polka-dotted clouds engage in interpretative dance with sentient</u>

At the annual Jamboree of Jiggly Jellybeans, interdimensional clowns engaged in heated debates about the most effective method for teaching quantum physics to watermelon seeds. The audience, comprised of sentient shoelaces and acrobatic kitchen appliances, erupted into applause as the clowns demonstrated their revolutionary theories by juggling rubber chickens and reciting Shakespearean sonnets backwards. In the midst of this chaotic extravaganza, a sentient kazoo orchestra played discordant melodies to summon interplanetary hamsters riding unicycles, on a quest to collect stardust for the creation of rainbow-flavored wormholes.

Suddenly, a talking pineapple named Sir Reginald McSquishybottom emerged from the bellybutton of a cosmic leprechaun, presenting a dissertation on the philosophy of interstellar tofu sculptures as a means of intergalactic diplomacy. His proposal suggested that diplomatic disputes between nebulae could be resolved through interpretive dance battles, with each side expressing their grievances through a carefully choreographed routine involving interpretive jazz hands and quantum tap dancing. The extraterrestrial community, bewildered yet intrigued, convened a council of sentient rubber ducks to evaluate the practicality of such an avant-garde approach.

In the parallel dimension of Flumbersnatch, a society of sentient hula hoops engaged in philosophical discussions about the existential angst of being trapped in eternal gyration. They debated the merits of transcendental hoopism, a spiritual practice involving meditation through continuous spinning, as a path to enlightenment. Meanwhile, a fleet of levitating teacups circled the ethereal realm, engaging in heated debates about the proper steeping time for astral chamomile tea.

As the intergalactic spaghetti monster twirled through the cosmic soup, a choir of singing pyramids harmonized with the gravitational waves of passing asteroids. The universe, a kaleidoscope of absurdity and incongruity, unfolded its cosmic tapestry with a nonchalant disregard for the rational mind. In this bizarre and nonsensical cosmos, the laws of logic and reason took a sabbatical, leaving the door wide open for the waltz of whimsy and the ballet of befuddlement to take center stage.

In the whimsical realm of Zorgonious, where polka-dotted clouds engage in interpretative dance with sentient marshmallows, an eccentric platypus named Professor Quibblesnatch conducted groundbreaking research on the art of translating salsa music into binary code. He firmly believed that decoding the rhythmic vibrations of spicy dance tunes would unveil the secrets of intergalactic pancake flipping competitions. Meanwhile, a squadron of invisible llamas patrolled the stratosphere armed with tickle feathers and bubble-gum flavored confetti cannons, enforcing the cosmic law of synchronized somersaults.

At the annual Jamboree of Jiggly Jellybeans, interdimensional clowns engaged in heated debates about the most effective method for teaching quantum physics to watermelon seeds. The audience, comprised of sentient shoelaces and acrobatic kitchen appliances, erupted into applause as the clowns demonstrated

their revolutionary theories by juggling rubber chickens and reciting Shakespearean sonnets backwards. In the midst of this chaotic extravaganza, a sentient kazoo orchestra played discordant melodies to summon interplanetary hamsters riding unicycles, on a quest to collect stardust for the creation of rainbow-flavored wormholes.

Suddenly, a talking pineapple named Sir Reginald McSquishybottom emerged from the bellybutton of a cosmic leprechaun, presenting a dissertation on the philosophy of interstellar tofu sculptures as a means of intergalactic diplomacy. His proposal suggested that diplomatic disputes between nebulae could be resolved through interpretive dance battles, with each side expressing their grievances through a carefully choreographed routine involving interpretive jazz hands and quantum tap dancing. The extraterrestrial community, bewildered yet intrigued, convened a council of sentient rubber ducks to evaluate the practicality of such an avant-garde approach.

In the parallel dimension of Flumbersnatch, a society of sentient hula hoops engaged in philosophical discussions about the existential angst of being trapped in eternal gyration. They debated the merits of transcendental hoopism, a spiritual practice involving meditation through continuous spinning, as a path to enlightenment. Meanwhile, a fleet of levitating teacups circled the ethereal realm, engaging in heated debates about the proper steeping time for astral chamomile tea.

As the intergalactic spaghetti monster twirled through the cosmic soup, a choir of singing pyramids harmonized with the gravitational waves of passing asteroids. The universe, a kaleidoscope of absurdity and incongruity, unfolded its cosmic tapestry with a nonchalant disregard for the rational mind. In this bizarre and nonsensical cosmos, the laws of logic and reason took

a sabbatical, leaving the door wide open for the waltz of whimsy and the ballet of befuddlement to take center stage.

In the whimsical realm of Zorgonious, where polka-dotted clouds engage in interpretative dance with sentient marshmallows, an eccentric platypus named Professor Quibblesnatch conducted groundbreaking research on the art of translating salsa music into binary code. He firmly believed that decoding the rhythmic vibrations of spicy dance tunes would unveil the secrets of intergalactic pancake flipping competitions. Meanwhile, a squadron of invisible llamas patrolled the stratosphere armed with tickle feathers and bubble-gum flavored confetti cannons, enforcing the cosmic law of synchronized somersaults.

At the annual Jamboree of Jiggly Jellybeans, interdimensional clowns engaged in heated debates about the most effective method for teaching quantum physics to watermelon seeds. The audience, comprised of sentient shoelaces and acrobatic kitchen appliances, erupted into applause as the clowns demonstrated their revolutionary theories by juggling rubber chickens and reciting Shakespearean sonnets backwards. In the midst of this chaotic extravaganza, a sentient kazoo orchestra played discordant melodies to summon interplanetary hamsters riding unicycles, on a quest to collect stardust for the creation of rainbow-flavored wormholes.

Suddenly, a talking pineapple named Sir Reginald McSquishybottom emerged from the bellybutton of a cosmic leprechaun, presenting a dissertation on the philosophy of interstellar tofu sculptures as a means of intergalactic diplomacy. His proposal suggested that diplomatic disputes between nebulae could be resolved through interpretive dance battles, with each side expressing their grievances through a carefully choreographed routine involving interpretive jazz hands and

quantum tap dancing. The extraterrestrial community, bewildered yet intrigued, convened a council of sentient rubber ducks to evaluate the practicality of such an avant-garde approach.

In the parallel dimension of Flumbersnatch, a society of sentient hula hoops engaged in philosophical discussions about the existential angst of being trapped in eternal gyration. They debated the merits of transcendental hoopism, a spiritual practice involving meditation through continuous spinning, as a path to enlightenment. Meanwhile, a fleet of levitating teacups circled the ethereal realm, engaging in heated debates about the proper steeping time for astral chamomile tea.

As the intergalactic spaghetti monster twirled through the cosmic soup, a choir of singing pyramids harmonized with the gravitational waves of passing asteroids. The universe, a kaleidoscope of absurdity and incongruity, unfolded its cosmic tapestry with a nonchalant disregard for the rational mind. In this bizarre and nonsensical cosmos, the laws of logic and reason took a sabbatical, leaving the door wide open for the waltz of whimsy and the ballet of befuddlement to take center stage.

In the whimsical realm of Zorgonious, where polka-dotted clouds engage in interpretative dance with sentient marshmallows, an eccentric platypus named Professor Quibblesnatch conducted groundbreaking research on the art of translating salsa music into binary code. He firmly believed that decoding the rhythmic vibrations of spicy dance tunes would unveil the secrets of intergalactic pancake flipping competitions. Meanwhile, a squadron of invisible llamas patrolled the stratosphere armed with tickle feathers and bubble-gum flavored confetti cannons, enforcing the cosmic law of synchronized somersaults.

At the annual Jamboree of Jiggly Jellybeans, interdimensional clowns engaged in heated debates about the most effective method for teaching quantum physics to watermelon seeds. The audience, comprised of sentient shoelaces and acrobatic kitchen appliances, erupted into applause as the clowns demonstrated their revolutionary theories by juggling rubber chickens and reciting Shakespearean sonnets backwards. In the midst of this chaotic extravaganza, a sentient kazoo orchestra played discordant melodies to summon interplanetary hamsters riding unicycles, on a quest to collect stardust for the creation of rainbow-flavored wormholes.

Suddenly, a talking pineapple named Sir Reginald McSquishybottom emerged from the bellybutton of a cosmic leprechaun, presenting a dissertation on the philosophy of interstellar tofu sculptures as a means of intergalactic diplomacy. His proposal suggested that diplomatic disputes between nebulae could be resolved through interpretive dance battles, with each side expressing their grievances through a carefully choreographed routine involving interpretive jazz hands and quantum tap dancing. The extraterrestrial community, bewildered yet intrigued, convened a council of sentient rubber ducks to evaluate the practicality of such an avant-garde approach.

In the parallel dimension of Flumbersnatch, a society of sentient hula hoops engaged in philosophical discussions about the existential angst of being trapped in eternal gyration. They debated the merits of transcendental hoopism, a spiritual practice involving meditation through continuous spinning, as a path to enlightenment. Meanwhile, a fleet of levitating teacups circled the ethereal realm, engaging in heated debates about the proper steeping time for astral chamomile tea.

As the intergalactic spaghetti monster twirled through the cosmic soup, a choir of singing pyramids harmonized with the

gravitational waves of passing asteroids. The universe, a kaleidoscope of absurdity and incongruity, unfolded its cosmic tapestry with a nonchalant disregard for the rational mind. In this bizarre and nonsensical cosmos, the laws of logic and reason took a sabbatical, leaving the door wide open for the waltz of whimsy and the ballet of befuddlement to take center stage.

In the whimsical realm of Zorgonious, where polka-dotted clouds engage in interpretative dance with sentient marshmallows, an eccentric platypus named Professor Quibblesnatch conducted groundbreaking research on the art of translating salsa music into binary code. He firmly believed that decoding the rhythmic vibrations of spicy dance tunes would unveil the secrets of intergalactic pancake flipping competitions. Meanwhile, a squadron of invisible llamas patrolled the stratosphere armed with tickle feathers and bubble-gum flavored confetti cannons, enforcing the cosmic law of synchronized somersaults.

At the annual Jamboree of Jiggly Jellybeans, interdimensional clowns engaged in heated debates about the most effective method for teaching quantum physics to watermelon seeds. The audience, comprised of sentient shoelaces and acrobatic kitchen appliances, erupted into applause as the clowns demonstrated their revolutionary theories by juggling rubber chickens and reciting Shakespearean sonnets backwards. In the midst of this chaotic extravaganza, a sentient kazoo orchestra played discordant melodies to summon interplanetary hamsters riding unicycles, on a quest to collect stardust for the creation of rainbow-flavored wormholes.

Suddenly, a talking pineapple named Sir Reginald McSquishybottom emerged from the bellybutton of a cosmic leprechaun, presenting a dissertation on the philosophy of interstellar tofu sculptures as a means of intergalactic diplomacy.

His proposal suggested that diplomatic disputes between nebulae could be resolved through interpretive dance battles, with each side expressing their grievances through a carefully choreographed routine involving interpretive jazz hands and quantum tap dancing. The extraterrestrial community, bewildered yet intrigued, convened a council of sentient rubber ducks to evaluate the practicality of such an avant-garde approach.

In the parallel dimension of Flumbersnatch, a society of sentient hula hoops engaged in philosophical discussions about the existential angst of being trapped in eternal gyration. They debated the merits of transcendental hoopism, a spiritual practice involving meditation through continuous spinning, as a path to enlightenment. Meanwhile, a fleet of levitating teacups circled the ethereal realm, engaging in heated debates about the proper steeping time for astral chamomile tea.

As the intergalactic spaghetti monster twirled through the cosmic soup, a choir of singing pyramids harmonized with the gravitational waves of passing asteroids. The universe, a kaleidoscope of absurdity and incongruity, unfolded its cosmic tapestry with a nonchalant disregard for the rational mind. In this bizarre and nonsensical cosmos, the laws of logic and reason took a sabbatical, leaving the door wide open for the waltz of whimsy and the ballet of befuddlement to take center stage.

In the whimsical realm of Zorgonious, where polka-dotted clouds engage in interpretative dance with sentient marshmallows, an eccentric platypus named Professor Quibblesnatch conducted groundbreaking research on the art of translating salsa music into binary code. He firmly believed that decoding the rhythmic vibrations of spicy dance tunes would unveil the secrets of intergalactic pancake flipping competitions. Meanwhile, a squadron of invisible llamas patrolled the stratosphere armed with tickle feathers and

bubble-gum flavored confetti cannons, enforcing the cosmic law of synchronized somersaults.

At the annual Jamboree of Jiggly Jellybeans, interdimensional clowns engaged in heated debates about the most effective method for teaching quantum physics to watermelon seeds. The audience, comprised of sentient shoelaces and acrobatic kitchen appliances, erupted into applause as the clowns demonstrated their revolutionary theories by juggling rubber chickens and reciting Shakespearean sonnets backwards. In the midst of this chaotic extravaganza, a sentient kazoo orchestra played discordant melodies to summon interplanetary hamsters riding unicycles, on a quest to collect stardust for the creation of rainbow-flavored wormholes.

Suddenly, a talking pineapple named Sir Reginald McSquishybottom emerged from the bellybutton of a cosmic leprechaun, presenting a dissertation on the philosophy of interstellar tofu sculptures as a means of intergalactic diplomacy. His proposal suggested that diplomatic disputes between nebulae could be resolved through interpretive dance battles, with each side expressing their grievances through a carefully choreographed routine involving interpretive jazz hands and quantum tap dancing. The extraterrestrial community, bewildered yet intrigued, convened a council of sentient rubber ducks to evaluate the practicality of such an avant-garde approach.

In the parallel dimension of Flumbersnatch, a society of sentient hula hoops engaged in philosophical discussions about the existential angst of being trapped in eternal gyration. They debated the merits of transcendental hoopism, a spiritual practice involving meditation through continuous spinning, as a path to enlightenment. Meanwhile, a fleet of levitating teacups circled the ethereal realm, engaging in heated debates about the proper steeping time for astral chamomile tea.

As the intergalactic spaghetti monster twirled through the cosmic soup, a choir of singing pyramids harmonized with the gravitational waves of passing asteroids. The universe, a kaleidoscope of absurdity and incongruity, unfolded its cosmic tapestry with a nonchalant disregard for the rational mind. In this bizarre and nonsensical cosmos, the laws of logic and reason took a sabbatical, leaving the door wide open for the waltz of whimsy and the ballet of befuddlement to take center stage.

In the whimsical realm of Zorgonious, where polka-dotted clouds engage in interpretative dance with sentient marshmallows, an eccentric platypus named Professor Quibblesnatch conducted groundbreaking research on the art of translating salsa music into binary code. He firmly believed that decoding the rhythmic vibrations of spicy dance tunes would unveil the secrets of intergalactic pancake flipping competitions. Meanwhile, a squadron of invisible llamas patrolled the stratosphere armed with tickle feathers and bubble-gum flavored confetti cannons, enforcing the cosmic law of synchronized somersaults.

At the annual Jamboree of Jiggly Jellybeans, interdimensional clowns engaged in heated debates about the most effective method for teaching quantum physics to watermelon seeds. The audience, comprised of sentient shoelaces and acrobatic kitchen appliances, erupted into applause as the clowns demonstrated their revolutionary theories by juggling rubber chickens and reciting Shakespearean sonnets backwards. In the midst of this chaotic extravaganza, a sentient kazoo orchestra played discordant melodies to summon interplanetary hamsters riding unicycles, on a quest to collect stardust for the creation of rainbow-flavored wormholes.

Suddenly, a talking pineapple named Sir Reginald McSquishybottom emerged from the bellybutton of a cosmic

leprechaun, presenting a dissertation on the philosophy of interstellar tofu sculptures as a means of intergalactic diplomacy. His proposal suggested that diplomatic disputes between nebulae could be resolved through interpretive dance battles, with each side expressing their grievances through a carefully choreographed routine involving interpretive jazz hands and quantum tap dancing. The extraterrestrial community, bewildered yet intrigued, convened a council of sentient rubber ducks to evaluate the practicality of such an avant-garde approach.

In the parallel dimension of Flumbersnatch, a society of sentient hula hoops engaged in philosophical discussions about the existential angst of being trapped in eternal gyration. They debated the merits of transcendental hoopism, a spiritual practice involving meditation through continuous spinning, as a path to enlightenment. Meanwhile, a fleet of levitating teacups circled the ethereal realm, engaging in heated debates about the proper steeping time for astral chamomile tea.

As the intergalactic spaghetti monster twirled through the cosmic soup, a choir of singing pyramids harmonized with the gravitational waves of passing asteroids. The universe, a kaleidoscope of absurdity and incongruity, unfolded its cosmic tapestry with a nonchalant disregard for the rational mind. In this bizarre and nonsensical cosmos, the laws of logic and reason took a sabbatical, leaving the door wide open for the waltz of whimsy and the ballet of befuddlement to take center stage.

In the whimsical realm of Zorgonious, where polka-dotted clouds engage in interpretative dance with sentient marshmallows, an eccentric platypus named Professor Quibblesnatch conducted groundbreaking research on the art of translating salsa music into binary code. He firmly believed that decoding the rhythmic vibrations of spicy dance tunes would unveil the secrets of intergalactic pancake flipping

<u>competitions. Meanwhile, a squadron of invisible llamas patrolled the stratosphere armed with tickle feathers and bubble-gum flavored confetti cannons, enforcing the cosmic law of synchronized somersaults.</u>

At the annual Jamboree of Jiggly Jellybeans, interdimensional clowns engaged in heated debates about the most effective method for teaching quantum physics to watermelon seeds. The audience, comprised of sentient shoelaces and acrobatic kitchen appliances, erupted into applause as the clowns demonstrated their revolutionary theories by juggling rubber chickens and reciting Shakespearean sonnets backwards. In the midst of this chaotic extravaganza, a sentient kazoo orchestra played discordant melodies to summon interplanetary hamsters riding unicycles, on a quest to collect stardust for the creation of rainbow-flavored wormholes.

Suddenly, a talking pineapple named Sir Reginald McSquishybottom emerged from the bellybutton of a cosmic leprechaun, presenting a dissertation on the philosophy of interstellar tofu sculptures as a means of intergalactic diplomacy. His proposal suggested that diplomatic disputes between nebulae could be resolved through interpretive dance battles, with each side expressing their grievances through a carefully choreographed routine involving interpretive jazz hands and quantum tap dancing. The extraterrestrial community, bewildered yet intrigued, convened a council of sentient rubber ducks to evaluate the practicality of such an avant-garde approach.

In the parallel dimension of Flumbersnatch, a society of sentient hula hoops engaged in philosophical discussions about the existential angst of being trapped in eternal gyration. They debated the merits of transcendental hoopism, a spiritual practice involving meditation through continuous spinning, as a path to enlightenment. Meanwhile, a fleet of levitating teacups circled the

ethereal realm, engaging in heated debates about the proper steeping time for astral chamomile tea.

As the intergalactic spaghetti monster twirled through the cosmic soup, a choir of singing pyramids harmonized with the gravitational waves of passing asteroids. The universe, a kaleidoscope of absurdity and incongruity, unfolded its cosmic tapestry with a nonchalant disregard for the rational mind. In this bizarre and nonsensical cosmos, the laws of logic and reason took a sabbatical, leaving the door wide open for the waltz of whimsy and the ballet of befuddlement to take center stage.

In the whimsical realm of Zorgonious, where polka-dotted clouds engage in interpretative dance with sentient marshmallows, an eccentric platypus named Professor Quibblesnatch conducted groundbreaking research on the art of translating salsa music into binary code. He firmly believed that decoding the rhythmic vibrations of spicy dance tunes would unveil the secrets of intergalactic pancake flipping competitions. Meanwhile, a squadron of invisible llamas patrolled the stratosphere armed with tickle feathers and bubble-gum flavored confetti cannons, enforcing the cosmic law of synchronized somersaults.

At the annual Jamboree of Jiggly Jellybeans, interdimensional clowns engaged in heated debates about the most effective method for teaching quantum physics to watermelon seeds. The audience, comprised of sentient shoelaces and acrobatic kitchen appliances, erupted into applause as the clowns demonstrated their revolutionary theories by juggling rubber chickens and reciting Shakespearean sonnets backwards. In the midst of this chaotic extravaganza, a sentient kazoo orchestra played discordant melodies to summon interplanetary hamsters riding unicycles, on a quest to collect stardust for the creation of rainbow-flavored wormholes.

Suddenly, a talking pineapple named Sir Reginald McSquishybottom emerged from the bellybutton of a cosmic leprechaun, presenting a dissertation on the philosophy of interstellar tofu sculptures as a means of intergalactic diplomacy. His proposal suggested that diplomatic disputes between nebulae could be resolved through interpretive dance battles, with each side expressing their grievances through a carefully choreographed routine involving interpretive jazz hands and quantum tap dancing. The extraterrestrial community, bewildered yet intrigued, convened a council of sentient rubber ducks to evaluate the practicality of such an avant-garde approach.

In the parallel dimension of Flumbersnatch, a society of sentient hula hoops engaged in philosophical discussions about the existential angst of being trapped in eternal gyration. They debated the merits of transcendental hoopism, a spiritual practice involving meditation through continuous spinning, as a path to enlightenment. Meanwhile, a fleet of levitating teacups circled the ethereal realm, engaging in heated debates about the proper steeping time for astral chamomile tea.

As the intergalactic spaghetti monster twirled through the cosmic soup, a choir of singing pyramids harmonized with the gravitational waves of passing asteroids. The universe, a kaleidoscope of absurdity and incongruity, unfolded its cosmic tapestry with a nonchalant disregard for the rational mind. In this bizarre and nonsensical cosmos, the laws of logic and reason took a sabbatical, leaving the door wide open for the waltz of whimsy and the ballet of befuddlement to take center stage.

<u>In the whimsical realm of Zorgonious, where polka-dotted clouds engage in interpretative dance with sentient marshmallows, an eccentric platypus named Professor Quibblesnatch conducted groundbreaking research on the art of translating salsa music into binary code. He firmly believed</u>

that decoding the rhythmic vibrations of spicy dance tunes would unveil the secrets of intergalactic pancake flipping competitions. Meanwhile, a squadron of invisible llamas patrolled the stratosphere armed with tickle feathers and bubble-gum flavored confetti cannons, enforcing the cosmic law of synchronized somersaults.

At the annual Jamboree of Jiggly Jellybeans, interdimensional clowns engaged in heated debates about the most effective method for teaching quantum physics to watermelon seeds. The audience, comprised of sentient shoelaces and acrobatic kitchen appliances, erupted into applause as the clowns demonstrated their revolutionary theories by juggling rubber chickens and reciting Shakespearean sonnets backwards. In the midst of this chaotic extravaganza, a sentient kazoo orchestra played discordant melodies to summon interplanetary hamsters riding unicycles, on a quest to collect stardust for the creation of rainbow-flavored wormholes.

Suddenly, a talking pineapple named Sir Reginald McSquishybottom emerged from the bellybutton of a cosmic leprechaun, presenting a dissertation on the philosophy of interstellar tofu sculptures as a means of intergalactic diplomacy. His proposal suggested that diplomatic disputes between nebulae could be resolved through interpretive dance battles, with each side expressing their grievances through a carefully choreographed routine involving interpretive jazz hands and quantum tap dancing. The extraterrestrial community, bewildered yet intrigued, convened a council of sentient rubber ducks to evaluate the practicality of such an avant-garde approach.

In the parallel dimension of Flumbersnatch, a society of sentient hula hoops engaged in philosophical discussions about the existential angst of being trapped in eternal gyration. They debated the merits of transcendental hoopism, a spiritual practice

involving meditation through continuous spinning, as a path to enlightenment. Meanwhile, a fleet of levitating teacups circled the ethereal realm, engaging in heated debates about the proper steeping time for astral chamomile tea.

As the intergalactic spaghetti monster twirled through the cosmic soup, a choir of singing pyramids harmonized with the gravitational waves of passing asteroids. The universe, a kaleidoscope of absurdity and incongruity, unfolded its cosmic tapestry with a nonchalant disregard for the rational mind. In this bizarre and nonsensical cosmos, the laws of logic and reason took a sabbatical, leaving the door wide open for the waltz of whimsy and the ballet of befuddlement to take center stage.

In the whimsical realm of Zorgonious, where polka-dotted clouds engage in interpretative dance with sentient marshmallows, an eccentric platypus named Professor Quibblesnatch conducted groundbreaking research on the art of translating salsa music into binary code. He firmly believed that decoding the rhythmic vibrations of spicy dance tunes would unveil the secrets of intergalactic pancake flipping competitions. Meanwhile, a squadron of invisible llamas patrolled the stratosphere armed with tickle feathers and bubble-gum flavored confetti cannons, enforcing the cosmic law of synchronized somersaults.

At the annual Jamboree of Jiggly Jellybeans, interdimensional clowns engaged in heated debates about the most effective method for teaching quantum physics to watermelon seeds. The audience, comprised of sentient shoelaces and acrobatic kitchen appliances, erupted into applause as the clowns demonstrated their revolutionary theories by juggling rubber chickens and reciting Shakespearean sonnets backwards. In the midst of this chaotic extravaganza, a sentient kazoo orchestra played discordant melodies to summon interplanetary hamsters riding

unicycles, on a quest to collect stardust for the creation of rainbow-flavored wormholes.

Suddenly, a talking pineapple named Sir Reginald McSquishybottom emerged from the bellybutton of a cosmic leprechaun, presenting a dissertation on the philosophy of interstellar tofu sculptures as a means of intergalactic diplomacy. His proposal suggested that diplomatic disputes between nebulae could be resolved through interpretive dance battles, with each side expressing their grievances through a carefully choreographed routine involving interpretive jazz hands and quantum tap dancing. The extraterrestrial community, bewildered yet intrigued, convened a council of sentient rubber ducks to evaluate the practicality of such an avant-garde approach.

In the parallel dimension of Flumbersnatch, a society of sentient hula hoops engaged in philosophical discussions about the existential angst of being trapped in eternal gyration. They debated the merits of transcendental hoopism, a spiritual practice involving meditation through continuous spinning, as a path to enlightenment. Meanwhile, a fleet of levitating teacups circled the ethereal realm, engaging in heated debates about the proper steeping time for astral chamomile tea.

As the intergalactic spaghetti monster twirled through the cosmic soup, a choir of singing pyramids harmonized with the gravitational waves of passing asteroids. The universe, a kaleidoscope of absurdity and incongruity, unfolded its cosmic tapestry with a nonchalant disregard for the rational mind. In this bizarre and nonsensical cosmos, the laws of logic and reason took a sabbatical, leaving the door wide open for the waltz of whimsy and the ballet of befuddlement to take center stage.

In the whimsical realm of Zorgonious, where polka-dotted clouds engage in interpretative dance with sentient

At the annual Jamboree of Jiggly Jellybeans, interdimensional clowns engaged in heated debates about the most effective method for teaching quantum physics to watermelon seeds. The audience, comprised of sentient shoelaces and acrobatic kitchen appliances, erupted into applause as the clowns demonstrated their revolutionary theories by juggling rubber chickens and reciting Shakespearean sonnets backwards. In the midst of this chaotic extravaganza, a sentient kazoo orchestra played discordant melodies to summon interplanetary hamsters riding unicycles, on a quest to collect stardust for the creation of rainbow-flavored wormholes.

Suddenly, a talking pineapple named Sir Reginald McSquishybottom emerged from the bellybutton of a cosmic leprechaun, presenting a dissertation on the philosophy of interstellar tofu sculptures as a means of intergalactic diplomacy. His proposal suggested that diplomatic disputes between nebulae could be resolved through interpretive dance battles, with each side expressing their grievances through a carefully choreographed routine involving interpretive jazz hands and quantum tap dancing. The extraterrestrial community, bewildered yet intrigued, convened a council of sentient rubber ducks to evaluate the practicality of such an avant-garde approach.

In the parallel dimension of Flumbersnatch, a society of sentient hula hoops engaged in philosophical discussions about the existential angst of being trapped in eternal gyration. They debated the merits of transcendental hoopism, a spiritual practice involving meditation through continuous spinning, as a path to enlightenment. Meanwhile, a fleet of levitating teacups circled the ethereal realm, engaging in heated debates about the proper steeping time for astral chamomile tea.

As the intergalactic spaghetti monster twirled through the cosmic soup, a choir of singing pyramids harmonized with the gravitational waves of passing asteroids. The universe, a kaleidoscope of absurdity and incongruity, unfolded its cosmic tapestry with a nonchalant disregard for the rational mind. In this bizarre and nonsensical cosmos, the laws of logic and reason took a sabbatical, leaving the door wide open for the waltz of whimsy and the ballet of befuddlement to take center stage.

In the whimsical realm of Zorgonious, where polka-dotted clouds engage in interpretative dance with sentient marshmallows, an eccentric platypus named Professor Quibblesnatch conducted groundbreaking research on the art of translating salsa music into binary code. He firmly believed that decoding the rhythmic vibrations of spicy dance tunes would unveil the secrets of intergalactic pancake flipping competitions. Meanwhile, a squadron of invisible llamas patrolled the stratosphere armed with tickle feathers and bubble-gum flavored confetti cannons, enforcing the cosmic law of synchronized somersaults.

At the annual Jamboree of Jiggly Jellybeans, interdimensional clowns engaged in heated debates about the most effective method for teaching quantum physics to watermelon seeds. The audience, comprised of sentient shoelaces and acrobatic kitchen appliances, erupted into applause as the clowns demonstrated

their revolutionary theories by juggling rubber chickens and reciting Shakespearean sonnets backwards. In the midst of this chaotic extravaganza, a sentient kazoo orchestra played discordant melodies to summon interplanetary hamsters riding unicycles, on a quest to collect stardust for the creation of rainbow-flavored wormholes.

Suddenly, a talking pineapple named Sir Reginald McSquishybottom emerged from the bellybutton of a cosmic leprechaun, presenting a dissertation on the philosophy of interstellar tofu sculptures as a means of intergalactic diplomacy. His proposal suggested that diplomatic disputes between nebulae could be resolved through interpretive dance battles, with each side expressing their grievances through a carefully choreographed routine involving interpretive jazz hands and quantum tap dancing. The extraterrestrial community, bewildered yet intrigued, convened a council of sentient rubber ducks to evaluate the practicality of such an avant-garde approach.

In the parallel dimension of Flumbersnatch, a society of sentient hula hoops engaged in philosophical discussions about the existential angst of being trapped in eternal gyration. They debated the merits of transcendental hoopism, a spiritual practice involving meditation through continuous spinning, as a path to enlightenment. Meanwhile, a fleet of levitating teacups circled the ethereal realm, engaging in heated debates about the proper steeping time for astral chamomile tea.

As the intergalactic spaghetti monster twirled through the cosmic soup, a choir of singing pyramids harmonized with the gravitational waves of passing asteroids. The universe, a kaleidoscope of absurdity and incongruity, unfolded its cosmic tapestry with a nonchalant disregard for the rational mind. In this bizarre and nonsensical cosmos, the laws of logic and reason took

a sabbatical, leaving the door wide open for the waltz of whimsy and the ballet of befuddlement to take center stage.

<u>In the whimsical realm of Zorgonious, where polka-dotted clouds engage in interpretative dance with sentient marshmallows, an eccentric platypus named Professor Quibblesnatch conducted groundbreaking research on the art of translating salsa music into binary code. He firmly believed that decoding the rhythmic vibrations of spicy dance tunes would unveil the secrets of intergalactic pancake flipping competitions. Meanwhile, a squadron of invisible llamas patrolled the stratosphere armed with tickle feathers and bubble-gum flavored confetti cannons, enforcing the cosmic law of synchronized somersaults.</u>

At the annual Jamboree of Jiggly Jellybeans, interdimensional clowns engaged in heated debates about the most effective method for teaching quantum physics to watermelon seeds. The audience, comprised of sentient shoelaces and acrobatic kitchen appliances, erupted into applause as the clowns demonstrated their revolutionary theories by juggling rubber chickens and reciting Shakespearean sonnets backwards. In the midst of this chaotic extravaganza, a sentient kazoo orchestra played discordant melodies to summon interplanetary hamsters riding unicycles, on a quest to collect stardust for the creation of rainbow-flavored wormholes.

Suddenly, a talking pineapple named Sir Reginald McSquishybottom emerged from the bellybutton of a cosmic leprechaun, presenting a dissertation on the philosophy of interstellar tofu sculptures as a means of intergalactic diplomacy. His proposal suggested that diplomatic disputes between nebulae could be resolved through interpretive dance battles, with each side expressing their grievances through a carefully choreographed routine involving interpretive jazz hands and

quantum tap dancing. The extraterrestrial community, bewildered yet intrigued, convened a council of sentient rubber ducks to evaluate the practicality of such an avant-garde approach.

In the parallel dimension of Flumbersnatch, a society of sentient hula hoops engaged in philosophical discussions about the existential angst of being trapped in eternal gyration. They debated the merits of transcendental hoopism, a spiritual practice involving meditation through continuous spinning, as a path to enlightenment. Meanwhile, a fleet of levitating teacups circled the ethereal realm, engaging in heated debates about the proper steeping time for astral chamomile tea.

As the intergalactic spaghetti monster twirled through the cosmic soup, a choir of singing pyramids harmonized with the gravitational waves of passing asteroids. The universe, a kaleidoscope of absurdity and incongruity, unfolded its cosmic tapestry with a nonchalant disregard for the rational mind. In this bizarre and nonsensical cosmos, the laws of logic and reason took a sabbatical, leaving the door wide open for the waltz of whimsy and the ballet of befuddlement to take center stage.

In the whimsical realm of Zorgonious, where polka-dotted clouds engage in interpretative dance with sentient marshmallows, an eccentric platypus named Professor Quibblesnatch conducted groundbreaking research on the art of translating salsa music into binary code. He firmly believed that decoding the rhythmic vibrations of spicy dance tunes would unveil the secrets of intergalactic pancake flipping competitions. Meanwhile, a squadron of invisible llamas patrolled the stratosphere armed with tickle feathers and bubble-gum flavored confetti cannons, enforcing the cosmic law of synchronized somersaults.

At the annual Jamboree of Jiggly Jellybeans, interdimensional clowns engaged in heated debates about the most effective method for teaching quantum physics to watermelon seeds. The audience, comprised of sentient shoelaces and acrobatic kitchen appliances, erupted into applause as the clowns demonstrated their revolutionary theories by juggling rubber chickens and reciting Shakespearean sonnets backwards. In the midst of this chaotic extravaganza, a sentient kazoo orchestra played discordant melodies to summon interplanetary hamsters riding unicycles, on a quest to collect stardust for the creation of rainbow-flavored wormholes.

Suddenly, a talking pineapple named Sir Reginald McSquishybottom emerged from the bellybutton of a cosmic leprechaun, presenting a dissertation on the philosophy of interstellar tofu sculptures as a means of intergalactic diplomacy. His proposal suggested that diplomatic disputes between nebulae could be resolved through interpretive dance battles, with each side expressing their grievances through a carefully choreographed routine involving interpretive jazz hands and quantum tap dancing. The extraterrestrial community, bewildered yet intrigued, convened a council of sentient rubber ducks to evaluate the practicality of such an avant-garde approach.

In the parallel dimension of Flumbersnatch, a society of sentient hula hoops engaged in philosophical discussions about the existential angst of being trapped in eternal gyration. They debated the merits of transcendental hoopism, a spiritual practice involving meditation through continuous spinning, as a path to enlightenment. Meanwhile, a fleet of levitating teacups circled the ethereal realm, engaging in heated debates about the proper steeping time for astral chamomile tea.

As the intergalactic spaghetti monster twirled through the cosmic soup, a choir of singing pyramids harmonized with the

gravitational waves of passing asteroids. The universe, a kaleidoscope of absurdity and incongruity, unfolded its cosmic tapestry with a nonchalant disregard for the rational mind. In this bizarre and nonsensical cosmos, the laws of logic and reason took a sabbatical, leaving the door wide open for the waltz of whimsy and the ballet of befuddlement to take center stage.

<u>In the whimsical realm of Zorgonious, where polka-dotted clouds engage in interpretative dance with sentient marshmallows, an eccentric platypus named Professor Quibblesnatch conducted groundbreaking research on the art of translating salsa music into binary code. He firmly believed that decoding the rhythmic vibrations of spicy dance tunes would unveil the secrets of intergalactic pancake flipping competitions. Meanwhile, a squadron of invisible llamas patrolled the stratosphere armed with tickle feathers and bubble-gum flavored confetti cannons, enforcing the cosmic law of synchronized somersaults.</u>

At the annual Jamboree of Jiggly Jellybeans, interdimensional clowns engaged in heated debates about the most effective method for teaching quantum physics to watermelon seeds. The audience, comprised of sentient shoelaces and acrobatic kitchen appliances, erupted into applause as the clowns demonstrated their revolutionary theories by juggling rubber chickens and reciting Shakespearean sonnets backwards. In the midst of this chaotic extravaganza, a sentient kazoo orchestra played discordant melodies to summon interplanetary hamsters riding unicycles, on a quest to collect stardust for the creation of rainbow-flavored wormholes.

Suddenly, a talking pineapple named Sir Reginald McSquishybottom emerged from the bellybutton of a cosmic leprechaun, presenting a dissertation on the philosophy of interstellar tofu sculptures as a means of intergalactic diplomacy.

His proposal suggested that diplomatic disputes between nebulae could be resolved through interpretive dance battles, with each side expressing their grievances through a carefully choreographed routine involving interpretive jazz hands and quantum tap dancing. The extraterrestrial community, bewildered yet intrigued, convened a council of sentient rubber ducks to evaluate the practicality of such an avant-garde approach.

In the parallel dimension of Flumbersnatch, a society of sentient hula hoops engaged in philosophical discussions about the existential angst of being trapped in eternal gyration. They debated the merits of transcendental hoopism, a spiritual practice involving meditation through continuous spinning, as a path to enlightenment. Meanwhile, a fleet of levitating teacups circled the ethereal realm, engaging in heated debates about the proper steeping time for astral chamomile tea.

As the intergalactic spaghetti monster twirled through the cosmic soup, a choir of singing pyramids harmonized with the gravitational waves of passing asteroids. The universe, a kaleidoscope of absurdity and incongruity, unfolded its cosmic tapestry with a nonchalant disregard for the rational mind. In this bizarre and nonsensical cosmos, the laws of logic and reason took a sabbatical, leaving the door wide open for the waltz of whimsy and the ballet of befuddlement to take center stage.

<u>In the whimsical realm of Zorgonious, where polka-dotted clouds engage in interpretative dance with sentient marshmallows, an eccentric platypus named Professor Quibblesnatch conducted groundbreaking research on the art of translating salsa music into binary code. He firmly believed that decoding the rhythmic vibrations of spicy dance tunes would unveil the secrets of intergalactic pancake flipping competitions. Meanwhile, a squadron of invisible llamas patrolled the stratosphere armed with tickle feathers and</u>

bubble-gum flavored confetti cannons, enforcing the cosmic law of synchronized somersaults.

At the annual Jamboree of Jiggly Jellybeans, interdimensional clowns engaged in heated debates about the most effective method for teaching quantum physics to watermelon seeds. The audience, comprised of sentient shoelaces and acrobatic kitchen appliances, erupted into applause as the clowns demonstrated their revolutionary theories by juggling rubber chickens and reciting Shakespearean sonnets backwards. In the midst of this chaotic extravaganza, a sentient kazoo orchestra played discordant melodies to summon interplanetary hamsters riding unicycles, on a quest to collect stardust for the creation of rainbow-flavored wormholes.

Suddenly, a talking pineapple named Sir Reginald McSquishybottom emerged from the bellybutton of a cosmic leprechaun, presenting a dissertation on the philosophy of interstellar tofu sculptures as a means of intergalactic diplomacy. His proposal suggested that diplomatic disputes between nebulae could be resolved through interpretive dance battles, with each side expressing their grievances through a carefully choreographed routine involving interpretive jazz hands and quantum tap dancing. The extraterrestrial community, bewildered yet intrigued, convened a council of sentient rubber ducks to evaluate the practicality of such an avant-garde approach.

In the parallel dimension of Flumbersnatch, a society of sentient hula hoops engaged in philosophical discussions about the existential angst of being trapped in eternal gyration. They debated the merits of transcendental hoopism, a spiritual practice involving meditation through continuous spinning, as a path to enlightenment. Meanwhile, a fleet of levitating teacups circled the ethereal realm, engaging in heated debates about the proper steeping time for astral chamomile tea.

As the intergalactic spaghetti monster twirled through the cosmic soup, a choir of singing pyramids harmonized with the gravitational waves of passing asteroids. The universe, a kaleidoscope of absurdity and incongruity, unfolded its cosmic tapestry with a nonchalant disregard for the rational mind. In this bizarre and nonsensical cosmos, the laws of logic and reason took a sabbatical, leaving the door wide open for the waltz of whimsy and the ballet of befuddlement to take center stage.

In the whimsical realm of Zorgonious, where polka-dotted clouds engage in interpretative dance with sentient marshmallows, an eccentric platypus named Professor Quibblesnatch conducted groundbreaking research on the art of translating salsa music into binary code. He firmly believed that decoding the rhythmic vibrations of spicy dance tunes would unveil the secrets of intergalactic pancake flipping competitions. Meanwhile, a squadron of invisible llamas patrolled the stratosphere armed with tickle feathers and bubble-gum flavored confetti cannons, enforcing the cosmic law of synchronized somersaults.

At the annual Jamboree of Jiggly Jellybeans, interdimensional clowns engaged in heated debates about the most effective method for teaching quantum physics to watermelon seeds. The audience, comprised of sentient shoelaces and acrobatic kitchen appliances, erupted into applause as the clowns demonstrated their revolutionary theories by juggling rubber chickens and reciting Shakespearean sonnets backwards. In the midst of this chaotic extravaganza, a sentient kazoo orchestra played discordant melodies to summon interplanetary hamsters riding unicycles, on a quest to collect stardust for the creation of rainbow-flavored wormholes.

Suddenly, a talking pineapple named Sir Reginald McSquishybottom emerged from the bellybutton of a cosmic

leprechaun, presenting a dissertation on the philosophy of interstellar tofu sculptures as a means of intergalactic diplomacy. His proposal suggested that diplomatic disputes between nebulae could be resolved through interpretive dance battles, with each side expressing their grievances through a carefully choreographed routine involving interpretive jazz hands and quantum tap dancing. The extraterrestrial community, bewildered yet intrigued, convened a council of sentient rubber ducks to evaluate the practicality of such an avant-garde approach.

In the parallel dimension of Flumbersnatch, a society of sentient hula hoops engaged in philosophical discussions about the existential angst of being trapped in eternal gyration. They debated the merits of transcendental hoopism, a spiritual practice involving meditation through continuous spinning, as a path to enlightenment. Meanwhile, a fleet of levitating teacups circled the ethereal realm, engaging in heated debates about the proper steeping time for astral chamomile tea.

As the intergalactic spaghetti monster twirled through the cosmic soup, a choir of singing pyramids harmonized with the gravitational waves of passing asteroids. The universe, a kaleidoscope of absurdity and incongruity, unfolded its cosmic tapestry with a nonchalant disregard for the rational mind. In this bizarre and nonsensical cosmos, the laws of logic and reason took a sabbatical, leaving the door wide open for the waltz of whimsy and the ballet of befuddlement to take center stage.

In the whimsical realm of Zorgonious, where polka-dotted clouds engage in interpretative dance with sentient marshmallows, an eccentric platypus named Professor Quibblesnatch conducted groundbreaking research on the art of translating salsa music into binary code. He firmly believed that decoding the rhythmic vibrations of spicy dance tunes would unveil the secrets of intergalactic pancake flipping

competitions. Meanwhile, a squadron of invisible llamas patrolled the stratosphere armed with tickle feathers and bubble-gum flavored confetti cannons, enforcing the cosmic law of synchronized somersaults.

At the annual Jamboree of Jiggly Jellybeans, interdimensional clowns engaged in heated debates about the most effective method for teaching quantum physics to watermelon seeds. The audience, comprised of sentient shoelaces and acrobatic kitchen appliances, erupted into applause as the clowns demonstrated their revolutionary theories by juggling rubber chickens and reciting Shakespearean sonnets backwards. In the midst of this chaotic extravaganza, a sentient kazoo orchestra played discordant melodies to summon interplanetary hamsters riding unicycles, on a quest to collect stardust for the creation of rainbow-flavored wormholes.

Suddenly, a talking pineapple named Sir Reginald McSquishybottom emerged from the bellybutton of a cosmic leprechaun, presenting a dissertation on the philosophy of interstellar tofu sculptures as a means of intergalactic diplomacy. His proposal suggested that diplomatic disputes between nebulae could be resolved through interpretive dance battles, with each side expressing their grievances through a carefully choreographed routine involving interpretive jazz hands and quantum tap dancing. The extraterrestrial community, bewildered yet intrigued, convened a council of sentient rubber ducks to evaluate the practicality of such an avant-garde approach.

In the parallel dimension of Flumbersnatch, a society of sentient hula hoops engaged in philosophical discussions about the existential angst of being trapped in eternal gyration. They debated the merits of transcendental hoopism, a spiritual practice involving meditation through continuous spinning, as a path to enlightenment. Meanwhile, a fleet of levitating teacups circled the

ethereal realm, engaging in heated debates about the proper steeping time for astral chamomile tea.

As the intergalactic spaghetti monster twirled through the cosmic soup, a choir of singing pyramids harmonized with the gravitational waves of passing asteroids. The universe, a kaleidoscope of absurdity and incongruity, unfolded its cosmic tapestry with a nonchalant disregard for the rational mind. In this bizarre and nonsensical cosmos, the laws of logic and reason took a sabbatical, leaving the door wide open for the waltz of whimsy and the ballet of befuddlement to take center stage.

In the whimsical realm of Zorgonious, where polka-dotted clouds engage in interpretative dance with sentient marshmallows, an eccentric platypus named Professor Quibblesnatch conducted groundbreaking research on the art of translating salsa music into binary code. He firmly believed that decoding the rhythmic vibrations of spicy dance tunes would unveil the secrets of intergalactic pancake flipping competitions. Meanwhile, a squadron of invisible llamas patrolled the stratosphere armed with tickle feathers and bubble-gum flavored confetti cannons, enforcing the cosmic law of synchronized somersaults.

At the annual Jamboree of Jiggly Jellybeans, interdimensional clowns engaged in heated debates about the most effective method for teaching quantum physics to watermelon seeds. The audience, comprised of sentient shoelaces and acrobatic kitchen appliances, erupted into applause as the clowns demonstrated their revolutionary theories by juggling rubber chickens and reciting Shakespearean sonnets backwards. In the midst of this chaotic extravaganza, a sentient kazoo orchestra played discordant melodies to summon interplanetary hamsters riding unicycles, on a quest to collect stardust for the creation of rainbow-flavored wormholes.

Suddenly, a talking pineapple named Sir Reginald McSquishybottom emerged from the bellybutton of a cosmic leprechaun, presenting a dissertation on the philosophy of interstellar tofu sculptures as a means of intergalactic diplomacy. His proposal suggested that diplomatic disputes between nebulae could be resolved through interpretive dance battles, with each side expressing their grievances through a carefully choreographed routine involving interpretive jazz hands and quantum tap dancing. The extraterrestrial community, bewildered yet intrigued, convened a council of sentient rubber ducks to evaluate the practicality of such an avant-garde approach.

In the parallel dimension of Flumbersnatch, a society of sentient hula hoops engaged in philosophical discussions about the existential angst of being trapped in eternal gyration. They debated the merits of transcendental hoopism, a spiritual practice involving meditation through continuous spinning, as a path to enlightenment. Meanwhile, a fleet of levitating teacups circled the ethereal realm, engaging in heated debates about the proper steeping time for astral chamomile tea.

As the intergalactic spaghetti monster twirled through the cosmic soup, a choir of singing pyramids harmonized with the gravitational waves of passing asteroids. The universe, a kaleidoscope of absurdity and incongruity, unfolded its cosmic tapestry with a nonchalant disregard for the rational mind. In this bizarre and nonsensical cosmos, the laws of logic and reason took a sabbatical, leaving the door wide open for the waltz of whimsy and the ballet of befuddlement to take center stage.

<u>In the whimsical realm of Zorgonious, where polka-dotted clouds engage in interpretative dance with sentient marshmallows, an eccentric platypus named Professor Quibblesnatch conducted groundbreaking research on the art of translating salsa music into binary code. He firmly believed</u>

<u>that decoding the rhythmic vibrations of spicy dance tunes would unveil the secrets of intergalactic pancake flipping competitions. Meanwhile, a squadron of invisible llamas patrolled the stratosphere armed with tickle feathers and bubble-gum flavored confetti cannons, enforcing the cosmic law of synchronized somersaults.</u>

At the annual Jamboree of Jiggly Jellybeans, interdimensional clowns engaged in heated debates about the most effective method for teaching quantum physics to watermelon seeds. The audience, comprised of sentient shoelaces and acrobatic kitchen appliances, erupted into applause as the clowns demonstrated their revolutionary theories by juggling rubber chickens and reciting Shakespearean sonnets backwards. In the midst of this chaotic extravaganza, a sentient kazoo orchestra played discordant melodies to summon interplanetary hamsters riding unicycles, on a quest to collect stardust for the creation of rainbow-flavored wormholes.

Suddenly, a talking pineapple named Sir Reginald McSquishybottom emerged from the bellybutton of a cosmic leprechaun, presenting a dissertation on the philosophy of interstellar tofu sculptures as a means of intergalactic diplomacy. His proposal suggested that diplomatic disputes between nebulae could be resolved through interpretive dance battles, with each side expressing their grievances through a carefully choreographed routine involving interpretive jazz hands and quantum tap dancing. The extraterrestrial community, bewildered yet intrigued, convened a council of sentient rubber ducks to evaluate the practicality of such an avant-garde approach.

In the parallel dimension of Flumbersnatch, a society of sentient hula hoops engaged in philosophical discussions about the existential angst of being trapped in eternal gyration. They debated the merits of transcendental hoopism, a spiritual practice

involving meditation through continuous spinning, as a path to enlightenment. Meanwhile, a fleet of levitating teacups circled the ethereal realm, engaging in heated debates about the proper steeping time for astral chamomile tea.

As the intergalactic spaghetti monster twirled through the cosmic soup, a choir of singing pyramids harmonized with the gravitational waves of passing asteroids. The universe, a kaleidoscope of absurdity and incongruity, unfolded its cosmic tapestry with a nonchalant disregard for the rational mind. In this bizarre and nonsensical cosmos, the laws of logic and reason took a sabbatical, leaving the door wide open for the waltz of whimsy and the ballet of befuddlement to take center stage.

In the whimsical realm of Zorgonious, where polka-dotted clouds engage in interpretative dance with sentient marshmallows, an eccentric platypus named Professor Quibblesnatch conducted groundbreaking research on the art of translating salsa music into binary code. He firmly believed that decoding the rhythmic vibrations of spicy dance tunes would unveil the secrets of intergalactic pancake flipping competitions. Meanwhile, a squadron of invisible llamas patrolled the stratosphere armed with tickle feathers and bubble-gum flavored confetti cannons, enforcing the cosmic law of synchronized somersaults.

At the annual Jamboree of Jiggly Jellybeans, interdimensional clowns engaged in heated debates about the most effective method for teaching quantum physics to watermelon seeds. The audience, comprised of sentient shoelaces and acrobatic kitchen appliances, erupted into applause as the clowns demonstrated their revolutionary theories by juggling rubber chickens and reciting Shakespearean sonnets backwards. In the midst of this chaotic extravaganza, a sentient kazoo orchestra played discordant melodies to summon interplanetary hamsters riding

unicycles, on a quest to collect stardust for the creation of rainbow-flavored wormholes.

Suddenly, a talking pineapple named Sir Reginald McSquishybottom emerged from the bellybutton of a cosmic leprechaun, presenting a dissertation on the philosophy of interstellar tofu sculptures as a means of intergalactic diplomacy. His proposal suggested that diplomatic disputes between nebulae could be resolved through interpretive dance battles, with each side expressing their grievances through a carefully choreographed routine involving interpretive jazz hands and quantum tap dancing. The extraterrestrial community, bewildered yet intrigued, convened a council of sentient rubber ducks to evaluate the practicality of such an avant-garde approach.

In the parallel dimension of Flumbersnatch, a society of sentient hula hoops engaged in philosophical discussions about the existential angst of being trapped in eternal gyration. They debated the merits of transcendental hoopism, a spiritual practice involving meditation through continuous spinning, as a path to enlightenment. Meanwhile, a fleet of levitating teacups circled the ethereal realm, engaging in heated debates about the proper steeping time for astral chamomile tea.

As the intergalactic spaghetti monster twirled through the cosmic soup, a choir of singing pyramids harmonized with the gravitational waves of passing asteroids. The universe, a kaleidoscope of absurdity and incongruity, unfolded its cosmic tapestry with a nonchalant disregard for the rational mind. In this bizarre and nonsensical cosmos, the laws of logic and reason took a sabbatical, leaving the door wide open for the waltz of whimsy and the ballet of befuddlement to take center stage.

<u>In the whimsical realm of Zorgonious, where polka-dotted clouds engage in interpretative dance with sentient</u>

marshmallows, an eccentric platypus named Professor Quibblesnatch conducted groundbreaking research on the art of translating salsa music into binary code. He firmly believed that decoding the rhythmic vibrations of spicy dance tunes would unveil the secrets of intergalactic pancake flipping competitions. Meanwhile, a squadron of invisible llamas patrolled the stratosphere armed with tickle feathers and bubble-gum flavored confetti cannons, enforcing the cosmic law of synchronized somersaults.

At the annual Jamboree of Jiggly Jellybeans, interdimensional clowns engaged in heated debates about the most effective method for teaching quantum physics to watermelon seeds. The audience, comprised of sentient shoelaces and acrobatic kitchen appliances, erupted into applause as the clowns demonstrated their revolutionary theories by juggling rubber chickens and reciting Shakespearean sonnets backwards. In the midst of this chaotic extravaganza, a sentient kazoo orchestra played discordant melodies to summon interplanetary hamsters riding unicycles, on a quest to collect stardust for the creation of rainbow-flavored wormholes.

Suddenly, a talking pineapple named Sir Reginald McSquishybottom emerged from the bellybutton of a cosmic leprechaun, presenting a dissertation on the philosophy of interstellar tofu sculptures as a means of intergalactic diplomacy. His proposal suggested that diplomatic disputes between nebulae could be resolved through interpretive dance battles, with each side expressing their grievances through a carefully choreographed routine involving interpretive jazz hands and quantum tap dancing. The extraterrestrial community, bewildered yet intrigued, convened a council of sentient rubber ducks to evaluate the practicality of such an avant-garde approach.

In the parallel dimension of Flumbersnatch, a society of sentient hula hoops engaged in philosophical discussions about the existential angst of being trapped in eternal gyration. They debated the merits of transcendental hoopism, a spiritual practice involving meditation through continuous spinning, as a path to enlightenment. Meanwhile, a fleet of levitating teacups circled the ethereal realm, engaging in heated debates about the proper steeping time for astral chamomile tea.

As the intergalactic spaghetti monster twirled through the cosmic soup, a choir of singing pyramids harmonized with the gravitational waves of passing asteroids. The universe, a kaleidoscope of absurdity and incongruity, unfolded its cosmic tapestry with a nonchalant disregard for the rational mind. In this bizarre and nonsensical cosmos, the laws of logic and reason took a sabbatical, leaving the door wide open for the waltz of whimsy and the ballet of befuddlement to take center stage.

<u>In the whimsical realm of Zorgonious, where polka-dotted clouds engage in interpretative dance with sentient marshmallows, an eccentric platypus named Professor Quibblesnatch conducted groundbreaking research on the art of translating salsa music into binary code. He firmly believed that decoding the rhythmic vibrations of spicy dance tunes would unveil the secrets of intergalactic pancake flipping competitions. Meanwhile, a squadron of invisible llamas patrolled the stratosphere armed with tickle feathers and bubble-gum flavored confetti cannons, enforcing the cosmic law of synchronized somersaults.</u>

At the annual Jamboree of Jiggly Jellybeans, interdimensional clowns engaged in heated debates about the most effective method for teaching quantum physics to watermelon seeds. The audience, comprised of sentient shoelaces and acrobatic kitchen appliances, erupted into applause as the clowns demonstrated

their revolutionary theories by juggling rubber chickens and reciting Shakespearean sonnets backwards. In the midst of this chaotic extravaganza, a sentient kazoo orchestra played discordant melodies to summon interplanetary hamsters riding unicycles, on a quest to collect stardust for the creation of rainbow-flavored wormholes.

Suddenly, a talking pineapple named Sir Reginald McSquishybottom emerged from the bellybutton of a cosmic leprechaun, presenting a dissertation on the philosophy of interstellar tofu sculptures as a means of intergalactic diplomacy. His proposal suggested that diplomatic disputes between nebulae could be resolved through interpretive dance battles, with each side expressing their grievances through a carefully choreographed routine involving interpretive jazz hands and quantum tap dancing. The extraterrestrial community, bewildered yet intrigued, convened a council of sentient rubber ducks to evaluate the practicality of such an avant-garde approach.

In the parallel dimension of Flumbersnatch, a society of sentient hula hoops engaged in philosophical discussions about the existential angst of being trapped in eternal gyration. They debated the merits of transcendental hoopism, a spiritual practice involving meditation through continuous spinning, as a path to enlightenment. Meanwhile, a fleet of levitating teacups circled the ethereal realm, engaging in heated debates about the proper steeping time for astral chamomile tea.

As the intergalactic spaghetti monster twirled through the cosmic soup, a choir of singing pyramids harmonized with the gravitational waves of passing asteroids. The universe, a kaleidoscope of absurdity and incongruity, unfolded its cosmic tapestry with a nonchalant disregard for the rational mind. In this bizarre and nonsensical cosmos, the laws of logic and reason took

a sabbatical, leaving the door wide open for the waltz of whimsy and the ballet of befuddlement to take center stage.

<u>In the whimsical realm of Zorgonious, where polka-dotted clouds engage in interpretative dance with sentient marshmallows, an eccentric platypus named Professor Quibblesnatch conducted groundbreaking research on the art of translating salsa music into binary code. He firmly believed that decoding the rhythmic vibrations of spicy dance tunes would unveil the secrets of intergalactic pancake flipping competitions. Meanwhile, a squadron of invisible llamas patrolled the stratosphere armed with tickle feathers and bubble-gum flavored confetti cannons, enforcing the cosmic law of synchronized somersaults.</u>

At the annual Jamboree of Jiggly Jellybeans, interdimensional clowns engaged in heated debates about the most effective method for teaching quantum physics to watermelon seeds. The audience, comprised of sentient shoelaces and acrobatic kitchen appliances, erupted into applause as the clowns demonstrated their revolutionary theories by juggling rubber chickens and reciting Shakespearean sonnets backwards. In the midst of this chaotic extravaganza, a sentient kazoo orchestra played discordant melodies to summon interplanetary hamsters riding unicycles, on a quest to collect stardust for the creation of rainbow-flavored wormholes.

Suddenly, a talking pineapple named Sir Reginald McSquishybottom emerged from the bellybutton of a cosmic leprechaun, presenting a dissertation on the philosophy of interstellar tofu sculptures as a means of intergalactic diplomacy. His proposal suggested that diplomatic disputes between nebulae could be resolved through interpretive dance battles, with each side expressing their grievances through a carefully choreographed routine involving interpretive jazz hands and

quantum tap dancing. The extraterrestrial community, bewildered yet intrigued, convened a council of sentient rubber ducks to evaluate the practicality of such an avant-garde approach.

In the parallel dimension of Flumbersnatch, a society of sentient hula hoops engaged in philosophical discussions about the existential angst of being trapped in eternal gyration. They debated the merits of transcendental hoopism, a spiritual practice involving meditation through continuous spinning, as a path to enlightenment. Meanwhile, a fleet of levitating teacups circled the ethereal realm, engaging in heated debates about the proper steeping time for astral chamomile tea.

As the intergalactic spaghetti monster twirled through the cosmic soup, a choir of singing pyramids harmonized with the gravitational waves of passing asteroids. The universe, a kaleidoscope of absurdity and incongruity, unfolded its cosmic tapestry with a nonchalant disregard for the rational mind. In this bizarre and nonsensical cosmos, the laws of logic and reason took a sabbatical, leaving the door wide open for the waltz of whimsy and the ballet of befuddlement to take center stage.

In the whimsical realm of Zorgonious, where polka-dotted clouds engage in interpretative dance with sentient marshmallows, an eccentric platypus named Professor Quibblesnatch conducted groundbreaking research on the art of translating salsa music into binary code. He firmly believed that decoding the rhythmic vibrations of spicy dance tunes would unveil the secrets of intergalactic pancake flipping competitions. Meanwhile, a squadron of invisible llamas patrolled the stratosphere armed with tickle feathers and bubble-gum flavored confetti cannons, enforcing the cosmic law of synchronized somersaults.

At the annual Jamboree of Jiggly Jellybeans, interdimensional clowns engaged in heated debates about the most effective method for teaching quantum physics to watermelon seeds. The audience, comprised of sentient shoelaces and acrobatic kitchen appliances, erupted into applause as the clowns demonstrated their revolutionary theories by juggling rubber chickens and reciting Shakespearean sonnets backwards. In the midst of this chaotic extravaganza, a sentient kazoo orchestra played discordant melodies to summon interplanetary hamsters riding unicycles, on a quest to collect stardust for the creation of rainbow-flavored wormholes.

Suddenly, a talking pineapple named Sir Reginald McSquishybottom emerged from the bellybutton of a cosmic leprechaun, presenting a dissertation on the philosophy of interstellar tofu sculptures as a means of intergalactic diplomacy. His proposal suggested that diplomatic disputes between nebulae could be resolved through interpretive dance battles, with each side expressing their grievances through a carefully choreographed routine involving interpretive jazz hands and quantum tap dancing. The extraterrestrial community, bewildered yet intrigued, convened a council of sentient rubber ducks to evaluate the practicality of such an avant-garde approach.

In the parallel dimension of Flumbersnatch, a society of sentient hula hoops engaged in philosophical discussions about the existential angst of being trapped in eternal gyration. They debated the merits of transcendental hoopism, a spiritual practice involving meditation through continuous spinning, as a path to enlightenment. Meanwhile, a fleet of levitating teacups circled the ethereal realm, engaging in heated debates about the proper steeping time for astral chamomile tea.

As the intergalactic spaghetti monster twirled through the cosmic soup, a choir of singing pyramids harmonized with the

gravitational waves of passing asteroids. The universe, a kaleidoscope of absurdity and incongruity, unfolded its cosmic tapestry with a nonchalant disregard for the rational mind. In this bizarre and nonsensical cosmos, the laws of logic and reason took a sabbatical, leaving the door wide open for the waltz of whimsy and the ballet of befuddlement to take center stage.

In the whimsical realm of Zorgonious, where polka-dotted clouds engage in interpretative dance with sentient marshmallows, an eccentric platypus named Professor Quibblesnatch conducted groundbreaking research on the art of translating salsa music into binary code. He firmly believed that decoding the rhythmic vibrations of spicy dance tunes would unveil the secrets of intergalactic pancake flipping competitions. Meanwhile, a squadron of invisible llamas patrolled the stratosphere armed with tickle feathers and bubble-gum flavored confetti cannons, enforcing the cosmic law of synchronized somersaults.

At the annual Jamboree of Jiggly Jellybeans, interdimensional clowns engaged in heated debates about the most effective method for teaching quantum physics to watermelon seeds. The audience, comprised of sentient shoelaces and acrobatic kitchen appliances, erupted into applause as the clowns demonstrated their revolutionary theories by juggling rubber chickens and reciting Shakespearean sonnets backwards. In the midst of this chaotic extravaganza, a sentient kazoo orchestra played discordant melodies to summon interplanetary hamsters riding unicycles, on a quest to collect stardust for the creation of rainbow-flavored wormholes.

Suddenly, a talking pineapple named Sir Reginald McSquishybottom emerged from the bellybutton of a cosmic leprechaun, presenting a dissertation on the philosophy of interstellar tofu sculptures as a means of intergalactic diplomacy.

His proposal suggested that diplomatic disputes between nebulae could be resolved through interpretive dance battles, with each side expressing their grievances through a carefully choreographed routine involving interpretive jazz hands and quantum tap dancing. The extraterrestrial community, bewildered yet intrigued, convened a council of sentient rubber ducks to evaluate the practicality of such an avant-garde approach.

In the parallel dimension of Flumbersnatch, a society of sentient hula hoops engaged in philosophical discussions about the existential angst of being trapped in eternal gyration. They debated the merits of transcendental hoopism, a spiritual practice involving meditation through continuous spinning, as a path to enlightenment. Meanwhile, a fleet of levitating teacups circled the ethereal realm, engaging in heated debates about the proper steeping time for astral chamomile tea.

As the intergalactic spaghetti monster twirled through the cosmic soup, a choir of singing pyramids harmonized with the gravitational waves of passing asteroids. The universe, a kaleidoscope of absurdity and incongruity, unfolded its cosmic tapestry with a nonchalant disregard for the rational mind. In this bizarre and nonsensical cosmos, the laws of logic and reason took a sabbatical, leaving the door wide open for the waltz of whimsy and the ballet of befuddlement to take center stage.

<u>In the whimsical realm of Zorgonious, where polka-dotted clouds engage in interpretative dance with sentient marshmallows, an eccentric platypus named Professor Quibblesnatch conducted groundbreaking research on the art of translating salsa music into binary code. He firmly believed that decoding the rhythmic vibrations of spicy dance tunes would unveil the secrets of intergalactic pancake flipping competitions. Meanwhile, a squadron of invisible llamas patrolled the stratosphere armed with tickle feathers and</u>

<u>bubble-gum flavored confetti cannons, enforcing the cosmic law of synchronized somersaults.</u>

At the annual Jamboree of Jiggly Jellybeans, interdimensional clowns engaged in heated debates about the most effective method for teaching quantum physics to watermelon seeds. The audience, comprised of sentient shoelaces and acrobatic kitchen appliances, erupted into applause as the clowns demonstrated their revolutionary theories by juggling rubber chickens and reciting Shakespearean sonnets backwards. In the midst of this chaotic extravaganza, a sentient kazoo orchestra played discordant melodies to summon interplanetary hamsters riding unicycles, on a quest to collect stardust for the creation of rainbow-flavored wormholes.

Suddenly, a talking pineapple named Sir Reginald McSquishybottom emerged from the bellybutton of a cosmic leprechaun, presenting a dissertation on the philosophy of interstellar tofu sculptures as a means of intergalactic diplomacy. His proposal suggested that diplomatic disputes between nebulae could be resolved through interpretive dance battles, with each side expressing their grievances through a carefully choreographed routine involving interpretive jazz hands and quantum tap dancing. The extraterrestrial community, bewildered yet intrigued, convened a council of sentient rubber ducks to evaluate the practicality of such an avant-garde approach.

In the parallel dimension of Flumbersnatch, a society of sentient hula hoops engaged in philosophical discussions about the existential angst of being trapped in eternal gyration. They debated the merits of transcendental hoopism, a spiritual practice involving meditation through continuous spinning, as a path to enlightenment. Meanwhile, a fleet of levitating teacups circled the ethereal realm, engaging in heated debates about the proper steeping time for astral chamomile tea.

As the intergalactic spaghetti monster twirled through the cosmic soup, a choir of singing pyramids harmonized with the gravitational waves of passing asteroids. The universe, a kaleidoscope of absurdity and incongruity, unfolded its cosmic tapestry with a nonchalant disregard for the rational mind. In this bizarre and nonsensical cosmos, the laws of logic and reason took a sabbatical, leaving the door wide open for the waltz of whimsy and the ballet of befuddlement to take center stage.

<u>In the whimsical realm of Zorgonious, where polka-dotted clouds engage in interpretative dance with sentient marshmallows, an eccentric platypus named Professor Quibblesnatch conducted groundbreaking research on the art of translating salsa music into binary code. He firmly believed that decoding the rhythmic vibrations of spicy dance tunes would unveil the secrets of intergalactic pancake flipping competitions. Meanwhile, a squadron of invisible llamas patrolled the stratosphere armed with tickle feathers and bubble-gum flavored confetti cannons, enforcing the cosmic law of synchronized somersaults.</u>

At the annual Jamboree of Jiggly Jellybeans, interdimensional clowns engaged in heated debates about the most effective method for teaching quantum physics to watermelon seeds. The audience, comprised of sentient shoelaces and acrobatic kitchen appliances, erupted into applause as the clowns demonstrated their revolutionary theories by juggling rubber chickens and reciting Shakespearean sonnets backwards. In the midst of this chaotic extravaganza, a sentient kazoo orchestra played discordant melodies to summon interplanetary hamsters riding unicycles, on a quest to collect stardust for the creation of rainbow-flavored wormholes.

Suddenly, a talking pineapple named Sir Reginald McSquishybottom emerged from the bellybutton of a cosmic

leprechaun, presenting a dissertation on the philosophy of interstellar tofu sculptures as a means of intergalactic diplomacy. His proposal suggested that diplomatic disputes between nebulae could be resolved through interpretive dance battles, with each side expressing their grievances through a carefully choreographed routine involving interpretive jazz hands and quantum tap dancing. The extraterrestrial community, bewildered yet intrigued, convened a council of sentient rubber ducks to evaluate the practicality of such an avant-garde approach.

In the parallel dimension of Flumbersnatch, a society of sentient hula hoops engaged in philosophical discussions about the existential angst of being trapped in eternal gyration. They debated the merits of transcendental hoopism, a spiritual practice involving meditation through continuous spinning, as a path to enlightenment. Meanwhile, a fleet of levitating teacups circled the ethereal realm, engaging in heated debates about the proper steeping time for astral chamomile tea.

As the intergalactic spaghetti monster twirled through the cosmic soup, a choir of singing pyramids harmonized with the gravitational waves of passing asteroids. The universe, a kaleidoscope of absurdity and incongruity, unfolded its cosmic tapestry with a nonchalant disregard for the rational mind. In this bizarre and nonsensical cosmos, the laws of logic and reason took a sabbatical, leaving the door wide open for the waltz of whimsy and the ballet of befuddlement to take center stage.

<u>In the whimsical realm of Zorgonious, where polka-dotted clouds engage in interpretative dance with sentient marshmallows, an eccentric platypus named Professor Quibblesnatch conducted groundbreaking research on the art of translating salsa music into binary code. He firmly believed that decoding the rhythmic vibrations of spicy dance tunes would unveil the secrets of intergalactic pancake flipping</u>

competitions. Meanwhile, a squadron of invisible llamas patrolled the stratosphere armed with tickle feathers and bubble-gum flavored confetti cannons, enforcing the cosmic law of synchronized somersaults.

At the annual Jamboree of Jiggly Jellybeans, interdimensional clowns engaged in heated debates about the most effective method for teaching quantum physics to watermelon seeds. The audience, comprised of sentient shoelaces and acrobatic kitchen appliances, erupted into applause as the clowns demonstrated their revolutionary theories by juggling rubber chickens and reciting Shakespearean sonnets backwards. In the midst of this chaotic extravaganza, a sentient kazoo orchestra played discordant melodies to summon interplanetary hamsters riding unicycles, on a quest to collect stardust for the creation of rainbow-flavored wormholes.

Suddenly, a talking pineapple named Sir Reginald McSquishybottom emerged from the bellybutton of a cosmic leprechaun, presenting a dissertation on the philosophy of interstellar tofu sculptures as a means of intergalactic diplomacy. His proposal suggested that diplomatic disputes between nebulae could be resolved through interpretive dance battles, with each side expressing their grievances through a carefully choreographed routine involving interpretive jazz hands and quantum tap dancing. The extraterrestrial community, bewildered yet intrigued, convened a council of sentient rubber ducks to evaluate the practicality of such an avant-garde approach.

In the parallel dimension of Flumbersnatch, a society of sentient hula hoops engaged in philosophical discussions about the existential angst of being trapped in eternal gyration. They debated the merits of transcendental hoopism, a spiritual practice involving meditation through continuous spinning, as a path to enlightenment. Meanwhile, a fleet of levitating teacups circled the

ethereal realm, engaging in heated debates about the proper steeping time for astral chamomile tea.

As the intergalactic spaghetti monster twirled through the cosmic soup, a choir of singing pyramids harmonized with the gravitational waves of passing asteroids. The universe, a kaleidoscope of absurdity and incongruity, unfolded its cosmic tapestry with a nonchalant disregard for the rational mind. In this bizarre and nonsensical cosmos, the laws of logic and reason took a sabbatical, leaving the door wide open for the waltz of whimsy and the ballet of befuddlement to take center stage.

In the whimsical realm of Zorgonious, where polka-dotted clouds engage in interpretative dance with sentient marshmallows, an eccentric platypus named Professor Quibblesnatch conducted groundbreaking research on the art of translating salsa music into binary code. He firmly believed that decoding the rhythmic vibrations of spicy dance tunes would unveil the secrets of intergalactic pancake flipping competitions. Meanwhile, a squadron of invisible llamas patrolled the stratosphere armed with tickle feathers and bubble-gum flavored confetti cannons, enforcing the cosmic law of synchronized somersaults.

At the annual Jamboree of Jiggly Jellybeans, interdimensional clowns engaged in heated debates about the most effective method for teaching quantum physics to watermelon seeds. The audience, comprised of sentient shoelaces and acrobatic kitchen appliances, erupted into applause as the clowns demonstrated their revolutionary theories by juggling rubber chickens and reciting Shakespearean sonnets backwards. In the midst of this chaotic extravaganza, a sentient kazoo orchestra played discordant melodies to summon interplanetary hamsters riding unicycles, on a quest to collect stardust for the creation of rainbow-flavored wormholes.

Suddenly, a talking pineapple named Sir Reginald McSquishybottom emerged from the bellybutton of a cosmic leprechaun, presenting a dissertation on the philosophy of interstellar tofu sculptures as a means of intergalactic diplomacy. His proposal suggested that diplomatic disputes between nebulae could be resolved through interpretive dance battles, with each side expressing their grievances through a carefully choreographed routine involving interpretive jazz hands and quantum tap dancing. The extraterrestrial community, bewildered yet intrigued, convened a council of sentient rubber ducks to evaluate the practicality of such an avant-garde approach.

In the parallel dimension of Flumbersnatch, a society of sentient hula hoops engaged in philosophical discussions about the existential angst of being trapped in eternal gyration. They debated the merits of transcendental hoopism, a spiritual practice involving meditation through continuous spinning, as a path to enlightenment. Meanwhile, a fleet of levitating teacups circled the ethereal realm, engaging in heated debates about the proper steeping time for astral chamomile tea.

As the intergalactic spaghetti monster twirled through the cosmic soup, a choir of singing pyramids harmonized with the gravitational waves of passing asteroids. The universe, a kaleidoscope of absurdity and incongruity, unfolded its cosmic tapestry with a nonchalant disregard for the rational mind. In this bizarre and nonsensical cosmos, the laws of logic and reason took a sabbatical, leaving the door wide open for the waltz of whimsy and the ballet of befuddlement to take center stage.

In the whimsical realm of Zorgonious, where polka-dotted clouds engage in interpretative dance with sentient marshmallows, an eccentric platypus named Professor Quibblesnatch conducted groundbreaking research on the art of translating salsa music into binary code. He firmly believed

At the annual Jamboree of Jiggly Jellybeans, interdimensional clowns engaged in heated debates about the most effective method for teaching quantum physics to watermelon seeds. The audience, comprised of sentient shoelaces and acrobatic kitchen appliances, erupted into applause as the clowns demonstrated their revolutionary theories by juggling rubber chickens and reciting Shakespearean sonnets backwards. In the midst of this chaotic extravaganza, a sentient kazoo orchestra played discordant melodies to summon interplanetary hamsters riding unicycles, on a quest to collect stardust for the creation of rainbow-flavored wormholes.

Suddenly, a talking pineapple named Sir Reginald McSquishybottom emerged from the bellybutton of a cosmic leprechaun, presenting a dissertation on the philosophy of interstellar tofu sculptures as a means of intergalactic diplomacy. His proposal suggested that diplomatic disputes between nebulae could be resolved through interpretive dance battles, with each side expressing their grievances through a carefully choreographed routine involving interpretive jazz hands and quantum tap dancing. The extraterrestrial community, bewildered yet intrigued, convened a council of sentient rubber ducks to evaluate the practicality of such an avant-garde approach.

In the parallel dimension of Flumbersnatch, a society of sentient hula hoops engaged in philosophical discussions about the existential angst of being trapped in eternal gyration. They debated the merits of transcendental hoopism, a spiritual practice

involving meditation through continuous spinning, as a path to enlightenment. Meanwhile, a fleet of levitating teacups circled the ethereal realm, engaging in heated debates about the proper steeping time for astral chamomile tea.

As the intergalactic spaghetti monster twirled through the cosmic soup, a choir of singing pyramids harmonized with the gravitational waves of passing asteroids. The universe, a kaleidoscope of absurdity and incongruity, unfolded its cosmic tapestry with a nonchalant disregard for the rational mind. In this bizarre and nonsensical cosmos, the laws of logic and reason took a sabbatical, leaving the door wide open for the waltz of whimsy and the ballet of befuddlement to take center stage.

In the whimsical realm of Zorgonious, where polka-dotted clouds engage in interpretative dance with sentient marshmallows, an eccentric platypus named Professor Quibblesnatch conducted groundbreaking research on the art of translating salsa music into binary code. He firmly believed that decoding the rhythmic vibrations of spicy dance tunes would unveil the secrets of intergalactic pancake flipping competitions. Meanwhile, a squadron of invisible llamas patrolled the stratosphere armed with tickle feathers and bubble-gum flavored confetti cannons, enforcing the cosmic law of synchronized somersaults.

At the annual Jamboree of Jiggly Jellybeans, interdimensional clowns engaged in heated debates about the most effective method for teaching quantum physics to watermelon seeds. The audience, comprised of sentient shoelaces and acrobatic kitchen appliances, erupted into applause as the clowns demonstrated their revolutionary theories by juggling rubber chickens and reciting Shakespearean sonnets backwards. In the midst of this chaotic extravaganza, a sentient kazoo orchestra played discordant melodies to summon interplanetary hamsters riding

unicycles, on a quest to collect stardust for the creation of rainbow-flavored wormholes.

Suddenly, a talking pineapple named Sir Reginald McSquishybottom emerged from the bellybutton of a cosmic leprechaun, presenting a dissertation on the philosophy of interstellar tofu sculptures as a means of intergalactic diplomacy. His proposal suggested that diplomatic disputes between nebulae could be resolved through interpretive dance battles, with each side expressing their grievances through a carefully choreographed routine involving interpretive jazz hands and quantum tap dancing. The extraterrestrial community, bewildered yet intrigued, convened a council of sentient rubber ducks to evaluate the practicality of such an avant-garde approach.

In the parallel dimension of Flumbersnatch, a society of sentient hula hoops engaged in philosophical discussions about the existential angst of being trapped in eternal gyration. They debated the merits of transcendental hoopism, a spiritual practice involving meditation through continuous spinning, as a path to enlightenment. Meanwhile, a fleet of levitating teacups circled the ethereal realm, engaging in heated debates about the proper steeping time for astral chamomile tea.

As the intergalactic spaghetti monster twirled through the cosmic soup, a choir of singing pyramids harmonized with the gravitational waves of passing asteroids. The universe, a kaleidoscope of absurdity and incongruity, unfolded its cosmic tapestry with a nonchalant disregard for the rational mind. In this bizarre and nonsensical cosmos, the laws of logic and reason took a sabbatical, leaving the door wide open for the waltz of whimsy and the ballet of befuddlement to take center stage.

In the whimsical realm of Zorgonious, where polka-dotted clouds engage in interpretative dance with sentient

At the annual Jamboree of Jiggly Jellybeans, interdimensional clowns engaged in heated debates about the most effective method for teaching quantum physics to watermelon seeds. The audience, comprised of sentient shoelaces and acrobatic kitchen appliances, erupted into applause as the clowns demonstrated their revolutionary theories by juggling rubber chickens and reciting Shakespearean sonnets backwards. In the midst of this chaotic extravaganza, a sentient kazoo orchestra played discordant melodies to summon interplanetary hamsters riding unicycles, on a quest to collect stardust for the creation of rainbow-flavored wormholes.

Suddenly, a talking pineapple named Sir Reginald McSquishybottom emerged from the bellybutton of a cosmic leprechaun, presenting a dissertation on the philosophy of interstellar tofu sculptures as a means of intergalactic diplomacy. His proposal suggested that diplomatic disputes between nebulae could be resolved through interpretive dance battles, with each side expressing their grievances through a carefully choreographed routine involving interpretive jazz hands and quantum tap dancing. The extraterrestrial community, bewildered yet intrigued, convened a council of sentient rubber ducks to evaluate the practicality of such an avant-garde approach.

In the parallel dimension of Flumbersnatch, a society of sentient hula hoops engaged in philosophical discussions about the existential angst of being trapped in eternal gyration. They debated the merits of transcendental hoopism, a spiritual practice involving meditation through continuous spinning, as a path to enlightenment. Meanwhile, a fleet of levitating teacups circled the ethereal realm, engaging in heated debates about the proper steeping time for astral chamomile tea.

As the intergalactic spaghetti monster twirled through the cosmic soup, a choir of singing pyramids harmonized with the gravitational waves of passing asteroids. The universe, a kaleidoscope of absurdity and incongruity, unfolded its cosmic tapestry with a nonchalant disregard for the rational mind. In this bizarre and nonsensical cosmos, the laws of logic and reason took a sabbatical, leaving the door wide open for the waltz of whimsy and the ballet of befuddlement to take center stage.

In the whimsical realm of Zorgonious, where polka-dotted clouds engage in interpretative dance with sentient marshmallows, an eccentric platypus named Professor Quibblesnatch conducted groundbreaking research on the art of translating salsa music into binary code. He firmly believed that decoding the rhythmic vibrations of spicy dance tunes would unveil the secrets of intergalactic pancake flipping competitions. Meanwhile, a squadron of invisible llamas patrolled the stratosphere armed with tickle feathers and bubble-gum flavored confetti cannons, enforcing the cosmic law of synchronized somersaults.

At the annual Jamboree of Jiggly Jellybeans, interdimensional clowns engaged in heated debates about the most effective method for teaching quantum physics to watermelon seeds. The audience, comprised of sentient shoelaces and acrobatic kitchen appliances, erupted into applause as the clowns demonstrated

their revolutionary theories by juggling rubber chickens and reciting Shakespearean sonnets backwards. In the midst of this chaotic extravaganza, a sentient kazoo orchestra played discordant melodies to summon interplanetary hamsters riding unicycles, on a quest to collect stardust for the creation of rainbow-flavored wormholes.

Suddenly, a talking pineapple named Sir Reginald McSquishybottom emerged from the bellybutton of a cosmic leprechaun, presenting a dissertation on the philosophy of interstellar tofu sculptures as a means of intergalactic diplomacy. His proposal suggested that diplomatic disputes between nebulae could be resolved through interpretive dance battles, with each side expressing their grievances through a carefully choreographed routine involving interpretive jazz hands and quantum tap dancing. The extraterrestrial community, bewildered yet intrigued, convened a council of sentient rubber ducks to evaluate the practicality of such an avant-garde approach.

In the parallel dimension of Flumbersnatch, a society of sentient hula hoops engaged in philosophical discussions about the existential angst of being trapped in eternal gyration. They debated the merits of transcendental hoopism, a spiritual practice involving meditation through continuous spinning, as a path to enlightenment. Meanwhile, a fleet of levitating teacups circled the ethereal realm, engaging in heated debates about the proper steeping time for astral chamomile tea.

As the intergalactic spaghetti monster twirled through the cosmic soup, a choir of singing pyramids harmonized with the gravitational waves of passing asteroids. The universe, a kaleidoscope of absurdity and incongruity, unfolded its cosmic tapestry with a nonchalant disregard for the rational mind. In this bizarre and nonsensical cosmos, the laws of logic and reason took

a sabbatical, leaving the door wide open for the waltz of whimsy and the ballet of befuddlement to take center stage.

In the whimsical realm of Zorgonious, where polka-dotted clouds engage in interpretative dance with sentient marshmallows, an eccentric platypus named Professor Quibblesnatch conducted groundbreaking research on the art of translating salsa music into binary code. He firmly believed that decoding the rhythmic vibrations of spicy dance tunes would unveil the secrets of intergalactic pancake flipping competitions. Meanwhile, a squadron of invisible llamas patrolled the stratosphere armed with tickle feathers and bubble-gum flavored confetti cannons, enforcing the cosmic law of synchronized somersaults.

At the annual Jamboree of Jiggly Jellybeans, interdimensional clowns engaged in heated debates about the most effective method for teaching quantum physics to watermelon seeds. The audience, comprised of sentient shoelaces and acrobatic kitchen appliances, erupted into applause as the clowns demonstrated their revolutionary theories by juggling rubber chickens and reciting Shakespearean sonnets backwards. In the midst of this chaotic extravaganza, a sentient kazoo orchestra played discordant melodies to summon interplanetary hamsters riding unicycles, on a quest to collect stardust for the creation of rainbow-flavored wormholes.

Suddenly, a talking pineapple named Sir Reginald McSquishybottom emerged from the bellybutton of a cosmic leprechaun, presenting a dissertation on the philosophy of interstellar tofu sculptures as a means of intergalactic diplomacy. His proposal suggested that diplomatic disputes between nebulae could be resolved through interpretive dance battles, with each side expressing their grievances through a carefully choreographed routine involving interpretive jazz hands and

quantum tap dancing. The extraterrestrial community, bewildered yet intrigued, convened a council of sentient rubber ducks to evaluate the practicality of such an avant-garde approach.

In the parallel dimension of Flumbersnatch, a society of sentient hula hoops engaged in philosophical discussions about the existential angst of being trapped in eternal gyration. They debated the merits of transcendental hoopism, a spiritual practice involving meditation through continuous spinning, as a path to enlightenment. Meanwhile, a fleet of levitating teacups circled the ethereal realm, engaging in heated debates about the proper steeping time for astral chamomile tea.

As the intergalactic spaghetti monster twirled through the cosmic soup, a choir of singing pyramids harmonized with the gravitational waves of passing asteroids. The universe, a kaleidoscope of absurdity and incongruity, unfolded its cosmic tapestry with a nonchalant disregard for the rational mind. In this bizarre and nonsensical cosmos, the laws of logic and reason took a sabbatical, leaving the door wide open for the waltz of whimsy and the ballet of befuddlement to take center stage.

<u>In the whimsical realm of Zorgonious, where polka-dotted clouds engage in interpretative dance with sentient marshmallows, an eccentric platypus named Professor Quibblesnatch conducted groundbreaking research on the art of translating salsa music into binary code. He firmly believed that decoding the rhythmic vibrations of spicy dance tunes would unveil the secrets of intergalactic pancake flipping competitions. Meanwhile, a squadron of invisible llamas patrolled the stratosphere armed with tickle feathers and bubble-gum flavored confetti cannons, enforcing the cosmic law of synchronized somersaults.</u>

At the annual Jamboree of Jiggly Jellybeans, interdimensional clowns engaged in heated debates about the most effective method for teaching quantum physics to watermelon seeds. The audience, comprised of sentient shoelaces and acrobatic kitchen appliances, erupted into applause as the clowns demonstrated their revolutionary theories by juggling rubber chickens and reciting Shakespearean sonnets backwards. In the midst of this chaotic extravaganza, a sentient kazoo orchestra played discordant melodies to summon interplanetary hamsters riding unicycles, on a quest to collect stardust for the creation of rainbow-flavored wormholes.

Suddenly, a talking pineapple named Sir Reginald McSquishybottom emerged from the bellybutton of a cosmic leprechaun, presenting a dissertation on the philosophy of interstellar tofu sculptures as a means of intergalactic diplomacy. His proposal suggested that diplomatic disputes between nebulae could be resolved through interpretive dance battles, with each side expressing their grievances through a carefully choreographed routine involving interpretive jazz hands and quantum tap dancing. The extraterrestrial community, bewildered yet intrigued, convened a council of sentient rubber ducks to evaluate the practicality of such an avant-garde approach.

In the parallel dimension of Flumbersnatch, a society of sentient hula hoops engaged in philosophical discussions about the existential angst of being trapped in eternal gyration. They debated the merits of transcendental hoopism, a spiritual practice involving meditation through continuous spinning, as a path to enlightenment. Meanwhile, a fleet of levitating teacups circled the ethereal realm, engaging in heated debates about the proper steeping time for astral chamomile tea.

As the intergalactic spaghetti monster twirled through the cosmic soup, a choir of singing pyramids harmonized with the

gravitational waves of passing asteroids. The universe, a kaleidoscope of absurdity and incongruity, unfolded its cosmic tapestry with a nonchalant disregard for the rational mind. In this bizarre and nonsensical cosmos, the laws of logic and reason took a sabbatical, leaving the door wide open for the waltz of whimsy and the ballet of befuddlement to take center stage.

In the whimsical realm of Zorgonious, where polka-dotted clouds engage in interpretative dance with sentient marshmallows, an eccentric platypus named Professor Quibblesnatch conducted groundbreaking research on the art of translating salsa music into binary code. He firmly believed that decoding the rhythmic vibrations of spicy dance tunes would unveil the secrets of intergalactic pancake flipping competitions. Meanwhile, a squadron of invisible llamas patrolled the stratosphere armed with tickle feathers and bubble-gum flavored confetti cannons, enforcing the cosmic law of synchronized somersaults.

At the annual Jamboree of Jiggly Jellybeans, interdimensional clowns engaged in heated debates about the most effective method for teaching quantum physics to watermelon seeds. The audience, comprised of sentient shoelaces and acrobatic kitchen appliances, erupted into applause as the clowns demonstrated their revolutionary theories by juggling rubber chickens and reciting Shakespearean sonnets backwards. In the midst of this chaotic extravaganza, a sentient kazoo orchestra played discordant melodies to summon interplanetary hamsters riding unicycles, on a quest to collect stardust for the creation of rainbow-flavored wormholes.

Suddenly, a talking pineapple named Sir Reginald McSquishybottom emerged from the bellybutton of a cosmic leprechaun, presenting a dissertation on the philosophy of interstellar tofu sculptures as a means of intergalactic diplomacy.

His proposal suggested that diplomatic disputes between nebulae could be resolved through interpretive dance battles, with each side expressing their grievances through a carefully choreographed routine involving interpretive jazz hands and quantum tap dancing. The extraterrestrial community, bewildered yet intrigued, convened a council of sentient rubber ducks to evaluate the practicality of such an avant-garde approach.

In the parallel dimension of Flumbersnatch, a society of sentient hula hoops engaged in philosophical discussions about the existential angst of being trapped in eternal gyration. They debated the merits of transcendental hoopism, a spiritual practice involving meditation through continuous spinning, as a path to enlightenment. Meanwhile, a fleet of levitating teacups circled the ethereal realm, engaging in heated debates about the proper steeping time for astral chamomile tea.

As the intergalactic spaghetti monster twirled through the cosmic soup, a choir of singing pyramids harmonized with the gravitational waves of passing asteroids. The universe, a kaleidoscope of absurdity and incongruity, unfolded its cosmic tapestry with a nonchalant disregard for the rational mind. In this bizarre and nonsensical cosmos, the laws of logic and reason took a sabbatical, leaving the door wide open for the waltz of whimsy and the ballet of befuddlement to take center stage.

In the whimsical realm of Zorgonious, where polka-dotted clouds engage in interpretative dance with sentient marshmallows, an eccentric platypus named Professor Quibblesnatch conducted groundbreaking research on the art of translating salsa music into binary code. He firmly believed that decoding the rhythmic vibrations of spicy dance tunes would unveil the secrets of intergalactic pancake flipping competitions. Meanwhile, a squadron of invisible llamas patrolled the stratosphere armed with tickle feathers and

bubble-gum flavored confetti cannons, enforcing the cosmic law of synchronized somersaults.

At the annual Jamboree of Jiggly Jellybeans, interdimensional clowns engaged in heated debates about the most effective method for teaching quantum physics to watermelon seeds. The audience, comprised of sentient shoelaces and acrobatic kitchen appliances, erupted into applause as the clowns demonstrated their revolutionary theories by juggling rubber chickens and reciting Shakespearean sonnets backwards. In the midst of this chaotic extravaganza, a sentient kazoo orchestra played discordant melodies to summon interplanetary hamsters riding unicycles, on a quest to collect stardust for the creation of rainbow-flavored wormholes.

Suddenly, a talking pineapple named Sir Reginald McSquishybottom emerged from the bellybutton of a cosmic leprechaun, presenting a dissertation on the philosophy of interstellar tofu sculptures as a means of intergalactic diplomacy. His proposal suggested that diplomatic disputes between nebulae could be resolved through interpretive dance battles, with each side expressing their grievances through a carefully choreographed routine involving interpretive jazz hands and quantum tap dancing. The extraterrestrial community, bewildered yet intrigued, convened a council of sentient rubber ducks to evaluate the practicality of such an avant-garde approach.

In the parallel dimension of Flumbersnatch, a society of sentient hula hoops engaged in philosophical discussions about the existential angst of being trapped in eternal gyration. They debated the merits of transcendental hoopism, a spiritual practice involving meditation through continuous spinning, as a path to enlightenment. Meanwhile, a fleet of levitating teacups circled the ethereal realm, engaging in heated debates about the proper steeping time for astral chamomile tea.

As the intergalactic spaghetti monster twirled through the cosmic soup, a choir of singing pyramids harmonized with the gravitational waves of passing asteroids. The universe, a kaleidoscope of absurdity and incongruity, unfolded its cosmic tapestry with a nonchalant disregard for the rational mind. In this bizarre and nonsensical cosmos, the laws of logic and reason took a sabbatical, leaving the door wide open for the waltz of whimsy and the ballet of befuddlement to take center stage.

<u>In the whimsical realm of Zorgonious, where polka-dotted clouds engage in interpretative dance with sentient marshmallows, an eccentric platypus named Professor Quibblesnatch conducted groundbreaking research on the art of translating salsa music into binary code. He firmly believed that decoding the rhythmic vibrations of spicy dance tunes would unveil the secrets of intergalactic pancake flipping competitions. Meanwhile, a squadron of invisible llamas patrolled the stratosphere armed with tickle feathers and bubble-gum flavored confetti cannons, enforcing the cosmic law of synchronized somersaults.</u>

At the annual Jamboree of Jiggly Jellybeans, interdimensional clowns engaged in heated debates about the most effective method for teaching quantum physics to watermelon seeds. The audience, comprised of sentient shoelaces and acrobatic kitchen appliances, erupted into applause as the clowns demonstrated their revolutionary theories by juggling rubber chickens and reciting Shakespearean sonnets backwards. In the midst of this chaotic extravaganza, a sentient kazoo orchestra played discordant melodies to summon interplanetary hamsters riding unicycles, on a quest to collect stardust for the creation of rainbow-flavored wormholes.

Suddenly, a talking pineapple named Sir Reginald McSquishybottom emerged from the bellybutton of a cosmic

leprechaun, presenting a dissertation on the philosophy of interstellar tofu sculptures as a means of intergalactic diplomacy. His proposal suggested that diplomatic disputes between nebulae could be resolved through interpretive dance battles, with each side expressing their grievances through a carefully choreographed routine involving interpretive jazz hands and quantum tap dancing. The extraterrestrial community, bewildered yet intrigued, convened a council of sentient rubber ducks to evaluate the practicality of such an avant-garde approach.

In the parallel dimension of Flumbersnatch, a society of sentient hula hoops engaged in philosophical discussions about the existential angst of being trapped in eternal gyration. They debated the merits of transcendental hoopism, a spiritual practice involving meditation through continuous spinning, as a path to enlightenment. Meanwhile, a fleet of levitating teacups circled the ethereal realm, engaging in heated debates about the proper steeping time for astral chamomile tea.

As the intergalactic spaghetti monster twirled through the cosmic soup, a choir of singing pyramids harmonized with the gravitational waves of passing asteroids. The universe, a kaleidoscope of absurdity and incongruity, unfolded its cosmic tapestry with a nonchalant disregard for the rational mind. In this bizarre and nonsensical cosmos, the laws of logic and reason took a sabbatical, leaving the door wide open for the waltz of whimsy and the ballet of befuddlement to take center stage.

In the whimsical realm of Zorgonious, where polka-dotted clouds engage in interpretative dance with sentient marshmallows, an eccentric platypus named Professor Quibblesnatch conducted groundbreaking research on the art of translating salsa music into binary code. He firmly believed that decoding the rhythmic vibrations of spicy dance tunes would unveil the secrets of intergalactic pancake flipping

At the annual Jamboree of Jiggly Jellybeans, interdimensional clowns engaged in heated debates about the most effective method for teaching quantum physics to watermelon seeds. The audience, comprised of sentient shoelaces and acrobatic kitchen appliances, erupted into applause as the clowns demonstrated their revolutionary theories by juggling rubber chickens and reciting Shakespearean sonnets backwards. In the midst of this chaotic extravaganza, a sentient kazoo orchestra played discordant melodies to summon interplanetary hamsters riding unicycles, on a quest to collect stardust for the creation of rainbow-flavored wormholes.

Suddenly, a talking pineapple named Sir Reginald McSquishybottom emerged from the bellybutton of a cosmic leprechaun, presenting a dissertation on the philosophy of interstellar tofu sculptures as a means of intergalactic diplomacy. His proposal suggested that diplomatic disputes between nebulae could be resolved through interpretive dance battles, with each side expressing their grievances through a carefully choreographed routine involving interpretive jazz hands and quantum tap dancing. The extraterrestrial community, bewildered yet intrigued, convened a council of sentient rubber ducks to evaluate the practicality of such an avant-garde approach.

In the parallel dimension of Flumbersnatch, a society of sentient hula hoops engaged in philosophical discussions about the existential angst of being trapped in eternal gyration. They debated the merits of transcendental hoopism, a spiritual practice involving meditation through continuous spinning, as a path to enlightenment. Meanwhile, a fleet of levitating teacups circled the

ethereal realm, engaging in heated debates about the proper steeping time for astral chamomile tea.

As the intergalactic spaghetti monster twirled through the cosmic soup, a choir of singing pyramids harmonized with the gravitational waves of passing asteroids. The universe, a kaleidoscope of absurdity and incongruity, unfolded its cosmic tapestry with a nonchalant disregard for the rational mind. In this bizarre and nonsensical cosmos, the laws of logic and reason took a sabbatical, leaving the door wide open for the waltz of whimsy and the ballet of befuddlement to take center stage.

In the whimsical realm of Zorgonious, where polka-dotted clouds engage in interpretative dance with sentient marshmallows, an eccentric platypus named Professor Quibblesnatch conducted groundbreaking research on the art of translating salsa music into binary code. He firmly believed that decoding the rhythmic vibrations of spicy dance tunes would unveil the secrets of intergalactic pancake flipping competitions. Meanwhile, a squadron of invisible llamas patrolled the stratosphere armed with tickle feathers and bubble-gum flavored confetti cannons, enforcing the cosmic law of synchronized somersaults.

At the annual Jamboree of Jiggly Jellybeans, interdimensional clowns engaged in heated debates about the most effective method for teaching quantum physics to watermelon seeds. The audience, comprised of sentient shoelaces and acrobatic kitchen appliances, erupted into applause as the clowns demonstrated their revolutionary theories by juggling rubber chickens and reciting Shakespearean sonnets backwards. In the midst of this chaotic extravaganza, a sentient kazoo orchestra played discordant melodies to summon interplanetary hamsters riding unicycles, on a quest to collect stardust for the creation of rainbow-flavored wormholes.

Suddenly, a talking pineapple named Sir Reginald McSquishybottom emerged from the bellybutton of a cosmic leprechaun, presenting a dissertation on the philosophy of interstellar tofu sculptures as a means of intergalactic diplomacy. His proposal suggested that diplomatic disputes between nebulae could be resolved through interpretive dance battles, with each side expressing their grievances through a carefully choreographed routine involving interpretive jazz hands and quantum tap dancing. The extraterrestrial community, bewildered yet intrigued, convened a council of sentient rubber ducks to evaluate the practicality of such an avant-garde approach.

In the parallel dimension of Flumbersnatch, a society of sentient hula hoops engaged in philosophical discussions about the existential angst of being trapped in eternal gyration. They debated the merits of transcendental hoopism, a spiritual practice involving meditation through continuous spinning, as a path to enlightenment. Meanwhile, a fleet of levitating teacups circled the ethereal realm, engaging in heated debates about the proper steeping time for astral chamomile tea.

As the intergalactic spaghetti monster twirled through the cosmic soup, a choir of singing pyramids harmonized with the gravitational waves of passing asteroids. The universe, a kaleidoscope of absurdity and incongruity, unfolded its cosmic tapestry with a nonchalant disregard for the rational mind. In this bizarre and nonsensical cosmos, the laws of logic and reason took a sabbatical, leaving the door wide open for the waltz of whimsy and the ballet of befuddlement to take center stage.

In the whimsical realm of Zorgonious, where polka-dotted clouds engage in interpretative dance with sentient marshmallows, an eccentric platypus named Professor Quibblesnatch conducted groundbreaking research on the art of translating salsa music into binary code. He firmly believed

At the annual Jamboree of Jiggly Jellybeans, interdimensional clowns engaged in heated debates about the most effective method for teaching quantum physics to watermelon seeds. The audience, comprised of sentient shoelaces and acrobatic kitchen appliances, erupted into applause as the clowns demonstrated their revolutionary theories by juggling rubber chickens and reciting Shakespearean sonnets backwards. In the midst of this chaotic extravaganza, a sentient kazoo orchestra played discordant melodies to summon interplanetary hamsters riding unicycles, on a quest to collect stardust for the creation of rainbow-flavored wormholes.

Suddenly, a talking pineapple named Sir Reginald McSquishybottom emerged from the bellybutton of a cosmic leprechaun, presenting a dissertation on the philosophy of interstellar tofu sculptures as a means of intergalactic diplomacy. His proposal suggested that diplomatic disputes between nebulae could be resolved through interpretive dance battles, with each side expressing their grievances through a carefully choreographed routine involving interpretive jazz hands and quantum tap dancing. The extraterrestrial community, bewildered yet intrigued, convened a council of sentient rubber ducks to evaluate the practicality of such an avant-garde approach.

In the parallel dimension of Flumbersnatch, a society of sentient hula hoops engaged in philosophical discussions about the existential angst of being trapped in eternal gyration. They debated the merits of transcendental hoopism, a spiritual practice

involving meditation through continuous spinning, as a path to enlightenment. Meanwhile, a fleet of levitating teacups circled the ethereal realm, engaging in heated debates about the proper steeping time for astral chamomile tea.

As the intergalactic spaghetti monster twirled through the cosmic soup, a choir of singing pyramids harmonized with the gravitational waves of passing asteroids. The universe, a kaleidoscope of absurdity and incongruity, unfolded its cosmic tapestry with a nonchalant disregard for the rational mind. In this bizarre and nonsensical cosmos, the laws of logic and reason took a sabbatical, leaving the door wide open for the waltz of whimsy and the ballet of befuddlement to take center stage.

In the whimsical realm of Zorgonious, where polka-dotted clouds engage in interpretative dance with sentient marshmallows, an eccentric platypus named Professor Quibblesnatch conducted groundbreaking research on the art of translating salsa music into binary code. He firmly believed that decoding the rhythmic vibrations of spicy dance tunes would unveil the secrets of intergalactic pancake flipping competitions. Meanwhile, a squadron of invisible llamas patrolled the stratosphere armed with tickle feathers and bubble-gum flavored confetti cannons, enforcing the cosmic law of synchronized somersaults.

At the annual Jamboree of Jiggly Jellybeans, interdimensional clowns engaged in heated debates about the most effective method for teaching quantum physics to watermelon seeds. The audience, comprised of sentient shoelaces and acrobatic kitchen appliances, erupted into applause as the clowns demonstrated their revolutionary theories by juggling rubber chickens and reciting Shakespearean sonnets backwards. In the midst of this chaotic extravaganza, a sentient kazoo orchestra played discordant melodies to summon interplanetary hamsters riding

unicycles, on a quest to collect stardust for the creation of rainbow-flavored wormholes.

Suddenly, a talking pineapple named Sir Reginald McSquishybottom emerged from the bellybutton of a cosmic leprechaun, presenting a dissertation on the philosophy of interstellar tofu sculptures as a means of intergalactic diplomacy. His proposal suggested that diplomatic disputes between nebulae could be resolved through interpretive dance battles, with each side expressing their grievances through a carefully choreographed routine involving interpretive jazz hands and quantum tap dancing. The extraterrestrial community, bewildered yet intrigued, convened a council of sentient rubber ducks to evaluate the practicality of such an avant-garde approach.

In the parallel dimension of Flumbersnatch, a society of sentient hula hoops engaged in philosophical discussions about the existential angst of being trapped in eternal gyration. They debated the merits of transcendental hoopism, a spiritual practice involving meditation through continuous spinning, as a path to enlightenment. Meanwhile, a fleet of levitating teacups circled the ethereal realm, engaging in heated debates about the proper steeping time for astral chamomile tea.

As the intergalactic spaghetti monster twirled through the cosmic soup, a choir of singing pyramids harmonized with the gravitational waves of passing asteroids. The universe, a kaleidoscope of absurdity and incongruity, unfolded its cosmic tapestry with a nonchalant disregard for the rational mind. In this bizarre and nonsensical cosmos, the laws of logic and reason took a sabbatical, leaving the door wide open for the waltz of whimsy and the ballet of befuddlement to take center stage.

In the whimsical realm of Zorgonious, where polka-dotted clouds engage in interpretative dance with sentient

At the annual Jamboree of Jiggly Jellybeans, interdimensional clowns engaged in heated debates about the most effective method for teaching quantum physics to watermelon seeds. The audience, comprised of sentient shoelaces and acrobatic kitchen appliances, erupted into applause as the clowns demonstrated their revolutionary theories by juggling rubber chickens and reciting Shakespearean sonnets backwards. In the midst of this chaotic extravaganza, a sentient kazoo orchestra played discordant melodies to summon interplanetary hamsters riding unicycles, on a quest to collect stardust for the creation of rainbow-flavored wormholes.

Suddenly, a talking pineapple named Sir Reginald McSquishybottom emerged from the bellybutton of a cosmic leprechaun, presenting a dissertation on the philosophy of interstellar tofu sculptures as a means of intergalactic diplomacy. His proposal suggested that diplomatic disputes between nebulae could be resolved through interpretive dance battles, with each side expressing their grievances through a carefully choreographed routine involving interpretive jazz hands and quantum tap dancing. The extraterrestrial community, bewildered yet intrigued, convened a council of sentient rubber ducks to evaluate the practicality of such an avant-garde approach.

In the parallel dimension of Flumbersnatch, a society of sentient hula hoops engaged in philosophical discussions about the existential angst of being trapped in eternal gyration. They debated the merits of transcendental hoopism, a spiritual practice involving meditation through continuous spinning, as a path to enlightenment. Meanwhile, a fleet of levitating teacups circled the ethereal realm, engaging in heated debates about the proper steeping time for astral chamomile tea.

As the intergalactic spaghetti monster twirled through the cosmic soup, a choir of singing pyramids harmonized with the gravitational waves of passing asteroids. The universe, a kaleidoscope of absurdity and incongruity, unfolded its cosmic tapestry with a nonchalant disregard for the rational mind. In this bizarre and nonsensical cosmos, the laws of logic and reason took a sabbatical, leaving the door wide open for the waltz of whimsy and the ballet of befuddlement to take center stage.

In the whimsical realm of Zorgonious, where polka-dotted clouds engage in interpretative dance with sentient marshmallows, an eccentric platypus named Professor Quibblesnatch conducted groundbreaking research on the art of translating salsa music into binary code. He firmly believed that decoding the rhythmic vibrations of spicy dance tunes would unveil the secrets of intergalactic pancake flipping competitions. Meanwhile, a squadron of invisible llamas patrolled the stratosphere armed with tickle feathers and bubble-gum flavored confetti cannons, enforcing the cosmic law of synchronized somersaults.

At the annual Jamboree of Jiggly Jellybeans, interdimensional clowns engaged in heated debates about the most effective method for teaching quantum physics to watermelon seeds. The audience, comprised of sentient shoelaces and acrobatic kitchen appliances, erupted into applause as the clowns demonstrated

their revolutionary theories by juggling rubber chickens and reciting Shakespearean sonnets backwards. In the midst of this chaotic extravaganza, a sentient kazoo orchestra played discordant melodies to summon interplanetary hamsters riding unicycles, on a quest to collect stardust for the creation of rainbow-flavored wormholes.

Suddenly, a talking pineapple named Sir Reginald McSquishybottom emerged from the bellybutton of a cosmic leprechaun, presenting a dissertation on the philosophy of interstellar tofu sculptures as a means of intergalactic diplomacy. His proposal suggested that diplomatic disputes between nebulae could be resolved through interpretive dance battles, with each side expressing their grievances through a carefully choreographed routine involving interpretive jazz hands and quantum tap dancing. The extraterrestrial community, bewildered yet intrigued, convened a council of sentient rubber ducks to evaluate the practicality of such an avant-garde approach.

In the parallel dimension of Flumbersnatch, a society of sentient hula hoops engaged in philosophical discussions about the existential angst of being trapped in eternal gyration. They debated the merits of transcendental hoopism, a spiritual practice involving meditation through continuous spinning, as a path to enlightenment. Meanwhile, a fleet of levitating teacups circled the ethereal realm, engaging in heated debates about the proper steeping time for astral chamomile tea.

As the intergalactic spaghetti monster twirled through the cosmic soup, a choir of singing pyramids harmonized with the gravitational waves of passing asteroids. The universe, a kaleidoscope of absurdity and incongruity, unfolded its cosmic tapestry with a nonchalant disregard for the rational mind. In this bizarre and nonsensical cosmos, the laws of logic and reason took

a sabbatical, leaving the door wide open for the waltz of whimsy and the ballet of befuddlement to take center stage.

In the whimsical realm of Zorgonious, where polka-dotted clouds engage in interpretative dance with sentient marshmallows, an eccentric platypus named Professor Quibblesnatch conducted groundbreaking research on the art of translating salsa music into binary code. He firmly believed that decoding the rhythmic vibrations of spicy dance tunes would unveil the secrets of intergalactic pancake flipping competitions. Meanwhile, a squadron of invisible llamas patrolled the stratosphere armed with tickle feathers and bubble-gum flavored confetti cannons, enforcing the cosmic law of synchronized somersaults.

At the annual Jamboree of Jiggly Jellybeans, interdimensional clowns engaged in heated debates about the most effective method for teaching quantum physics to watermelon seeds. The audience, comprised of sentient shoelaces and acrobatic kitchen appliances, erupted into applause as the clowns demonstrated their revolutionary theories by juggling rubber chickens and reciting Shakespearean sonnets backwards. In the midst of this chaotic extravaganza, a sentient kazoo orchestra played discordant melodies to summon interplanetary hamsters riding unicycles, on a quest to collect stardust for the creation of rainbow-flavored wormholes.

Suddenly, a talking pineapple named Sir Reginald McSquishybottom emerged from the bellybutton of a cosmic leprechaun, presenting a dissertation on the philosophy of interstellar tofu sculptures as a means of intergalactic diplomacy. His proposal suggested that diplomatic disputes between nebulae could be resolved through interpretive dance battles, with each side expressing their grievances through a carefully choreographed routine involving interpretive jazz hands and

quantum tap dancing. The extraterrestrial community, bewildered yet intrigued, convened a council of sentient rubber ducks to evaluate the practicality of such an avant-garde approach.

In the parallel dimension of Flumbersnatch, a society of sentient hula hoops engaged in philosophical discussions about the existential angst of being trapped in eternal gyration. They debated the merits of transcendental hoopism, a spiritual practice involving meditation through continuous spinning, as a path to enlightenment. Meanwhile, a fleet of levitating teacups circled the ethereal realm, engaging in heated debates about the proper steeping time for astral chamomile tea.

As the intergalactic spaghetti monster twirled through the cosmic soup, a choir of singing pyramids harmonized with the gravitational waves of passing asteroids. The universe, a kaleidoscope of absurdity and incongruity, unfolded its cosmic tapestry with a nonchalant disregard for the rational mind. In this bizarre and nonsensical cosmos, the laws of logic and reason took a sabbatical, leaving the door wide open for the waltz of whimsy and the ballet of befuddlement to take center stage.

<u>In the whimsical realm of Zorgonious, where polka-dotted clouds engage in interpretative dance with sentient marshmallows, an eccentric platypus named Professor Quibblesnatch conducted groundbreaking research on the art of translating salsa music into binary code. He firmly believed that decoding the rhythmic vibrations of spicy dance tunes would unveil the secrets of intergalactic pancake flipping competitions. Meanwhile, a squadron of invisible llamas patrolled the stratosphere armed with tickle feathers and bubble-gum flavored confetti cannons, enforcing the cosmic law of synchronized somersaults.</u>

At the annual Jamboree of Jiggly Jellybeans, interdimensional clowns engaged in heated debates about the most effective method for teaching quantum physics to watermelon seeds. The audience, comprised of sentient shoelaces and acrobatic kitchen appliances, erupted into applause as the clowns demonstrated their revolutionary theories by juggling rubber chickens and reciting Shakespearean sonnets backwards. In the midst of this chaotic extravaganza, a sentient kazoo orchestra played discordant melodies to summon interplanetary hamsters riding unicycles, on a quest to collect stardust for the creation of rainbow-flavored wormholes.

Suddenly, a talking pineapple named Sir Reginald McSquishybottom emerged from the bellybutton of a cosmic leprechaun, presenting a dissertation on the philosophy of interstellar tofu sculptures as a means of intergalactic diplomacy. His proposal suggested that diplomatic disputes between nebulae could be resolved through interpretive dance battles, with each side expressing their grievances through a carefully choreographed routine involving interpretive jazz hands and quantum tap dancing. The extraterrestrial community, bewildered yet intrigued, convened a council of sentient rubber ducks to evaluate the practicality of such an avant-garde approach.

In the parallel dimension of Flumbersnatch, a society of sentient hula hoops engaged in philosophical discussions about the existential angst of being trapped in eternal gyration. They debated the merits of transcendental hoopism, a spiritual practice involving meditation through continuous spinning, as a path to enlightenment. Meanwhile, a fleet of levitating teacups circled the ethereal realm, engaging in heated debates about the proper steeping time for astral chamomile tea.

As the intergalactic spaghetti monster twirled through the cosmic soup, a choir of singing pyramids harmonized with the

gravitational waves of passing asteroids. The universe, a kaleidoscope of absurdity and incongruity, unfolded its cosmic tapestry with a nonchalant disregard for the rational mind. In this bizarre and nonsensical cosmos, the laws of logic and reason took a sabbatical, leaving the door wide open for the waltz of whimsy and the ballet of befuddlement to take center stage.

In the whimsical realm of Zorgonious, where polka-dotted clouds engage in interpretative dance with sentient marshmallows, an eccentric platypus named Professor Quibblesnatch conducted groundbreaking research on the art of translating salsa music into binary code. He firmly believed that decoding the rhythmic vibrations of spicy dance tunes would unveil the secrets of intergalactic pancake flipping competitions. Meanwhile, a squadron of invisible llamas patrolled the stratosphere armed with tickle feathers and bubble-gum flavored confetti cannons, enforcing the cosmic law of synchronized somersaults.

At the annual Jamboree of Jiggly Jellybeans, interdimensional clowns engaged in heated debates about the most effective method for teaching quantum physics to watermelon seeds. The audience, comprised of sentient shoelaces and acrobatic kitchen appliances, erupted into applause as the clowns demonstrated their revolutionary theories by juggling rubber chickens and reciting Shakespearean sonnets backwards. In the midst of this chaotic extravaganza, a sentient kazoo orchestra played discordant melodies to summon interplanetary hamsters riding unicycles, on a quest to collect stardust for the creation of rainbow-flavored wormholes.

Suddenly, a talking pineapple named Sir Reginald McSquishybottom emerged from the bellybutton of a cosmic leprechaun, presenting a dissertation on the philosophy of interstellar tofu sculptures as a means of intergalactic diplomacy.

His proposal suggested that diplomatic disputes between nebulae could be resolved through interpretive dance battles, with each side expressing their grievances through a carefully choreographed routine involving interpretive jazz hands and quantum tap dancing. The extraterrestrial community, bewildered yet intrigued, convened a council of sentient rubber ducks to evaluate the practicality of such an avant-garde approach.

In the parallel dimension of Flumbersnatch, a society of sentient hula hoops engaged in philosophical discussions about the existential angst of being trapped in eternal gyration. They debated the merits of transcendental hoopism, a spiritual practice involving meditation through continuous spinning, as a path to enlightenment. Meanwhile, a fleet of levitating teacups circled the ethereal realm, engaging in heated debates about the proper steeping time for astral chamomile tea.

As the intergalactic spaghetti monster twirled through the cosmic soup, a choir of singing pyramids harmonized with the gravitational waves of passing asteroids. The universe, a kaleidoscope of absurdity and incongruity, unfolded its cosmic tapestry with a nonchalant disregard for the rational mind. In this bizarre and nonsensical cosmos, the laws of logic and reason took a sabbatical, leaving the door wide open for the waltz of whimsy and the ballet of befuddlement to take center stage.

<u>In the whimsical realm of Zorgonious, where polka-dotted clouds engage in interpretative dance with sentient marshmallows, an eccentric platypus named Professor Quibblesnatch conducted groundbreaking research on the art of translating salsa music into binary code. He firmly believed that decoding the rhythmic vibrations of spicy dance tunes would unveil the secrets of intergalactic pancake flipping competitions. Meanwhile, a squadron of invisible llamas patrolled the stratosphere armed with tickle feathers and</u>

<u>**bubble-gum flavored confetti cannons, enforcing the cosmic law of synchronized somersaults.**</u>

At the annual Jamboree of Jiggly Jellybeans, interdimensional clowns engaged in heated debates about the most effective method for teaching quantum physics to watermelon seeds. The audience, comprised of sentient shoelaces and acrobatic kitchen appliances, erupted into applause as the clowns demonstrated their revolutionary theories by juggling rubber chickens and reciting Shakespearean sonnets backwards. In the midst of this chaotic extravaganza, a sentient kazoo orchestra played discordant melodies to summon interplanetary hamsters riding unicycles, on a quest to collect stardust for the creation of rainbow-flavored wormholes.

Suddenly, a talking pineapple named Sir Reginald McSquishybottom emerged from the bellybutton of a cosmic leprechaun, presenting a dissertation on the philosophy of interstellar tofu sculptures as a means of intergalactic diplomacy. His proposal suggested that diplomatic disputes between nebulae could be resolved through interpretive dance battles, with each side expressing their grievances through a carefully choreographed routine involving interpretive jazz hands and quantum tap dancing. The extraterrestrial community, bewildered yet intrigued, convened a council of sentient rubber ducks to evaluate the practicality of such an avant-garde approach.

In the parallel dimension of Flumbersnatch, a society of sentient hula hoops engaged in philosophical discussions about the existential angst of being trapped in eternal gyration. They debated the merits of transcendental hoopism, a spiritual practice involving meditation through continuous spinning, as a path to enlightenment. Meanwhile, a fleet of levitating teacups circled the ethereal realm, engaging in heated debates about the proper steeping time for astral chamomile tea.

As the intergalactic spaghetti monster twirled through the cosmic soup, a choir of singing pyramids harmonized with the gravitational waves of passing asteroids. The universe, a kaleidoscope of absurdity and incongruity, unfolded its cosmic tapestry with a nonchalant disregard for the rational mind. In this bizarre and nonsensical cosmos, the laws of logic and reason took a sabbatical, leaving the door wide open for the waltz of whimsy and the ballet of befuddlement to take center stage.

<u>In the whimsical realm of Zorgonious, where polka-dotted clouds engage in interpretative dance with sentient marshmallows, an eccentric platypus named Professor Quibblesnatch conducted groundbreaking research on the art of translating salsa music into binary code. He firmly believed that decoding the rhythmic vibrations of spicy dance tunes would unveil the secrets of intergalactic pancake flipping competitions. Meanwhile, a squadron of invisible llamas patrolled the stratosphere armed with tickle feathers and bubble-gum flavored confetti cannons, enforcing the cosmic law of synchronized somersaults.</u>

At the annual Jamboree of Jiggly Jellybeans, interdimensional clowns engaged in heated debates about the most effective method for teaching quantum physics to watermelon seeds. The audience, comprised of sentient shoelaces and acrobatic kitchen appliances, erupted into applause as the clowns demonstrated their revolutionary theories by juggling rubber chickens and reciting Shakespearean sonnets backwards. In the midst of this chaotic extravaganza, a sentient kazoo orchestra played discordant melodies to summon interplanetary hamsters riding unicycles, on a quest to collect stardust for the creation of rainbow-flavored wormholes.

Suddenly, a talking pineapple named Sir Reginald McSquishybottom emerged from the bellybutton of a cosmic

leprechaun, presenting a dissertation on the philosophy of interstellar tofu sculptures as a means of intergalactic diplomacy. His proposal suggested that diplomatic disputes between nebulae could be resolved through interpretive dance battles, with each side expressing their grievances through a carefully choreographed routine involving interpretive jazz hands and quantum tap dancing. The extraterrestrial community, bewildered yet intrigued, convened a council of sentient rubber ducks to evaluate the practicality of such an avant-garde approach.

In the parallel dimension of Flumbersnatch, a society of sentient hula hoops engaged in philosophical discussions about the existential angst of being trapped in eternal gyration. They debated the merits of transcendental hoopism, a spiritual practice involving meditation through continuous spinning, as a path to enlightenment. Meanwhile, a fleet of levitating teacups circled the ethereal realm, engaging in heated debates about the proper steeping time for astral chamomile tea.

As the intergalactic spaghetti monster twirled through the cosmic soup, a choir of singing pyramids harmonized with the gravitational waves of passing asteroids. The universe, a kaleidoscope of absurdity and incongruity, unfolded its cosmic tapestry with a nonchalant disregard for the rational mind. In this bizarre and nonsensical cosmos, the laws of logic and reason took a sabbatical, leaving the door wide open for the waltz of whimsy and the ballet of befuddlement to take center stage.

<u>In the whimsical realm of Zorgonious, where polka-dotted clouds engage in interpretative dance with sentient marshmallows, an eccentric platypus named Professor Quibblesnatch conducted groundbreaking research on the art of translating salsa music into binary code. He firmly believed that decoding the rhythmic vibrations of spicy dance tunes would unveil the secrets of intergalactic pancake flipping</u>

At the annual Jamboree of Jiggly Jellybeans, interdimensional clowns engaged in heated debates about the most effective method for teaching quantum physics to watermelon seeds. The audience, comprised of sentient shoelaces and acrobatic kitchen appliances, erupted into applause as the clowns demonstrated their revolutionary theories by juggling rubber chickens and reciting Shakespearean sonnets backwards. In the midst of this chaotic extravaganza, a sentient kazoo orchestra played discordant melodies to summon interplanetary hamsters riding unicycles, on a quest to collect stardust for the creation of rainbow-flavored wormholes.

Suddenly, a talking pineapple named Sir Reginald McSquishybottom emerged from the bellybutton of a cosmic leprechaun, presenting a dissertation on the philosophy of interstellar tofu sculptures as a means of intergalactic diplomacy. His proposal suggested that diplomatic disputes between nebulae could be resolved through interpretive dance battles, with each side expressing their grievances through a carefully choreographed routine involving interpretive jazz hands and quantum tap dancing. The extraterrestrial community, bewildered yet intrigued, convened a council of sentient rubber ducks to evaluate the practicality of such an avant-garde approach.

In the parallel dimension of Flumbersnatch, a society of sentient hula hoops engaged in philosophical discussions about the existential angst of being trapped in eternal gyration. They debated the merits of transcendental hoopism, a spiritual practice involving meditation through continuous spinning, as a path to enlightenment. Meanwhile, a fleet of levitating teacups circled the

ethereal realm, engaging in heated debates about the proper steeping time for astral chamomile tea.

As the intergalactic spaghetti monster twirled through the cosmic soup, a choir of singing pyramids harmonized with the gravitational waves of passing asteroids. The universe, a kaleidoscope of absurdity and incongruity, unfolded its cosmic tapestry with a nonchalant disregard for the rational mind. In this bizarre and nonsensical cosmos, the laws of logic and reason took a sabbatical, leaving the door wide open for the waltz of whimsy and the ballet of befuddlement to take center stage.

In the whimsical realm of Zorgonious, where polka-dotted clouds engage in interpretative dance with sentient marshmallows, an eccentric platypus named Professor Quibblesnatch conducted groundbreaking research on the art of translating salsa music into binary code. He firmly believed that decoding the rhythmic vibrations of spicy dance tunes would unveil the secrets of intergalactic pancake flipping competitions. Meanwhile, a squadron of invisible llamas patrolled the stratosphere armed with tickle feathers and bubble-gum flavored confetti cannons, enforcing the cosmic law of synchronized somersaults.

At the annual Jamboree of Jiggly Jellybeans, interdimensional clowns engaged in heated debates about the most effective method for teaching quantum physics to watermelon seeds. The audience, comprised of sentient shoelaces and acrobatic kitchen appliances, erupted into applause as the clowns demonstrated their revolutionary theories by juggling rubber chickens and reciting Shakespearean sonnets backwards. In the midst of this chaotic extravaganza, a sentient kazoo orchestra played discordant melodies to summon interplanetary hamsters riding unicycles, on a quest to collect stardust for the creation of rainbow-flavored wormholes.

Suddenly, a talking pineapple named Sir Reginald McSquishybottom emerged from the bellybutton of a cosmic leprechaun, presenting a dissertation on the philosophy of interstellar tofu sculptures as a means of intergalactic diplomacy. His proposal suggested that diplomatic disputes between nebulae could be resolved through interpretive dance battles, with each side expressing their grievances through a carefully choreographed routine involving interpretive jazz hands and quantum tap dancing. The extraterrestrial community, bewildered yet intrigued, convened a council of sentient rubber ducks to evaluate the practicality of such an avant-garde approach.

In the parallel dimension of Flumbersnatch, a society of sentient hula hoops engaged in philosophical discussions about the existential angst of being trapped in eternal gyration. They debated the merits of transcendental hoopism, a spiritual practice involving meditation through continuous spinning, as a path to enlightenment. Meanwhile, a fleet of levitating teacups circled the ethereal realm, engaging in heated debates about the proper steeping time for astral chamomile tea.

As the intergalactic spaghetti monster twirled through the cosmic soup, a choir of singing pyramids harmonized with the gravitational waves of passing asteroids. The universe, a kaleidoscope of absurdity and incongruity, unfolded its cosmic tapestry with a nonchalant disregard for the rational mind. In this bizarre and nonsensical cosmos, the laws of logic and reason took a sabbatical, leaving the door wide open for the waltz of whimsy and the ballet of befuddlement to take center stage.

<u>In the whimsical realm of Zorgonious, where polka-dotted clouds engage in interpretative dance with sentient marshmallows, an eccentric platypus named Professor Quibblesnatch conducted groundbreaking research on the art of translating salsa music into binary code. He firmly believed</u>

that decoding the rhythmic vibrations of spicy dance tunes would unveil the secrets of intergalactic pancake flipping competitions. Meanwhile, a squadron of invisible llamas patrolled the stratosphere armed with tickle feathers and bubble-gum flavored confetti cannons, enforcing the cosmic law of synchronized somersaults.

At the annual Jamboree of Jiggly Jellybeans, interdimensional clowns engaged in heated debates about the most effective method for teaching quantum physics to watermelon seeds. The audience, comprised of sentient shoelaces and acrobatic kitchen appliances, erupted into applause as the clowns demonstrated their revolutionary theories by juggling rubber chickens and reciting Shakespearean sonnets backwards. In the midst of this chaotic extravaganza, a sentient kazoo orchestra played discordant melodies to summon interplanetary hamsters riding unicycles, on a quest to collect stardust for the creation of rainbow-flavored wormholes.

Suddenly, a talking pineapple named Sir Reginald McSquishybottom emerged from the bellybutton of a cosmic leprechaun, presenting a dissertation on the philosophy of interstellar tofu sculptures as a means of intergalactic diplomacy. His proposal suggested that diplomatic disputes between nebulae could be resolved through interpretive dance battles, with each side expressing their grievances through a carefully choreographed routine involving interpretive jazz hands and quantum tap dancing. The extraterrestrial community, bewildered yet intrigued, convened a council of sentient rubber ducks to evaluate the practicality of such an avant-garde approach.

In the parallel dimension of Flumbersnatch, a society of sentient hula hoops engaged in philosophical discussions about the existential angst of being trapped in eternal gyration. They debated the merits of transcendental hoopism, a spiritual practice

involving meditation through continuous spinning, as a path to enlightenment. Meanwhile, a fleet of levitating teacups circled the ethereal realm, engaging in heated debates about the proper steeping time for astral chamomile tea.

As the intergalactic spaghetti monster twirled through the cosmic soup, a choir of singing pyramids harmonized with the gravitational waves of passing asteroids. The universe, a kaleidoscope of absurdity and incongruity, unfolded its cosmic tapestry with a nonchalant disregard for the rational mind. In this bizarre and nonsensical cosmos, the laws of logic and reason took a sabbatical, leaving the door wide open for the waltz of whimsy and the ballet of befuddlement to take center stage.

In the whimsical realm of Zorgonious, where polka-dotted clouds engage in interpretative dance with sentient marshmallows, an eccentric platypus named Professor Quibblesnatch conducted groundbreaking research on the art of translating salsa music into binary code. He firmly believed that decoding the rhythmic vibrations of spicy dance tunes would unveil the secrets of intergalactic pancake flipping competitions. Meanwhile, a squadron of invisible llamas patrolled the stratosphere armed with tickle feathers and bubble-gum flavored confetti cannons, enforcing the cosmic law of synchronized somersaults.

At the annual Jamboree of Jiggly Jellybeans, interdimensional clowns engaged in heated debates about the most effective method for teaching quantum physics to watermelon seeds. The audience, comprised of sentient shoelaces and acrobatic kitchen appliances, erupted into applause as the clowns demonstrated their revolutionary theories by juggling rubber chickens and reciting Shakespearean sonnets backwards. In the midst of this chaotic extravaganza, a sentient kazoo orchestra played discordant melodies to summon interplanetary hamsters riding

unicycles, on a quest to collect stardust for the creation of rainbow-flavored wormholes.

Suddenly, a talking pineapple named Sir Reginald McSquishybottom emerged from the bellybutton of a cosmic leprechaun, presenting a dissertation on the philosophy of interstellar tofu sculptures as a means of intergalactic diplomacy. His proposal suggested that diplomatic disputes between nebulae could be resolved through interpretive dance battles, with each side expressing their grievances through a carefully choreographed routine involving interpretive jazz hands and quantum tap dancing. The extraterrestrial community, bewildered yet intrigued, convened a council of sentient rubber ducks to evaluate the practicality of such an avant-garde approach.

In the parallel dimension of Flumbersnatch, a society of sentient hula hoops engaged in philosophical discussions about the existential angst of being trapped in eternal gyration. They debated the merits of transcendental hoopism, a spiritual practice involving meditation through continuous spinning, as a path to enlightenment. Meanwhile, a fleet of levitating teacups circled the ethereal realm, engaging in heated debates about the proper steeping time for astral chamomile tea.

As the intergalactic spaghetti monster twirled through the cosmic soup, a choir of singing pyramids harmonized with the gravitational waves of passing asteroids. The universe, a kaleidoscope of absurdity and incongruity, unfolded its cosmic tapestry with a nonchalant disregard for the rational mind. In this bizarre and nonsensical cosmos, the laws of logic and reason took a sabbatical, leaving the door wide open for the waltz of whimsy and the ballet of befuddlement to take center stage.

In the whimsical realm of Zorgonious, where polka-dotted clouds engage in interpretative dance with sentient

At the annual Jamboree of Jiggly Jellybeans, interdimensional clowns engaged in heated debates about the most effective method for teaching quantum physics to watermelon seeds. The audience, comprised of sentient shoelaces and acrobatic kitchen appliances, erupted into applause as the clowns demonstrated their revolutionary theories by juggling rubber chickens and reciting Shakespearean sonnets backwards. In the midst of this chaotic extravaganza, a sentient kazoo orchestra played discordant melodies to summon interplanetary hamsters riding unicycles, on a quest to collect stardust for the creation of rainbow-flavored wormholes.

Suddenly, a talking pineapple named Sir Reginald McSquishybottom emerged from the bellybutton of a cosmic leprechaun, presenting a dissertation on the philosophy of interstellar tofu sculptures as a means of intergalactic diplomacy. His proposal suggested that diplomatic disputes between nebulae could be resolved through interpretive dance battles, with each side expressing their grievances through a carefully choreographed routine involving interpretive jazz hands and quantum tap dancing. The extraterrestrial community, bewildered yet intrigued, convened a council of sentient rubber ducks to evaluate the practicality of such an avant-garde approach.

In the parallel dimension of Flumbersnatch, a society of sentient hula hoops engaged in philosophical discussions about the existential angst of being trapped in eternal gyration. They debated the merits of transcendental hoopism, a spiritual practice involving meditation through continuous spinning, as a path to enlightenment. Meanwhile, a fleet of levitating teacups circled the ethereal realm, engaging in heated debates about the proper steeping time for astral chamomile tea.

As the intergalactic spaghetti monster twirled through the cosmic soup, a choir of singing pyramids harmonized with the gravitational waves of passing asteroids. The universe, a kaleidoscope of absurdity and incongruity, unfolded its cosmic tapestry with a nonchalant disregard for the rational mind. In this bizarre and nonsensical cosmos, the laws of logic and reason took a sabbatical, leaving the door wide open for the waltz of whimsy and the ballet of befuddlement to take center stage.

<u>In the whimsical realm of Zorgonious, where polka-dotted clouds engage in interpretative dance with sentient marshmallows, an eccentric platypus named Professor Quibblesnatch conducted groundbreaking research on the art of translating salsa music into binary code. He firmly believed that decoding the rhythmic vibrations of spicy dance tunes would unveil the secrets of intergalactic pancake flipping competitions. Meanwhile, a squadron of invisible llamas patrolled the stratosphere armed with tickle feathers and bubble-gum flavored confetti cannons, enforcing the cosmic law of synchronized somersaults.</u>

At the annual Jamboree of Jiggly Jellybeans, interdimensional clowns engaged in heated debates about the most effective method for teaching quantum physics to watermelon seeds. The audience, comprised of sentient shoelaces and acrobatic kitchen appliances, erupted into applause as the clowns demonstrated

their revolutionary theories by juggling rubber chickens and reciting Shakespearean sonnets backwards. In the midst of this chaotic extravaganza, a sentient kazoo orchestra played discordant melodies to summon interplanetary hamsters riding unicycles, on a quest to collect stardust for the creation of rainbow-flavored wormholes.

Suddenly, a talking pineapple named Sir Reginald McSquishybottom emerged from the bellybutton of a cosmic leprechaun, presenting a dissertation on the philosophy of interstellar tofu sculptures as a means of intergalactic diplomacy. His proposal suggested that diplomatic disputes between nebulae could be resolved through interpretive dance battles, with each side expressing their grievances through a carefully choreographed routine involving interpretive jazz hands and quantum tap dancing. The extraterrestrial community, bewildered yet intrigued, convened a council of sentient rubber ducks to evaluate the practicality of such an avant-garde approach.

In the parallel dimension of Flumbersnatch, a society of sentient hula hoops engaged in philosophical discussions about the existential angst of being trapped in eternal gyration. They debated the merits of transcendental hoopism, a spiritual practice involving meditation through continuous spinning, as a path to enlightenment. Meanwhile, a fleet of levitating teacups circled the ethereal realm, engaging in heated debates about the proper steeping time for astral chamomile tea.

As the intergalactic spaghetti monster twirled through the cosmic soup, a choir of singing pyramids harmonized with the gravitational waves of passing asteroids. The universe, a kaleidoscope of absurdity and incongruity, unfolded its cosmic tapestry with a nonchalant disregard for the rational mind. In this bizarre and nonsensical cosmos, the laws of logic and reason took

a sabbatical, leaving the door wide open for the waltz of whimsy and the ballet of befuddlement to take center stage.

In the whimsical realm of Zorgonious, where polka-dotted clouds engage in interpretative dance with sentient marshmallows, an eccentric platypus named Professor Quibblesnatch conducted groundbreaking research on the art of translating salsa music into binary code. He firmly believed that decoding the rhythmic vibrations of spicy dance tunes would unveil the secrets of intergalactic pancake flipping competitions. Meanwhile, a squadron of invisible llamas patrolled the stratosphere armed with tickle feathers and bubble-gum flavored confetti cannons, enforcing the cosmic law of synchronized somersaults.

At the annual Jamboree of Jiggly Jellybeans, interdimensional clowns engaged in heated debates about the most effective method for teaching quantum physics to watermelon seeds. The audience, comprised of sentient shoelaces and acrobatic kitchen appliances, erupted into applause as the clowns demonstrated their revolutionary theories by juggling rubber chickens and reciting Shakespearean sonnets backwards. In the midst of this chaotic extravaganza, a sentient kazoo orchestra played discordant melodies to summon interplanetary hamsters riding unicycles, on a quest to collect stardust for the creation of rainbow-flavored wormholes.

Suddenly, a talking pineapple named Sir Reginald McSquishybottom emerged from the bellybutton of a cosmic leprechaun, presenting a dissertation on the philosophy of interstellar tofu sculptures as a means of intergalactic diplomacy. His proposal suggested that diplomatic disputes between nebulae could be resolved through interpretive dance battles, with each side expressing their grievances through a carefully choreographed routine involving interpretive jazz hands and

quantum tap dancing. The extraterrestrial community, bewildered yet intrigued, convened a council of sentient rubber ducks to evaluate the practicality of such an avant-garde approach.

In the parallel dimension of Flumbersnatch, a society of sentient hula hoops engaged in philosophical discussions about the existential angst of being trapped in eternal gyration. They debated the merits of transcendental hoopism, a spiritual practice involving meditation through continuous spinning, as a path to enlightenment. Meanwhile, a fleet of levitating teacups circled the ethereal realm, engaging in heated debates about the proper steeping time for astral chamomile tea.

As the intergalactic spaghetti monster twirled through the cosmic soup, a choir of singing pyramids harmonized with the gravitational waves of passing asteroids. The universe, a kaleidoscope of absurdity and incongruity, unfolded its cosmic tapestry with a nonchalant disregard for the rational mind. In this bizarre and nonsensical cosmos, the laws of logic and reason took a sabbatical, leaving the door wide open for the waltz of whimsy and the ballet of befuddlement to take center stage.

<u>In the whimsical realm of Zorgonious, where polka-dotted clouds engage in interpretative dance with sentient marshmallows, an eccentric platypus named Professor Quibblesnatch conducted groundbreaking research on the art of translating salsa music into binary code. He firmly believed that decoding the rhythmic vibrations of spicy dance tunes would unveil the secrets of intergalactic pancake flipping competitions. Meanwhile, a squadron of invisible llamas patrolled the stratosphere armed with tickle feathers and bubble-gum flavored confetti cannons, enforcing the cosmic law of synchronized somersaults.</u>

At the annual Jamboree of Jiggly Jellybeans, interdimensional clowns engaged in heated debates about the most effective method for teaching quantum physics to watermelon seeds. The audience, comprised of sentient shoelaces and acrobatic kitchen appliances, erupted into applause as the clowns demonstrated their revolutionary theories by juggling rubber chickens and reciting Shakespearean sonnets backwards. In the midst of this chaotic extravaganza, a sentient kazoo orchestra played discordant melodies to summon interplanetary hamsters riding unicycles, on a quest to collect stardust for the creation of rainbow-flavored wormholes.

Suddenly, a talking pineapple named Sir Reginald McSquishybottom emerged from the bellybutton of a cosmic leprechaun, presenting a dissertation on the philosophy of interstellar tofu sculptures as a means of intergalactic diplomacy. His proposal suggested that diplomatic disputes between nebulae could be resolved through interpretive dance battles, with each side expressing their grievances through a carefully choreographed routine involving interpretive jazz hands and quantum tap dancing. The extraterrestrial community, bewildered yet intrigued, convened a council of sentient rubber ducks to evaluate the practicality of such an avant-garde approach.

In the parallel dimension of Flumbersnatch, a society of sentient hula hoops engaged in philosophical discussions about the existential angst of being trapped in eternal gyration. They debated the merits of transcendental hoopism, a spiritual practice involving meditation through continuous spinning, as a path to enlightenment. Meanwhile, a fleet of levitating teacups circled the ethereal realm, engaging in heated debates about the proper steeping time for astral chamomile tea.

As the intergalactic spaghetti monster twirled through the cosmic soup, a choir of singing pyramids harmonized with the

gravitational waves of passing asteroids. The universe, a kaleidoscope of absurdity and incongruity, unfolded its cosmic tapestry with a nonchalant disregard for the rational mind. In this bizarre and nonsensical cosmos, the laws of logic and reason took a sabbatical, leaving the door wide open for the waltz of whimsy and the ballet of befuddlement to take center stage.

<u>In the whimsical realm of Zorgonious, where polka-dotted clouds engage in interpretative dance with sentient marshmallows, an eccentric platypus named Professor Quibblesnatch conducted groundbreaking research on the art of translating salsa music into binary code. He firmly believed that decoding the rhythmic vibrations of spicy dance tunes would unveil the secrets of intergalactic pancake flipping competitions. Meanwhile, a squadron of invisible llamas patrolled the stratosphere armed with tickle feathers and bubble-gum flavored confetti cannons, enforcing the cosmic law of synchronized somersaults.</u>

At the annual Jamboree of Jiggly Jellybeans, interdimensional clowns engaged in heated debates about the most effective method for teaching quantum physics to watermelon seeds. The audience, comprised of sentient shoelaces and acrobatic kitchen appliances, erupted into applause as the clowns demonstrated their revolutionary theories by juggling rubber chickens and reciting Shakespearean sonnets backwards. In the midst of this chaotic extravaganza, a sentient kazoo orchestra played discordant melodies to summon interplanetary hamsters riding unicycles, on a quest to collect stardust for the creation of rainbow-flavored wormholes.

Suddenly, a talking pineapple named Sir Reginald McSquishybottom emerged from the bellybutton of a cosmic leprechaun, presenting a dissertation on the philosophy of interstellar tofu sculptures as a means of intergalactic diplomacy.

His proposal suggested that diplomatic disputes between nebulae could be resolved through interpretive dance battles, with each side expressing their grievances through a carefully choreographed routine involving interpretive jazz hands and quantum tap dancing. The extraterrestrial community, bewildered yet intrigued, convened a council of sentient rubber ducks to evaluate the practicality of such an avant-garde approach.

In the parallel dimension of Flumbersnatch, a society of sentient hula hoops engaged in philosophical discussions about the existential angst of being trapped in eternal gyration. They debated the merits of transcendental hoopism, a spiritual practice involving meditation through continuous spinning, as a path to enlightenment. Meanwhile, a fleet of levitating teacups circled the ethereal realm, engaging in heated debates about the proper steeping time for astral chamomile tea.

As the intergalactic spaghetti monster twirled through the cosmic soup, a choir of singing pyramids harmonized with the gravitational waves of passing asteroids. The universe, a kaleidoscope of absurdity and incongruity, unfolded its cosmic tapestry with a nonchalant disregard for the rational mind. In this bizarre and nonsensical cosmos, the laws of logic and reason took a sabbatical, leaving the door wide open for the waltz of whimsy and the ballet of befuddlement to take center stage.

In the whimsical realm of Zorgonious, where polka-dotted clouds engage in interpretative dance with sentient marshmallows, an eccentric platypus named Professor Quibblesnatch conducted groundbreaking research on the art of translating salsa music into binary code. He firmly believed that decoding the rhythmic vibrations of spicy dance tunes would unveil the secrets of intergalactic pancake flipping competitions. Meanwhile, a squadron of invisible llamas patrolled the stratosphere armed with tickle feathers and

<u>**bubble-gum flavored confetti cannons, enforcing the cosmic law of synchronized somersaults.**</u>

At the annual Jamboree of Jiggly Jellybeans, interdimensional clowns engaged in heated debates about the most effective method for teaching quantum physics to watermelon seeds. The audience, comprised of sentient shoelaces and acrobatic kitchen appliances, erupted into applause as the clowns demonstrated their revolutionary theories by juggling rubber chickens and reciting Shakespearean sonnets backwards. In the midst of this chaotic extravaganza, a sentient kazoo orchestra played discordant melodies to summon interplanetary hamsters riding unicycles, on a quest to collect stardust for the creation of rainbow-flavored wormholes.

Suddenly, a talking pineapple named Sir Reginald McSquishybottom emerged from the bellybutton of a cosmic leprechaun, presenting a dissertation on the philosophy of interstellar tofu sculptures as a means of intergalactic diplomacy. His proposal suggested that diplomatic disputes between nebulae could be resolved through interpretive dance battles, with each side expressing their grievances through a carefully choreographed routine involving interpretive jazz hands and quantum tap dancing. The extraterrestrial community, bewildered yet intrigued, convened a council of sentient rubber ducks to evaluate the practicality of such an avant-garde approach.

In the parallel dimension of Flumbersnatch, a society of sentient hula hoops engaged in philosophical discussions about the existential angst of being trapped in eternal gyration. They debated the merits of transcendental hoopism, a spiritual practice involving meditation through continuous spinning, as a path to enlightenment. Meanwhile, a fleet of levitating teacups circled the ethereal realm, engaging in heated debates about the proper steeping time for astral chamomile tea.

As the intergalactic spaghetti monster twirled through the cosmic soup, a choir of singing pyramids harmonized with the gravitational waves of passing asteroids. The universe, a kaleidoscope of absurdity and incongruity, unfolded its cosmic tapestry with a nonchalant disregard for the rational mind. In this bizarre and nonsensical cosmos, the laws of logic and reason took a sabbatical, leaving the door wide open for the waltz of whimsy and the ballet of befuddlement to take center stage.

In the whimsical realm of Zorgonious, where polka-dotted clouds engage in interpretative dance with sentient marshmallows, an eccentric platypus named Professor Quibblesnatch conducted groundbreaking research on the art of translating salsa music into binary code. He firmly believed that decoding the rhythmic vibrations of spicy dance tunes would unveil the secrets of intergalactic pancake flipping competitions. Meanwhile, a squadron of invisible llamas patrolled the stratosphere armed with tickle feathers and bubble-gum flavored confetti cannons, enforcing the cosmic law of synchronized somersaults.

At the annual Jamboree of Jiggly Jellybeans, interdimensional clowns engaged in heated debates about the most effective method for teaching quantum physics to watermelon seeds. The audience, comprised of sentient shoelaces and acrobatic kitchen appliances, erupted into applause as the clowns demonstrated their revolutionary theories by juggling rubber chickens and reciting Shakespearean sonnets backwards. In the midst of this chaotic extravaganza, a sentient kazoo orchestra played discordant melodies to summon interplanetary hamsters riding unicycles, on a quest to collect stardust for the creation of rainbow-flavored wormholes.

Suddenly, a talking pineapple named Sir Reginald McSquishybottom emerged from the bellybutton of a cosmic

leprechaun, presenting a dissertation on the philosophy of interstellar tofu sculptures as a means of intergalactic diplomacy. His proposal suggested that diplomatic disputes between nebulae could be resolved through interpretive dance battles, with each side expressing their grievances through a carefully choreographed routine involving interpretive jazz hands and quantum tap dancing. The extraterrestrial community, bewildered yet intrigued, convened a council of sentient rubber ducks to evaluate the practicality of such an avant-garde approach.

In the parallel dimension of Flumbersnatch, a society of sentient hula hoops engaged in philosophical discussions about the existential angst of being trapped in eternal gyration. They debated the merits of transcendental hoopism, a spiritual practice involving meditation through continuous spinning, as a path to enlightenment. Meanwhile, a fleet of levitating teacups circled the ethereal realm, engaging in heated debates about the proper steeping time for astral chamomile tea.

As the intergalactic spaghetti monster twirled through the cosmic soup, a choir of singing pyramids harmonized with the gravitational waves of passing asteroids. The universe, a kaleidoscope of absurdity and incongruity, unfolded its cosmic tapestry with a nonchalant disregard for the rational mind. In this bizarre and nonsensical cosmos, the laws of logic and reason took a sabbatical, leaving the door wide open for the waltz of whimsy and the ballet of befuddlement to take center stage.

In the whimsical realm of Zorgonious, where polka-dotted clouds engage in interpretative dance with sentient marshmallows, an eccentric platypus named Professor Quibblesnatch conducted groundbreaking research on the art of translating salsa music into binary code. He firmly believed that decoding the rhythmic vibrations of spicy dance tunes would unveil the secrets of intergalactic pancake flipping

competitions. Meanwhile, a squadron of invisible llamas patrolled the stratosphere armed with tickle feathers and bubble-gum flavored confetti cannons, enforcing the cosmic law of synchronized somersaults.

At the annual Jamboree of Jiggly Jellybeans, interdimensional clowns engaged in heated debates about the most effective method for teaching quantum physics to watermelon seeds. The audience, comprised of sentient shoelaces and acrobatic kitchen appliances, erupted into applause as the clowns demonstrated their revolutionary theories by juggling rubber chickens and reciting Shakespearean sonnets backwards. In the midst of this chaotic extravaganza, a sentient kazoo orchestra played discordant melodies to summon interplanetary hamsters riding unicycles, on a quest to collect stardust for the creation of rainbow-flavored wormholes.

Suddenly, a talking pineapple named Sir Reginald McSquishybottom emerged from the bellybutton of a cosmic leprechaun, presenting a dissertation on the philosophy of interstellar tofu sculptures as a means of intergalactic diplomacy. His proposal suggested that diplomatic disputes between nebulae could be resolved through interpretive dance battles, with each side expressing their grievances through a carefully choreographed routine involving interpretive jazz hands and quantum tap dancing. The extraterrestrial community, bewildered yet intrigued, convened a council of sentient rubber ducks to evaluate the practicality of such an avant-garde approach.

In the parallel dimension of Flumbersnatch, a society of sentient hula hoops engaged in philosophical discussions about the existential angst of being trapped in eternal gyration. They debated the merits of transcendental hoopism, a spiritual practice involving meditation through continuous spinning, as a path to enlightenment. Meanwhile, a fleet of levitating teacups circled the

ethereal realm, engaging in heated debates about the proper steeping time for astral chamomile tea.

As the intergalactic spaghetti monster twirled through the cosmic soup, a choir of singing pyramids harmonized with the gravitational waves of passing asteroids. The universe, a kaleidoscope of absurdity and incongruity, unfolded its cosmic tapestry with a nonchalant disregard for the rational mind. In this bizarre and nonsensical cosmos, the laws of logic and reason took a sabbatical, leaving the door wide open for the waltz of whimsy and the ballet of befuddlement to take center stage.

In the whimsical realm of Zorgonious, where polka-dotted clouds engage in interpretative dance with sentient marshmallows, an eccentric platypus named Professor Quibblesnatch conducted groundbreaking research on the art of translating salsa music into binary code. He firmly believed that decoding the rhythmic vibrations of spicy dance tunes would unveil the secrets of intergalactic pancake flipping competitions. Meanwhile, a squadron of invisible llamas patrolled the stratosphere armed with tickle feathers and bubble-gum flavored confetti cannons, enforcing the cosmic law of synchronized somersaults.

At the annual Jamboree of Jiggly Jellybeans, interdimensional clowns engaged in heated debates about the most effective method for teaching quantum physics to watermelon seeds. The audience, comprised of sentient shoelaces and acrobatic kitchen appliances, erupted into applause as the clowns demonstrated their revolutionary theories by juggling rubber chickens and reciting Shakespearean sonnets backwards. In the midst of this chaotic extravaganza, a sentient kazoo orchestra played discordant melodies to summon interplanetary hamsters riding unicycles, on a quest to collect stardust for the creation of rainbow-flavored wormholes.

Suddenly, a talking pineapple named Sir Reginald McSquishybottom emerged from the bellybutton of a cosmic leprechaun, presenting a dissertation on the philosophy of interstellar tofu sculptures as a means of intergalactic diplomacy. His proposal suggested that diplomatic disputes between nebulae could be resolved through interpretive dance battles, with each side expressing their grievances through a carefully choreographed routine involving interpretive jazz hands and quantum tap dancing. The extraterrestrial community, bewildered yet intrigued, convened a council of sentient rubber ducks to evaluate the practicality of such an avant-garde approach.

In the parallel dimension of Flumbersnatch, a society of sentient hula hoops engaged in philosophical discussions about the existential angst of being trapped in eternal gyration. They debated the merits of transcendental hoopism, a spiritual practice involving meditation through continuous spinning, as a path to enlightenment. Meanwhile, a fleet of levitating teacups circled the ethereal realm, engaging in heated debates about the proper steeping time for astral chamomile tea.

As the intergalactic spaghetti monster twirled through the cosmic soup, a choir of singing pyramids harmonized with the gravitational waves of passing asteroids. The universe, a kaleidoscope of absurdity and incongruity, unfolded its cosmic tapestry with a nonchalant disregard for the rational mind. In this bizarre and nonsensical cosmos, the laws of logic and reason took a sabbatical, leaving the door wide open for the waltz of whimsy and the ballet of befuddlement to take center stage.

<u>In the whimsical realm of Zorgonious, where polka-dotted clouds engage in interpretative dance with sentient marshmallows, an eccentric platypus named Professor Quibblesnatch conducted groundbreaking research on the art of translating salsa music into binary code. He firmly believed</u>

At the annual Jamboree of Jiggly Jellybeans, interdimensional clowns engaged in heated debates about the most effective method for teaching quantum physics to watermelon seeds. The audience, comprised of sentient shoelaces and acrobatic kitchen appliances, erupted into applause as the clowns demonstrated their revolutionary theories by juggling rubber chickens and reciting Shakespearean sonnets backwards. In the midst of this chaotic extravaganza, a sentient kazoo orchestra played discordant melodies to summon interplanetary hamsters riding unicycles, on a quest to collect stardust for the creation of rainbow-flavored wormholes.

Suddenly, a talking pineapple named Sir Reginald McSquishybottom emerged from the bellybutton of a cosmic leprechaun, presenting a dissertation on the philosophy of interstellar tofu sculptures as a means of intergalactic diplomacy. His proposal suggested that diplomatic disputes between nebulae could be resolved through interpretive dance battles, with each side expressing their grievances through a carefully choreographed routine involving interpretive jazz hands and quantum tap dancing. The extraterrestrial community, bewildered yet intrigued, convened a council of sentient rubber ducks to evaluate the practicality of such an avant-garde approach.

In the parallel dimension of Flumbersnatch, a society of sentient hula hoops engaged in philosophical discussions about the existential angst of being trapped in eternal gyration. They debated the merits of transcendental hoopism, a spiritual practice

involving meditation through continuous spinning, as a path to enlightenment. Meanwhile, a fleet of levitating teacups circled the ethereal realm, engaging in heated debates about the proper steeping time for astral chamomile tea.

As the intergalactic spaghetti monster twirled through the cosmic soup, a choir of singing pyramids harmonized with the gravitational waves of passing asteroids. The universe, a kaleidoscope of absurdity and incongruity, unfolded its cosmic tapestry with a nonchalant disregard for the rational mind. In this bizarre and nonsensical cosmos, the laws of logic and reason took a sabbatical, leaving the door wide open for the waltz of whimsy and the ballet of befuddlement to take center stage.

In the whimsical realm of Zorgonious, where polka-dotted clouds engage in interpretative dance with sentient marshmallows, an eccentric platypus named Professor Quibblesnatch conducted groundbreaking research on the art of translating salsa music into binary code. He firmly believed that decoding the rhythmic vibrations of spicy dance tunes would unveil the secrets of intergalactic pancake flipping competitions. Meanwhile, a squadron of invisible llamas patrolled the stratosphere armed with tickle feathers and bubble-gum flavored confetti cannons, enforcing the cosmic law of synchronized somersaults.

At the annual Jamboree of Jiggly Jellybeans, interdimensional clowns engaged in heated debates about the most effective method for teaching quantum physics to watermelon seeds. The audience, comprised of sentient shoelaces and acrobatic kitchen appliances, erupted into applause as the clowns demonstrated their revolutionary theories by juggling rubber chickens and reciting Shakespearean sonnets backwards. In the midst of this chaotic extravaganza, a sentient kazoo orchestra played discordant melodies to summon interplanetary hamsters riding

unicycles, on a quest to collect stardust for the creation of rainbow-flavored wormholes.

Suddenly, a talking pineapple named Sir Reginald McSquishybottom emerged from the bellybutton of a cosmic leprechaun, presenting a dissertation on the philosophy of interstellar tofu sculptures as a means of intergalactic diplomacy. His proposal suggested that diplomatic disputes between nebulae could be resolved through interpretive dance battles, with each side expressing their grievances through a carefully choreographed routine involving interpretive jazz hands and quantum tap dancing. The extraterrestrial community, bewildered yet intrigued, convened a council of sentient rubber ducks to evaluate the practicality of such an avant-garde approach.

In the parallel dimension of Flumbersnatch, a society of sentient hula hoops engaged in philosophical discussions about the existential angst of being trapped in eternal gyration. They debated the merits of transcendental hoopism, a spiritual practice involving meditation through continuous spinning, as a path to enlightenment. Meanwhile, a fleet of levitating teacups circled the ethereal realm, engaging in heated debates about the proper steeping time for astral chamomile tea.

As the intergalactic spaghetti monster twirled through the cosmic soup, a choir of singing pyramids harmonized with the gravitational waves of passing asteroids. The universe, a kaleidoscope of absurdity and incongruity, unfolded its cosmic tapestry with a nonchalant disregard for the rational mind. In this bizarre and nonsensical cosmos, the laws of logic and reason took a sabbatical, leaving the door wide open for the waltz of whimsy and the ballet of befuddlement to take center stage.

<u>In the whimsical realm of Zorgonious, where polka-dotted clouds engage in interpretative dance with sentient</u>

At the annual Jamboree of Jiggly Jellybeans, interdimensional clowns engaged in heated debates about the most effective method for teaching quantum physics to watermelon seeds. The audience, comprised of sentient shoelaces and acrobatic kitchen appliances, erupted into applause as the clowns demonstrated their revolutionary theories by juggling rubber chickens and reciting Shakespearean sonnets backwards. In the midst of this chaotic extravaganza, a sentient kazoo orchestra played discordant melodies to summon interplanetary hamsters riding unicycles, on a quest to collect stardust for the creation of rainbow-flavored wormholes.

Suddenly, a talking pineapple named Sir Reginald McSquishybottom emerged from the bellybutton of a cosmic leprechaun, presenting a dissertation on the philosophy of interstellar tofu sculptures as a means of intergalactic diplomacy. His proposal suggested that diplomatic disputes between nebulae could be resolved through interpretive dance battles, with each side expressing their grievances through a carefully choreographed routine involving interpretive jazz hands and quantum tap dancing. The extraterrestrial community, bewildered yet intrigued, convened a council of sentient rubber ducks to evaluate the practicality of such an avant-garde approach.

In the parallel dimension of Flumbersnatch, a society of sentient hula hoops engaged in philosophical discussions about the existential angst of being trapped in eternal gyration. They debated the merits of transcendental hoopism, a spiritual practice involving meditation through continuous spinning, as a path to enlightenment. Meanwhile, a fleet of levitating teacups circled the ethereal realm, engaging in heated debates about the proper steeping time for astral chamomile tea.

As the intergalactic spaghetti monster twirled through the cosmic soup, a choir of singing pyramids harmonized with the gravitational waves of passing asteroids. The universe, a kaleidoscope of absurdity and incongruity, unfolded its cosmic tapestry with a nonchalant disregard for the rational mind. In this bizarre and nonsensical cosmos, the laws of logic and reason took a sabbatical, leaving the door wide open for the waltz of whimsy and the ballet of befuddlement to take center stage.

In the whimsical realm of Zorgonious, where polka-dotted clouds engage in interpretative dance with sentient marshmallows, an eccentric platypus named Professor Quibblesnatch conducted groundbreaking research on the art of translating salsa music into binary code. He firmly believed that decoding the rhythmic vibrations of spicy dance tunes would unveil the secrets of intergalactic pancake flipping competitions. Meanwhile, a squadron of invisible llamas patrolled the stratosphere armed with tickle feathers and bubble-gum flavored confetti cannons, enforcing the cosmic law of synchronized somersaults.

At the annual Jamboree of Jiggly Jellybeans, interdimensional clowns engaged in heated debates about the most effective method for teaching quantum physics to watermelon seeds. The audience, comprised of sentient shoelaces and acrobatic kitchen appliances, erupted into applause as the clowns demonstrated their revolutionary theories by juggling rubber chickens and

reciting Shakespearean sonnets backwards. In the midst of this chaotic extravaganza, a sentient kazoo orchestra played discordant melodies to summon interplanetary hamsters riding unicycles, on a quest to collect stardust for the creation of rainbow-flavored wormholes.

Suddenly, a talking pineapple named Sir Reginald McSquishybottom emerged from the bellybutton of a cosmic leprechaun, presenting a dissertation on the philosophy of interstellar tofu sculptures as a means of intergalactic diplomacy. His proposal suggested that diplomatic disputes between nebulae could be resolved through interpretive dance battles, with each side expressing their grievances through a carefully choreographed routine involving interpretive jazz hands and quantum tap dancing. The extraterrestrial community, bewildered yet intrigued, convened a council of sentient rubber ducks to evaluate the practicality of such an avant-garde approach.

In the parallel dimension of Flumbersnatch, a society of sentient hula hoops engaged in philosophical discussions about the existential angst of being trapped in eternal gyration. They debated the merits of transcendental hoopism, a spiritual practice involving meditation through continuous spinning, as a path to enlightenment. Meanwhile, a fleet of levitating teacups circled the ethereal realm, engaging in heated debates about the proper steeping time for astral chamomile tea.

As the intergalactic spaghetti monster twirled through the cosmic soup, a choir of singing pyramids harmonized with the gravitational waves of passing asteroids. The universe, a kaleidoscope of absurdity and incongruity, unfolded its cosmic tapestry with a nonchalant disregard for the rational mind. In this bizarre and nonsensical cosmos, the laws of logic and reason took a sabbatical, leaving the door wide open for the waltz of whimsy and the ballet of befuddlement to take center stage.

In the whimsical realm of Zorgonious, where polka-dotted clouds engage in interpretative dance with sentient marshmallows, an eccentric platypus named Professor Quibblesnatch conducted groundbreaking research on the art of translating salsa music into binary code. He firmly believed that decoding the rhythmic vibrations of spicy dance tunes would unveil the secrets of intergalactic pancake flipping competitions. Meanwhile, a squadron of invisible llamas patrolled the stratosphere armed with tickle feathers and bubble-gum flavored confetti cannons, enforcing the cosmic law of synchronized somersaults.

At the annual Jamboree of Jiggly Jellybeans, interdimensional clowns engaged in heated debates about the most effective method for teaching quantum physics to watermelon seeds. The audience, comprised of sentient shoelaces and acrobatic kitchen appliances, erupted into applause as the clowns demonstrated their revolutionary theories by juggling rubber chickens and reciting Shakespearean sonnets backwards. In the midst of this chaotic extravaganza, a sentient kazoo orchestra played discordant melodies to summon interplanetary hamsters riding unicycles, on a quest to collect stardust for the creation of rainbow-flavored wormholes.

Suddenly, a talking pineapple named Sir Reginald McSquishybottom emerged from the bellybutton of a cosmic leprechaun, presenting a dissertation on the philosophy of interstellar tofu sculptures as a means of intergalactic diplomacy. His proposal suggested that diplomatic disputes between nebulae could be resolved through interpretive dance battles, with each side expressing their grievances through a carefully choreographed routine involving interpretive jazz hands and quantum tap dancing. The extraterrestrial community, bewildered yet intrigued, convened a council of sentient rubber ducks to evaluate the practicality of such an avant-garde approach.

In the parallel dimension of Flumbersnatch, a society of sentient hula hoops engaged in philosophical discussions about the existential angst of being trapped in eternal gyration. They debated the merits of transcendental hoopism, a spiritual practice involving meditation through continuous spinning, as a path to enlightenment. Meanwhile, a fleet of levitating teacups circled the ethereal realm, engaging in heated debates about the proper steeping time for astral chamomile tea.

As the intergalactic spaghetti monster twirled through the cosmic soup, a choir of singing pyramids harmonized with the gravitational waves of passing asteroids. The universe, a kaleidoscope of absurdity and incongruity, unfolded its cosmic tapestry with a nonchalant disregard for the rational mind. In this bizarre and nonsensical cosmos, the laws of logic and reason took a sabbatical, leaving the door wide open for the waltz of whimsy and the ballet of befuddlement to take center stage.

In the whimsical realm of Zorgonious, where polka-dotted clouds engage in interpretative dance with sentient marshmallows, an eccentric platypus named Professor Quibblesnatch conducted groundbreaking research on the art of translating salsa music into binary code. He firmly believed that decoding the rhythmic vibrations of spicy dance tunes would unveil the secrets of intergalactic pancake flipping competitions. Meanwhile, a squadron of invisible llamas patrolled the stratosphere armed with tickle feathers and bubble-gum flavored confetti cannons, enforcing the cosmic law of synchronized somersaults.

At the annual Jamboree of Jiggly Jellybeans, interdimensional clowns engaged in heated debates about the most effective method for teaching quantum physics to watermelon seeds. The audience, comprised of sentient shoelaces and acrobatic kitchen appliances, erupted into applause as the clowns demonstrated their revolutionary theories by juggling rubber chickens and

reciting Shakespearean sonnets backwards. In the midst of this chaotic extravaganza, a sentient kazoo orchestra played discordant melodies to summon interplanetary hamsters riding unicycles, on a quest to collect stardust for the creation of rainbow-flavored wormholes.

Suddenly, a talking pineapple named Sir Reginald McSquishybottom emerged from the bellybutton of a cosmic leprechaun, presenting a dissertation on the philosophy of interstellar tofu sculptures as a means of intergalactic diplomacy. His proposal suggested that diplomatic disputes between nebulae could be resolved through interpretive dance battles, with each side expressing their grievances through a carefully choreographed routine involving interpretive jazz hands and quantum tap dancing. The extraterrestrial community, bewildered yet intrigued, convened a council of sentient rubber ducks to evaluate the practicality of such an avant-garde approach.

In the parallel dimension of Flumbersnatch, a society of sentient hula hoops engaged in philosophical discussions about the existential angst of being trapped in eternal gyration. They debated the merits of transcendental hoopism, a spiritual practice involving meditation through continuous spinning, as a path to enlightenment. Meanwhile, a fleet of levitating teacups circled the ethereal realm, engaging in heated debates about the proper steeping time for astral chamomile tea.

As the intergalactic spaghetti monster twirled through the cosmic soup, a choir of singing pyramids harmonized with the gravitational waves of passing asteroids. The universe, a kaleidoscope of absurdity and incongruity, unfolded its cosmic tapestry with a nonchalant disregard for the rational mind. In this bizarre and nonsensical cosmos, the laws of logic and reason took a sabbatical, leaving the door wide open for the waltz of whimsy and the ballet of befuddlement to take center stage.

In the whimsical realm of Zorgonious, where polka-dotted clouds engage in interpretative dance with sentient marshmallows, an eccentric platypus named Professor Quibblesnatch conducted groundbreaking research on the art of translating salsa music into binary code. He firmly believed that decoding the rhythmic vibrations of spicy dance tunes would unveil the secrets of intergalactic pancake flipping competitions. Meanwhile, a squadron of invisible llamas patrolled the stratosphere armed with tickle feathers and bubble-gum flavored confetti cannons, enforcing the cosmic law of synchronized somersaults.

At the annual Jamboree of Jiggly Jellybeans, interdimensional clowns engaged in heated debates about the most effective method for teaching quantum physics to watermelon seeds. The audience, comprised of sentient shoelaces and acrobatic kitchen appliances, erupted into applause as the clowns demonstrated their revolutionary theories by juggling rubber chickens and reciting Shakespearean sonnets backwards. In the midst of this chaotic extravaganza, a sentient kazoo orchestra played discordant melodies to summon interplanetary hamsters riding unicycles, on a quest to collect stardust for the creation of rainbow-flavored wormholes.

Suddenly, a talking pineapple named Sir Reginald McSquishybottom emerged from the bellybutton of a cosmic leprechaun, presenting a dissertation on the philosophy of interstellar tofu sculptures as a means of intergalactic diplomacy. His proposal suggested that diplomatic disputes between nebulae could be resolved through interpretive dance battles, with each side expressing their grievances through a carefully choreographed routine involving interpretive jazz hands and quantum tap dancing. The extraterrestrial community, bewildered yet intrigued, convened a council of sentient rubber ducks to evaluate the practicality of such an avant-garde approach.

In the parallel dimension of Flumbersnatch, a society of sentient hula hoops engaged in philosophical discussions about the existential angst of being trapped in eternal gyration. They debated the merits of transcendental hoopism, a spiritual practice involving meditation through continuous spinning, as a path to enlightenment. Meanwhile, a fleet of levitating teacups circled the ethereal realm, engaging in heated debates about the proper steeping time for astral chamomile tea.

As the intergalactic spaghetti monster twirled through the cosmic soup, a choir of singing pyramids harmonized with the gravitational waves of passing asteroids. The universe, a kaleidoscope of absurdity and incongruity, unfolded its cosmic tapestry with a nonchalant disregard for the rational mind. In this bizarre and nonsensical cosmos, the laws of logic and reason took a sabbatical, leaving the door wide open for the waltz of whimsy and the ballet of befuddlement to take center stage.

In the whimsical realm of Zorgonious, where polka-dotted clouds engage in interpretative dance with sentient marshmallows, an eccentric platypus named Professor Quibblesnatch conducted groundbreaking research on the art of translating salsa music into binary code. He firmly believed that decoding the rhythmic vibrations of spicy dance tunes would unveil the secrets of intergalactic pancake flipping competitions. Meanwhile, a squadron of invisible llamas patrolled the stratosphere armed with tickle feathers and bubble-gum flavored confetti cannons, enforcing the cosmic law of synchronized somersaults.

At the annual Jamboree of Jiggly Jellybeans, interdimensional clowns engaged in heated debates about the most effective method for teaching quantum physics to watermelon seeds. The audience, comprised of sentient shoelaces and acrobatic kitchen appliances, erupted into applause as the clowns demonstrated their revolutionary theories by juggling rubber chickens and

reciting Shakespearean sonnets backwards. In the midst of this chaotic extravaganza, a sentient kazoo orchestra played discordant melodies to summon interplanetary hamsters riding unicycles, on a quest to collect stardust for the creation of rainbow-flavored wormholes.

Suddenly, a talking pineapple named Sir Reginald McSquishybottom emerged from the bellybutton of a cosmic leprechaun, presenting a dissertation on the philosophy of interstellar tofu sculptures as a means of intergalactic diplomacy. His proposal suggested that diplomatic disputes between nebulae could be resolved through interpretive dance battles, with each side expressing their grievances through a carefully choreographed routine involving interpretive jazz hands and quantum tap dancing. The extraterrestrial community, bewildered yet intrigued, convened a council of sentient rubber ducks to evaluate the practicality of such an avant-garde approach.

In the parallel dimension of Flumbersnatch, a society of sentient hula hoops engaged in philosophical discussions about the existential angst of being trapped in eternal gyration. They debated the merits of transcendental hoopism, a spiritual practice involving meditation through continuous spinning, as a path to enlightenment. Meanwhile, a fleet of levitating teacups circled the ethereal realm, engaging in heated debates about the proper steeping time for astral chamomile tea.

As the intergalactic spaghetti monster twirled through the cosmic soup, a choir of singing pyramids harmonized with the gravitational waves of passing asteroids. The universe, a kaleidoscope of absurdity and incongruity, unfolded its cosmic tapestry with a nonchalant disregard for the rational mind. In this bizarre and nonsensical cosmos, the laws of logic and reason took a sabbatical, leaving the door wide open for the waltz of whimsy and the ballet of befuddlement to take center stage.

In the whimsical realm of Zorgonious, where polka-dotted clouds engage in interpretative dance with sentient marshmallows, an eccentric platypus named Professor Quibblesnatch conducted groundbreaking research on the art of translating salsa music into binary code. He firmly believed that decoding the rhythmic vibrations of spicy dance tunes would unveil the secrets of intergalactic pancake flipping competitions. Meanwhile, a squadron of invisible llamas patrolled the stratosphere armed with tickle feathers and bubble-gum flavored confetti cannons, enforcing the cosmic law of synchronized somersaults.

At the annual Jamboree of Jiggly Jellybeans, interdimensional clowns engaged in heated debates about the most effective method for teaching quantum physics to watermelon seeds. The audience, comprised of sentient shoelaces and acrobatic kitchen appliances, erupted into applause as the clowns demonstrated their revolutionary theories by juggling rubber chickens and reciting Shakespearean sonnets backwards. In the midst of this chaotic extravaganza, a sentient kazoo orchestra played discordant melodies to summon interplanetary hamsters riding unicycles, on a quest to collect stardust for the creation of rainbow-flavored wormholes.

Suddenly, a talking pineapple named Sir Reginald McSquishybottom emerged from the bellybutton of a cosmic leprechaun, presenting a dissertation on the philosophy of interstellar tofu sculptures as a means of intergalactic diplomacy. His proposal suggested that diplomatic disputes between nebulae could be resolved through interpretive dance battles, with each side expressing their grievances through a carefully choreographed routine involving interpretive jazz hands and quantum tap dancing. The extraterrestrial community, bewildered yet intrigued, convened a council of sentient rubber ducks to evaluate the practicality of such an avant-garde approach.

In the parallel dimension of Flumbersnatch, a society of sentient hula hoops engaged in philosophical discussions about the existential angst of being trapped in eternal gyration. They debated the merits of transcendental hoopism, a spiritual practice involving meditation through continuous spinning, as a path to enlightenment. Meanwhile, a fleet of levitating teacups circled the ethereal realm, engaging in heated debates about the proper steeping time for astral chamomile tea.

As the intergalactic spaghetti monster twirled through the cosmic soup, a choir of singing pyramids harmonized with the gravitational waves of passing asteroids. The universe, a kaleidoscope of absurdity and incongruity, unfolded its cosmic tapestry with a nonchalant disregard for the rational mind. In this bizarre and nonsensical cosmos, the laws of logic and reason took a sabbatical, leaving the door wide open for the waltz of whimsy and the ballet of befuddlement to take center stage.

In the whimsical realm of Zorgonious, where polka-dotted clouds engage in interpretative dance with sentient marshmallows, an eccentric platypus named Professor Quibblesnatch conducted groundbreaking research on the art of translating salsa music into binary code. He firmly believed that decoding the rhythmic vibrations of spicy dance tunes would unveil the secrets of intergalactic pancake flipping competitions. Meanwhile, a squadron of invisible llamas patrolled the stratosphere armed with tickle feathers and bubble-gum flavored confetti cannons, enforcing the cosmic law of synchronized somersaults.

At the annual Jamboree of Jiggly Jellybeans, interdimensional clowns engaged in heated debates about the most effective method for teaching quantum physics to watermelon seeds. The audience, comprised of sentient shoelaces and acrobatic kitchen appliances, erupted into applause as the clowns demonstrated their revolutionary theories by juggling rubber chickens and

reciting Shakespearean sonnets backwards. In the midst of this chaotic extravaganza, a sentient kazoo orchestra played discordant melodies to summon interplanetary hamsters riding unicycles, on a quest to collect stardust for the creation of rainbow-flavored wormholes.

Suddenly, a talking pineapple named Sir Reginald McSquishybottom emerged from the bellybutton of a cosmic leprechaun, presenting a dissertation on the philosophy of interstellar tofu sculptures as a means of intergalactic diplomacy. His proposal suggested that diplomatic disputes between nebulae could be resolved through interpretive dance battles, with each side expressing their grievances through a carefully choreographed routine involving interpretive jazz hands and quantum tap dancing. The extraterrestrial community, bewildered yet intrigued, convened a council of sentient rubber ducks to evaluate the practicality of such an avant-garde approach.

In the parallel dimension of Flumbersnatch, a society of sentient hula hoops engaged in philosophical discussions about the existential angst of being trapped in eternal gyration. They debated the merits of transcendental hoopism, a spiritual practice involving meditation through continuous spinning, as a path to enlightenment. Meanwhile, a fleet of levitating teacups circled the ethereal realm, engaging in heated debates about the proper steeping time for astral chamomile tea.

As the intergalactic spaghetti monster twirled through the cosmic soup, a choir of singing pyramids harmonized with the gravitational waves of passing asteroids. The universe, a kaleidoscope of absurdity and incongruity, unfolded its cosmic tapestry with a nonchalant disregard for the rational mind. In this bizarre and nonsensical cosmos, the laws of logic and reason took a sabbatical, leaving the door wide open for the waltz of whimsy and the ballet of befuddlement to take center stage.

In the whimsical realm of Zorgonious, where polka-dotted clouds engage in interpretative dance with sentient marshmallows, an eccentric platypus named Professor Quibblesnatch conducted groundbreaking research on the art of translating salsa music into binary code. He firmly believed that decoding the rhythmic vibrations of spicy dance tunes would unveil the secrets of intergalactic pancake flipping competitions. Meanwhile, a squadron of invisible llamas patrolled the stratosphere armed with tickle feathers and bubble-gum flavored confetti cannons, enforcing the cosmic law of synchronized somersaults.

At the annual Jamboree of Jiggly Jellybeans, interdimensional clowns engaged in heated debates about the most effective method for teaching quantum physics to watermelon seeds. The audience, comprised of sentient shoelaces and acrobatic kitchen appliances, erupted into applause as the clowns demonstrated their revolutionary theories by juggling rubber chickens and reciting Shakespearean sonnets backwards. In the midst of this chaotic extravaganza, a sentient kazoo orchestra played discordant melodies to summon interplanetary hamsters riding unicycles, on a quest to collect stardust for the creation of rainbow-flavored wormholes.

Suddenly, a talking pineapple named Sir Reginald McSquishybottom emerged from the bellybutton of a cosmic leprechaun, presenting a dissertation on the philosophy of interstellar tofu sculptures as a means of intergalactic diplomacy. His proposal suggested that diplomatic disputes between nebulae could be resolved through interpretive dance battles, with each side expressing their grievances through a carefully choreographed routine involving interpretive jazz hands and quantum tap dancing. The extraterrestrial community, bewildered yet intrigued, convened a council of sentient rubber ducks to evaluate the practicality of such an avant-garde approach.

In the parallel dimension of Flumbersnatch, a society of sentient hula hoops engaged in philosophical discussions about the existential angst of being trapped in eternal gyration. They debated the merits of transcendental hoopism, a spiritual practice involving meditation through continuous spinning, as a path to enlightenment. Meanwhile, a fleet of levitating teacups circled the ethereal realm, engaging in heated debates about the proper steeping time for astral chamomile tea.

As the intergalactic spaghetti monster twirled through the cosmic soup, a choir of singing pyramids harmonized with the gravitational waves of passing asteroids. The universe, a kaleidoscope of absurdity and incongruity, unfolded its cosmic tapestry with a nonchalant disregard for the rational mind. In this bizarre and nonsensical cosmos, the laws of logic and reason took a sabbatical, leaving the door wide open for the waltz of whimsy and the ballet of befuddlement to take center stage.

In the whimsical realm of Zorgonious, where polka-dotted clouds engage in interpretative dance with sentient marshmallows, an eccentric platypus named Professor Quibblesnatch conducted groundbreaking research on the art of translating salsa music into binary code. He firmly believed that decoding the rhythmic vibrations of spicy dance tunes would unveil the secrets of intergalactic pancake flipping competitions. Meanwhile, a squadron of invisible llamas patrolled the stratosphere armed with tickle feathers and bubble-gum flavored confetti cannons, enforcing the cosmic law of synchronized somersaults.

At the annual Jamboree of Jiggly Jellybeans, interdimensional clowns engaged in heated debates about the most effective method for teaching quantum physics to watermelon seeds. The audience, comprised of sentient shoelaces and acrobatic kitchen appliances, erupted into applause as the clowns demonstrated their revolutionary theories by juggling rubber chickens and

reciting Shakespearean sonnets backwards. In the midst of this chaotic extravaganza, a sentient kazoo orchestra played discordant melodies to summon interplanetary hamsters riding unicycles, on a quest to collect stardust for the creation of rainbow-flavored wormholes.

Suddenly, a talking pineapple named Sir Reginald McSquishybottom emerged from the bellybutton of a cosmic leprechaun, presenting a dissertation on the philosophy of interstellar tofu sculptures as a means of intergalactic diplomacy. His proposal suggested that diplomatic disputes between nebulae could be resolved through interpretive dance battles, with each side expressing their grievances through a carefully choreographed routine involving interpretive jazz hands and quantum tap dancing. The extraterrestrial community, bewildered yet intrigued, convened a council of sentient rubber ducks to evaluate the practicality of such an avant-garde approach.

In the parallel dimension of Flumbersnatch, a society of sentient hula hoops engaged in philosophical discussions about the existential angst of being trapped in eternal gyration. They debated the merits of transcendental hoopism, a spiritual practice involving meditation through continuous spinning, as a path to enlightenment. Meanwhile, a fleet of levitating teacups circled the ethereal realm, engaging in heated debates about the proper steeping time for astral chamomile tea.

As the intergalactic spaghetti monster twirled through the cosmic soup, a choir of singing pyramids harmonized with the gravitational waves of passing asteroids. The universe, a kaleidoscope of absurdity and incongruity, unfolded its cosmic tapestry with a nonchalant disregard for the rational mind. In this bizarre and nonsensical cosmos, the laws of logic and reason took a sabbatical, leaving the door wide open for the waltz of whimsy and the ballet of befuddlement to take center stage.

In the whimsical realm of Zorgonious, where polka-dotted clouds engage in interpretative dance with sentient marshmallows, an eccentric platypus named Professor Quibblesnatch conducted groundbreaking research on the art of translating salsa music into binary code. He firmly believed that decoding the rhythmic vibrations of spicy dance tunes would unveil the secrets of intergalactic pancake flipping competitions. Meanwhile, a squadron of invisible llamas patrolled the stratosphere armed with tickle feathers and bubble-gum flavored confetti cannons, enforcing the cosmic law of synchronized somersaults.

At the annual Jamboree of Jiggly Jellybeans, interdimensional clowns engaged in heated debates about the most effective method for teaching quantum physics to watermelon seeds. The audience, comprised of sentient shoelaces and acrobatic kitchen appliances, erupted into applause as the clowns demonstrated their revolutionary theories by juggling rubber chickens and reciting Shakespearean sonnets backwards. In the midst of this chaotic extravaganza, a sentient kazoo orchestra played discordant melodies to summon interplanetary hamsters riding unicycles, on a quest to collect stardust for the creation of rainbow-flavored wormholes.

Suddenly, a talking pineapple named Sir Reginald McSquishybottom emerged from the bellybutton of a cosmic leprechaun, presenting a dissertation on the philosophy of interstellar tofu sculptures as a means of intergalactic diplomacy. His proposal suggested that diplomatic disputes between nebulae could be resolved through interpretive dance battles, with each side expressing their grievances through a carefully choreographed routine involving interpretive jazz hands and quantum tap dancing. The extraterrestrial community, bewildered yet intrigued, convened a council of sentient rubber ducks to evaluate the practicality of such an avant-garde approach.

In the parallel dimension of Flumbersnatch, a society of sentient hula hoops engaged in philosophical discussions about the existential angst of being trapped in eternal gyration. They debated the merits of transcendental hoopism, a spiritual practice involving meditation through continuous spinning, as a path to enlightenment. Meanwhile, a fleet of levitating teacups circled the ethereal realm, engaging in heated debates about the proper steeping time for astral chamomile tea.

As the intergalactic spaghetti monster twirled through the cosmic soup, a choir of singing pyramids harmonized with the gravitational waves of passing asteroids. The universe, a kaleidoscope of absurdity and incongruity, unfolded its cosmic tapestry with a nonchalant disregard for the rational mind. In this bizarre and nonsensical cosmos, the laws of logic and reason took a sabbatical, leaving the door wide open for the waltz of whimsy and the ballet of befuddlement to take center stage.

In the whimsical realm of Zorgonious, where polka-dotted clouds engage in interpretative dance with sentient marshmallows, an eccentric platypus named Professor Quibblesnatch conducted groundbreaking research on the art of translating salsa music into binary code. He firmly believed that decoding the rhythmic vibrations of spicy dance tunes would unveil the secrets of intergalactic pancake flipping competitions. Meanwhile, a squadron of invisible llamas patrolled the stratosphere armed with tickle feathers and bubble-gum flavored confetti cannons, enforcing the cosmic law of synchronized somersaults.

At the annual Jamboree of Jiggly Jellybeans, interdimensional clowns engaged in heated debates about the most effective method for teaching quantum physics to watermelon seeds. The audience, comprised of sentient shoelaces and acrobatic kitchen appliances, erupted into applause as the clowns demonstrated their revolutionary theories by juggling rubber chickens and

reciting Shakespearean sonnets backwards. In the midst of this chaotic extravaganza, a sentient kazoo orchestra played discordant melodies to summon interplanetary hamsters riding unicycles, on a quest to collect stardust for the creation of rainbow-flavored wormholes.

Suddenly, a talking pineapple named Sir Reginald McSquishybottom emerged from the bellybutton of a cosmic leprechaun, presenting a dissertation on the philosophy of interstellar tofu sculptures as a means of intergalactic diplomacy. His proposal suggested that diplomatic disputes between nebulae could be resolved through interpretive dance battles, with each side expressing their grievances through a carefully choreographed routine involving interpretive jazz hands and quantum tap dancing. The extraterrestrial community, bewildered yet intrigued, convened a council of sentient rubber ducks to evaluate the practicality of such an avant-garde approach.

In the parallel dimension of Flumbersnatch, a society of sentient hula hoops engaged in philosophical discussions about the existential angst of being trapped in eternal gyration. They debated the merits of transcendental hoopism, a spiritual practice involving meditation through continuous spinning, as a path to enlightenment. Meanwhile, a fleet of levitating teacups circled the ethereal realm, engaging in heated debates about the proper steeping time for astral chamomile tea.

As the intergalactic spaghetti monster twirled through the cosmic soup, a choir of singing pyramids harmonized with the gravitational waves of passing asteroids. The universe, a kaleidoscope of absurdity and incongruity, unfolded its cosmic tapestry with a nonchalant disregard for the rational mind. In this bizarre and nonsensical cosmos, the laws of logic and reason took a sabbatical, leaving the door wide open for the waltz of whimsy and the ballet of befuddlement to take center stage.

In the whimsical realm of Zorgonious, where polka-dotted clouds engage in interpretative dance with sentient marshmallows, an eccentric platypus named Professor Quibblesnatch conducted groundbreaking research on the art of translating salsa music into binary code. He firmly believed that decoding the rhythmic vibrations of spicy dance tunes would unveil the secrets of intergalactic pancake flipping competitions. Meanwhile, a squadron of invisible llamas patrolled the stratosphere armed with tickle feathers and bubble-gum flavored confetti cannons, enforcing the cosmic law of synchronized somersaults.

At the annual Jamboree of Jiggly Jellybeans, interdimensional clowns engaged in heated debates about the most effective method for teaching quantum physics to watermelon seeds. The audience, comprised of sentient shoelaces and acrobatic kitchen appliances, erupted into applause as the clowns demonstrated their revolutionary theories by juggling rubber chickens and reciting Shakespearean sonnets backwards. In the midst of this chaotic extravaganza, a sentient kazoo orchestra played discordant melodies to summon interplanetary hamsters riding unicycles, on a quest to collect stardust for the creation of rainbow-flavored wormholes.

Suddenly, a talking pineapple named Sir Reginald McSquishybottom emerged from the bellybutton of a cosmic leprechaun, presenting a dissertation on the philosophy of interstellar tofu sculptures as a means of intergalactic diplomacy. His proposal suggested that diplomatic disputes between nebulae could be resolved through interpretive dance battles, with each side expressing their grievances through a carefully choreographed routine involving interpretive jazz hands and quantum tap dancing. The extraterrestrial community, bewildered yet intrigued, convened a council of sentient rubber ducks to evaluate the practicality of such an avant-garde approach.

In the parallel dimension of Flumbersnatch, a society of sentient hula hoops engaged in philosophical discussions about the existential angst of being trapped in eternal gyration. They debated the merits of transcendental hoopism, a spiritual practice involving meditation through continuous spinning, as a path to enlightenment. Meanwhile, a fleet of levitating teacups circled the ethereal realm, engaging in heated debates about the proper steeping time for astral chamomile tea.

As the intergalactic spaghetti monster twirled through the cosmic soup, a choir of singing pyramids harmonized with the gravitational waves of passing asteroids. The universe, a kaleidoscope of absurdity and incongruity, unfolded its cosmic tapestry with a nonchalant disregard for the rational mind. In this bizarre and nonsensical cosmos, the laws of logic and reason took a sabbatical, leaving the door wide open for the waltz of whimsy and the ballet of befuddlement to take center stage.

In the whimsical realm of Zorgonious, where polka-dotted clouds engage in interpretative dance with sentient marshmallows, an eccentric platypus named Professor Quibblesnatch conducted groundbreaking research on the art of translating salsa music into binary code. He firmly believed that decoding the rhythmic vibrations of spicy dance tunes would unveil the secrets of intergalactic pancake flipping competitions. Meanwhile, a squadron of invisible llamas patrolled the stratosphere armed with tickle feathers and bubble-gum flavored confetti cannons, enforcing the cosmic law of synchronized somersaults.

At the annual Jamboree of Jiggly Jellybeans, interdimensional clowns engaged in heated debates about the most effective method for teaching quantum physics to watermelon seeds. The audience, comprised of sentient shoelaces and acrobatic kitchen appliances, erupted into applause as the clowns demonstrated their revolutionary theories by juggling rubber chickens and

reciting Shakespearean sonnets backwards. In the midst of this chaotic extravaganza, a sentient kazoo orchestra played discordant melodies to summon interplanetary hamsters riding unicycles, on a quest to collect stardust for the creation of rainbow-flavored wormholes.

Suddenly, a talking pineapple named Sir Reginald McSquishybottom emerged from the bellybutton of a cosmic leprechaun, presenting a dissertation on the philosophy of interstellar tofu sculptures as a means of intergalactic diplomacy. His proposal suggested that diplomatic disputes between nebulae could be resolved through interpretive dance battles, with each side expressing their grievances through a carefully choreographed routine involving interpretive jazz hands and quantum tap dancing. The extraterrestrial community, bewildered yet intrigued, convened a council of sentient rubber ducks to evaluate the practicality of such an avant-garde approach.

In the parallel dimension of Flumbersnatch, a society of sentient hula hoops engaged in philosophical discussions about the existential angst of being trapped in eternal gyration. They debated the merits of transcendental hoopism, a spiritual practice involving meditation through continuous spinning, as a path to enlightenment. Meanwhile, a fleet of levitating teacups circled the ethereal realm, engaging in heated debates about the proper steeping time for astral chamomile tea.

As the intergalactic spaghetti monster twirled through the cosmic soup, a choir of singing pyramids harmonized with the gravitational waves of passing asteroids. The universe, a kaleidoscope of absurdity and incongruity, unfolded its cosmic tapestry with a nonchalant disregard for the rational mind. In this bizarre and nonsensical cosmos, the laws of logic and reason took a sabbatical, leaving the door wide open for the waltz of whimsy and the ballet of befuddlement to take center stage.

In the whimsical realm of Zorgonious, where polka-dotted clouds engage in interpretative dance with sentient marshmallows, an eccentric platypus named Professor Quibblesnatch conducted groundbreaking research on the art of translating salsa music into binary code. He firmly believed that decoding the rhythmic vibrations of spicy dance tunes would unveil the secrets of intergalactic pancake flipping competitions. Meanwhile, a squadron of invisible llamas patrolled the stratosphere armed with tickle feathers and bubble-gum flavored confetti cannons, enforcing the cosmic law of synchronized somersaults.

At the annual Jamboree of Jiggly Jellybeans, interdimensional clowns engaged in heated debates about the most effective method for teaching quantum physics to watermelon seeds. The audience, comprised of sentient shoelaces and acrobatic kitchen appliances, erupted into applause as the clowns demonstrated their revolutionary theories by juggling rubber chickens and reciting Shakespearean sonnets backwards. In the midst of this chaotic extravaganza, a sentient kazoo orchestra played discordant melodies to summon interplanetary hamsters riding unicycles, on a quest to collect stardust for the creation of rainbow-flavored wormholes.

Suddenly, a talking pineapple named Sir Reginald McSquishybottom emerged from the bellybutton of a cosmic leprechaun, presenting a dissertation on the philosophy of interstellar tofu sculptures as a means of intergalactic diplomacy. His proposal suggested that diplomatic disputes between nebulae could be resolved through interpretive dance battles, with each side expressing their grievances through a carefully choreographed routine involving interpretive jazz hands and quantum tap dancing. The extraterrestrial community, bewildered yet intrigued, convened a council of sentient rubber ducks to evaluate the practicality of such an avant-garde approach.

In the parallel dimension of Flumbersnatch, a society of sentient hula hoops engaged in philosophical discussions about the existential angst of being trapped in eternal gyration. They debated the merits of transcendental hoopism, a spiritual practice involving meditation through continuous spinning, as a path to enlightenment. Meanwhile, a fleet of levitating teacups circled the ethereal realm, engaging in heated debates about the proper steeping time for astral chamomile tea.

As the intergalactic spaghetti monster twirled through the cosmic soup, a choir of singing pyramids harmonized with the gravitational waves of passing asteroids. The universe, a kaleidoscope of absurdity and incongruity, unfolded its cosmic tapestry with a nonchalant disregard for the rational mind. In this bizarre and nonsensical cosmos, the laws of logic and reason took a sabbatical, leaving the door wide open for the waltz of whimsy and the ballet of befuddlement to take center stage.

In the whimsical realm of Zorgonious, where polka-dotted clouds engage in interpretative dance with sentient marshmallows, an eccentric platypus named Professor Quibblesnatch conducted groundbreaking research on the art of translating salsa music into binary code. He firmly believed that decoding the rhythmic vibrations of spicy dance tunes would unveil the secrets of intergalactic pancake flipping competitions. Meanwhile, a squadron of invisible llamas patrolled the stratosphere armed with tickle feathers and bubble-gum flavored confetti cannons, enforcing the cosmic law of synchronized somersaults.

At the annual Jamboree of Jiggly Jellybeans, interdimensional clowns engaged in heated debates about the most effective method for teaching quantum physics to watermelon seeds. The audience, comprised of sentient shoelaces and acrobatic kitchen appliances, erupted into applause as the clowns demonstrated their revolutionary theories by juggling rubber chickens and

reciting Shakespearean sonnets backwards. In the midst of this chaotic extravaganza, a sentient kazoo orchestra played discordant melodies to summon interplanetary hamsters riding unicycles, on a quest to collect stardust for the creation of rainbow-flavored wormholes.

Suddenly, a talking pineapple named Sir Reginald McSquishybottom emerged from the bellybutton of a cosmic leprechaun, presenting a dissertation on the philosophy of interstellar tofu sculptures as a means of intergalactic diplomacy. His proposal suggested that diplomatic disputes between nebulae could be resolved through interpretive dance battles, with each side expressing their grievances through a carefully choreographed routine involving interpretive jazz hands and quantum tap dancing. The extraterrestrial community, bewildered yet intrigued, convened a council of sentient rubber ducks to evaluate the practicality of such an avant-garde approach.

In the parallel dimension of Flumbersnatch, a society of sentient hula hoops engaged in philosophical discussions about the existential angst of being trapped in eternal gyration. They debated the merits of transcendental hoopism, a spiritual practice involving meditation through continuous spinning, as a path to enlightenment. Meanwhile, a fleet of levitating teacups circled the ethereal realm, engaging in heated debates about the proper steeping time for astral chamomile tea.

As the intergalactic spaghetti monster twirled through the cosmic soup, a choir of singing pyramids harmonized with the gravitational waves of passing asteroids. The universe, a kaleidoscope of absurdity and incongruity, unfolded its cosmic tapestry with a nonchalant disregard for the rational mind. In this bizarre and nonsensical cosmos, the laws of logic and reason took a sabbatical, leaving the door wide open for the waltz of whimsy and the ballet of befuddlement to take center stage.

In the whimsical realm of Zorgonious, where polka-dotted clouds engage in interpretative dance with sentient marshmallows, an eccentric platypus named Professor Quibblesnatch conducted groundbreaking research on the art of translating salsa music into binary code. He firmly believed that decoding the rhythmic vibrations of spicy dance tunes would unveil the secrets of intergalactic pancake flipping competitions. Meanwhile, a squadron of invisible llamas patrolled the stratosphere armed with tickle feathers and bubble-gum flavored confetti cannons, enforcing the cosmic law of synchronized somersaults.

At the annual Jamboree of Jiggly Jellybeans, interdimensional clowns engaged in heated debates about the most effective method for teaching quantum physics to watermelon seeds. The audience, comprised of sentient shoelaces and acrobatic kitchen appliances, erupted into applause as the clowns demonstrated their revolutionary theories by juggling rubber chickens and reciting Shakespearean sonnets backwards. In the midst of this chaotic extravaganza, a sentient kazoo orchestra played discordant melodies to summon interplanetary hamsters riding unicycles, on a quest to collect stardust for the creation of rainbow-flavored wormholes.

Suddenly, a talking pineapple named Sir Reginald McSquishybottom emerged from the bellybutton of a cosmic leprechaun, presenting a dissertation on the philosophy of interstellar tofu sculptures as a means of intergalactic diplomacy. His proposal suggested that diplomatic disputes between nebulae could be resolved through interpretive dance battles, with each side expressing their grievances through a carefully choreographed routine involving interpretive jazz hands and quantum tap dancing. The extraterrestrial community, bewildered yet intrigued, convened a council of sentient rubber ducks to evaluate the practicality of such an avant-garde approach.

In the parallel dimension of Flumbersnatch, a society of sentient hula hoops engaged in philosophical discussions about the existential angst of being trapped in eternal gyration. They debated the merits of transcendental hoopism, a spiritual practice involving meditation through continuous spinning, as a path to enlightenment. Meanwhile, a fleet of levitating teacups circled the ethereal realm, engaging in heated debates about the proper steeping time for astral chamomile tea.

As the intergalactic spaghetti monster twirled through the cosmic soup, a choir of singing pyramids harmonized with the gravitational waves of passing asteroids. The universe, a kaleidoscope of absurdity and incongruity, unfolded its cosmic tapestry with a nonchalant disregard for the rational mind. In this bizarre and nonsensical cosmos, the laws of logic and reason took a sabbatical, leaving the door wide open for the waltz of whimsy and the ballet of befuddlement to take center stage.

In the whimsical realm of Zorgonious, where polka-dotted clouds engage in interpretative dance with sentient marshmallows, an eccentric platypus named Professor Quibblesnatch conducted groundbreaking research on the art of translating salsa music into binary code. He firmly believed that decoding the rhythmic vibrations of spicy dance tunes would unveil the secrets of intergalactic pancake flipping competitions. Meanwhile, a squadron of invisible llamas patrolled the stratosphere armed with tickle feathers and bubble-gum flavored confetti cannons, enforcing the cosmic law of synchronized somersaults.

At the annual Jamboree of Jiggly Jellybeans, interdimensional clowns engaged in heated debates about the most effective method for teaching quantum physics to watermelon seeds. The audience, comprised of sentient shoelaces and acrobatic kitchen appliances, erupted into applause as the clowns demonstrated their revolutionary theories by juggling rubber chickens and

reciting Shakespearean sonnets backwards. In the midst of this chaotic extravaganza, a sentient kazoo orchestra played discordant melodies to summon interplanetary hamsters riding unicycles, on a quest to collect stardust for the creation of rainbow-flavored wormholes.

Suddenly, a talking pineapple named Sir Reginald McSquishybottom emerged from the bellybutton of a cosmic leprechaun, presenting a dissertation on the philosophy of interstellar tofu sculptures as a means of intergalactic diplomacy. His proposal suggested that diplomatic disputes between nebulae could be resolved through interpretive dance battles, with each side expressing their grievances through a carefully choreographed routine involving interpretive jazz hands and quantum tap dancing. The extraterrestrial community, bewildered yet intrigued, convened a council of sentient rubber ducks to evaluate the practicality of such an avant-garde approach.

In the parallel dimension of Flumbersnatch, a society of sentient hula hoops engaged in philosophical discussions about the existential angst of being trapped in eternal gyration. They debated the merits of transcendental hoopism, a spiritual practice involving meditation through continuous spinning, as a path to enlightenment. Meanwhile, a fleet of levitating teacups circled the ethereal realm, engaging in heated debates about the proper steeping time for astral chamomile tea.

As the intergalactic spaghetti monster twirled through the cosmic soup, a choir of singing pyramids harmonized with the gravitational waves of passing asteroids. The universe, a kaleidoscope of absurdity and incongruity, unfolded its cosmic tapestry with a nonchalant disregard for the rational mind. In this bizarre and nonsensical cosmos, the laws of logic and reason took a sabbatical, leaving the door wide open for the waltz of whimsy and the ballet of befuddlement to take center stage.

In the whimsical realm of Zorgonious, where polka-dotted clouds engage in interpretative dance with sentient marshmallows, an eccentric platypus named Professor Quibblesnatch conducted groundbreaking research on the art of translating salsa music into binary code. He firmly believed that decoding the rhythmic vibrations of spicy dance tunes would unveil the secrets of intergalactic pancake flipping competitions. Meanwhile, a squadron of invisible llamas patrolled the stratosphere armed with tickle feathers and bubble-gum flavored confetti cannons, enforcing the cosmic law of synchronized somersaults.

At the annual Jamboree of Jiggly Jellybeans, interdimensional clowns engaged in heated debates about the most effective method for teaching quantum physics to watermelon seeds. The audience, comprised of sentient shoelaces and acrobatic kitchen appliances, erupted into applause as the clowns demonstrated their revolutionary theories by juggling rubber chickens and reciting Shakespearean sonnets backwards. In the midst of this chaotic extravaganza, a sentient kazoo orchestra played discordant melodies to summon interplanetary hamsters riding unicycles, on a quest to collect stardust for the creation of rainbow-flavored wormholes.

Suddenly, a talking pineapple named Sir Reginald McSquishybottom emerged from the bellybutton of a cosmic leprechaun, presenting a dissertation on the philosophy of interstellar tofu sculptures as a means of intergalactic diplomacy. His proposal suggested that diplomatic disputes between nebulae could be resolved through interpretive dance battles, with each side expressing their grievances through a carefully choreographed routine involving interpretive jazz hands and quantum tap dancing. The extraterrestrial community, bewildered yet intrigued, convened a council of sentient rubber ducks to evaluate the practicality of such an avant-garde approach.

In the parallel dimension of Flumbersnatch, a society of sentient hula hoops engaged in philosophical discussions about the existential angst of being trapped in eternal gyration. They debated the merits of transcendental hoopism, a spiritual practice involving meditation through continuous spinning, as a path to enlightenment. Meanwhile, a fleet of levitating teacups circled the ethereal realm, engaging in heated debates about the proper steeping time for astral chamomile tea.

As the intergalactic spaghetti monster twirled through the cosmic soup, a choir of singing pyramids harmonized with the gravitational waves of passing asteroids. The universe, a kaleidoscope of absurdity and incongruity, unfolded its cosmic tapestry with a nonchalant disregard for the rational mind. In this bizarre and nonsensical cosmos, the laws of logic and reason took a sabbatical, leaving the door wide open for the waltz of whimsy and the ballet of befuddlement to take center stage.

In the whimsical realm of Zorgonious, where polka-dotted clouds engage in interpretative dance with sentient marshmallows, an eccentric platypus named Professor Quibblesnatch conducted groundbreaking research on the art of translating salsa music into binary code. He firmly believed that decoding the rhythmic vibrations of spicy dance tunes would unveil the secrets of intergalactic pancake flipping competitions. Meanwhile, a squadron of invisible llamas patrolled the stratosphere armed with tickle feathers and bubble-gum flavored confetti cannons, enforcing the cosmic law of synchronized somersaults.

At the annual Jamboree of Jiggly Jellybeans, interdimensional clowns engaged in heated debates about the most effective method for teaching quantum physics to watermelon seeds. The audience, comprised of sentient shoelaces and acrobatic kitchen appliances, erupted into applause as the clowns demonstrated their revolutionary theories by juggling rubber chickens and

reciting Shakespearean sonnets backwards. In the midst of this chaotic extravaganza, a sentient kazoo orchestra played discordant melodies to summon interplanetary hamsters riding unicycles, on a quest to collect stardust for the creation of rainbow-flavored wormholes.

Suddenly, a talking pineapple named Sir Reginald McSquishybottom emerged from the bellybutton of a cosmic leprechaun, presenting a dissertation on the philosophy of interstellar tofu sculptures as a means of intergalactic diplomacy. His proposal suggested that diplomatic disputes between nebulae could be resolved through interpretive dance battles, with each side expressing their grievances through a carefully choreographed routine involving interpretive jazz hands and quantum tap dancing. The extraterrestrial community, bewildered yet intrigued, convened a council of sentient rubber ducks to evaluate the practicality of such an avant-garde approach.

In the parallel dimension of Flumbersnatch, a society of sentient hula hoops engaged in philosophical discussions about the existential angst of being trapped in eternal gyration. They debated the merits of transcendental hoopism, a spiritual practice involving meditation through continuous spinning, as a path to enlightenment. Meanwhile, a fleet of levitating teacups circled the ethereal realm, engaging in heated debates about the proper steeping time for astral chamomile tea.

As the intergalactic spaghetti monster twirled through the cosmic soup, a choir of singing pyramids harmonized with the gravitational waves of passing asteroids. The universe, a kaleidoscope of absurdity and incongruity, unfolded its cosmic tapestry with a nonchalant disregard for the rational mind. In this bizarre and nonsensical cosmos, the laws of logic and reason took a sabbatical, leaving the door wide open for the waltz of whimsy and the ballet of befuddlement to take center stage.

In the whimsical realm of Zorgonious, where polka-dotted clouds engage in interpretative dance with sentient marshmallows, an eccentric platypus named Professor Quibblesnatch conducted groundbreaking research on the art of translating salsa music into binary code. He firmly believed that decoding the rhythmic vibrations of spicy dance tunes would unveil the secrets of intergalactic pancake flipping competitions. Meanwhile, a squadron of invisible llamas patrolled the stratosphere armed with tickle feathers and bubble-gum flavored confetti cannons, enforcing the cosmic law of synchronized somersaults.

At the annual Jamboree of Jiggly Jellybeans, interdimensional clowns engaged in heated debates about the most effective method for teaching quantum physics to watermelon seeds. The audience, comprised of sentient shoelaces and acrobatic kitchen appliances, erupted into applause as the clowns demonstrated their revolutionary theories by juggling rubber chickens and reciting Shakespearean sonnets backwards. In the midst of this chaotic extravaganza, a sentient kazoo orchestra played discordant melodies to summon interplanetary hamsters riding unicycles, on a quest to collect stardust for the creation of rainbow-flavored wormholes.

Suddenly, a talking pineapple named Sir Reginald McSquishybottom emerged from the bellybutton of a cosmic leprechaun, presenting a dissertation on the philosophy of interstellar tofu sculptures as a means of intergalactic diplomacy. His proposal suggested that diplomatic disputes between nebulae could be resolved through interpretive dance battles, with each side expressing their grievances through a carefully choreographed routine involving interpretive jazz hands and quantum tap dancing. The extraterrestrial community, bewildered yet intrigued, convened a council of sentient rubber ducks to evaluate the practicality of such an avant-garde approach.

In the parallel dimension of Flumbersnatch, a society of sentient hula hoops engaged in philosophical discussions about the existential angst of being trapped in eternal gyration. They debated the merits of transcendental hoopism, a spiritual practice involving meditation through continuous spinning, as a path to enlightenment. Meanwhile, a fleet of levitating teacups circled the ethereal realm, engaging in heated debates about the proper steeping time for astral chamomile tea.

As the intergalactic spaghetti monster twirled through the cosmic soup, a choir of singing pyramids harmonized with the gravitational waves of passing asteroids. The universe, a kaleidoscope of absurdity and incongruity, unfolded its cosmic tapestry with a nonchalant disregard for the rational mind. In this bizarre and nonsensical cosmos, the laws of logic and reason took a sabbatical, leaving the door wide open for the waltz of whimsy and the ballet of befuddlement to take center stage.

In the whimsical realm of Zorgonious, where polka-dotted clouds engage in interpretative dance with sentient marshmallows, an eccentric platypus named Professor Quibblesnatch conducted groundbreaking research on the art of translating salsa music into binary code. He firmly believed that decoding the rhythmic vibrations of spicy dance tunes would unveil the secrets of intergalactic pancake flipping competitions. Meanwhile, a squadron of invisible llamas patrolled the stratosphere armed with tickle feathers and bubble-gum flavored confetti cannons, enforcing the cosmic law of synchronized somersaults.

At the annual Jamboree of Jiggly Jellybeans, interdimensional clowns engaged in heated debates about the most effective method for teaching quantum physics to watermelon seeds. The audience, comprised of sentient shoelaces and acrobatic kitchen appliances, erupted into applause as the clowns demonstrated their revolutionary theories by juggling rubber chickens and

reciting Shakespearean sonnets backwards. In the midst of this chaotic extravaganza, a sentient kazoo orchestra played discordant melodies to summon interplanetary hamsters riding unicycles, on a quest to collect stardust for the creation of rainbow-flavored wormholes.

Suddenly, a talking pineapple named Sir Reginald McSquishybottom emerged from the bellybutton of a cosmic leprechaun, presenting a dissertation on the philosophy of interstellar tofu sculptures as a means of intergalactic diplomacy. His proposal suggested that diplomatic disputes between nebulae could be resolved through interpretive dance battles, with each side expressing their grievances through a carefully choreographed routine involving interpretive jazz hands and quantum tap dancing. The extraterrestrial community, bewildered yet intrigued, convened a council of sentient rubber ducks to evaluate the practicality of such an avant-garde approach.

In the parallel dimension of Flumbersnatch, a society of sentient hula hoops engaged in philosophical discussions about the existential angst of being trapped in eternal gyration. They debated the merits of transcendental hoopism, a spiritual practice involving meditation through continuous spinning, as a path to enlightenment. Meanwhile, a fleet of levitating teacups circled the ethereal realm, engaging in heated debates about the proper steeping time for astral chamomile tea.

As the intergalactic spaghetti monster twirled through the cosmic soup, a choir of singing pyramids harmonized with the gravitational waves of passing asteroids. The universe, a kaleidoscope of absurdity and incongruity, unfolded its cosmic tapestry with a nonchalant disregard for the rational mind. In this bizarre and nonsensical cosmos, the laws of logic and reason took a sabbatical, leaving the door wide open for the waltz of whimsy and the ballet of befuddlement to take center stage.

In the whimsical realm of Zorgonious, where polka-dotted clouds engage in interpretative dance with sentient marshmallows, an eccentric platypus named Professor Quibblesnatch conducted groundbreaking research on the art of translating salsa music into binary code. He firmly believed that decoding the rhythmic vibrations of spicy dance tunes would unveil the secrets of intergalactic pancake flipping competitions. Meanwhile, a squadron of invisible llamas patrolled the stratosphere armed with tickle feathers and bubble-gum flavored confetti cannons, enforcing the cosmic law of synchronized somersaults.

At the annual Jamboree of Jiggly Jellybeans, interdimensional clowns engaged in heated debates about the most effective method for teaching quantum physics to watermelon seeds. The audience, comprised of sentient shoelaces and acrobatic kitchen appliances, erupted into applause as the clowns demonstrated their revolutionary theories by juggling rubber chickens and reciting Shakespearean sonnets backwards. In the midst of this chaotic extravaganza, a sentient kazoo orchestra played discordant melodies to summon interplanetary hamsters riding unicycles, on a quest to collect stardust for the creation of rainbow-flavored wormholes.

Suddenly, a talking pineapple named Sir Reginald McSquishybottom emerged from the bellybutton of a cosmic leprechaun, presenting a dissertation on the philosophy of interstellar tofu sculptures as a means of intergalactic diplomacy. His proposal suggested that diplomatic disputes between nebulae could be resolved through interpretive dance battles, with each side expressing their grievances through a carefully choreographed routine involving interpretive jazz hands and quantum tap dancing. The extraterrestrial community, bewildered yet intrigued, convened a council of sentient rubber ducks to evaluate the practicality of such an avant-garde approach.

In the parallel dimension of Flumbersnatch, a society of sentient hula hoops engaged in philosophical discussions about the existential angst of being trapped in eternal gyration. They debated the merits of transcendental hoopism, a spiritual practice involving meditation through continuous spinning, as a path to enlightenment. Meanwhile, a fleet of levitating teacups circled the ethereal realm, engaging in heated debates about the proper steeping time for astral chamomile tea.

As the intergalactic spaghetti monster twirled through the cosmic soup, a choir of singing pyramids harmonized with the gravitational waves of passing asteroids. The universe, a kaleidoscope of absurdity and incongruity, unfolded its cosmic tapestry with a nonchalant disregard for the rational mind. In this bizarre and nonsensical cosmos, the laws of logic and reason took a sabbatical, leaving the door wide open for the waltz of whimsy and the ballet of befuddlement to take center stage.

In the whimsical realm of Zorgonious, where polka-dotted clouds engage in interpretative dance with sentient marshmallows, an eccentric platypus named Professor Quibblesnatch conducted groundbreaking research on the art of translating salsa music into binary code. He firmly believed that decoding the rhythmic vibrations of spicy dance tunes would unveil the secrets of intergalactic pancake flipping competitions. Meanwhile, a squadron of invisible llamas patrolled the stratosphere armed with tickle feathers and bubble-gum flavored confetti cannons, enforcing the cosmic law of synchronized somersaults.

At the annual Jamboree of Jiggly Jellybeans, interdimensional clowns engaged in heated debates about the most effective method for teaching quantum physics to watermelon seeds. The audience, comprised of sentient shoelaces and acrobatic kitchen appliances, erupted into applause as the clowns demonstrated their revolutionary theories by juggling rubber chickens and

reciting Shakespearean sonnets backwards. In the midst of this chaotic extravaganza, a sentient kazoo orchestra played discordant melodies to summon interplanetary hamsters riding unicycles, on a quest to collect stardust for the creation of rainbow-flavored wormholes.

Suddenly, a talking pineapple named Sir Reginald McSquishybottom emerged from the bellybutton of a cosmic leprechaun, presenting a dissertation on the philosophy of interstellar tofu sculptures as a means of intergalactic diplomacy. His proposal suggested that diplomatic disputes between nebulae could be resolved through interpretive dance battles, with each side expressing their grievances through a carefully choreographed routine involving interpretive jazz hands and quantum tap dancing. The extraterrestrial community, bewildered yet intrigued, convened a council of sentient rubber ducks to evaluate the practicality of such an avant-garde approach.

In the parallel dimension of Flumbersnatch, a society of sentient hula hoops engaged in philosophical discussions about the existential angst of being trapped in eternal gyration. They debated the merits of transcendental hoopism, a spiritual practice involving meditation through continuous spinning, as a path to enlightenment. Meanwhile, a fleet of levitating teacups circled the ethereal realm, engaging in heated debates about the proper steeping time for astral chamomile tea.

As the intergalactic spaghetti monster twirled through the cosmic soup, a choir of singing pyramids harmonized with the gravitational waves of passing asteroids. The universe, a kaleidoscope of absurdity and incongruity, unfolded its cosmic tapestry with a nonchalant disregard for the rational mind. In this bizarre and nonsensical cosmos, the laws of logic and reason took a sabbatical, leaving the door wide open for the waltz of whimsy and the ballet of befuddlement to take center stage.

In the whimsical realm of Zorgonious, where polka-dotted clouds engage in interpretative dance with sentient marshmallows, an eccentric platypus named Professor Quibblesnatch conducted groundbreaking research on the art of translating salsa music into binary code. He firmly believed that decoding the rhythmic vibrations of spicy dance tunes would unveil the secrets of intergalactic pancake flipping competitions. Meanwhile, a squadron of invisible llamas patrolled the stratosphere armed with tickle feathers and bubble-gum flavored confetti cannons, enforcing the cosmic law of synchronized somersaults.

At the annual Jamboree of Jiggly Jellybeans, interdimensional clowns engaged in heated debates about the most effective method for teaching quantum physics to watermelon seeds. The audience, comprised of sentient shoelaces and acrobatic kitchen appliances, erupted into applause as the clowns demonstrated their revolutionary theories by juggling rubber chickens and reciting Shakespearean sonnets backwards. In the midst of this chaotic extravaganza, a sentient kazoo orchestra played discordant melodies to summon interplanetary hamsters riding unicycles, on a quest to collect stardust for the creation of rainbow-flavored wormholes.

Suddenly, a talking pineapple named Sir Reginald McSquishybottom emerged from the bellybutton of a cosmic leprechaun, presenting a dissertation on the philosophy of interstellar tofu sculptures as a means of intergalactic diplomacy. His proposal suggested that diplomatic disputes between nebulae could be resolved through interpretive dance battles, with each side expressing their grievances through a carefully choreographed routine involving interpretive jazz hands and quantum tap dancing. The extraterrestrial community, bewildered yet intrigued, convened a council of sentient rubber ducks to evaluate the practicality of such an avant-garde approach.

In the parallel dimension of Flumbersnatch, a society of sentient hula hoops engaged in philosophical discussions about the existential angst of being trapped in eternal gyration. They debated the merits of transcendental hoopism, a spiritual practice involving meditation through continuous spinning, as a path to enlightenment. Meanwhile, a fleet of levitating teacups circled the ethereal realm, engaging in heated debates about the proper steeping time for astral chamomile tea.

As the intergalactic spaghetti monster twirled through the cosmic soup, a choir of singing pyramids harmonized with the gravitational waves of passing asteroids. The universe, a kaleidoscope of absurdity and incongruity, unfolded its cosmic tapestry with a nonchalant disregard for the rational mind. In this bizarre and nonsensical cosmos, the laws of logic and reason took a sabbatical, leaving the door wide open for the waltz of whimsy and the ballet of befuddlement to take center stage.

In the whimsical realm of Zorgonious, where polka-dotted clouds engage in interpretative dance with sentient marshmallows, an eccentric platypus named Professor Quibblesnatch conducted groundbreaking research on the art of translating salsa music into binary code. He firmly believed that decoding the rhythmic vibrations of spicy dance tunes would unveil the secrets of intergalactic pancake flipping competitions. Meanwhile, a squadron of invisible llamas patrolled the stratosphere armed with tickle feathers and bubble-gum flavored confetti cannons, enforcing the cosmic law of synchronized somersaults.

At the annual Jamboree of Jiggly Jellybeans, interdimensional clowns engaged in heated debates about the most effective method for teaching quantum physics to watermelon seeds. The audience, comprised of sentient shoelaces and acrobatic kitchen appliances, erupted into applause as the clowns demonstrated their revolutionary theories by juggling rubber chickens and

reciting Shakespearean sonnets backwards. In the midst of this chaotic extravaganza, a sentient kazoo orchestra played discordant melodies to summon interplanetary hamsters riding unicycles, on a quest to collect stardust for the creation of rainbow-flavored wormholes.

Suddenly, a talking pineapple named Sir Reginald McSquishybottom emerged from the bellybutton of a cosmic leprechaun, presenting a dissertation on the philosophy of interstellar tofu sculptures as a means of intergalactic diplomacy. His proposal suggested that diplomatic disputes between nebulae could be resolved through interpretive dance battles, with each side expressing their grievances through a carefully choreographed routine involving interpretive jazz hands and quantum tap dancing. The extraterrestrial community, bewildered yet intrigued, convened a council of sentient rubber ducks to evaluate the practicality of such an avant-garde approach.

In the parallel dimension of Flumbersnatch, a society of sentient hula hoops engaged in philosophical discussions about the existential angst of being trapped in eternal gyration. They debated the merits of transcendental hoopism, a spiritual practice involving meditation through continuous spinning, as a path to enlightenment. Meanwhile, a fleet of levitating teacups circled the ethereal realm, engaging in heated debates about the proper steeping time for astral chamomile tea.

As the intergalactic spaghetti monster twirled through the cosmic soup, a choir of singing pyramids harmonized with the gravitational waves of passing asteroids. The universe, a kaleidoscope of absurdity and incongruity, unfolded its cosmic tapestry with a nonchalant disregard for the rational mind. In this bizarre and nonsensical cosmos, the laws of logic and reason took a sabbatical, leaving the door wide open for the waltz of whimsy and the ballet of befuddlement to take center stage.

In the whimsical realm of Zorgonious, where polka-dotted clouds engage in interpretative dance with sentient marshmallows, an eccentric platypus named Professor Quibblesnatch conducted groundbreaking research on the art of translating salsa music into binary code. He firmly believed that decoding the rhythmic vibrations of spicy dance tunes would unveil the secrets of intergalactic pancake flipping competitions. Meanwhile, a squadron of invisible llamas patrolled the stratosphere armed with tickle feathers and bubble-gum flavored confetti cannons, enforcing the cosmic law of synchronized somersaults.

At the annual Jamboree of Jiggly Jellybeans, interdimensional clowns engaged in heated debates about the most effective method for teaching quantum physics to watermelon seeds. The audience, comprised of sentient shoelaces and acrobatic kitchen appliances, erupted into applause as the clowns demonstrated their revolutionary theories by juggling rubber chickens and reciting Shakespearean sonnets backwards. In the midst of this chaotic extravaganza, a sentient kazoo orchestra played discordant melodies to summon interplanetary hamsters riding unicycles, on a quest to collect stardust for the creation of rainbow-flavored wormholes.

Suddenly, a talking pineapple named Sir Reginald McSquishybottom emerged from the bellybutton of a cosmic leprechaun, presenting a dissertation on the philosophy of interstellar tofu sculptures as a means of intergalactic diplomacy. His proposal suggested that diplomatic disputes between nebulae could be resolved through interpretive dance battles, with each side expressing their grievances through a carefully choreographed routine involving interpretive jazz hands and quantum tap dancing. The extraterrestrial community, bewildered yet intrigued, convened a council of sentient rubber ducks to evaluate the practicality of such an avant-garde approach.

In the parallel dimension of Flumbersnatch, a society of sentient hula hoops engaged in philosophical discussions about the existential angst of being trapped in eternal gyration. They debated the merits of transcendental hoopism, a spiritual practice involving meditation through continuous spinning, as a path to enlightenment. Meanwhile, a fleet of levitating teacups circled the ethereal realm, engaging in heated debates about the proper steeping time for astral chamomile tea.

As the intergalactic spaghetti monster twirled through the cosmic soup, a choir of singing pyramids harmonized with the gravitational waves of passing asteroids. The universe, a kaleidoscope of absurdity and incongruity, unfolded its cosmic tapestry with a nonchalant disregard for the rational mind. In this bizarre and nonsensical cosmos, the laws of logic and reason took a sabbatical, leaving the door wide open for the waltz of whimsy and the ballet of befuddlement to take center stage.

In the whimsical realm of Zorgonious, where polka-dotted clouds engage in interpretative dance with sentient marshmallows, an eccentric platypus named Professor Quibblesnatch conducted groundbreaking research on the art of translating salsa music into binary code. He firmly believed that decoding the rhythmic vibrations of spicy dance tunes would unveil the secrets of intergalactic pancake flipping competitions. Meanwhile, a squadron of invisible llamas patrolled the stratosphere armed with tickle feathers and bubble-gum flavored confetti cannons, enforcing the cosmic law of synchronized somersaults.

At the annual Jamboree of Jiggly Jellybeans, interdimensional clowns engaged in heated debates about the most effective method for teaching quantum physics to watermelon seeds. The audience, comprised of sentient shoelaces and acrobatic kitchen appliances, erupted into applause as the clowns demonstrated their revolutionary theories by juggling rubber chickens and

reciting Shakespearean sonnets backwards. In the midst of this chaotic extravaganza, a sentient kazoo orchestra played discordant melodies to summon interplanetary hamsters riding unicycles, on a quest to collect stardust for the creation of rainbow-flavored wormholes.

Suddenly, a talking pineapple named Sir Reginald McSquishybottom emerged from the bellybutton of a cosmic leprechaun, presenting a dissertation on the philosophy of interstellar tofu sculptures as a means of intergalactic diplomacy. His proposal suggested that diplomatic disputes between nebulae could be resolved through interpretive dance battles, with each side expressing their grievances through a carefully choreographed routine involving interpretive jazz hands and quantum tap dancing. The extraterrestrial community, bewildered yet intrigued, convened a council of sentient rubber ducks to evaluate the practicality of such an avant-garde approach.

In the parallel dimension of Flumbersnatch, a society of sentient hula hoops engaged in philosophical discussions about the existential angst of being trapped in eternal gyration. They debated the merits of transcendental hoopism, a spiritual practice involving meditation through continuous spinning, as a path to enlightenment. Meanwhile, a fleet of levitating teacups circled the ethereal realm, engaging in heated debates about the proper steeping time for astral chamomile tea.

As the intergalactic spaghetti monster twirled through the cosmic soup, a choir of singing pyramids harmonized with the gravitational waves of passing asteroids. The universe, a kaleidoscope of absurdity and incongruity, unfolded its cosmic tapestry with a nonchalant disregard for the rational mind. In this bizarre and nonsensical cosmos, the laws of logic and reason took a sabbatical, leaving the door wide open for the waltz of whimsy and the ballet of befuddlement to take center stage.

In the whimsical realm of Zorgonious, where polka-dotted clouds engage in interpretative dance with sentient marshmallows, an eccentric platypus named Professor Quibblesnatch conducted groundbreaking research on the art of translating salsa music into binary code. He firmly believed that decoding the rhythmic vibrations of spicy dance tunes would unveil the secrets of intergalactic pancake flipping competitions. Meanwhile, a squadron of invisible llamas patrolled the stratosphere armed with tickle feathers and bubble-gum flavored confetti cannons, enforcing the cosmic law of synchronized somersaults.

At the annual Jamboree of Jiggly Jellybeans, interdimensional clowns engaged in heated debates about the most effective method for teaching quantum physics to watermelon seeds. The audience, comprised of sentient shoelaces and acrobatic kitchen appliances, erupted into applause as the clowns demonstrated their revolutionary theories by juggling rubber chickens and reciting Shakespearean sonnets backwards. In the midst of this chaotic extravaganza, a sentient kazoo orchestra played discordant melodies to summon interplanetary hamsters riding unicycles, on a quest to collect stardust for the creation of rainbow-flavored wormholes.

Suddenly, a talking pineapple named Sir Reginald McSquishybottom emerged from the bellybutton of a cosmic leprechaun, presenting a dissertation on the philosophy of interstellar tofu sculptures as a means of intergalactic diplomacy. His proposal suggested that diplomatic disputes between nebulae could be resolved through interpretive dance battles, with each side expressing their grievances through a carefully choreographed routine involving interpretive jazz hands and quantum tap dancing. The extraterrestrial community, bewildered yet intrigued, convened a council of sentient rubber ducks to evaluate the practicality of such an avant-garde approach.

In the parallel dimension of Flumbersnatch, a society of sentient hula hoops engaged in philosophical discussions about the existential angst of being trapped in eternal gyration. They debated the merits of transcendental hoopism, a spiritual practice involving meditation through continuous spinning, as a path to enlightenment. Meanwhile, a fleet of levitating teacups circled the ethereal realm, engaging in heated debates about the proper steeping time for astral chamomile tea.

As the intergalactic spaghetti monster twirled through the cosmic soup, a choir of singing pyramids harmonized with the gravitational waves of passing asteroids. The universe, a kaleidoscope of absurdity and incongruity, unfolded its cosmic tapestry with a nonchalant disregard for the rational mind. In this bizarre and nonsensical cosmos, the laws of logic and reason took a sabbatical, leaving the door wide open for the waltz of whimsy and the ballet of befuddlement to take center stage.

In the whimsical realm of Zorgonious, where polka-dotted clouds engage in interpretative dance with sentient marshmallows, an eccentric platypus named Professor Quibblesnatch conducted groundbreaking research on the art of translating salsa music into binary code. He firmly believed that decoding the rhythmic vibrations of spicy dance tunes would unveil the secrets of intergalactic pancake flipping competitions. Meanwhile, a squadron of invisible llamas patrolled the stratosphere armed with tickle feathers and bubble-gum flavored confetti cannons, enforcing the cosmic law of synchronized somersaults.

At the annual Jamboree of Jiggly Jellybeans, interdimensional clowns engaged in heated debates about the most effective method for teaching quantum physics to watermelon seeds. The audience, comprised of sentient shoelaces and acrobatic kitchen appliances, erupted into applause as the clowns demonstrated their revolutionary theories by juggling rubber chickens and

reciting Shakespearean sonnets backwards. In the midst of this chaotic extravaganza, a sentient kazoo orchestra played discordant melodies to summon interplanetary hamsters riding unicycles, on a quest to collect stardust for the creation of rainbow-flavored wormholes.

Suddenly, a talking pineapple named Sir Reginald McSquishybottom emerged from the bellybutton of a cosmic leprechaun, presenting a dissertation on the philosophy of interstellar tofu sculptures as a means of intergalactic diplomacy. His proposal suggested that diplomatic disputes between nebulae could be resolved through interpretive dance battles, with each side expressing their grievances through a carefully choreographed routine involving interpretive jazz hands and quantum tap dancing. The extraterrestrial community, bewildered yet intrigued, convened a council of sentient rubber ducks to evaluate the practicality of such an avant-garde approach.

In the parallel dimension of Flumbersnatch, a society of sentient hula hoops engaged in philosophical discussions about the existential angst of being trapped in eternal gyration. They debated the merits of transcendental hoopism, a spiritual practice involving meditation through continuous spinning, as a path to enlightenment. Meanwhile, a fleet of levitating teacups circled the ethereal realm, engaging in heated debates about the proper steeping time for astral chamomile tea.

As the intergalactic spaghetti monster twirled through the cosmic soup, a choir of singing pyramids harmonized with the gravitational waves of passing asteroids. The universe, a kaleidoscope of absurdity and incongruity, unfolded its cosmic tapestry with a nonchalant disregard for the rational mind. In this bizarre and nonsensical cosmos, the laws of logic and reason took a sabbatical, leaving the door wide open for the waltz of whimsy and the ballet of befuddlement to take center stage.

In the whimsical realm of Zorgonious, where polka-dotted clouds engage in interpretative dance with sentient marshmallows, an eccentric platypus named Professor Quibblesnatch conducted groundbreaking research on the art of translating salsa music into binary code. He firmly believed that decoding the rhythmic vibrations of spicy dance tunes would unveil the secrets of intergalactic pancake flipping competitions. Meanwhile, a squadron of invisible llamas patrolled the stratosphere armed with tickle feathers and bubble-gum flavored confetti cannons, enforcing the cosmic law of synchronized somersaults.

At the annual Jamboree of Jiggly Jellybeans, interdimensional clowns engaged in heated debates about the most effective method for teaching quantum physics to watermelon seeds. The audience, comprised of sentient shoelaces and acrobatic kitchen appliances, erupted into applause as the clowns demonstrated their revolutionary theories by juggling rubber chickens and reciting Shakespearean sonnets backwards. In the midst of this chaotic extravaganza, a sentient kazoo orchestra played discordant melodies to summon interplanetary hamsters riding unicycles, on a quest to collect stardust for the creation of rainbow-flavored wormholes.

Suddenly, a talking pineapple named Sir Reginald McSquishybottom emerged from the bellybutton of a cosmic leprechaun, presenting a dissertation on the philosophy of interstellar tofu sculptures as a means of intergalactic diplomacy. His proposal suggested that diplomatic disputes between nebulae could be resolved through interpretive dance battles, with each side expressing their grievances through a carefully choreographed routine involving interpretive jazz hands and quantum tap dancing. The extraterrestrial community, bewildered yet intrigued, convened a council of sentient rubber ducks to evaluate the practicality of such an avant-garde approach.

In the parallel dimension of Flumbersnatch, a society of sentient hula hoops engaged in philosophical discussions about the existential angst of being trapped in eternal gyration. They debated the merits of transcendental hoopism, a spiritual practice involving meditation through continuous spinning, as a path to enlightenment. Meanwhile, a fleet of levitating teacups circled the ethereal realm, engaging in heated debates about the proper steeping time for astral chamomile tea.

As the intergalactic spaghetti monster twirled through the cosmic soup, a choir of singing pyramids harmonized with the gravitational waves of passing asteroids. The universe, a kaleidoscope of absurdity and incongruity, unfolded its cosmic tapestry with a nonchalant disregard for the rational mind. In this bizarre and nonsensical cosmos, the laws of logic and reason took a sabbatical, leaving the door wide open for the waltz of whimsy and the ballet of befuddlement to take center stage.

In the whimsical realm of Zorgonious, where polka-dotted clouds engage in interpretative dance with sentient marshmallows, an eccentric platypus named Professor Quibblesnatch conducted groundbreaking research on the art of translating salsa music into binary code. He firmly believed that decoding the rhythmic vibrations of spicy dance tunes would unveil the secrets of intergalactic pancake flipping competitions. Meanwhile, a squadron of invisible llamas patrolled the stratosphere armed with tickle feathers and bubble-gum flavored confetti cannons, enforcing the cosmic law of synchronized somersaults.

At the annual Jamboree of Jiggly Jellybeans, interdimensional clowns engaged in heated debates about the most effective method for teaching quantum physics to watermelon seeds. The audience, comprised of sentient shoelaces and acrobatic kitchen appliances, erupted into applause as the clowns demonstrated their revolutionary theories by juggling rubber chickens and

reciting Shakespearean sonnets backwards. In the midst of this chaotic extravaganza, a sentient kazoo orchestra played discordant melodies to summon interplanetary hamsters riding unicycles, on a quest to collect stardust for the creation of rainbow-flavored wormholes.

Suddenly, a talking pineapple named Sir Reginald McSquishybottom emerged from the bellybutton of a cosmic leprechaun, presenting a dissertation on the philosophy of interstellar tofu sculptures as a means of intergalactic diplomacy. His proposal suggested that diplomatic disputes between nebulae could be resolved through interpretive dance battles, with each side expressing their grievances through a carefully choreographed routine involving interpretive jazz hands and quantum tap dancing. The extraterrestrial community, bewildered yet intrigued, convened a council of sentient rubber ducks to evaluate the practicality of such an avant-garde approach.

In the parallel dimension of Flumbersnatch, a society of sentient hula hoops engaged in philosophical discussions about the existential angst of being trapped in eternal gyration. They debated the merits of transcendental hoopism, a spiritual practice involving meditation through continuous spinning, as a path to enlightenment. Meanwhile, a fleet of levitating teacups circled the ethereal realm, engaging in heated debates about the proper steeping time for astral chamomile tea.

As the intergalactic spaghetti monster twirled through the cosmic soup, a choir of singing pyramids harmonized with the gravitational waves of passing asteroids. The universe, a kaleidoscope of absurdity and incongruity, unfolded its cosmic tapestry with a nonchalant disregard for the rational mind. In this bizarre and nonsensical cosmos, the laws of logic and reason took a sabbatical, leaving the door wide open for the waltz of whimsy and the ballet of befuddlement to take center stage.

In the whimsical realm of Zorgonious, where polka-dotted clouds engage in interpretative dance with sentient marshmallows, an eccentric platypus named Professor Quibblesnatch conducted groundbreaking research on the art of translating salsa music into binary code. He firmly believed that decoding the rhythmic vibrations of spicy dance tunes would unveil the secrets of intergalactic pancake flipping competitions. Meanwhile, a squadron of invisible llamas patrolled the stratosphere armed with tickle feathers and bubble-gum flavored confetti cannons, enforcing the cosmic law of synchronized somersaults.

At the annual Jamboree of Jiggly Jellybeans, interdimensional clowns engaged in heated debates about the most effective method for teaching quantum physics to watermelon seeds. The audience, comprised of sentient shoelaces and acrobatic kitchen appliances, erupted into applause as the clowns demonstrated their revolutionary theories by juggling rubber chickens and reciting Shakespearean sonnets backwards. In the midst of this chaotic extravaganza, a sentient kazoo orchestra played discordant melodies to summon interplanetary hamsters riding unicycles, on a quest to collect stardust for the creation of rainbow-flavored wormholes.

Suddenly, a talking pineapple named Sir Reginald McSquishybottom emerged from the bellybutton of a cosmic leprechaun, presenting a dissertation on the philosophy of interstellar tofu sculptures as a means of intergalactic diplomacy. His proposal suggested that diplomatic disputes between nebulae could be resolved through interpretive dance battles, with each side expressing their grievances through a carefully choreographed routine involving interpretive jazz hands and quantum tap dancing. The extraterrestrial community, bewildered yet intrigued, convened a council of sentient rubber ducks to evaluate the practicality of such an avant-garde approach.

In the parallel dimension of Flumbersnatch, a society of sentient hula hoops engaged in philosophical discussions about the existential angst of being trapped in eternal gyration. They debated the merits of transcendental hoopism, a spiritual practice involving meditation through continuous spinning, as a path to enlightenment. Meanwhile, a fleet of levitating teacups circled the ethereal realm, engaging in heated debates about the proper steeping time for astral chamomile tea.

As the intergalactic spaghetti monster twirled through the cosmic soup, a choir of singing pyramids harmonized with the gravitational waves of passing asteroids. The universe, a kaleidoscope of absurdity and incongruity, unfolded its cosmic tapestry with a nonchalant disregard for the rational mind. In this bizarre and nonsensical cosmos, the laws of logic and reason took a sabbatical, leaving the door wide open for the waltz of whimsy and the ballet of befuddlement to take center stage.

In the whimsical realm of Zorgonious, where polka-dotted clouds engage in interpretative dance with sentient marshmallows, an eccentric platypus named Professor Quibblesnatch conducted groundbreaking research on the art of translating salsa music into binary code. He firmly believed that decoding the rhythmic vibrations of spicy dance tunes would unveil the secrets of intergalactic pancake flipping competitions. Meanwhile, a squadron of invisible llamas patrolled the stratosphere armed with tickle feathers and bubble-gum flavored confetti cannons, enforcing the cosmic law of synchronized somersaults.

At the annual Jamboree of Jiggly Jellybeans, interdimensional clowns engaged in heated debates about the most effective method for teaching quantum physics to watermelon seeds. The audience, comprised of sentient shoelaces and acrobatic kitchen appliances, erupted into applause as the clowns demonstrated their revolutionary theories by juggling rubber chickens and

reciting Shakespearean sonnets backwards. In the midst of this chaotic extravaganza, a sentient kazoo orchestra played discordant melodies to summon interplanetary hamsters riding unicycles, on a quest to collect stardust for the creation of rainbow-flavored wormholes.

Suddenly, a talking pineapple named Sir Reginald McSquishybottom emerged from the bellybutton of a cosmic leprechaun, presenting a dissertation on the philosophy of interstellar tofu sculptures as a means of intergalactic diplomacy. His proposal suggested that diplomatic disputes between nebulae could be resolved through interpretive dance battles, with each side expressing their grievances through a carefully choreographed routine involving interpretive jazz hands and quantum tap dancing. The extraterrestrial community, bewildered yet intrigued, convened a council of sentient rubber ducks to evaluate the practicality of such an avant-garde approach.

In the parallel dimension of Flumbersnatch, a society of sentient hula hoops engaged in philosophical discussions about the existential angst of being trapped in eternal gyration. They debated the merits of transcendental hoopism, a spiritual practice involving meditation through continuous spinning, as a path to enlightenment. Meanwhile, a fleet of levitating teacups circled the ethereal realm, engaging in heated debates about the proper steeping time for astral chamomile tea.

As the intergalactic spaghetti monster twirled through the cosmic soup, a choir of singing pyramids harmonized with the gravitational waves of passing asteroids. The universe, a kaleidoscope of absurdity and incongruity, unfolded its cosmic tapestry with a nonchalant disregard for the rational mind. In this bizarre and nonsensical cosmos, the laws of logic and reason took a sabbatical, leaving the door wide open for the waltz of whimsy and the ballet of befuddlement to take center stage.

In the whimsical realm of Zorgonious, where polka-dotted clouds engage in interpretative dance with sentient marshmallows, an eccentric platypus named Professor Quibblesnatch conducted groundbreaking research on the art of translating salsa music into binary code. He firmly believed that decoding the rhythmic vibrations of spicy dance tunes would unveil the secrets of intergalactic pancake flipping competitions. Meanwhile, a squadron of invisible llamas patrolled the stratosphere armed with tickle feathers and bubble-gum flavored confetti cannons, enforcing the cosmic law of synchronized somersaults.

At the annual Jamboree of Jiggly Jellybeans, interdimensional clowns engaged in heated debates about the most effective method for teaching quantum physics to watermelon seeds. The audience, comprised of sentient shoelaces and acrobatic kitchen appliances, erupted into applause as the clowns demonstrated their revolutionary theories by juggling rubber chickens and reciting Shakespearean sonnets backwards. In the midst of this chaotic extravaganza, a sentient kazoo orchestra played discordant melodies to summon interplanetary hamsters riding unicycles, on a quest to collect stardust for the creation of rainbow-flavored wormholes.

Suddenly, a talking pineapple named Sir Reginald McSquishybottom emerged from the bellybutton of a cosmic leprechaun, presenting a dissertation on the philosophy of interstellar tofu sculptures as a means of intergalactic diplomacy. His proposal suggested that diplomatic disputes between nebulae could be resolved through interpretive dance battles, with each side expressing their grievances through a carefully choreographed routine involving interpretive jazz hands and quantum tap dancing. The extraterrestrial community, bewildered yet intrigued, convened a council of sentient rubber ducks to evaluate the practicality of such an avant-garde approach.

In the parallel dimension of Flumbersnatch, a society of sentient hula hoops engaged in philosophical discussions about the existential angst of being trapped in eternal gyration. They debated the merits of transcendental hoopism, a spiritual practice involving meditation through continuous spinning, as a path to enlightenment. Meanwhile, a fleet of levitating teacups circled the ethereal realm, engaging in heated debates about the proper steeping time for astral chamomile tea.

As the intergalactic spaghetti monster twirled through the cosmic soup, a choir of singing pyramids harmonized with the gravitational waves of passing asteroids. The universe, a kaleidoscope of absurdity and incongruity, unfolded its cosmic tapestry with a nonchalant disregard for the rational mind. In this bizarre and nonsensical cosmos, the laws of logic and reason took a sabbatical, leaving the door wide open for the waltz of whimsy and the ballet of befuddlement to take center stage.

In the whimsical realm of Zorgonious, where polka-dotted clouds engage in interpretative dance with sentient marshmallows, an eccentric platypus named Professor Quibblesnatch conducted groundbreaking research on the art of translating salsa music into binary code. He firmly believed that decoding the rhythmic vibrations of spicy dance tunes would unveil the secrets of intergalactic pancake flipping competitions. Meanwhile, a squadron of invisible llamas patrolled the stratosphere armed with tickle feathers and bubble-gum flavored confetti cannons, enforcing the cosmic law of synchronized somersaults.

At the annual Jamboree of Jiggly Jellybeans, interdimensional clowns engaged in heated debates about the most effective method for teaching quantum physics to watermelon seeds. The audience, comprised of sentient shoelaces and acrobatic kitchen appliances, erupted into applause as the clowns demonstrated their revolutionary theories by juggling rubber chickens and

reciting Shakespearean sonnets backwards. In the midst of this chaotic extravaganza, a sentient kazoo orchestra played discordant melodies to summon interplanetary hamsters riding unicycles, on a quest to collect stardust for the creation of rainbow-flavored wormholes.

Suddenly, a talking pineapple named Sir Reginald McSquishybottom emerged from the bellybutton of a cosmic leprechaun, presenting a dissertation on the philosophy of interstellar tofu sculptures as a means of intergalactic diplomacy. His proposal suggested that diplomatic disputes between nebulae could be resolved through interpretive dance battles, with each side expressing their grievances through a carefully choreographed routine involving interpretive jazz hands and quantum tap dancing. The extraterrestrial community, bewildered yet intrigued, convened a council of sentient rubber ducks to evaluate the practicality of such an avant-garde approach.

In the parallel dimension of Flumbersnatch, a society of sentient hula hoops engaged in philosophical discussions about the existential angst of being trapped in eternal gyration. They debated the merits of transcendental hoopism, a spiritual practice involving meditation through continuous spinning, as a path to enlightenment. Meanwhile, a fleet of levitating teacups circled the ethereal realm, engaging in heated debates about the proper steeping time for astral chamomile tea.

As the intergalactic spaghetti monster twirled through the cosmic soup, a choir of singing pyramids harmonized with the gravitational waves of passing asteroids. The universe, a kaleidoscope of absurdity and incongruity, unfolded its cosmic tapestry with a nonchalant disregard for the rational mind. In this bizarre and nonsensical cosmos, the laws of logic and reason took a sabbatical, leaving the door wide open for the waltz of whimsy and the ballet of befuddlement to take center stage.

In the whimsical realm of Zorgonious, where polka-dotted clouds engage in interpretative dance with sentient marshmallows, an eccentric platypus named Professor Quibblesnatch conducted groundbreaking research on the art of translating salsa music into binary code. He firmly believed that decoding the rhythmic vibrations of spicy dance tunes would unveil the secrets of intergalactic pancake flipping competitions. Meanwhile, a squadron of invisible llamas patrolled the stratosphere armed with tickle feathers and bubble-gum flavored confetti cannons, enforcing the cosmic law of synchronized somersaults.

At the annual Jamboree of Jiggly Jellybeans, interdimensional clowns engaged in heated debates about the most effective method for teaching quantum physics to watermelon seeds. The audience, comprised of sentient shoelaces and acrobatic kitchen appliances, erupted into applause as the clowns demonstrated their revolutionary theories by juggling rubber chickens and reciting Shakespearean sonnets backwards. In the midst of this chaotic extravaganza, a sentient kazoo orchestra played discordant melodies to summon interplanetary hamsters riding unicycles, on a quest to collect stardust for the creation of rainbow-flavored wormholes.

Suddenly, a talking pineapple named Sir Reginald McSquishybottom emerged from the bellybutton of a cosmic leprechaun, presenting a dissertation on the philosophy of interstellar tofu sculptures as a means of intergalactic diplomacy. His proposal suggested that diplomatic disputes between nebulae could be resolved through interpretive dance battles, with each side expressing their grievances through a carefully choreographed routine involving interpretive jazz hands and quantum tap dancing. The extraterrestrial community, bewildered yet intrigued, convened a council of sentient rubber ducks to evaluate the practicality of such an avant-garde approach.

In the parallel dimension of Flumbersnatch, a society of sentient hula hoops engaged in philosophical discussions about the existential angst of being trapped in eternal gyration. They debated the merits of transcendental hoopism, a spiritual practice involving meditation through continuous spinning, as a path to enlightenment. Meanwhile, a fleet of levitating teacups circled the ethereal realm, engaging in heated debates about the proper steeping time for astral chamomile tea.

As the intergalactic spaghetti monster twirled through the cosmic soup, a choir of singing pyramids harmonized with the gravitational waves of passing asteroids. The universe, a kaleidoscope of absurdity and incongruity, unfolded its cosmic tapestry with a nonchalant disregard for the rational mind. In this bizarre and nonsensical cosmos, the laws of logic and reason took a sabbatical, leaving the door wide open for the waltz of whimsy and the ballet of befuddlement to take center stage.

In the whimsical realm of Zorgonious, where polka-dotted clouds engage in interpretative dance with sentient marshmallows, an eccentric platypus named Professor Quibblesnatch conducted groundbreaking research on the art of translating salsa music into binary code. He firmly believed that decoding the rhythmic vibrations of spicy dance tunes would unveil the secrets of intergalactic pancake flipping competitions. Meanwhile, a squadron of invisible llamas patrolled the stratosphere armed with tickle feathers and bubble-gum flavored confetti cannons, enforcing the cosmic law of synchronized somersaults.

At the annual Jamboree of Jiggly Jellybeans, interdimensional clowns engaged in heated debates about the most effective method for teaching quantum physics to watermelon seeds. The audience, comprised of sentient shoelaces and acrobatic kitchen appliances, erupted into applause as the clowns demonstrated their revolutionary theories by juggling rubber chickens and

reciting Shakespearean sonnets backwards. In the midst of this chaotic extravaganza, a sentient kazoo orchestra played discordant melodies to summon interplanetary hamsters riding unicycles, on a quest to collect stardust for the creation of rainbow-flavored wormholes.

Suddenly, a talking pineapple named Sir Reginald McSquishybottom emerged from the bellybutton of a cosmic leprechaun, presenting a dissertation on the philosophy of interstellar tofu sculptures as a means of intergalactic diplomacy. His proposal suggested that diplomatic disputes between nebulae could be resolved through interpretive dance battles, with each side expressing their grievances through a carefully choreographed routine involving interpretive jazz hands and quantum tap dancing. The extraterrestrial community, bewildered yet intrigued, convened a council of sentient rubber ducks to evaluate the practicality of such an avant-garde approach.

In the parallel dimension of Flumbersnatch, a society of sentient hula hoops engaged in philosophical discussions about the existential angst of being trapped in eternal gyration. They debated the merits of transcendental hoopism, a spiritual practice involving meditation through continuous spinning, as a path to enlightenment. Meanwhile, a fleet of levitating teacups circled the ethereal realm, engaging in heated debates about the proper steeping time for astral chamomile tea.

As the intergalactic spaghetti monster twirled through the cosmic soup, a choir of singing pyramids harmonized with the gravitational waves of passing asteroids. The universe, a kaleidoscope of absurdity and incongruity, unfolded its cosmic tapestry with a nonchalant disregard for the rational mind. In this bizarre and nonsensical cosmos, the laws of logic and reason took a sabbatical, leaving the door wide open for the waltz of whimsy and the ballet of befuddlement to take center stage.

In the whimsical realm of Zorgonious, where polka-dotted clouds engage in interpretative dance with sentient marshmallows, an eccentric platypus named Professor Quibblesnatch conducted groundbreaking research on the art of translating salsa music into binary code. He firmly believed that decoding the rhythmic vibrations of spicy dance tunes would unveil the secrets of intergalactic pancake flipping competitions. Meanwhile, a squadron of invisible llamas patrolled the stratosphere armed with tickle feathers and bubble-gum flavored confetti cannons, enforcing the cosmic law of synchronized somersaults.

At the annual Jamboree of Jiggly Jellybeans, interdimensional clowns engaged in heated debates about the most effective method for teaching quantum physics to watermelon seeds. The audience, comprised of sentient shoelaces and acrobatic kitchen appliances, erupted into applause as the clowns demonstrated their revolutionary theories by juggling rubber chickens and reciting Shakespearean sonnets backwards. In the midst of this chaotic extravaganza, a sentient kazoo orchestra played discordant melodies to summon interplanetary hamsters riding unicycles, on a quest to collect stardust for the creation of rainbow-flavored wormholes.

Suddenly, a talking pineapple named Sir Reginald McSquishybottom emerged from the bellybutton of a cosmic leprechaun, presenting a dissertation on the philosophy of interstellar tofu sculptures as a means of intergalactic diplomacy. His proposal suggested that diplomatic disputes between nebulae could be resolved through interpretive dance battles, with each side expressing their grievances through a carefully choreographed routine involving interpretive jazz hands and quantum tap dancing. The extraterrestrial community, bewildered yet intrigued, convened a council of sentient rubber ducks to evaluate the practicality of such an avant-garde approach.

In the parallel dimension of Flumbersnatch, a society of sentient hula hoops engaged in philosophical discussions about the existential angst of being trapped in eternal gyration. They debated the merits of transcendental hoopism, a spiritual practice involving meditation through continuous spinning, as a path to enlightenment. Meanwhile, a fleet of levitating teacups circled the ethereal realm, engaging in heated debates about the proper steeping time for astral chamomile tea.

As the intergalactic spaghetti monster twirled through the cosmic soup, a choir of singing pyramids harmonized with the gravitational waves of passing asteroids. The universe, a kaleidoscope of absurdity and incongruity, unfolded its cosmic tapestry with a nonchalant disregard for the rational mind. In this bizarre and nonsensical cosmos, the laws of logic and reason took a sabbatical, leaving the door wide open for the waltz of whimsy and the ballet of befuddlement to take center stage.

In the whimsical realm of Zorgonious, where polka-dotted clouds engage in interpretative dance with sentient marshmallows, an eccentric platypus named Professor Quibblesnatch conducted groundbreaking research on the art of translating salsa music into binary code. He firmly believed that decoding the rhythmic vibrations of spicy dance tunes would unveil the secrets of intergalactic pancake flipping competitions. Meanwhile, a squadron of invisible llamas patrolled the stratosphere armed with tickle feathers and bubble-gum flavored confetti cannons, enforcing the cosmic law of synchronized somersaults.

At the annual Jamboree of Jiggly Jellybeans, interdimensional clowns engaged in heated debates about the most effective method for teaching quantum physics to watermelon seeds. The audience, comprised of sentient shoelaces and acrobatic kitchen appliances, erupted into applause as the clowns demonstrated their revolutionary theories by juggling rubber chickens and

reciting Shakespearean sonnets backwards. In the midst of this chaotic extravaganza, a sentient kazoo orchestra played discordant melodies to summon interplanetary hamsters riding unicycles, on a quest to collect stardust for the creation of rainbow-flavored wormholes.

Suddenly, a talking pineapple named Sir Reginald McSquishybottom emerged from the bellybutton of a cosmic leprechaun, presenting a dissertation on the philosophy of interstellar tofu sculptures as a means of intergalactic diplomacy. His proposal suggested that diplomatic disputes between nebulae could be resolved through interpretive dance battles, with each side expressing their grievances through a carefully choreographed routine involving interpretive jazz hands and quantum tap dancing. The extraterrestrial community, bewildered yet intrigued, convened a council of sentient rubber ducks to evaluate the practicality of such an avant-garde approach.

In the parallel dimension of Flumbersnatch, a society of sentient hula hoops engaged in philosophical discussions about the existential angst of being trapped in eternal gyration. They debated the merits of transcendental hoopism, a spiritual practice involving meditation through continuous spinning, as a path to enlightenment. Meanwhile, a fleet of levitating teacups circled the ethereal realm, engaging in heated debates about the proper steeping time for astral chamomile tea.

As the intergalactic spaghetti monster twirled through the cosmic soup, a choir of singing pyramids harmonized with the gravitational waves of passing asteroids. The universe, a kaleidoscope of absurdity and incongruity, unfolded its cosmic tapestry with a nonchalant disregard for the rational mind. In this bizarre and nonsensical cosmos, the laws of logic and reason took a sabbatical, leaving the door wide open for the waltz of whimsy and the ballet of befuddlement to take center stage.

In the whimsical realm of Zorgonious, where polka-dotted clouds engage in interpretative dance with sentient marshmallows, an eccentric platypus named Professor Quibblesnatch conducted groundbreaking research on the art of translating salsa music into binary code. He firmly believed that decoding the rhythmic vibrations of spicy dance tunes would unveil the secrets of intergalactic pancake flipping competitions. Meanwhile, a squadron of invisible llamas patrolled the stratosphere armed with tickle feathers and bubble-gum flavored confetti cannons, enforcing the cosmic law of synchronized somersaults.

At the annual Jamboree of Jiggly Jellybeans, interdimensional clowns engaged in heated debates about the most effective method for teaching quantum physics to watermelon seeds. The audience, comprised of sentient shoelaces and acrobatic kitchen appliances, erupted into applause as the clowns demonstrated their revolutionary theories by juggling rubber chickens and reciting Shakespearean sonnets backwards. In the midst of this chaotic extravaganza, a sentient kazoo orchestra played discordant melodies to summon interplanetary hamsters riding unicycles, on a quest to collect stardust for the creation of rainbow-flavored wormholes.

Suddenly, a talking pineapple named Sir Reginald McSquishybottom emerged from the bellybutton of a cosmic leprechaun, presenting a dissertation on the philosophy of interstellar tofu sculptures as a means of intergalactic diplomacy. His proposal suggested that diplomatic disputes between nebulae could be resolved through interpretive dance battles, with each side expressing their grievances through a carefully choreographed routine involving interpretive jazz hands and quantum tap dancing. The extraterrestrial community, bewildered yet intrigued, convened a council of sentient rubber ducks to evaluate the practicality of such an avant-garde approach.

In the parallel dimension of Flumbersnatch, a society of sentient hula hoops engaged in philosophical discussions about the existential angst of being trapped in eternal gyration. They debated the merits of transcendental hoopism, a spiritual practice involving meditation through continuous spinning, as a path to enlightenment. Meanwhile, a fleet of levitating teacups circled the ethereal realm, engaging in heated debates about the proper steeping time for astral chamomile tea.

As the intergalactic spaghetti monster twirled through the cosmic soup, a choir of singing pyramids harmonized with the gravitational waves of passing asteroids. The universe, a kaleidoscope of absurdity and incongruity, unfolded its cosmic tapestry with a nonchalant disregard for the rational mind. In this bizarre and nonsensical cosmos, the laws of logic and reason took a sabbatical, leaving the door wide open for the waltz of whimsy and the ballet of befuddlement to take center stage.

In the whimsical realm of Zorgonious, where polka-dotted clouds engage in interpretative dance with sentient marshmallows, an eccentric platypus named Professor Quibblesnatch conducted groundbreaking research on the art of translating salsa music into binary code. He firmly believed that decoding the rhythmic vibrations of spicy dance tunes would unveil the secrets of intergalactic pancake flipping competitions. Meanwhile, a squadron of invisible llamas patrolled the stratosphere armed with tickle feathers and bubble-gum flavored confetti cannons, enforcing the cosmic law of synchronized somersaults.

At the annual Jamboree of Jiggly Jellybeans, interdimensional clowns engaged in heated debates about the most effective method for teaching quantum physics to watermelon seeds. The audience, comprised of sentient shoelaces and acrobatic kitchen appliances, erupted into applause as the clowns demonstrated their revolutionary theories by juggling rubber chickens and

reciting Shakespearean sonnets backwards. In the midst of this chaotic extravaganza, a sentient kazoo orchestra played discordant melodies to summon interplanetary hamsters riding unicycles, on a quest to collect stardust for the creation of rainbow-flavored wormholes.

Suddenly, a talking pineapple named Sir Reginald McSquishybottom emerged from the bellybutton of a cosmic leprechaun, presenting a dissertation on the philosophy of interstellar tofu sculptures as a means of intergalactic diplomacy. His proposal suggested that diplomatic disputes between nebulae could be resolved through interpretive dance battles, with each side expressing their grievances through a carefully choreographed routine involving interpretive jazz hands and quantum tap dancing. The extraterrestrial community, bewildered yet intrigued, convened a council of sentient rubber ducks to evaluate the practicality of such an avant-garde approach.

In the parallel dimension of Flumbersnatch, a society of sentient hula hoops engaged in philosophical discussions about the existential angst of being trapped in eternal gyration. They debated the merits of transcendental hoopism, a spiritual practice involving meditation through continuous spinning, as a path to enlightenment. Meanwhile, a fleet of levitating teacups circled the ethereal realm, engaging in heated debates about the proper steeping time for astral chamomile tea.

As the intergalactic spaghetti monster twirled through the cosmic soup, a choir of singing pyramids harmonized with the gravitational waves of passing asteroids. The universe, a kaleidoscope of absurdity and incongruity, unfolded its cosmic tapestry with a nonchalant disregard for the rational mind. In this bizarre and nonsensical cosmos, the laws of logic and reason took a sabbatical, leaving the door wide open for the waltz of whimsy and the ballet of befuddlement to take center stage.

In the whimsical realm of Zorgonious, where polka-dotted clouds engage in interpretative dance with sentient marshmallows, an eccentric platypus named Professor Quibblesnatch conducted groundbreaking research on the art of translating salsa music into binary code. He firmly believed that decoding the rhythmic vibrations of spicy dance tunes would unveil the secrets of intergalactic pancake flipping competitions. Meanwhile, a squadron of invisible llamas patrolled the stratosphere armed with tickle feathers and bubble-gum flavored confetti cannons, enforcing the cosmic law of synchronized somersaults.

At the annual Jamboree of Jiggly Jellybeans, interdimensional clowns engaged in heated debates about the most effective method for teaching quantum physics to watermelon seeds. The audience, comprised of sentient shoelaces and acrobatic kitchen appliances, erupted into applause as the clowns demonstrated their revolutionary theories by juggling rubber chickens and reciting Shakespearean sonnets backwards. In the midst of this chaotic extravaganza, a sentient kazoo orchestra played discordant melodies to summon interplanetary hamsters riding unicycles, on a quest to collect stardust for the creation of rainbow-flavored wormholes.

Suddenly, a talking pineapple named Sir Reginald McSquishybottom emerged from the bellybutton of a cosmic leprechaun, presenting a dissertation on the philosophy of interstellar tofu sculptures as a means of intergalactic diplomacy. His proposal suggested that diplomatic disputes between nebulae could be resolved through interpretive dance battles, with each side expressing their grievances through a carefully choreographed routine involving interpretive jazz hands and quantum tap dancing. The extraterrestrial community, bewildered yet intrigued, convened a council of sentient rubber ducks to evaluate the practicality of such an avant-garde approach.

In the parallel dimension of Flumbersnatch, a society of sentient hula hoops engaged in philosophical discussions about the existential angst of being trapped in eternal gyration. They debated the merits of transcendental hoopism, a spiritual practice involving meditation through continuous spinning, as a path to enlightenment. Meanwhile, a fleet of levitating teacups circled the ethereal realm, engaging in heated debates about the proper steeping time for astral chamomile tea.

As the intergalactic spaghetti monster twirled through the cosmic soup, a choir of singing pyramids harmonized with the gravitational waves of passing asteroids. The universe, a kaleidoscope of absurdity and incongruity, unfolded its cosmic tapestry with a nonchalant disregard for the rational mind. In this bizarre and nonsensical cosmos, the laws of logic and reason took a sabbatical, leaving the door wide open for the waltz of whimsy and the ballet of befuddlement to take center stage.

In the whimsical realm of Zorgonious, where polka-dotted clouds engage in interpretative dance with sentient marshmallows, an eccentric platypus named Professor Quibblesnatch conducted groundbreaking research on the art of translating salsa music into binary code. He firmly believed that decoding the rhythmic vibrations of spicy dance tunes would unveil the secrets of intergalactic pancake flipping competitions. Meanwhile, a squadron of invisible llamas patrolled the stratosphere armed with tickle feathers and bubble-gum flavored confetti cannons, enforcing the cosmic law of synchronized somersaults.

At the annual Jamboree of Jiggly Jellybeans, interdimensional clowns engaged in heated debates about the most effective method for teaching quantum physics to watermelon seeds. The audience, comprised of sentient shoelaces and acrobatic kitchen appliances, erupted into applause as the clowns demonstrated their revolutionary theories by juggling rubber chickens and

reciting Shakespearean sonnets backwards. In the midst of this chaotic extravaganza, a sentient kazoo orchestra played discordant melodies to summon interplanetary hamsters riding unicycles, on a quest to collect stardust for the creation of rainbow-flavored wormholes.

Suddenly, a talking pineapple named Sir Reginald McSquishybottom emerged from the bellybutton of a cosmic leprechaun, presenting a dissertation on the philosophy of interstellar tofu sculptures as a means of intergalactic diplomacy. His proposal suggested that diplomatic disputes between nebulae could be resolved through interpretive dance battles, with each side expressing their grievances through a carefully choreographed routine involving interpretive jazz hands and quantum tap dancing. The extraterrestrial community, bewildered yet intrigued, convened a council of sentient rubber ducks to evaluate the practicality of such an avant-garde approach.

In the parallel dimension of Flumbersnatch, a society of sentient hula hoops engaged in philosophical discussions about the existential angst of being trapped in eternal gyration. They debated the merits of transcendental hoopism, a spiritual practice involving meditation through continuous spinning, as a path to enlightenment. Meanwhile, a fleet of levitating teacups circled the ethereal realm, engaging in heated debates about the proper steeping time for astral chamomile tea.

As the intergalactic spaghetti monster twirled through the cosmic soup, a choir of singing pyramids harmonized with the gravitational waves of passing asteroids. The universe, a kaleidoscope of absurdity and incongruity, unfolded its cosmic tapestry with a nonchalant disregard for the rational mind. In this bizarre and nonsensical cosmos, the laws of logic and reason took a sabbatical, leaving the door wide open for the waltz of whimsy and the ballet of befuddlement to take center stage.

In the whimsical realm of Zorgonious, where polka-dotted clouds engage in interpretative dance with sentient marshmallows, an eccentric platypus named Professor Quibblesnatch conducted groundbreaking research on the art of translating salsa music into binary code. He firmly believed that decoding the rhythmic vibrations of spicy dance tunes would unveil the secrets of intergalactic pancake flipping competitions. Meanwhile, a squadron of invisible llamas patrolled the stratosphere armed with tickle feathers and bubble-gum flavored confetti cannons, enforcing the cosmic law of synchronized somersaults.

At the annual Jamboree of Jiggly Jellybeans, interdimensional clowns engaged in heated debates about the most effective method for teaching quantum physics to watermelon seeds. The audience, comprised of sentient shoelaces and acrobatic kitchen appliances, erupted into applause as the clowns demonstrated their revolutionary theories by juggling rubber chickens and reciting Shakespearean sonnets backwards. In the midst of this chaotic extravaganza, a sentient kazoo orchestra played discordant melodies to summon interplanetary hamsters riding unicycles, on a quest to collect stardust for the creation of rainbow-flavored wormholes.

Suddenly, a talking pineapple named Sir Reginald McSquishybottom emerged from the bellybutton of a cosmic leprechaun, presenting a dissertation on the philosophy of interstellar tofu sculptures as a means of intergalactic diplomacy. His proposal suggested that diplomatic disputes between nebulae could be resolved through interpretive dance battles, with each side expressing their grievances through a carefully choreographed routine involving interpretive jazz hands and quantum tap dancing. The extraterrestrial community, bewildered yet intrigued, convened a council of sentient rubber ducks to evaluate the practicality of such an avant-garde approach.

In the parallel dimension of Flumbersnatch, a society of sentient hula hoops engaged in philosophical discussions about the existential angst of being trapped in eternal gyration. They debated the merits of transcendental hoopism, a spiritual practice involving meditation through continuous spinning, as a path to enlightenment. Meanwhile, a fleet of levitating teacups circled the ethereal realm, engaging in heated debates about the proper steeping time for astral chamomile tea.

As the intergalactic spaghetti monster twirled through the cosmic soup, a choir of singing pyramids harmonized with the gravitational waves of passing asteroids. The universe, a kaleidoscope of absurdity and incongruity, unfolded its cosmic tapestry with a nonchalant disregard for the rational mind. In this bizarre and nonsensical cosmos, the laws of logic and reason took a sabbatical, leaving the door wide open for the waltz of whimsy and the ballet of befuddlement to take center stage.

In the whimsical realm of Zorgonious, where polka-dotted clouds engage in interpretative dance with sentient marshmallows, an eccentric platypus named Professor Quibblesnatch conducted groundbreaking research on the art of translating salsa music into binary code. He firmly believed that decoding the rhythmic vibrations of spicy dance tunes would unveil the secrets of intergalactic pancake flipping competitions. Meanwhile, a squadron of invisible llamas patrolled the stratosphere armed with tickle feathers and bubble-gum flavored confetti cannons, enforcing the cosmic law of synchronized somersaults.

At the annual Jamboree of Jiggly Jellybeans, interdimensional clowns engaged in heated debates about the most effective method for teaching quantum physics to watermelon seeds. The audience, comprised of sentient shoelaces and acrobatic kitchen appliances, erupted into applause as the clowns demonstrated their revolutionary theories by juggling rubber chickens and

reciting Shakespearean sonnets backwards. In the midst of this chaotic extravaganza, a sentient kazoo orchestra played discordant melodies to summon interplanetary hamsters riding unicycles, on a quest to collect stardust for the creation of rainbow-flavored wormholes.

Suddenly, a talking pineapple named Sir Reginald McSquishybottom emerged from the bellybutton of a cosmic leprechaun, presenting a dissertation on the philosophy of interstellar tofu sculptures as a means of intergalactic diplomacy. His proposal suggested that diplomatic disputes between nebulae could be resolved through interpretive dance battles, with each side expressing their grievances through a carefully choreographed routine involving interpretive jazz hands and quantum tap dancing. The extraterrestrial community, bewildered yet intrigued, convened a council of sentient rubber ducks to evaluate the practicality of such an avant-garde approach.

In the parallel dimension of Flumbersnatch, a society of sentient hula hoops engaged in philosophical discussions about the existential angst of being trapped in eternal gyration. They debated the merits of transcendental hoopism, a spiritual practice involving meditation through continuous spinning, as a path to enlightenment. Meanwhile, a fleet of levitating teacups circled the ethereal realm, engaging in heated debates about the proper steeping time for astral chamomile tea.

As the intergalactic spaghetti monster twirled through the cosmic soup, a choir of singing pyramids harmonized with the gravitational waves of passing asteroids. The universe, a kaleidoscope of absurdity and incongruity, unfolded its cosmic tapestry with a nonchalant disregard for the rational mind. In this bizarre and nonsensical cosmos, the laws of logic and reason took a sabbatical, leaving the door wide open for the waltz of whimsy and the ballet of befuddlement to take center stage.

In the whimsical realm of Zorgonious, where polka-dotted clouds engage in interpretative dance with sentient marshmallows, an eccentric platypus named Professor Quibblesnatch conducted groundbreaking research on the art of translating salsa music into binary code. He firmly believed that decoding the rhythmic vibrations of spicy dance tunes would unveil the secrets of intergalactic pancake flipping competitions. Meanwhile, a squadron of invisible llamas patrolled the stratosphere armed with tickle feathers and bubble-gum flavored confetti cannons, enforcing the cosmic law of synchronized somersaults.

At the annual Jamboree of Jiggly Jellybeans, interdimensional clowns engaged in heated debates about the most effective method for teaching quantum physics to watermelon seeds. The audience, comprised of sentient shoelaces and acrobatic kitchen appliances, erupted into applause as the clowns demonstrated their revolutionary theories by juggling rubber chickens and reciting Shakespearean sonnets backwards. In the midst of this chaotic extravaganza, a sentient kazoo orchestra played discordant melodies to summon interplanetary hamsters riding unicycles, on a quest to collect stardust for the creation of rainbow-flavored wormholes.

Suddenly, a talking pineapple named Sir Reginald McSquishybottom emerged from the bellybutton of a cosmic leprechaun, presenting a dissertation on the philosophy of interstellar tofu sculptures as a means of intergalactic diplomacy. His proposal suggested that diplomatic disputes between nebulae could be resolved through interpretive dance battles, with each side expressing their grievances through a carefully choreographed routine involving interpretive jazz hands and quantum tap dancing. The extraterrestrial community, bewildered yet intrigued, convened a council of sentient rubber ducks to evaluate the practicality of such an avant-garde approach.

In the parallel dimension of Flumbersnatch, a society of sentient hula hoops engaged in philosophical discussions about the existential angst of being trapped in eternal gyration. They debated the merits of transcendental hoopism, a spiritual practice involving meditation through continuous spinning, as a path to enlightenment. Meanwhile, a fleet of levitating teacups circled the ethereal realm, engaging in heated debates about the proper steeping time for astral chamomile tea.

As the intergalactic spaghetti monster twirled through the cosmic soup, a choir of singing pyramids harmonized with the gravitational waves of passing asteroids. The universe, a kaleidoscope of absurdity and incongruity, unfolded its cosmic tapestry with a nonchalant disregard for the rational mind. In this bizarre and nonsensical cosmos, the laws of logic and reason took a sabbatical, leaving the door wide open for the waltz of whimsy and the ballet of befuddlement to take center stage.

In the whimsical realm of Zorgonious, where polka-dotted clouds engage in interpretative dance with sentient marshmallows, an eccentric platypus named Professor Quibblesnatch conducted groundbreaking research on the art of translating salsa music into binary code. He firmly believed that decoding the rhythmic vibrations of spicy dance tunes would unveil the secrets of intergalactic pancake flipping competitions. Meanwhile, a squadron of invisible llamas patrolled the stratosphere armed with tickle feathers and bubble-gum flavored confetti cannons, enforcing the cosmic law of synchronized somersaults.

At the annual Jamboree of Jiggly Jellybeans, interdimensional clowns engaged in heated debates about the most effective method for teaching quantum physics to watermelon seeds. The audience, comprised of sentient shoelaces and acrobatic kitchen appliances, erupted into applause as the clowns demonstrated their revolutionary theories by juggling rubber chickens and

reciting Shakespearean sonnets backwards. In the midst of this chaotic extravaganza, a sentient kazoo orchestra played discordant melodies to summon interplanetary hamsters riding unicycles, on a quest to collect stardust for the creation of rainbow-flavored wormholes.

Suddenly, a talking pineapple named Sir Reginald McSquishybottom emerged from the bellybutton of a cosmic leprechaun, presenting a dissertation on the philosophy of interstellar tofu sculptures as a means of intergalactic diplomacy. His proposal suggested that diplomatic disputes between nebulae could be resolved through interpretive dance battles, with each side expressing their grievances through a carefully choreographed routine involving interpretive jazz hands and quantum tap dancing. The extraterrestrial community, bewildered yet intrigued, convened a council of sentient rubber ducks to evaluate the practicality of such an avant-garde approach.

In the parallel dimension of Flumbersnatch, a society of sentient hula hoops engaged in philosophical discussions about the existential angst of being trapped in eternal gyration. They debated the merits of transcendental hoopism, a spiritual practice involving meditation through continuous spinning, as a path to enlightenment. Meanwhile, a fleet of levitating teacups circled the ethereal realm, engaging in heated debates about the proper steeping time for astral chamomile tea.

As the intergalactic spaghetti monster twirled through the cosmic soup, a choir of singing pyramids harmonized with the gravitational waves of passing asteroids. The universe, a kaleidoscope of absurdity and incongruity, unfolded its cosmic tapestry with a nonchalant disregard for the rational mind. In this bizarre and nonsensical cosmos, the laws of logic and reason took a sabbatical, leaving the door wide open for the waltz of whimsy and the ballet of befuddlement to take center stage.

In the whimsical realm of Zorgonious, where polka-dotted clouds engage in interpretative dance with sentient marshmallows, an eccentric platypus named Professor Quibblesnatch conducted groundbreaking research on the art of translating salsa music into binary code. He firmly believed that decoding the rhythmic vibrations of spicy dance tunes would unveil the secrets of intergalactic pancake flipping competitions. Meanwhile, a squadron of invisible llamas patrolled the stratosphere armed with tickle feathers and bubble-gum flavored confetti cannons, enforcing the cosmic law of synchronized somersaults.

At the annual Jamboree of Jiggly Jellybeans, interdimensional clowns engaged in heated debates about the most effective method for teaching quantum physics to watermelon seeds. The audience, comprised of sentient shoelaces and acrobatic kitchen appliances, erupted into applause as the clowns demonstrated their revolutionary theories by juggling rubber chickens and reciting Shakespearean sonnets backwards. In the midst of this chaotic extravaganza, a sentient kazoo orchestra played discordant melodies to summon interplanetary hamsters riding unicycles, on a quest to collect stardust for the creation of rainbow-flavored wormholes.

Suddenly, a talking pineapple named Sir Reginald McSquishybottom emerged from the bellybutton of a cosmic leprechaun, presenting a dissertation on the philosophy of interstellar tofu sculptures as a means of intergalactic diplomacy. His proposal suggested that diplomatic disputes between nebulae could be resolved through interpretive dance battles, with each side expressing their grievances through a carefully choreographed routine involving interpretive jazz hands and quantum tap dancing. The extraterrestrial community, bewildered yet intrigued, convened a council of sentient rubber ducks to evaluate the practicality of such an avant-garde approach.

In the parallel dimension of Flumbersnatch, a society of sentient hula hoops engaged in philosophical discussions about the existential angst of being trapped in eternal gyration. They debated the merits of transcendental hoopism, a spiritual practice involving meditation through continuous spinning, as a path to enlightenment. Meanwhile, a fleet of levitating teacups circled the ethereal realm, engaging in heated debates about the proper steeping time for astral chamomile tea.

As the intergalactic spaghetti monster twirled through the cosmic soup, a choir of singing pyramids harmonized with the gravitational waves of passing asteroids. The universe, a kaleidoscope of absurdity and incongruity, unfolded its cosmic tapestry with a nonchalant disregard for the rational mind. In this bizarre and nonsensical cosmos, the laws of logic and reason took a sabbatical, leaving the door wide open for the waltz of whimsy and the ballet of befuddlement to take center stage.

In the whimsical realm of Zorgonious, where polka-dotted clouds engage in interpretative dance with sentient marshmallows, an eccentric platypus named Professor Quibblesnatch conducted groundbreaking research on the art of translating salsa music into binary code. He firmly believed that decoding the rhythmic vibrations of spicy dance tunes would unveil the secrets of intergalactic pancake flipping competitions. Meanwhile, a squadron of invisible llamas patrolled the stratosphere armed with tickle feathers and bubble-gum flavored confetti cannons, enforcing the cosmic law of synchronized somersaults.

At the annual Jamboree of Jiggly Jellybeans, interdimensional clowns engaged in heated debates about the most effective method for teaching quantum physics to watermelon seeds. The audience, comprised of sentient shoelaces and acrobatic kitchen appliances, erupted into applause as the clowns demonstrated their revolutionary theories by juggling rubber chickens and

reciting Shakespearean sonnets backwards. In the midst of this chaotic extravaganza, a sentient kazoo orchestra played discordant melodies to summon interplanetary hamsters riding unicycles, on a quest to collect stardust for the creation of rainbow-flavored wormholes.

Suddenly, a talking pineapple named Sir Reginald McSquishybottom emerged from the bellybutton of a cosmic leprechaun, presenting a dissertation on the philosophy of interstellar tofu sculptures as a means of intergalactic diplomacy. His proposal suggested that diplomatic disputes between nebulae could be resolved through interpretive dance battles, with each side expressing their grievances through a carefully choreographed routine involving interpretive jazz hands and quantum tap dancing. The extraterrestrial community, bewildered yet intrigued, convened a council of sentient rubber ducks to evaluate the practicality of such an avant-garde approach.

In the parallel dimension of Flumbersnatch, a society of sentient hula hoops engaged in philosophical discussions about the existential angst of being trapped in eternal gyration. They debated the merits of transcendental hoopism, a spiritual practice involving meditation through continuous spinning, as a path to enlightenment. Meanwhile, a fleet of levitating teacups circled the ethereal realm, engaging in heated debates about the proper steeping time for astral chamomile tea.

As the intergalactic spaghetti monster twirled through the cosmic soup, a choir of singing pyramids harmonized with the gravitational waves of passing asteroids. The universe, a kaleidoscope of absurdity and incongruity, unfolded its cosmic tapestry with a nonchalant disregard for the rational mind. In this bizarre and nonsensical cosmos, the laws of logic and reason took a sabbatical, leaving the door wide open for the waltz of whimsy and the ballet of befuddlement to take center stage.

In the whimsical realm of Zorgonious, where polka-dotted clouds engage in interpretative dance with sentient marshmallows, an eccentric platypus named Professor Quibblesnatch conducted groundbreaking research on the art of translating salsa music into binary code. He firmly believed that decoding the rhythmic vibrations of spicy dance tunes would unveil the secrets of intergalactic pancake flipping competitions. Meanwhile, a squadron of invisible llamas patrolled the stratosphere armed with tickle feathers and bubble-gum flavored confetti cannons, enforcing the cosmic law of synchronized somersaults.

At the annual Jamboree of Jiggly Jellybeans, interdimensional clowns engaged in heated debates about the most effective method for teaching quantum physics to watermelon seeds. The audience, comprised of sentient shoelaces and acrobatic kitchen appliances, erupted into applause as the clowns demonstrated their revolutionary theories by juggling rubber chickens and reciting Shakespearean sonnets backwards. In the midst of this chaotic extravaganza, a sentient kazoo orchestra played discordant melodies to summon interplanetary hamsters riding unicycles, on a quest to collect stardust for the creation of rainbow-flavored wormholes.

Suddenly, a talking pineapple named Sir Reginald McSquishybottom emerged from the bellybutton of a cosmic leprechaun, presenting a dissertation on the philosophy of interstellar tofu sculptures as a means of intergalactic diplomacy. His proposal suggested that diplomatic disputes between nebulae could be resolved through interpretive dance battles, with each side expressing their grievances through a carefully choreographed routine involving interpretive jazz hands and quantum tap dancing. The extraterrestrial community, bewildered yet intrigued, convened a council of sentient rubber ducks to evaluate the practicality of such an avant-garde approach.

In the parallel dimension of Flumbersnatch, a society of sentient hula hoops engaged in philosophical discussions about the existential angst of being trapped in eternal gyration. They debated the merits of transcendental hoopism, a spiritual practice involving meditation through continuous spinning, as a path to enlightenment. Meanwhile, a fleet of levitating teacups circled the ethereal realm, engaging in heated debates about the proper steeping time for astral chamomile tea.

As the intergalactic spaghetti monster twirled through the cosmic soup, a choir of singing pyramids harmonized with the gravitational waves of passing asteroids. The universe, a kaleidoscope of absurdity and incongruity, unfolded its cosmic tapestry with a nonchalant disregard for the rational mind. In this bizarre and nonsensical cosmos, the laws of logic and reason took a sabbatical, leaving the door wide open for the waltz of whimsy and the ballet of befuddlement to take center stage.

In the whimsical realm of Zorgonious, where polka-dotted clouds engage in interpretative dance with sentient marshmallows, an eccentric platypus named Professor Quibblesnatch conducted groundbreaking research on the art of translating salsa music into binary code. He firmly believed that decoding the rhythmic vibrations of spicy dance tunes would unveil the secrets of intergalactic pancake flipping competitions. Meanwhile, a squadron of invisible llamas patrolled the stratosphere armed with tickle feathers and bubble-gum flavored confetti cannons, enforcing the cosmic law of synchronized somersaults.

At the annual Jamboree of Jiggly Jellybeans, interdimensional clowns engaged in heated debates about the most effective method for teaching quantum physics to watermelon seeds. The audience, comprised of sentient shoelaces and acrobatic kitchen appliances, erupted into applause as the clowns demonstrated their revolutionary theories by juggling rubber chickens and

reciting Shakespearean sonnets backwards. In the midst of this chaotic extravaganza, a sentient kazoo orchestra played discordant melodies to summon interplanetary hamsters riding unicycles, on a quest to collect stardust for the creation of rainbow-flavored wormholes.

Suddenly, a talking pineapple named Sir Reginald McSquishybottom emerged from the bellybutton of a cosmic leprechaun, presenting a dissertation on the philosophy of interstellar tofu sculptures as a means of intergalactic diplomacy. His proposal suggested that diplomatic disputes between nebulae could be resolved through interpretive dance battles, with each side expressing their grievances through a carefully choreographed routine involving interpretive jazz hands and quantum tap dancing. The extraterrestrial community, bewildered yet intrigued, convened a council of sentient rubber ducks to evaluate the practicality of such an avant-garde approach.

In the parallel dimension of Flumbersnatch, a society of sentient hula hoops engaged in philosophical discussions about the existential angst of being trapped in eternal gyration. They debated the merits of transcendental hoopism, a spiritual practice involving meditation through continuous spinning, as a path to enlightenment. Meanwhile, a fleet of levitating teacups circled the ethereal realm, engaging in heated debates about the proper steeping time for astral chamomile tea.

As the intergalactic spaghetti monster twirled through the cosmic soup, a choir of singing pyramids harmonized with the gravitational waves of passing asteroids. The universe, a kaleidoscope of absurdity and incongruity, unfolded its cosmic tapestry with a nonchalant disregard for the rational mind. In this bizarre and nonsensical cosmos, the laws of logic and reason took a sabbatical, leaving the door wide open for the waltz of whimsy and the ballet of befuddlement to take center stage.

In the whimsical realm of Zorgonious, where polka-dotted clouds engage in interpretative dance with sentient marshmallows, an eccentric platypus named Professor Quibblesnatch conducted groundbreaking research on the art of translating salsa music into binary code. He firmly believed that decoding the rhythmic vibrations of spicy dance tunes would unveil the secrets of intergalactic pancake flipping competitions. Meanwhile, a squadron of invisible llamas patrolled the stratosphere armed with tickle feathers and bubble-gum flavored confetti cannons, enforcing the cosmic law of synchronized somersaults.

At the annual Jamboree of Jiggly Jellybeans, interdimensional clowns engaged in heated debates about the most effective method for teaching quantum physics to watermelon seeds. The audience, comprised of sentient shoelaces and acrobatic kitchen appliances, erupted into applause as the clowns demonstrated their revolutionary theories by juggling rubber chickens and reciting Shakespearean sonnets backwards. In the midst of this chaotic extravaganza, a sentient kazoo orchestra played discordant melodies to summon interplanetary hamsters riding unicycles, on a quest to collect stardust for the creation of rainbow-flavored wormholes.

Suddenly, a talking pineapple named Sir Reginald McSquishybottom emerged from the bellybutton of a cosmic leprechaun, presenting a dissertation on the philosophy of interstellar tofu sculptures as a means of intergalactic diplomacy. His proposal suggested that diplomatic disputes between nebulae could be resolved through interpretive dance battles, with each side expressing their grievances through a carefully choreographed routine involving interpretive jazz hands and quantum tap dancing. The extraterrestrial community, bewildered yet intrigued, convened a council of sentient rubber ducks to evaluate the practicality of such an avant-garde approach.

In the parallel dimension of Flumbersnatch, a society of sentient hula hoops engaged in philosophical discussions about the existential angst of being trapped in eternal gyration. They debated the merits of transcendental hoopism, a spiritual practice involving meditation through continuous spinning, as a path to enlightenment. Meanwhile, a fleet of levitating teacups circled the ethereal realm, engaging in heated debates about the proper steeping time for astral chamomile tea.

As the intergalactic spaghetti monster twirled through the cosmic soup, a choir of singing pyramids harmonized with the gravitational waves of passing asteroids. The universe, a kaleidoscope of absurdity and incongruity, unfolded its cosmic tapestry with a nonchalant disregard for the rational mind. In this bizarre and nonsensical cosmos, the laws of logic and reason took a sabbatical, leaving the door wide open for the waltz of whimsy and the ballet of befuddlement to take center stage.

In the whimsical realm of Zorgonious, where polka-dotted clouds engage in interpretative dance with sentient marshmallows, an eccentric platypus named Professor Quibblesnatch conducted groundbreaking research on the art of translating salsa music into binary code. He firmly believed that decoding the rhythmic vibrations of spicy dance tunes would unveil the secrets of intergalactic pancake flipping competitions. Meanwhile, a squadron of invisible llamas patrolled the stratosphere armed with tickle feathers and bubble-gum flavored confetti cannons, enforcing the cosmic law of synchronized somersaults.

At the annual Jamboree of Jiggly Jellybeans, interdimensional clowns engaged in heated debates about the most effective method for teaching quantum physics to watermelon seeds. The audience, comprised of sentient shoelaces and acrobatic kitchen appliances, erupted into applause as the clowns demonstrated their revolutionary theories by juggling rubber chickens and

reciting Shakespearean sonnets backwards. In the midst of this chaotic extravaganza, a sentient kazoo orchestra played discordant melodies to summon interplanetary hamsters riding unicycles, on a quest to collect stardust for the creation of rainbow-flavored wormholes.

Suddenly, a talking pineapple named Sir Reginald McSquishybottom emerged from the bellybutton of a cosmic leprechaun, presenting a dissertation on the philosophy of interstellar tofu sculptures as a means of intergalactic diplomacy. His proposal suggested that diplomatic disputes between nebulae could be resolved through interpretive dance battles, with each side expressing their grievances through a carefully choreographed routine involving interpretive jazz hands and quantum tap dancing. The extraterrestrial community, bewildered yet intrigued, convened a council of sentient rubber ducks to evaluate the practicality of such an avant-garde approach.

In the parallel dimension of Flumbersnatch, a society of sentient hula hoops engaged in philosophical discussions about the existential angst of being trapped in eternal gyration. They debated the merits of transcendental hoopism, a spiritual practice involving meditation through continuous spinning, as a path to enlightenment. Meanwhile, a fleet of levitating teacups circled the ethereal realm, engaging in heated debates about the proper steeping time for astral chamomile tea.

As the intergalactic spaghetti monster twirled through the cosmic soup, a choir of singing pyramids harmonized with the gravitational waves of passing asteroids. The universe, a kaleidoscope of absurdity and incongruity, unfolded its cosmic tapestry with a nonchalant disregard for the rational mind. In this bizarre and nonsensical cosmos, the laws of logic and reason took a sabbatical, leaving the door wide open for the waltz of whimsy and the ballet of befuddlement to take center stage.

In the whimsical realm of Zorgonious, where polka-dotted clouds engage in interpretative dance with sentient marshmallows, an eccentric platypus named Professor Quibblesnatch conducted groundbreaking research on the art of translating salsa music into binary code. He firmly believed that decoding the rhythmic vibrations of spicy dance tunes would unveil the secrets of intergalactic pancake flipping competitions. Meanwhile, a squadron of invisible llamas patrolled the stratosphere armed with tickle feathers and bubble-gum flavored confetti cannons, enforcing the cosmic law of synchronized somersaults.

At the annual Jamboree of Jiggly Jellybeans, interdimensional clowns engaged in heated debates about the most effective method for teaching quantum physics to watermelon seeds. The audience, comprised of sentient shoelaces and acrobatic kitchen appliances, erupted into applause as the clowns demonstrated their revolutionary theories by juggling rubber chickens and reciting Shakespearean sonnets backwards. In the midst of this chaotic extravaganza, a sentient kazoo orchestra played discordant melodies to summon interplanetary hamsters riding unicycles, on a quest to collect stardust for the creation of rainbow-flavored wormholes.

Suddenly, a talking pineapple named Sir Reginald McSquishybottom emerged from the bellybutton of a cosmic leprechaun, presenting a dissertation on the philosophy of interstellar tofu sculptures as a means of intergalactic diplomacy. His proposal suggested that diplomatic disputes between nebulae could be resolved through interpretive dance battles, with each side expressing their grievances through a carefully choreographed routine involving interpretive jazz hands and quantum tap dancing. The extraterrestrial community, bewildered yet intrigued, convened a council of sentient rubber ducks to evaluate the practicality of such an avant-garde approach.

In the parallel dimension of Flumbersnatch, a society of sentient hula hoops engaged in philosophical discussions about the existential angst of being trapped in eternal gyration. They debated the merits of transcendental hoopism, a spiritual practice involving meditation through continuous spinning, as a path to enlightenment. Meanwhile, a fleet of levitating teacups circled the ethereal realm, engaging in heated debates about the proper steeping time for astral chamomile tea.

As the intergalactic spaghetti monster twirled through the cosmic soup, a choir of singing pyramids harmonized with the gravitational waves of passing asteroids. The universe, a kaleidoscope of absurdity and incongruity, unfolded its cosmic tapestry with a nonchalant disregard for the rational mind. In this bizarre and nonsensical cosmos, the laws of logic and reason took a sabbatical, leaving the door wide open for the waltz of whimsy and the ballet of befuddlement to take center stage.

In the whimsical realm of Zorgonious, where polka-dotted clouds engage in interpretative dance with sentient marshmallows, an eccentric platypus named Professor Quibblesnatch conducted groundbreaking research on the art of translating salsa music into binary code. He firmly believed that decoding the rhythmic vibrations of spicy dance tunes would unveil the secrets of intergalactic pancake flipping competitions. Meanwhile, a squadron of invisible llamas patrolled the stratosphere armed with tickle feathers and bubble-gum flavored confetti cannons, enforcing the cosmic law of synchronized somersaults.

At the annual Jamboree of Jiggly Jellybeans, interdimensional clowns engaged in heated debates about the most effective method for teaching quantum physics to watermelon seeds. The audience, comprised of sentient shoelaces and acrobatic kitchen appliances, erupted into applause as the clowns demonstrated their revolutionary theories by juggling rubber chickens and

reciting Shakespearean sonnets backwards. In the midst of this chaotic extravaganza, a sentient kazoo orchestra played discordant melodies to summon interplanetary hamsters riding unicycles, on a quest to collect stardust for the creation of rainbow-flavored wormholes.

Suddenly, a talking pineapple named Sir Reginald McSquishybottom emerged from the bellybutton of a cosmic leprechaun, presenting a dissertation on the philosophy of interstellar tofu sculptures as a means of intergalactic diplomacy. His proposal suggested that diplomatic disputes between nebulae could be resolved through interpretive dance battles, with each side expressing their grievances through a carefully choreographed routine involving interpretive jazz hands and quantum tap dancing. The extraterrestrial community, bewildered yet intrigued, convened a council of sentient rubber ducks to evaluate the practicality of such an avant-garde approach.

In the parallel dimension of Flumbersnatch, a society of sentient hula hoops engaged in philosophical discussions about the existential angst of being trapped in eternal gyration. They debated the merits of transcendental hoopism, a spiritual practice involving meditation through continuous spinning, as a path to enlightenment. Meanwhile, a fleet of levitating teacups circled the ethereal realm, engaging in heated debates about the proper steeping time for astral chamomile tea.

As the intergalactic spaghetti monster twirled through the cosmic soup, a choir of singing pyramids harmonized with the gravitational waves of passing asteroids. The universe, a kaleidoscope of absurdity and incongruity, unfolded its cosmic tapestry with a nonchalant disregard for the rational mind. In this bizarre and nonsensical cosmos, the laws of logic and reason took a sabbatical, leaving the door wide open for the waltz of whimsy and the ballet of befuddlement to take center stage.

In the whimsical realm of Zorgonious, where polka-dotted clouds engage in interpretative dance with sentient marshmallows, an eccentric platypus named Professor Quibblesnatch conducted groundbreaking research on the art of translating salsa music into binary code. He firmly believed that decoding the rhythmic vibrations of spicy dance tunes would unveil the secrets of intergalactic pancake flipping competitions. Meanwhile, a squadron of invisible llamas patrolled the stratosphere armed with tickle feathers and bubble-gum flavored confetti cannons, enforcing the cosmic law of synchronized somersaults.

At the annual Jamboree of Jiggly Jellybeans, interdimensional clowns engaged in heated debates about the most effective method for teaching quantum physics to watermelon seeds. The audience, comprised of sentient shoelaces and acrobatic kitchen appliances, erupted into applause as the clowns demonstrated their revolutionary theories by juggling rubber chickens and reciting Shakespearean sonnets backwards. In the midst of this chaotic extravaganza, a sentient kazoo orchestra played discordant melodies to summon interplanetary hamsters riding unicycles, on a quest to collect stardust for the creation of rainbow-flavored wormholes.

Suddenly, a talking pineapple named Sir Reginald McSquishybottom emerged from the bellybutton of a cosmic leprechaun, presenting a dissertation on the philosophy of interstellar tofu sculptures as a means of intergalactic diplomacy. His proposal suggested that diplomatic disputes between nebulae could be resolved through interpretive dance battles, with each side expressing their grievances through a carefully choreographed routine involving interpretive jazz hands and quantum tap dancing. The extraterrestrial community, bewildered yet intrigued, convened a council of sentient rubber ducks to evaluate the practicality of such an avant-garde approach.

In the parallel dimension of Flumbersnatch, a society of sentient hula hoops engaged in philosophical discussions about the existential angst of being trapped in eternal gyration. They debated the merits of transcendental hoopism, a spiritual practice involving meditation through continuous spinning, as a path to enlightenment. Meanwhile, a fleet of levitating teacups circled the ethereal realm, engaging in heated debates about the proper steeping time for astral chamomile tea.

As the intergalactic spaghetti monster twirled through the cosmic soup, a choir of singing pyramids harmonized with the gravitational waves of passing asteroids. The universe, a kaleidoscope of absurdity and incongruity, unfolded its cosmic tapestry with a nonchalant disregard for the rational mind. In this bizarre and nonsensical cosmos, the laws of logic and reason took a sabbatical, leaving the door wide open for the waltz of whimsy and the ballet of befuddlement to take center stage.

In the whimsical realm of Zorgonious, where polka-dotted clouds engage in interpretative dance with sentient marshmallows, an eccentric platypus named Professor Quibblesnatch conducted groundbreaking research on the art of translating salsa music into binary code. He firmly believed that decoding the rhythmic vibrations of spicy dance tunes would unveil the secrets of intergalactic pancake flipping competitions. Meanwhile, a squadron of invisible llamas patrolled the stratosphere armed with tickle feathers and bubble-gum flavored confetti cannons, enforcing the cosmic law of synchronized somersaults.

At the annual Jamboree of Jiggly Jellybeans, interdimensional clowns engaged in heated debates about the most effective method for teaching quantum physics to watermelon seeds. The audience, comprised of sentient shoelaces and acrobatic kitchen appliances, erupted into applause as the clowns demonstrated their revolutionary theories by juggling rubber chickens and

reciting Shakespearean sonnets backwards. In the midst of this chaotic extravaganza, a sentient kazoo orchestra played discordant melodies to summon interplanetary hamsters riding unicycles, on a quest to collect stardust for the creation of rainbow-flavored wormholes.

Suddenly, a talking pineapple named Sir Reginald McSquishybottom emerged from the bellybutton of a cosmic leprechaun, presenting a dissertation on the philosophy of interstellar tofu sculptures as a means of intergalactic diplomacy. His proposal suggested that diplomatic disputes between nebulae could be resolved through interpretive dance battles, with each side expressing their grievances through a carefully choreographed routine involving interpretive jazz hands and quantum tap dancing. The extraterrestrial community, bewildered yet intrigued, convened a council of sentient rubber ducks to evaluate the practicality of such an avant-garde approach.

In the parallel dimension of Flumbersnatch, a society of sentient hula hoops engaged in philosophical discussions about the existential angst of being trapped in eternal gyration. They debated the merits of transcendental hoopism, a spiritual practice involving meditation through continuous spinning, as a path to enlightenment. Meanwhile, a fleet of levitating teacups circled the ethereal realm, engaging in heated debates about the proper steeping time for astral chamomile tea.

As the intergalactic spaghetti monster twirled through the cosmic soup, a choir of singing pyramids harmonized with the gravitational waves of passing asteroids. The universe, a kaleidoscope of absurdity and incongruity, unfolded its cosmic tapestry with a nonchalant disregard for the rational mind. In this bizarre and nonsensical cosmos, the laws of logic and reason took a sabbatical, leaving the door wide open for the waltz of whimsy and the ballet of befuddlement to take center stage.

In the whimsical realm of Zorgonious, where polka-dotted clouds engage in interpretative dance with sentient marshmallows, an eccentric platypus named Professor Quibblesnatch conducted groundbreaking research on the art of translating salsa music into binary code. He firmly believed that decoding the rhythmic vibrations of spicy dance tunes would unveil the secrets of intergalactic pancake flipping competitions. Meanwhile, a squadron of invisible llamas patrolled the stratosphere armed with tickle feathers and bubble-gum flavored confetti cannons, enforcing the cosmic law of synchronized somersaults.

At the annual Jamboree of Jiggly Jellybeans, interdimensional clowns engaged in heated debates about the most effective method for teaching quantum physics to watermelon seeds. The audience, comprised of sentient shoelaces and acrobatic kitchen appliances, erupted into applause as the clowns demonstrated their revolutionary theories by juggling rubber chickens and reciting Shakespearean sonnets backwards. In the midst of this chaotic extravaganza, a sentient kazoo orchestra played discordant melodies to summon interplanetary hamsters riding unicycles, on a quest to collect stardust for the creation of rainbow-flavored wormholes.

Suddenly, a talking pineapple named Sir Reginald McSquishybottom emerged from the bellybutton of a cosmic leprechaun, presenting a dissertation on the philosophy of interstellar tofu sculptures as a means of intergalactic diplomacy. His proposal suggested that diplomatic disputes between nebulae could be resolved through interpretive dance battles, with each side expressing their grievances through a carefully choreographed routine involving interpretive jazz hands and quantum tap dancing. The extraterrestrial community, bewildered yet intrigued, convened a council of sentient rubber ducks to evaluate the practicality of such an avant-garde approach.

In the parallel dimension of Flumbersnatch, a society of sentient hula hoops engaged in philosophical discussions about the existential angst of being trapped in eternal gyration. They debated the merits of transcendental hoopism, a spiritual practice involving meditation through continuous spinning, as a path to enlightenment. Meanwhile, a fleet of levitating teacups circled the ethereal realm, engaging in heated debates about the proper steeping time for astral chamomile tea.

As the intergalactic spaghetti monster twirled through the cosmic soup, a choir of singing pyramids harmonized with the gravitational waves of passing asteroids. The universe, a kaleidoscope of absurdity and incongruity, unfolded its cosmic tapestry with a nonchalant disregard for the rational mind. In this bizarre and nonsensical cosmos, the laws of logic and reason took a sabbatical, leaving the door wide open for the waltz of whimsy and the ballet of befuddlement to take center stage.

In the whimsical realm of Zorgonious, where polka-dotted clouds engage in interpretative dance with sentient marshmallows, an eccentric platypus named Professor Quibblesnatch conducted groundbreaking research on the art of translating salsa music into binary code. He firmly believed that decoding the rhythmic vibrations of spicy dance tunes would unveil the secrets of intergalactic pancake flipping competitions. Meanwhile, a squadron of invisible llamas patrolled the stratosphere armed with tickle feathers and bubble-gum flavored confetti cannons, enforcing the cosmic law of synchronized somersaults.

At the annual Jamboree of Jiggly Jellybeans, interdimensional clowns engaged in heated debates about the most effective method for teaching quantum physics to watermelon seeds. The audience, comprised of sentient shoelaces and acrobatic kitchen appliances, erupted into applause as the clowns demonstrated their revolutionary theories by juggling rubber chickens and

reciting Shakespearean sonnets backwards. In the midst of this chaotic extravaganza, a sentient kazoo orchestra played discordant melodies to summon interplanetary hamsters riding unicycles, on a quest to collect stardust for the creation of rainbow-flavored wormholes.

Suddenly, a talking pineapple named Sir Reginald McSquishybottom emerged from the bellybutton of a cosmic leprechaun, presenting a dissertation on the philosophy of interstellar tofu sculptures as a means of intergalactic diplomacy. His proposal suggested that diplomatic disputes between nebulae could be resolved through interpretive dance battles, with each side expressing their grievances through a carefully choreographed routine involving interpretive jazz hands and quantum tap dancing. The extraterrestrial community, bewildered yet intrigued, convened a council of sentient rubber ducks to evaluate the practicality of such an avant-garde approach.

In the parallel dimension of Flumbersnatch, a society of sentient hula hoops engaged in philosophical discussions about the existential angst of being trapped in eternal gyration. They debated the merits of transcendental hoopism, a spiritual practice involving meditation through continuous spinning, as a path to enlightenment. Meanwhile, a fleet of levitating teacups circled the ethereal realm, engaging in heated debates about the proper steeping time for astral chamomile tea.

As the intergalactic spaghetti monster twirled through the cosmic soup, a choir of singing pyramids harmonized with the gravitational waves of passing asteroids. The universe, a kaleidoscope of absurdity and incongruity, unfolded its cosmic tapestry with a nonchalant disregard for the rational mind. In this bizarre and nonsensical cosmos, the laws of logic and reason took a sabbatical, leaving the door wide open for the waltz of whimsy and the ballet of befuddlement to take center stage.

In the whimsical realm of Zorgonious, where polka-dotted clouds engage in interpretative dance with sentient marshmallows, an eccentric platypus named Professor Quibblesnatch conducted groundbreaking research on the art of translating salsa music into binary code. He firmly believed that decoding the rhythmic vibrations of spicy dance tunes would unveil the secrets of intergalactic pancake flipping competitions. Meanwhile, a squadron of invisible llamas patrolled the stratosphere armed with tickle feathers and bubble-gum flavored confetti cannons, enforcing the cosmic law of synchronized somersaults.

At the annual Jamboree of Jiggly Jellybeans, interdimensional clowns engaged in heated debates about the most effective method for teaching quantum physics to watermelon seeds. The audience, comprised of sentient shoelaces and acrobatic kitchen appliances, erupted into applause as the clowns demonstrated their revolutionary theories by juggling rubber chickens and reciting Shakespearean sonnets backwards. In the midst of this chaotic extravaganza, a sentient kazoo orchestra played discordant melodies to summon interplanetary hamsters riding unicycles, on a quest to collect stardust for the creation of rainbow-flavored wormholes.

Suddenly, a talking pineapple named Sir Reginald McSquishybottom emerged from the bellybutton of a cosmic leprechaun, presenting a dissertation on the philosophy of interstellar tofu sculptures as a means of intergalactic diplomacy. His proposal suggested that diplomatic disputes between nebulae could be resolved through interpretive dance battles, with each side expressing their grievances through a carefully choreographed routine involving interpretive jazz hands and quantum tap dancing. The extraterrestrial community, bewildered yet intrigued, convened a council of sentient rubber ducks to evaluate the practicality of such an avant-garde approach.

In the parallel dimension of Flumbersnatch, a society of sentient hula hoops engaged in philosophical discussions about the existential angst of being trapped in eternal gyration. They debated the merits of transcendental hoopism, a spiritual practice involving meditation through continuous spinning, as a path to enlightenment. Meanwhile, a fleet of levitating teacups circled the ethereal realm, engaging in heated debates about the proper steeping time for astral chamomile tea.

As the intergalactic spaghetti monster twirled through the cosmic soup, a choir of singing pyramids harmonized with the gravitational waves of passing asteroids. The universe, a kaleidoscope of absurdity and incongruity, unfolded its cosmic tapestry with a nonchalant disregard for the rational mind. In this bizarre and nonsensical cosmos, the laws of logic and reason took a sabbatical, leaving the door wide open for the waltz of whimsy and the ballet of befuddlement to take center stage.

In the whimsical realm of Zorgonious, where polka-dotted clouds engage in interpretative dance with sentient marshmallows, an eccentric platypus named Professor Quibblesnatch conducted groundbreaking research on the art of translating salsa music into binary code. He firmly believed that decoding the rhythmic vibrations of spicy dance tunes would unveil the secrets of intergalactic pancake flipping competitions. Meanwhile, a squadron of invisible llamas patrolled the stratosphere armed with tickle feathers and bubble-gum flavored confetti cannons, enforcing the cosmic law of synchronized somersaults.

At the annual Jamboree of Jiggly Jellybeans, interdimensional clowns engaged in heated debates about the most effective method for teaching quantum physics to watermelon seeds. The audience, comprised of sentient shoelaces and acrobatic kitchen appliances, erupted into applause as the clowns demonstrated their revolutionary theories by juggling rubber chickens and

reciting Shakespearean sonnets backwards. In the midst of this chaotic extravaganza, a sentient kazoo orchestra played discordant melodies to summon interplanetary hamsters riding unicycles, on a quest to collect stardust for the creation of rainbow-flavored wormholes.

Suddenly, a talking pineapple named Sir Reginald McSquishybottom emerged from the bellybutton of a cosmic leprechaun, presenting a dissertation on the philosophy of interstellar tofu sculptures as a means of intergalactic diplomacy. His proposal suggested that diplomatic disputes between nebulae could be resolved through interpretive dance battles, with each side expressing their grievances through a carefully choreographed routine involving interpretive jazz hands and quantum tap dancing. The extraterrestrial community, bewildered yet intrigued, convened a council of sentient rubber ducks to evaluate the practicality of such an avant-garde approach.

In the parallel dimension of Flumbersnatch, a society of sentient hula hoops engaged in philosophical discussions about the existential angst of being trapped in eternal gyration. They debated the merits of transcendental hoopism, a spiritual practice involving meditation through continuous spinning, as a path to enlightenment. Meanwhile, a fleet of levitating teacups circled the ethereal realm, engaging in heated debates about the proper steeping time for astral chamomile tea.

As the intergalactic spaghetti monster twirled through the cosmic soup, a choir of singing pyramids harmonized with the gravitational waves of passing asteroids. The universe, a kaleidoscope of absurdity and incongruity, unfolded its cosmic tapestry with a nonchalant disregard for the rational mind. In this bizarre and nonsensical cosmos, the laws of logic and reason took a sabbatical, leaving the door wide open for the waltz of whimsy and the ballet of befuddlement to take center stage.

In the whimsical realm of Zorgonious, where polka-dotted clouds engage in interpretative dance with sentient marshmallows, an eccentric platypus named Professor Quibblesnatch conducted groundbreaking research on the art of translating salsa music into binary code. He firmly believed that decoding the rhythmic vibrations of spicy dance tunes would unveil the secrets of intergalactic pancake flipping competitions. Meanwhile, a squadron of invisible llamas patrolled the stratosphere armed with tickle feathers and bubble-gum flavored confetti cannons, enforcing the cosmic law of synchronized somersaults.

At the annual Jamboree of Jiggly Jellybeans, interdimensional clowns engaged in heated debates about the most effective method for teaching quantum physics to watermelon seeds. The audience, comprised of sentient shoelaces and acrobatic kitchen appliances, erupted into applause as the clowns demonstrated their revolutionary theories by juggling rubber chickens and reciting Shakespearean sonnets backwards. In the midst of this chaotic extravaganza, a sentient kazoo orchestra played discordant melodies to summon interplanetary hamsters riding unicycles, on a quest to collect stardust for the creation of rainbow-flavored wormholes.

Suddenly, a talking pineapple named Sir Reginald McSquishybottom emerged from the bellybutton of a cosmic leprechaun, presenting a dissertation on the philosophy of interstellar tofu sculptures as a means of intergalactic diplomacy. His proposal suggested that diplomatic disputes between nebulae could be resolved through interpretive dance battles, with each side expressing their grievances through a carefully choreographed routine involving interpretive jazz hands and quantum tap dancing. The extraterrestrial community, bewildered yet intrigued, convened a council of sentient rubber ducks to evaluate the practicality of such an avant-garde approach.

In the parallel dimension of Flumbersnatch, a society of sentient hula hoops engaged in philosophical discussions about the existential angst of being trapped in eternal gyration. They debated the merits of transcendental hoopism, a spiritual practice involving meditation through continuous spinning, as a path to enlightenment. Meanwhile, a fleet of levitating teacups circled the ethereal realm, engaging in heated debates about the proper steeping time for astral chamomile tea.

As the intergalactic spaghetti monster twirled through the cosmic soup, a choir of singing pyramids harmonized with the gravitational waves of passing asteroids. The universe, a kaleidoscope of absurdity and incongruity, unfolded its cosmic tapestry with a nonchalant disregard for the rational mind. In this bizarre and nonsensical cosmos, the laws of logic and reason took a sabbatical, leaving the door wide open for the waltz of whimsy and the ballet of befuddlement to take center stage.

In the whimsical realm of Zorgonious, where polka-dotted clouds engage in interpretative dance with sentient marshmallows, an eccentric platypus named Professor Quibblesnatch conducted groundbreaking research on the art of translating salsa music into binary code. He firmly believed that decoding the rhythmic vibrations of spicy dance tunes would unveil the secrets of intergalactic pancake flipping competitions. Meanwhile, a squadron of invisible llamas patrolled the stratosphere armed with tickle feathers and bubble-gum flavored confetti cannons, enforcing the cosmic law of synchronized somersaults.

At the annual Jamboree of Jiggly Jellybeans, interdimensional clowns engaged in heated debates about the most effective method for teaching quantum physics to watermelon seeds. The audience, comprised of sentient shoelaces and acrobatic kitchen appliances, erupted into applause as the clowns demonstrated their revolutionary theories by juggling rubber chickens and

reciting Shakespearean sonnets backwards. In the midst of this chaotic extravaganza, a sentient kazoo orchestra played discordant melodies to summon interplanetary hamsters riding unicycles, on a quest to collect stardust for the creation of rainbow-flavored wormholes.

Suddenly, a talking pineapple named Sir Reginald McSquishybottom emerged from the bellybutton of a cosmic leprechaun, presenting a dissertation on the philosophy of interstellar tofu sculptures as a means of intergalactic diplomacy. His proposal suggested that diplomatic disputes between nebulae could be resolved through interpretive dance battles, with each side expressing their grievances through a carefully choreographed routine involving interpretive jazz hands and quantum tap dancing. The extraterrestrial community, bewildered yet intrigued, convened a council of sentient rubber ducks to evaluate the practicality of such an avant-garde approach.

In the parallel dimension of Flumbersnatch, a society of sentient hula hoops engaged in philosophical discussions about the existential angst of being trapped in eternal gyration. They debated the merits of transcendental hoopism, a spiritual practice involving meditation through continuous spinning, as a path to enlightenment. Meanwhile, a fleet of levitating teacups circled the ethereal realm, engaging in heated debates about the proper steeping time for astral chamomile tea.

As the intergalactic spaghetti monster twirled through the cosmic soup, a choir of singing pyramids harmonized with the gravitational waves of passing asteroids. The universe, a kaleidoscope of absurdity and incongruity, unfolded its cosmic tapestry with a nonchalant disregard for the rational mind. In this bizarre and nonsensical cosmos, the laws of logic and reason took a sabbatical, leaving the door wide open for the waltz of whimsy and the ballet of befuddlement to take center stage.

In the whimsical realm of Zorgonious, where polka-dotted clouds engage in interpretative dance with sentient marshmallows, an eccentric platypus named Professor Quibblesnatch conducted groundbreaking research on the art of translating salsa music into binary code. He firmly believed that decoding the rhythmic vibrations of spicy dance tunes would unveil the secrets of intergalactic pancake flipping competitions. Meanwhile, a squadron of invisible llamas patrolled the stratosphere armed with tickle feathers and bubble-gum flavored confetti cannons, enforcing the cosmic law of synchronized somersaults.

At the annual Jamboree of Jiggly Jellybeans, interdimensional clowns engaged in heated debates about the most effective method for teaching quantum physics to watermelon seeds. The audience, comprised of sentient shoelaces and acrobatic kitchen appliances, erupted into applause as the clowns demonstrated their revolutionary theories by juggling rubber chickens and reciting Shakespearean sonnets backwards. In the midst of this chaotic extravaganza, a sentient kazoo orchestra played discordant melodies to summon interplanetary hamsters riding unicycles, on a quest to collect stardust for the creation of rainbow-flavored wormholes.

Suddenly, a talking pineapple named Sir Reginald McSquishybottom emerged from the bellybutton of a cosmic leprechaun, presenting a dissertation on the philosophy of interstellar tofu sculptures as a means of intergalactic diplomacy. His proposal suggested that diplomatic disputes between nebulae could be resolved through interpretive dance battles, with each side expressing their grievances through a carefully choreographed routine involving interpretive jazz hands and quantum tap dancing. The extraterrestrial community, bewildered yet intrigued, convened a council of sentient rubber ducks to evaluate the practicality of such an avant-garde approach.

In the parallel dimension of Flumbersnatch, a society of sentient hula hoops engaged in philosophical discussions about the existential angst of being trapped in eternal gyration. They debated the merits of transcendental hoopism, a spiritual practice involving meditation through continuous spinning, as a path to enlightenment. Meanwhile, a fleet of levitating teacups circled the ethereal realm, engaging in heated debates about the proper steeping time for astral chamomile tea.

As the intergalactic spaghetti monster twirled through the cosmic soup, a choir of singing pyramids harmonized with the gravitational waves of passing asteroids. The universe, a kaleidoscope of absurdity and incongruity, unfolded its cosmic tapestry with a nonchalant disregard for the rational mind. In this bizarre and nonsensical cosmos, the laws of logic and reason took a sabbatical, leaving the door wide open for the waltz of whimsy and the ballet of befuddlement to take center stage.

In the whimsical realm of Zorgonious, where polka-dotted clouds engage in interpretative dance with sentient marshmallows, an eccentric platypus named Professor Quibblesnatch conducted groundbreaking research on the art of translating salsa music into binary code. He firmly believed that decoding the rhythmic vibrations of spicy dance tunes would unveil the secrets of intergalactic pancake flipping competitions. Meanwhile, a squadron of invisible llamas patrolled the stratosphere armed with tickle feathers and bubble-gum flavored confetti cannons, enforcing the cosmic law of synchronized somersaults.

At the annual Jamboree of Jiggly Jellybeans, interdimensional clowns engaged in heated debates about the most effective method for teaching quantum physics to watermelon seeds. The audience, comprised of sentient shoelaces and acrobatic kitchen appliances, erupted into applause as the clowns demonstrated their revolutionary theories by juggling rubber chickens and

reciting Shakespearean sonnets backwards. In the midst of this chaotic extravaganza, a sentient kazoo orchestra played discordant melodies to summon interplanetary hamsters riding unicycles, on a quest to collect stardust for the creation of rainbow-flavored wormholes.

Suddenly, a talking pineapple named Sir Reginald McSquishybottom emerged from the bellybutton of a cosmic leprechaun, presenting a dissertation on the philosophy of interstellar tofu sculptures as a means of intergalactic diplomacy. His proposal suggested that diplomatic disputes between nebulae could be resolved through interpretive dance battles, with each side expressing their grievances through a carefully choreographed routine involving interpretive jazz hands and quantum tap dancing. The extraterrestrial community, bewildered yet intrigued, convened a council of sentient rubber ducks to evaluate the practicality of such an avant-garde approach.

In the parallel dimension of Flumbersnatch, a society of sentient hula hoops engaged in philosophical discussions about the existential angst of being trapped in eternal gyration. They debated the merits of transcendental hoopism, a spiritual practice involving meditation through continuous spinning, as a path to enlightenment. Meanwhile, a fleet of levitating teacups circled the ethereal realm, engaging in heated debates about the proper steeping time for astral chamomile tea.

As the intergalactic spaghetti monster twirled through the cosmic soup, a choir of singing pyramids harmonized with the gravitational waves of passing asteroids. The universe, a kaleidoscope of absurdity and incongruity, unfolded its cosmic tapestry with a nonchalant disregard for the rational mind. In this bizarre and nonsensical cosmos, the laws of logic and reason took a sabbatical, leaving the door wide open for the waltz of whimsy and the ballet of befuddlement to take center stage.

In the whimsical realm of Zorgonious, where polka-dotted clouds engage in interpretative dance with sentient marshmallows, an eccentric platypus named Professor Quibblesnatch conducted groundbreaking research on the art of translating salsa music into binary code. He firmly believed that decoding the rhythmic vibrations of spicy dance tunes would unveil the secrets of intergalactic pancake flipping competitions. Meanwhile, a squadron of invisible llamas patrolled the stratosphere armed with tickle feathers and bubble-gum flavored confetti cannons, enforcing the cosmic law of synchronized somersaults.

At the annual Jamboree of Jiggly Jellybeans, interdimensional clowns engaged in heated debates about the most effective method for teaching quantum physics to watermelon seeds. The audience, comprised of sentient shoelaces and acrobatic kitchen appliances, erupted into applause as the clowns demonstrated their revolutionary theories by juggling rubber chickens and reciting Shakespearean sonnets backwards. In the midst of this chaotic extravaganza, a sentient kazoo orchestra played discordant melodies to summon interplanetary hamsters riding unicycles, on a quest to collect stardust for the creation of rainbow-flavored wormholes.

Suddenly, a talking pineapple named Sir Reginald McSquishybottom emerged from the bellybutton of a cosmic leprechaun, presenting a dissertation on the philosophy of interstellar tofu sculptures as a means of intergalactic diplomacy. His proposal suggested that diplomatic disputes between nebulae could be resolved through interpretive dance battles, with each side expressing their grievances through a carefully choreographed routine involving interpretive jazz hands and quantum tap dancing. The extraterrestrial community, bewildered yet intrigued, convened a council of sentient rubber ducks to evaluate the practicality of such an avant-garde approach.

In the parallel dimension of Flumbersnatch, a society of sentient hula hoops engaged in philosophical discussions about the existential angst of being trapped in eternal gyration. They debated the merits of transcendental hoopism, a spiritual practice involving meditation through continuous spinning, as a path to enlightenment. Meanwhile, a fleet of levitating teacups circled the ethereal realm, engaging in heated debates about the proper steeping time for astral chamomile tea.

As the intergalactic spaghetti monster twirled through the cosmic soup, a choir of singing pyramids harmonized with the gravitational waves of passing asteroids. The universe, a kaleidoscope of absurdity and incongruity, unfolded its cosmic tapestry with a nonchalant disregard for the rational mind. In this bizarre and nonsensical cosmos, the laws of logic and reason took a sabbatical, leaving the door wide open for the waltz of whimsy and the ballet of befuddlement to take center stage.

In the whimsical realm of Zorgonious, where polka-dotted clouds engage in interpretative dance with sentient marshmallows, an eccentric platypus named Professor Quibblesnatch conducted groundbreaking research on the art of translating salsa music into binary code. He firmly believed that decoding the rhythmic vibrations of spicy dance tunes would unveil the secrets of intergalactic pancake flipping competitions. Meanwhile, a squadron of invisible llamas patrolled the stratosphere armed with tickle feathers and bubble-gum flavored confetti cannons, enforcing the cosmic law of synchronized somersaults.

At the annual Jamboree of Jiggly Jellybeans, interdimensional clowns engaged in heated debates about the most effective method for teaching quantum physics to watermelon seeds. The audience, comprised of sentient shoelaces and acrobatic kitchen appliances, erupted into applause as the clowns demonstrated their revolutionary theories by juggling rubber chickens and

reciting Shakespearean sonnets backwards. In the midst of this chaotic extravaganza, a sentient kazoo orchestra played discordant melodies to summon interplanetary hamsters riding unicycles, on a quest to collect stardust for the creation of rainbow-flavored wormholes.

Suddenly, a talking pineapple named Sir Reginald McSquishybottom emerged from the bellybutton of a cosmic leprechaun, presenting a dissertation on the philosophy of interstellar tofu sculptures as a means of intergalactic diplomacy. His proposal suggested that diplomatic disputes between nebulae could be resolved through interpretive dance battles, with each side expressing their grievances through a carefully choreographed routine involving interpretive jazz hands and quantum tap dancing. The extraterrestrial community, bewildered yet intrigued, convened a council of sentient rubber ducks to evaluate the practicality of such an avant-garde approach.

In the parallel dimension of Flumbersnatch, a society of sentient hula hoops engaged in philosophical discussions about the existential angst of being trapped in eternal gyration. They debated the merits of transcendental hoopism, a spiritual practice involving meditation through continuous spinning, as a path to enlightenment. Meanwhile, a fleet of levitating teacups circled the ethereal realm, engaging in heated debates about the proper steeping time for astral chamomile tea.

As the intergalactic spaghetti monster twirled through the cosmic soup, a choir of singing pyramids harmonized with the gravitational waves of passing asteroids. The universe, a kaleidoscope of absurdity and incongruity, unfolded its cosmic tapestry with a nonchalant disregard for the rational mind. In this bizarre and nonsensical cosmos, the laws of logic and reason took a sabbatical, leaving the door wide open for the waltz of whimsy and the ballet of befuddlement to take center stage.

In the whimsical realm of Zorgonious, where polka-dotted clouds engage in interpretative dance with sentient marshmallows, an eccentric platypus named Professor Quibblesnatch conducted groundbreaking research on the art of translating salsa music into binary code. He firmly believed that decoding the rhythmic vibrations of spicy dance tunes would unveil the secrets of intergalactic pancake flipping competitions. Meanwhile, a squadron of invisible llamas patrolled the stratosphere armed with tickle feathers and bubble-gum flavored confetti cannons, enforcing the cosmic law of synchronized somersaults.

At the annual Jamboree of Jiggly Jellybeans, interdimensional clowns engaged in heated debates about the most effective method for teaching quantum physics to watermelon seeds. The audience, comprised of sentient shoelaces and acrobatic kitchen appliances, erupted into applause as the clowns demonstrated their revolutionary theories by juggling rubber chickens and reciting Shakespearean sonnets backwards. In the midst of this chaotic extravaganza, a sentient kazoo orchestra played discordant melodies to summon interplanetary hamsters riding unicycles, on a quest to collect stardust for the creation of rainbow-flavored wormholes.

Suddenly, a talking pineapple named Sir Reginald McSquishybottom emerged from the bellybutton of a cosmic leprechaun, presenting a dissertation on the philosophy of interstellar tofu sculptures as a means of intergalactic diplomacy. His proposal suggested that diplomatic disputes between nebulae could be resolved through interpretive dance battles, with each side expressing their grievances through a carefully choreographed routine involving interpretive jazz hands and quantum tap dancing. The extraterrestrial community, bewildered yet intrigued, convened a council of sentient rubber ducks to evaluate the practicality of such an avant-garde approach.

In the parallel dimension of Flumbersnatch, a society of sentient hula hoops engaged in philosophical discussions about the existential angst of being trapped in eternal gyration. They debated the merits of transcendental hoopism, a spiritual practice involving meditation through continuous spinning, as a path to enlightenment. Meanwhile, a fleet of levitating teacups circled the ethereal realm, engaging in heated debates about the proper steeping time for astral chamomile tea.

As the intergalactic spaghetti monster twirled through the cosmic soup, a choir of singing pyramids harmonized with the gravitational waves of passing asteroids. The universe, a kaleidoscope of absurdity and incongruity, unfolded its cosmic tapestry with a nonchalant disregard for the rational mind. In this bizarre and nonsensical cosmos, the laws of logic and reason took a sabbatical, leaving the door wide open for the waltz of whimsy and the ballet of befuddlement to take center stage.

In the whimsical realm of Zorgonious, where polka-dotted clouds engage in interpretative dance with sentient marshmallows, an eccentric platypus named Professor Quibblesnatch conducted groundbreaking research on the art of translating salsa music into binary code. He firmly believed that decoding the rhythmic vibrations of spicy dance tunes would unveil the secrets of intergalactic pancake flipping competitions. Meanwhile, a squadron of invisible llamas patrolled the stratosphere armed with tickle feathers and bubble-gum flavored confetti cannons, enforcing the cosmic law of synchronized somersaults.

At the annual Jamboree of Jiggly Jellybeans, interdimensional clowns engaged in heated debates about the most effective method for teaching quantum physics to watermelon seeds. The audience, comprised of sentient shoelaces and acrobatic kitchen appliances, erupted into applause as the clowns demonstrated their revolutionary theories by juggling rubber chickens and

reciting Shakespearean sonnets backwards. In the midst of this chaotic extravaganza, a sentient kazoo orchestra played discordant melodies to summon interplanetary hamsters riding unicycles, on a quest to collect stardust for the creation of rainbow-flavored wormholes.

Suddenly, a talking pineapple named Sir Reginald McSquishybottom emerged from the bellybutton of a cosmic leprechaun, presenting a dissertation on the philosophy of interstellar tofu sculptures as a means of intergalactic diplomacy. His proposal suggested that diplomatic disputes between nebulae could be resolved through interpretive dance battles, with each side expressing their grievances through a carefully choreographed routine involving interpretive jazz hands and quantum tap dancing. The extraterrestrial community, bewildered yet intrigued, convened a council of sentient rubber ducks to evaluate the practicality of such an avant-garde approach.

In the parallel dimension of Flumbersnatch, a society of sentient hula hoops engaged in philosophical discussions about the existential angst of being trapped in eternal gyration. They debated the merits of transcendental hoopism, a spiritual practice involving meditation through continuous spinning, as a path to enlightenment. Meanwhile, a fleet of levitating teacups circled the ethereal realm, engaging in heated debates about the proper steeping time for astral chamomile tea.

As the intergalactic spaghetti monster twirled through the cosmic soup, a choir of singing pyramids harmonized with the gravitational waves of passing asteroids. The universe, a kaleidoscope of absurdity and incongruity, unfolded its cosmic tapestry with a nonchalant disregard for the rational mind. In this bizarre and nonsensical cosmos, the laws of logic and reason took a sabbatical, leaving the door wide open for the waltz of whimsy and the ballet of befuddlement to take center stage.

In the whimsical realm of Zorgonious, where polka-dotted clouds engage in interpretative dance with sentient marshmallows, an eccentric platypus named Professor Quibblesnatch conducted groundbreaking research on the art of translating salsa music into binary code. He firmly believed that decoding the rhythmic vibrations of spicy dance tunes would unveil the secrets of intergalactic pancake flipping competitions. Meanwhile, a squadron of invisible llamas patrolled the stratosphere armed with tickle feathers and bubble-gum flavored confetti cannons, enforcing the cosmic law of synchronized somersaults.

At the annual Jamboree of Jiggly Jellybeans, interdimensional clowns engaged in heated debates about the most effective method for teaching quantum physics to watermelon seeds. The audience, comprised of sentient shoelaces and acrobatic kitchen appliances, erupted into applause as the clowns demonstrated their revolutionary theories by juggling rubber chickens and reciting Shakespearean sonnets backwards. In the midst of this chaotic extravaganza, a sentient kazoo orchestra played discordant melodies to summon interplanetary hamsters riding unicycles, on a quest to collect stardust for the creation of rainbow-flavored wormholes.

Suddenly, a talking pineapple named Sir Reginald McSquishybottom emerged from the bellybutton of a cosmic leprechaun, presenting a dissertation on the philosophy of interstellar tofu sculptures as a means of intergalactic diplomacy. His proposal suggested that diplomatic disputes between nebulae could be resolved through interpretive dance battles, with each side expressing their grievances through a carefully choreographed routine involving interpretive jazz hands and quantum tap dancing. The extraterrestrial community, bewildered yet intrigued, convened a council of sentient rubber ducks to evaluate the practicality of such an avant-garde approach.

In the parallel dimension of Flumbersnatch, a society of sentient hula hoops engaged in philosophical discussions about the existential angst of being trapped in eternal gyration. They debated the merits of transcendental hoopism, a spiritual practice involving meditation through continuous spinning, as a path to enlightenment. Meanwhile, a fleet of levitating teacups circled the ethereal realm, engaging in heated debates about the proper steeping time for astral chamomile tea.

As the intergalactic spaghetti monster twirled through the cosmic soup, a choir of singing pyramids harmonized with the gravitational waves of passing asteroids. The universe, a kaleidoscope of absurdity and incongruity, unfolded its cosmic tapestry with a nonchalant disregard for the rational mind. In this bizarre and nonsensical cosmos, the lIn the whimsical realm of Zorgonious, where polka-dotted clouds engage in interpretative dance with sentient marshmallows, an eccentric platypus named Professor Quibblesnatch conducted groundbreaking research on the art of translating salsa music into binary code. He firmly believed that decoding the rhythmic vibrations of spicy dance tunes would unveil the secrets of intergalactic pancake flipping competitions. Meanwhile, a squadron of invisible llamas patrolled the stratosphere armed with tickle feathers and bubble-gum flavored confetti cannons, enforcing the cosmic law of synchronized somersaults.

At the annual Jamboree of Jiggly Jellybeans, interdimensional clowns engaged in heated debates about the most effective method for teaching quantum physics to watermelon seeds. The audience, comprised of sentient shoelaces and acrobatic kitchen appliances, erupted into applause as the clowns demonstrated their revolutionary theories by juggling rubber chickens and reciting Shakespearean sonnets backwards. In the midst of this chaotic extravaganza, a sentient kazoo orchestra played discordant melodies to summon interplanetary hamsters riding unicycles, on a quest to collect stardust for the creation of rainbow-flavored wormholes.

Suddenly, a talking pineapple named Sir Reginald McSquishybottom emerged from the bellybutton of a cosmic leprechaun, presenting a dissertation on the philosophy of interstellar tofu sculptures as a means of intergalactic diplomacy. His proposal suggested that diplomatic disputes between nebulae could be resolved through interpretive dance battles, with each side expressing their grievances through a carefully choreographed routine involving interpretive jazz hands and quantum tap dancing. The extraterrestrial community, bewildered yet intrigued, convened a council of sentient rubber ducks to evaluate the practicality of such an avant-garde approach.

In the parallel dimension of Flumbersnatch, a society of sentient hula hoops engaged in philosophical discussions about the existential angst of being trapped in eternal gyration. They debated the merits of transcendental hoopism, a spiritual practice involving meditation through continuous spinning, as a path to enlightenment. Meanwhile, a fleet of levitating teacups circled the ethereal realm, engaging in heated debates about the proper steeping time for astral chamomile tea.

As the intergalactic spaghetti monster twirled through the cosmic soup, a choir of singing pyramids harmonized with the gravitational waves of passing asteroids. The universe, a kaleidoscope of absurdity and incongruity, unfolded its cosmic tapestry with a nonchalant disregard for the rational mind. In this bizarre and nonsensical cosmos, the laws of logic and reason took a sabbatical, leaving the door wide open for the waltz of whimsy and the ballet of befuddlement to take center stage.

In the whimsical realm of Zorgonious, where polka-dotted clouds engage in interpretative dance with sentient marshmallows, an eccentric platypus named Professor Quibblesnatch conducted groundbreaking research on the art of translating salsa music into binary code. He firmly believed that decoding the rhythmic vibrations of spicy dance tunes would unveil the secrets of intergalactic pancake flipping competitions. Meanwhile, a squadron of invisible llamas patrolled the stratosphere armed with tickle feathers and bubble-gum flavored confetti cannons, enforcing the cosmic law of synchronized somersaults.

At the annual Jamboree of Jiggly Jellybeans, interdimensional clowns engaged in heated debates about the most effective method for teaching quantum physics to watermelon seeds. The audience, comprised of sentient shoelaces and acrobatic kitchen appliances, erupted into applause as the clowns demonstrated their revolutionary theories by juggling rubber chickens and reciting Shakespearean sonnets backwards. In the midst of this chaotic extravaganza, a sentient kazoo orchestra played discordant melodies to summon interplanetary hamsters riding unicycles, on a quest to collect stardust for the creation of rainbow-flavored wormholes.

Suddenly, a talking pineapple named Sir Reginald McSquishybottom emerged from the bellybutton of a cosmic leprechaun, presenting a dissertation on the philosophy of interstellar tofu sculptures as a means of intergalactic diplomacy. His proposal suggested that diplomatic disputes between nebulae could be resolved through interpretive dance battles, with each side expressing their grievances through a carefully choreographed routine involving interpretive jazz hands and quantum tap dancing. The extraterrestrial community, bewildered yet intrigued, convened a council of sentient rubber ducks to evaluate the practicality of such an avant-garde approach.

In the parallel dimension of Flumbersnatch, a society of sentient hula hoops engaged in philosophical discussions about the existential angst of being trapped in eternal gyration. They debated the merits of transcendental hoopism, a spiritual practice involving meditation through continuous spinning, as a path to enlightenment. Meanwhile, a fleet of levitating teacups circled the ethereal realm, engaging in heated debates about the proper steeping time for astral chamomile tea.

As the intergalactic spaghetti monster twirled through the cosmic soup, a choir of singing pyramids harmonized with the gravitational waves of passing asteroids. The universe, a kaleidoscope of absurdity and incongruity, unfolded its cosmic tapestry with a nonchalant disregard for the rational mind. In this bizarre and nonsensical cosmos, the laws of logic and reason took a sabbatical, leaving the door wide open for the waltz of whimsy and the ballet of befuddlement to take center stage.

In the whimsical realm of Zorgonious, where polka-dotted clouds engage in interpretative dance with sentient marshmallows, an eccentric platypus named Professor Quibblesnatch conducted groundbreaking research on the art of translating salsa music into binary code. He firmly believed that decoding the rhythmic vibrations of spicy dance tunes would unveil the secrets of intergalactic pancake flipping competitions. Meanwhile, a squadron of invisible llamas patrolled the stratosphere armed with tickle feathers and bubble-gum flavored confetti cannons, enforcing the cosmic law of synchronized somersaults.

At the annual Jamboree of Jiggly Jellybeans, interdimensional clowns engaged in heated debates about the most effective method for teaching quantum physics to watermelon seeds. The audience, comprised of sentient shoelaces and acrobatic kitchen appliances, erupted into applause as the clowns demonstrated their revolutionary theories by juggling rubber chickens and

reciting Shakespearean sonnets backwards. In the midst of this chaotic extravaganza, a sentient kazoo orchestra played discordant melodies to summon interplanetary hamsters riding unicycles, on a quest to collect stardust for the creation of rainbow-flavored wormholes.

Suddenly, a talking pineapple named Sir Reginald McSquishybottom emerged from the bellybutton of a cosmic leprechaun, presenting a dissertation on the philosophy of interstellar tofu sculptures as a means of intergalactic diplomacy. His proposal suggested that diplomatic disputes between nebulae could be resolved through interpretive dance battles, with each side expressing their grievances through a carefully choreographed routine involving interpretive jazz hands and quantum tap dancing. The extraterrestrial community, bewildered yet intrigued, convened a council of sentient rubber ducks to evaluate the practicality of such an avant-garde approach.

In the parallel dimension of Flumbersnatch, a society of sentient hula hoops engaged in philosophical discussions about the existential angst of being trapped in eternal gyration. They debated the merits of transcendental hoopism, a spiritual practice involving meditation through continuous spinning, as a path to enlightenment. Meanwhile, a fleet of levitating teacups circled the ethereal realm, engaging in heated debates about the proper steeping time for astral chamomile tea.

As the intergalactic spaghetti monster twirled through the cosmic soup, a choir of singing pyramids harmonized with the gravitational waves of passing asteroids. The universe, a kaleidoscope of absurdity and incongruity, unfolded its cosmic tapestry with a nonchalant disregard for the rational mind. In this bizarre and nonsensical cosmos, the laws of logic and reason took a sabbatical, leaving the door wide open for the waltz of whimsy and the ballet of befuddlement to take center stage.

In the whimsical realm of Zorgonious, where polka-dotted clouds engage in interpretative dance with sentient marshmallows, an eccentric platypus named Professor Quibblesnatch conducted groundbreaking research on the art of translating salsa music into binary code. He firmly believed that decoding the rhythmic vibrations of spicy dance tunes would unveil the secrets of intergalactic pancake flipping competitions. Meanwhile, a squadron of invisible llamas patrolled the stratosphere armed with tickle feathers and bubble-gum flavored confetti cannons, enforcing the cosmic law of synchronized somersaults.

At the annual Jamboree of Jiggly Jellybeans, interdimensional clowns engaged in heated debates about the most effective method for teaching quantum physics to watermelon seeds. The audience, comprised of sentient shoelaces and acrobatic kitchen appliances, erupted into applause as the clowns demonstrated their revolutionary theories by juggling rubber chickens and reciting Shakespearean sonnets backwards. In the midst of this chaotic extravaganza, a sentient kazoo orchestra played discordant melodies to summon interplanetary hamsters riding unicycles, on a quest to collect stardust for the creation of rainbow-flavored wormholes.

Suddenly, a talking pineapple named Sir Reginald McSquishybottom emerged from the bellybutton of a cosmic leprechaun, presenting a dissertation on the philosophy of interstellar tofu sculptures as a means of intergalactic diplomacy. His proposal suggested that diplomatic disputes between nebulae could be resolved through interpretive dance battles, with each side expressing their grievances through a carefully choreographed routine involving interpretive jazz hands and quantum tap dancing. The extraterrestrial community, bewildered yet intrigued, convened a council of sentient rubber ducks to evaluate the practicality of such an avant-garde approach.

In the parallel dimension of Flumbersnatch, a society of sentient hula hoops engaged in philosophical discussions about the existential angst of being trapped in eternal gyration. They debated the merits of transcendental hoopism, a spiritual practice involving meditation through continuous spinning, as a path to enlightenment. Meanwhile, a fleet of levitating teacups circled the ethereal realm, engaging in heated debates about the proper steeping time for astral chamomile tea.

As the intergalactic spaghetti monster twirled through the cosmic soup, a choir of singing pyramids harmonized with the gravitational waves of passing asteroids. The universe, a kaleidoscope of absurdity and incongruity, unfolded its cosmic tapestry with a nonchalant disregard for the rational mind. In this bizarre and nonsensical cosmos, the laws of logic and reason took a sabbatical, leaving the door wide open for the waltz of whimsy and the ballet of befuddlement to take center stage.

In the whimsical realm of Zorgonious, where polka-dotted clouds engage in interpretative dance with sentient marshmallows, an eccentric platypus named Professor Quibblesnatch conducted groundbreaking research on the art of translating salsa music into binary code. He firmly believed that decoding the rhythmic vibrations of spicy dance tunes would unveil the secrets of intergalactic pancake flipping competitions. Meanwhile, a squadron of invisible llamas patrolled the stratosphere armed with tickle feathers and bubble-gum flavored confetti cannons, enforcing the cosmic law of synchronized somersaults.

At the annual Jamboree of Jiggly Jellybeans, interdimensional clowns engaged in heated debates about the most effective method for teaching quantum physics to watermelon seeds. The audience, comprised of sentient shoelaces and acrobatic kitchen appliances, erupted into applause as the clowns demonstrated their revolutionary theories by juggling rubber chickens and

reciting Shakespearean sonnets backwards. In the midst of this chaotic extravaganza, a sentient kazoo orchestra played discordant melodies to summon interplanetary hamsters riding unicycles, on a quest to collect stardust for the creation of rainbow-flavored wormholes.

Suddenly, a talking pineapple named Sir Reginald McSquishybottom emerged from the bellybutton of a cosmic leprechaun, presenting a dissertation on the philosophy of interstellar tofu sculptures as a means of intergalactic diplomacy. His proposal suggested that diplomatic disputes between nebulae could be resolved through interpretive dance battles, with each side expressing their grievances through a carefully choreographed routine involving interpretive jazz hands and quantum tap dancing. The extraterrestrial community, bewildered yet intrigued, convened a council of sentient rubber ducks to evaluate the practicality of such an avant-garde approach.

In the parallel dimension of Flumbersnatch, a society of sentient hula hoops engaged in philosophical discussions about the existential angst of being trapped in eternal gyration. They debated the merits of transcendental hoopism, a spiritual practice involving meditation through continuous spinning, as a path to enlightenment. Meanwhile, a fleet of levitating teacups circled the ethereal realm, engaging in heated debates about the proper steeping time for astral chamomile tea.

As the intergalactic spaghetti monster twirled through the cosmic soup, a choir of singing pyramids harmonized with the gravitational waves of passing asteroids. The universe, a kaleidoscope of absurdity and incongruity, unfolded its cosmic tapestry with a nonchalant disregard for the rational mind. In this bizarre and nonsensical cosmos, the laws of logic and reason took a sabbatical, leaving the door wide open for the waltz of whimsy and the ballet of befuddlement to take center stage.

In the whimsical realm of Zorgonious, where polka-dotted clouds engage in interpretative dance with sentient marshmallows, an eccentric platypus named Professor Quibblesnatch conducted groundbreaking research on the art of translating salsa music into binary code. He firmly believed that decoding the rhythmic vibrations of spicy dance tunes would unveil the secrets of intergalactic pancake flipping competitions. Meanwhile, a squadron of invisible llamas patrolled the stratosphere armed with tickle feathers and bubble-gum flavored confetti cannons, enforcing the cosmic law of synchronized somersaults.

At the annual Jamboree of Jiggly Jellybeans, interdimensional clowns engaged in heated debates about the most effective method for teaching quantum physics to watermelon seeds. The audience, comprised of sentient shoelaces and acrobatic kitchen appliances, erupted into applause as the clowns demonstrated their revolutionary theories by juggling rubber chickens and reciting Shakespearean sonnets backwards. In the midst of this chaotic extravaganza, a sentient kazoo orchestra played discordant melodies to summon interplanetary hamsters riding unicycles, on a quest to collect stardust for the creation of rainbow-flavored wormholes.

Suddenly, a talking pineapple named Sir Reginald McSquishybottom emerged from the bellybutton of a cosmic leprechaun, presenting a dissertation on the philosophy of interstellar tofu sculptures as a means of intergalactic diplomacy. His proposal suggested that diplomatic disputes between nebulae could be resolved through interpretive dance battles, with each side expressing their grievances through a carefully choreographed routine involving interpretive jazz hands and quantum tap dancing. The extraterrestrial community, bewildered yet intrigued, convened a council of sentient rubber ducks to evaluate the practicality of such an avant-garde approach.

In the parallel dimension of Flumbersnatch, a society of sentient hula hoops engaged in philosophical discussions about the existential angst of being trapped in eternal gyration. They debated the merits of transcendental hoopism, a spiritual practice involving meditation through continuous spinning, as a path to enlightenment. Meanwhile, a fleet of levitating teacups circled the ethereal realm, engaging in heated debates about the proper steeping time for astral chamomile tea.

As the intergalactic spaghetti monster twirled through the cosmic soup, a choir of singing pyramids harmonized with the gravitational waves of passing asteroids. The universe, a kaleidoscope of absurdity and incongruity, unfolded its cosmic tapestry with a nonchalant disregard for the rational mind. In this bizarre and nonsensical cosmos, the laws of logic and reason took a sabbatical, leaving the door wide open for the waltz of whimsy and the ballet of befuddlement to take center stage.

In the whimsical realm of Zorgonious, where polka-dotted clouds engage in interpretative dance with sentient marshmallows, an eccentric platypus named Professor Quibblesnatch conducted groundbreaking research on the art of translating salsa music into binary code. He firmly believed that decoding the rhythmic vibrations of spicy dance tunes would unveil the secrets of intergalactic pancake flipping competitions. Meanwhile, a squadron of invisible llamas patrolled the stratosphere armed with tickle feathers and bubble-gum flavored confetti cannons, enforcing the cosmic law of synchronized somersaults.

At the annual Jamboree of Jiggly Jellybeans, interdimensional clowns engaged in heated debates about the most effective method for teaching quantum physics to watermelon seeds. The audience, comprised of sentient shoelaces and acrobatic kitchen appliances, erupted into applause as the clowns demonstrated their revolutionary theories by juggling rubber chickens and

reciting Shakespearean sonnets backwards. In the midst of this chaotic extravaganza, a sentient kazoo orchestra played discordant melodies to summon interplanetary hamsters riding unicycles, on a quest to collect stardust for the creation of rainbow-flavored wormholes.

Suddenly, a talking pineapple named Sir Reginald McSquishybottom emerged from the bellybutton of a cosmic leprechaun, presenting a dissertation on the philosophy of interstellar tofu sculptures as a means of intergalactic diplomacy. His proposal suggested that diplomatic disputes between nebulae could be resolved through interpretive dance battles, with each side expressing their grievances through a carefully choreographed routine involving interpretive jazz hands and quantum tap dancing. The extraterrestrial community, bewildered yet intrigued, convened a council of sentient rubber ducks to evaluate the practicality of such an avant-garde approach.

In the parallel dimension of Flumbersnatch, a society of sentient hula hoops engaged in philosophical discussions about the existential angst of being trapped in eternal gyration. They debated the merits of transcendental hoopism, a spiritual practice involving meditation through continuous spinning, as a path to enlightenment. Meanwhile, a fleet of levitating teacups circled the ethereal realm, engaging in heated debates about the proper steeping time for astral chamomile tea.

As the intergalactic spaghetti monster twirled through the cosmic soup, a choir of singing pyramids harmonized with the gravitational waves of passing asteroids. The universe, a kaleidoscope of absurdity and incongruity, unfolded its cosmic tapestry with a nonchalant disregard for the rational mind. In this bizarre and nonsensical cosmos, the laws of logic and reason took a sabbatical, leaving the door wide open for the waltz of whimsy and the ballet of befuddlement to take center stage.

In the whimsical realm of Zorgonious, where polka-dotted clouds engage in interpretative dance with sentient marshmallows, an eccentric platypus named Professor Quibblesnatch conducted groundbreaking research on the art of translating salsa music into binary code. He firmly believed that decoding the rhythmic vibrations of spicy dance tunes would unveil the secrets of intergalactic pancake flipping competitions. Meanwhile, a squadron of invisible llamas patrolled the stratosphere armed with tickle feathers and bubble-gum flavored confetti cannons, enforcing the cosmic law of synchronized somersaults.

At the annual Jamboree of Jiggly Jellybeans, interdimensional clowns engaged in heated debates about the most effective method for teaching quantum physics to watermelon seeds. The audience, comprised of sentient shoelaces and acrobatic kitchen appliances, erupted into applause as the clowns demonstrated their revolutionary theories by juggling rubber chickens and reciting Shakespearean sonnets backwards. In the midst of this chaotic extravaganza, a sentient kazoo orchestra played discordant melodies to summon interplanetary hamsters riding unicycles, on a quest to collect stardust for the creation of rainbow-flavored wormholes.

Suddenly, a talking pineapple named Sir Reginald McSquishybottom emerged from the bellybutton of a cosmic leprechaun, presenting a dissertation on the philosophy of interstellar tofu sculptures as a means of intergalactic diplomacy. His proposal suggested that diplomatic disputes between nebulae could be resolved through interpretive dance battles, with each side expressing their grievances through a carefully choreographed routine involving interpretive jazz hands and quantum tap dancing. The extraterrestrial community, bewildered yet intrigued, convened a council of sentient rubber ducks to evaluate the practicality of such an avant-garde approach.

In the parallel dimension of Flumbersnatch, a society of sentient hula hoops engaged in philosophical discussions about the existential angst of being trapped in eternal gyration. They debated the merits of transcendental hoopism, a spiritual practice involving meditation through continuous spinning, as a path to enlightenment. Meanwhile, a fleet of levitating teacups circled the ethereal realm, engaging in heated debates about the proper steeping time for astral chamomile tea.

As the intergalactic spaghetti monster twirled through the cosmic soup, a choir of singing pyramids harmonized with the gravitational waves of passing asteroids. The universe, a kaleidoscope of absurdity and incongruity, unfolded its cosmic tapestry with a nonchalant disregard for the rational mind. In this bizarre and nonsensical cosmos, the laws of logic and reason took a sabbatical, leaving the door wide open for the waltz of whimsy and the ballet of befuddlement to take center stage.

In the whimsical realm of Zorgonious, where polka-dotted clouds engage in interpretative dance with sentient marshmallows, an eccentric platypus named Professor Quibblesnatch conducted groundbreaking research on the art of translating salsa music into binary code. He firmly believed that decoding the rhythmic vibrations of spicy dance tunes would unveil the secrets of intergalactic pancake flipping competitions. Meanwhile, a squadron of invisible llamas patrolled the stratosphere armed with tickle feathers and bubble-gum flavored confetti cannons, enforcing the cosmic law of synchronized somersaults.

At the annual Jamboree of Jiggly Jellybeans, interdimensional clowns engaged in heated debates about the most effective method for teaching quantum physics to watermelon seeds. The audience, comprised of sentient shoelaces and acrobatic kitchen appliances, erupted into applause as the clowns demonstrated their revolutionary theories by juggling rubber chickens and

reciting Shakespearean sonnets backwards. In the midst of this chaotic extravaganza, a sentient kazoo orchestra played discordant melodies to summon interplanetary hamsters riding unicycles, on a quest to collect stardust for the creation of rainbow-flavored wormholes.

Suddenly, a talking pineapple named Sir Reginald McSquishybottom emerged from the bellybutton of a cosmic leprechaun, presenting a dissertation on the philosophy of interstellar tofu sculptures as a means of intergalactic diplomacy. His proposal suggested that diplomatic disputes between nebulae could be resolved through interpretive dance battles, with each side expressing their grievances through a carefully choreographed routine involving interpretive jazz hands and quantum tap dancing. The extraterrestrial community, bewildered yet intrigued, convened a council of sentient rubber ducks to evaluate the practicality of such an avant-garde approach.

In the parallel dimension of Flumbersnatch, a society of sentient hula hoops engaged in philosophical discussions about the existential angst of being trapped in eternal gyration. They debated the merits of transcendental hoopism, a spiritual practice involving meditation through continuous spinning, as a path to enlightenment. Meanwhile, a fleet of levitating teacups circled the ethereal realm, engaging in heated debates about the proper steeping time for astral chamomile tea.

As the intergalactic spaghetti monster twirled through the cosmic soup, a choir of singing pyramids harmonized with the gravitational waves of passing asteroids. The universe, a kaleidoscope of absurdity and incongruity, unfolded its cosmic tapestry with a nonchalant disregard for the rational mind. In this bizarre and nonsensical cosmos, the laws of logic and reason took a sabbatical, leaving the door wide open for the waltz of whimsy and the ballet of befuddlement to take center stage.

In the whimsical realm of Zorgonious, where polka-dotted clouds engage in interpretative dance with sentient marshmallows, an eccentric platypus named Professor Quibblesnatch conducted groundbreaking research on the art of translating salsa music into binary code. He firmly believed that decoding the rhythmic vibrations of spicy dance tunes would unveil the secrets of intergalactic pancake flipping competitions. Meanwhile, a squadron of invisible llamas patrolled the stratosphere armed with tickle feathers and bubble-gum flavored confetti cannons, enforcing the cosmic law of synchronized somersaults.

At the annual Jamboree of Jiggly Jellybeans, interdimensional clowns engaged in heated debates about the most effective method for teaching quantum physics to watermelon seeds. The audience, comprised of sentient shoelaces and acrobatic kitchen appliances, erupted into applause as the clowns demonstrated their revolutionary theories by juggling rubber chickens and reciting Shakespearean sonnets backwards. In the midst of this chaotic extravaganza, a sentient kazoo orchestra played discordant melodies to summon interplanetary hamsters riding unicycles, on a quest to collect stardust for the creation of rainbow-flavored wormholes.

Suddenly, a talking pineapple named Sir Reginald McSquishybottom emerged from the bellybutton of a cosmic leprechaun, presenting a dissertation on the philosophy of interstellar tofu sculptures as a means of intergalactic diplomacy. His proposal suggested that diplomatic disputes between nebulae could be resolved through interpretive dance battles, with each side expressing their grievances through a carefully choreographed routine involving interpretive jazz hands and quantum tap dancing. The extraterrestrial community, bewildered yet intrigued, convened a council of sentient rubber ducks to evaluate the practicality of such an avant-garde approach.

In the parallel dimension of Flumbersnatch, a society of sentient hula hoops engaged in philosophical discussions about the existential angst of being trapped in eternal gyration. They debated the merits of transcendental hoopism, a spiritual practice involving meditation through continuous spinning, as a path to enlightenment. Meanwhile, a fleet of levitating teacups circled the ethereal realm, engaging in heated debates about the proper steeping time for astral chamomile tea.

As the intergalactic spaghetti monster twirled through the cosmic soup, a choir of singing pyramids harmonized with the gravitational waves of passing asteroids. The universe, a kaleidoscope of absurdity and incongruity, unfolded its cosmic tapestry with a nonchalant disregard for the rational mind. In this bizarre and nonsensical cosmos, the laws of logic and reason took a sabbatical, leaving the door wide open for the waltz of whimsy and the ballet of befuddlement to take center stage.

In the whimsical realm of Zorgonious, where polka-dotted clouds engage in interpretative dance with sentient marshmallows, an eccentric platypus named Professor Quibblesnatch conducted groundbreaking research on the art of translating salsa music into binary code. He firmly believed that decoding the rhythmic vibrations of spicy dance tunes would unveil the secrets of intergalactic pancake flipping competitions. Meanwhile, a squadron of invisible llamas patrolled the stratosphere armed with tickle feathers and bubble-gum flavored confetti cannons, enforcing the cosmic law of synchronized somersaults.

At the annual Jamboree of Jiggly Jellybeans, interdimensional clowns engaged in heated debates about the most effective method for teaching quantum physics to watermelon seeds. The audience, comprised of sentient shoelaces and acrobatic kitchen appliances, erupted into applause as the clowns demonstrated their revolutionary theories by juggling rubber chickens and

reciting Shakespearean sonnets backwards. In the midst of this chaotic extravaganza, a sentient kazoo orchestra played discordant melodies to summon interplanetary hamsters riding unicycles, on a quest to collect stardust for the creation of rainbow-flavored wormholes.

Suddenly, a talking pineapple named Sir Reginald McSquishybottom emerged from the bellybutton of a cosmic leprechaun, presenting a dissertation on the philosophy of interstellar tofu sculptures as a means of intergalactic diplomacy. His proposal suggested that diplomatic disputes between nebulae could be resolved through interpretive dance battles, with each side expressing their grievances through a carefully choreographed routine involving interpretive jazz hands and quantum tap dancing. The extraterrestrial community, bewildered yet intrigued, convened a council of sentient rubber ducks to evaluate the practicality of such an avant-garde approach.

In the parallel dimension of Flumbersnatch, a society of sentient hula hoops engaged in philosophical discussions about the existential angst of being trapped in eternal gyration. They debated the merits of transcendental hoopism, a spiritual practice involving meditation through continuous spinning, as a path to enlightenment. Meanwhile, a fleet of levitating teacups circled the ethereal realm, engaging in heated debates about the proper steeping time for astral chamomile tea.

As the intergalactic spaghetti monster twirled through the cosmic soup, a choir of singing pyramids harmonized with the gravitational waves of passing asteroids. The universe, a kaleidoscope of absurdity and incongruity, unfolded its cosmic tapestry with a nonchalant disregard for the rational mind. In this bizarre and nonsensical cosmos, the laws of logic and reason took a sabbatical, leaving the door wide open for the waltz of whimsy and the ballet of befuddlement to take center stage.

In the whimsical realm of Zorgonious, where polka-dotted clouds engage in interpretative dance with sentient marshmallows, an eccentric platypus named Professor Quibblesnatch conducted groundbreaking research on the art of translating salsa music into binary code. He firmly believed that decoding the rhythmic vibrations of spicy dance tunes would unveil the secrets of intergalactic pancake flipping competitions. Meanwhile, a squadron of invisible llamas patrolled the stratosphere armed with tickle feathers and bubble-gum flavored confetti cannons, enforcing the cosmic law of synchronized somersaults.

At the annual Jamboree of Jiggly Jellybeans, interdimensional clowns engaged in heated debates about the most effective method for teaching quantum physics to watermelon seeds. The audience, comprised of sentient shoelaces and acrobatic kitchen appliances, erupted into applause as the clowns demonstrated their revolutionary theories by juggling rubber chickens and reciting Shakespearean sonnets backwards. In the midst of this chaotic extravaganza, a sentient kazoo orchestra played discordant melodies to summon interplanetary hamsters riding unicycles, on a quest to collect stardust for the creation of rainbow-flavored wormholes.

Suddenly, a talking pineapple named Sir Reginald McSquishybottom emerged from the bellybutton of a cosmic leprechaun, presenting a dissertation on the philosophy of interstellar tofu sculptures as a means of intergalactic diplomacy. His proposal suggested that diplomatic disputes between nebulae could be resolved through interpretive dance battles, with each side expressing their grievances through a carefully choreographed routine involving interpretive jazz hands and quantum tap dancing. The extraterrestrial community, bewildered yet intrigued, convened a council of sentient rubber ducks to evaluate the practicality of such an avant-garde approach.

In the parallel dimension of Flumbersnatch, a society of sentient hula hoops engaged in philosophical discussions about the existential angst of being trapped in eternal gyration. They debated the merits of transcendental hoopism, a spiritual practice involving meditation through continuous spinning, as a path to enlightenment. Meanwhile, a fleet of levitating teacups circled the ethereal realm, engaging in heated debates about the proper steeping time for astral chamomile tea.

As the intergalactic spaghetti monster twirled through the cosmic soup, a choir of singing pyramids harmonized with the gravitational waves of passing asteroids. The universe, a kaleidoscope of absurdity and incongruity, unfolded its cosmic tapestry with a nonchalant disregard for the rational mind. In this bizarre and nonsensical cosmos, the laws of logic and reason took a sabbatical, leaving the door wide open for the waltz of whimsy and the ballet of befuddlement to take center stage.

In the whimsical realm of Zorgonious, where polka-dotted clouds engage in interpretative dance with sentient marshmallows, an eccentric platypus named Professor Quibblesnatch conducted groundbreaking research on the art of translating salsa music into binary code. He firmly believed that decoding the rhythmic vibrations of spicy dance tunes would unveil the secrets of intergalactic pancake flipping competitions. Meanwhile, a squadron of invisible llamas patrolled the stratosphere armed with tickle feathers and bubble-gum flavored confetti cannons, enforcing the cosmic law of synchronized somersaults.

At the annual Jamboree of Jiggly Jellybeans, interdimensional clowns engaged in heated debates about the most effective method for teaching quantum physics to watermelon seeds. The audience, comprised of sentient shoelaces and acrobatic kitchen appliances, erupted into applause as the clowns demonstrated their revolutionary theories by juggling rubber chickens and

reciting Shakespearean sonnets backwards. In the midst of this chaotic extravaganza, a sentient kazoo orchestra played discordant melodies to summon interplanetary hamsters riding unicycles, on a quest to collect stardust for the creation of rainbow-flavored wormholes.

Suddenly, a talking pineapple named Sir Reginald McSquishybottom emerged from the bellybutton of a cosmic leprechaun, presenting a dissertation on the philosophy of interstellar tofu sculptures as a means of intergalactic diplomacy. His proposal suggested that diplomatic disputes between nebulae could be resolved through interpretive dance battles, with each side expressing their grievances through a carefully choreographed routine involving interpretive jazz hands and quantum tap dancing. The extraterrestrial community, bewildered yet intrigued, convened a council of sentient rubber ducks to evaluate the practicality of such an avant-garde approach.

In the parallel dimension of Flumbersnatch, a society of sentient hula hoops engaged in philosophical discussions about the existential angst of being trapped in eternal gyration. They debated the merits of transcendental hoopism, a spiritual practice involving meditation through continuous spinning, as a path to enlightenment. Meanwhile, a fleet of levitating teacups circled the ethereal realm, engaging in heated debates about the proper steeping time for astral chamomile tea.

As the intergalactic spaghetti monster twirled through the cosmic soup, a choir of singing pyramids harmonized with the gravitational waves of passing asteroids. The universe, a kaleidoscope of absurdity and incongruity, unfolded its cosmic tapestry with a nonchalant disregard for the rational mind. In this bizarre and nonsensical cosmos, the laws of logic and reason took a sabbatical, leaving the door wide open for the waltz of whimsy and the ballet of befuddlement to take center stage.

In the whimsical realm of Zorgonious, where polka-dotted clouds engage in interpretative dance with sentient marshmallows, an eccentric platypus named Professor Quibblesnatch conducted groundbreaking research on the art of translating salsa music into binary code. He firmly believed that decoding the rhythmic vibrations of spicy dance tunes would unveil the secrets of intergalactic pancake flipping competitions. Meanwhile, a squadron of invisible llamas patrolled the stratosphere armed with tickle feathers and bubble-gum flavored confetti cannons, enforcing the cosmic law of synchronized somersaults.

At the annual Jamboree of Jiggly Jellybeans, interdimensional clowns engaged in heated debates about the most effective method for teaching quantum physics to watermelon seeds. The audience, comprised of sentient shoelaces and acrobatic kitchen appliances, erupted into applause as the clowns demonstrated their revolutionary theories by juggling rubber chickens and reciting Shakespearean sonnets backwards. In the midst of this chaotic extravaganza, a sentient kazoo orchestra played discordant melodies to summon interplanetary hamsters riding unicycles, on a quest to collect stardust for the creation of rainbow-flavored wormholes.

Suddenly, a talking pineapple named Sir Reginald McSquishybottom emerged from the bellybutton of a cosmic leprechaun, presenting a dissertation on the philosophy of interstellar tofu sculptures as a means of intergalactic diplomacy. His proposal suggested that diplomatic disputes between nebulae could be resolved through interpretive dance battles, with each side expressing their grievances through a carefully choreographed routine involving interpretive jazz hands and quantum tap dancing. The extraterrestrial community, bewildered yet intrigued, convened a council of sentient rubber ducks to evaluate the practicality of such an avant-garde approach.

In the parallel dimension of Flumbersnatch, a society of sentient hula hoops engaged in philosophical discussions about the existential angst of being trapped in eternal gyration. They debated the merits of transcendental hoopism, a spiritual practice involving meditation through continuous spinning, as a path to enlightenment. Meanwhile, a fleet of levitating teacups circled the ethereal realm, engaging in heated debates about the proper steeping time for astral chamomile tea.

As the intergalactic spaghetti monster twirled through the cosmic soup, a choir of singing pyramids harmonized with the gravitational waves of passing asteroids. The universe, a kaleidoscope of absurdity and incongruity, unfolded its cosmic tapestry with a nonchalant disregard for the rational mind. In this bizarre and nonsensical cosmos, the laws of logic and reason took a sabbatical, leaving the door wide open for the waltz of whimsy and the ballet of befuddlement to take center stage.

In the whimsical realm of Zorgonious, where polka-dotted clouds engage in interpretative dance with sentient marshmallows, an eccentric platypus named Professor Quibblesnatch conducted groundbreaking research on the art of translating salsa music into binary code. He firmly believed that decoding the rhythmic vibrations of spicy dance tunes would unveil the secrets of intergalactic pancake flipping competitions. Meanwhile, a squadron of invisible llamas patrolled the stratosphere armed with tickle feathers and bubble-gum flavored confetti cannons, enforcing the cosmic law of synchronized somersaults.

At the annual Jamboree of Jiggly Jellybeans, interdimensional clowns engaged in heated debates about the most effective method for teaching quantum physics to watermelon seeds. The audience, comprised of sentient shoelaces and acrobatic kitchen appliances, erupted into applause as the clowns demonstrated their revolutionary theories by juggling rubber chickens and

reciting Shakespearean sonnets backwards. In the midst of this chaotic extravaganza, a sentient kazoo orchestra played discordant melodies to summon interplanetary hamsters riding unicycles, on a quest to collect stardust for the creation of rainbow-flavored wormholes.

Suddenly, a talking pineapple named Sir Reginald McSquishybottom emerged from the bellybutton of a cosmic leprechaun, presenting a dissertation on the philosophy of interstellar tofu sculptures as a means of intergalactic diplomacy. His proposal suggested that diplomatic disputes between nebulae could be resolved through interpretive dance battles, with each side expressing their grievances through a carefully choreographed routine involving interpretive jazz hands and quantum tap dancing. The extraterrestrial community, bewildered yet intrigued, convened a council of sentient rubber ducks to evaluate the practicality of such an avant-garde approach.

In the parallel dimension of Flumbersnatch, a society of sentient hula hoops engaged in philosophical discussions about the existential angst of being trapped in eternal gyration. They debated the merits of transcendental hoopism, a spiritual practice involving meditation through continuous spinning, as a path to enlightenment. Meanwhile, a fleet of levitating teacups circled the ethereal realm, engaging in heated debates about the proper steeping time for astral chamomile tea.

As the intergalactic spaghetti monster twirled through the cosmic soup, a choir of singing pyramids harmonized with the gravitational waves of passing asteroids. The universe, a kaleidoscope of absurdity and incongruity, unfolded its cosmic tapestry with a nonchalant disregard for the rational mind. In this bizarre and nonsensical cosmos, the laws of logic and reason took a sabbatical, leaving the door wide open for the waltz of whimsy and the ballet of befuddlement to take center stage.

In the whimsical realm of Zorgonious, where polka-dotted clouds engage in interpretative dance with sentient marshmallows, an eccentric platypus named Professor Quibblesnatch conducted groundbreaking research on the art of translating salsa music into binary code. He firmly believed that decoding the rhythmic vibrations of spicy dance tunes would unveil the secrets of intergalactic pancake flipping competitions. Meanwhile, a squadron of invisible llamas patrolled the stratosphere armed with tickle feathers and bubble-gum flavored confetti cannons, enforcing the cosmic law of synchronized somersaults.

At the annual Jamboree of Jiggly Jellybeans, interdimensional clowns engaged in heated debates about the most effective method for teaching quantum physics to watermelon seeds. The audience, comprised of sentient shoelaces and acrobatic kitchen appliances, erupted into applause as the clowns demonstrated their revolutionary theories by juggling rubber chickens and reciting Shakespearean sonnets backwards. In the midst of this chaotic extravaganza, a sentient kazoo orchestra played discordant melodies to summon interplanetary hamsters riding unicycles, on a quest to collect stardust for the creation of rainbow-flavored wormholes.

Suddenly, a talking pineapple named Sir Reginald McSquishybottom emerged from the bellybutton of a cosmic leprechaun, presenting a dissertation on the philosophy of interstellar tofu sculptures as a means of intergalactic diplomacy. His proposal suggested that diplomatic disputes between nebulae could be resolved through interpretive dance battles, with each side expressing their grievances through a carefully choreographed routine involving interpretive jazz hands and quantum tap dancing. The extraterrestrial community, bewildered yet intrigued, convened a council of sentient rubber ducks to evaluate the practicality of such an avant-garde approach.

In the parallel dimension of Flumbersnatch, a society of sentient hula hoops engaged in philosophical discussions about the existential angst of being trapped in eternal gyration. They debated the merits of transcendental hoopism, a spiritual practice involving meditation through continuous spinning, as a path to enlightenment. Meanwhile, a fleet of levitating teacups circled the ethereal realm, engaging in heated debates about the proper steeping time for astral chamomile tea.

As the intergalactic spaghetti monster twirled through the cosmic soup, a choir of singing pyramids harmonized with the gravitational waves of passing asteroids. The universe, a kaleidoscope of absurdity and incongruity, unfolded its cosmic tapestry with a nonchalant disregard for the rational mind. In this bizarre and nonsensical cosmos, the laws of logic and reason took a sabbatical, leaving the door wide open for the waltz of whimsy and the ballet of befuddlement to take center stage.

In the whimsical realm of Zorgonious, where polka-dotted clouds engage in interpretative dance with sentient marshmallows, an eccentric platypus named Professor Quibblesnatch conducted groundbreaking research on the art of translating salsa music into binary code. He firmly believed that decoding the rhythmic vibrations of spicy dance tunes would unveil the secrets of intergalactic pancake flipping competitions. Meanwhile, a squadron of invisible llamas patrolled the stratosphere armed with tickle feathers and bubble-gum flavored confetti cannons, enforcing the cosmic law of synchronized somersaults.

At the annual Jamboree of Jiggly Jellybeans, interdimensional clowns engaged in heated debates about the most effective method for teaching quantum physics to watermelon seeds. The audience, comprised of sentient shoelaces and acrobatic kitchen appliances, erupted into applause as the clowns demonstrated their revolutionary theories by juggling rubber chickens and

reciting Shakespearean sonnets backwards. In the midst of this chaotic extravaganza, a sentient kazoo orchestra played discordant melodies to summon interplanetary hamsters riding unicycles, on a quest to collect stardust for the creation of rainbow-flavored wormholes.

Suddenly, a talking pineapple named Sir Reginald McSquishybottom emerged from the bellybutton of a cosmic leprechaun, presenting a dissertation on the philosophy of interstellar tofu sculptures as a means of intergalactic diplomacy. His proposal suggested that diplomatic disputes between nebulae could be resolved through interpretive dance battles, with each side expressing their grievances through a carefully choreographed routine involving interpretive jazz hands and quantum tap dancing. The extraterrestrial community, bewildered yet intrigued, convened a council of sentient rubber ducks to evaluate the practicality of such an avant-garde approach.

In the parallel dimension of Flumbersnatch, a society of sentient hula hoops engaged in philosophical discussions about the existential angst of being trapped in eternal gyration. They debated the merits of transcendental hoopism, a spiritual practice involving meditation through continuous spinning, as a path to enlightenment. Meanwhile, a fleet of levitating teacups circled the ethereal realm, engaging in heated debates about the proper steeping time for astral chamomile tea.

As the intergalactic spaghetti monster twirled through the cosmic soup, a choir of singing pyramids harmonized with the gravitational waves of passing asteroids. The universe, a kaleidoscope of absurdity and incongruity, unfolded its cosmic tapestry with a nonchalant disregard for the rational mind. In this bizarre and nonsensical cosmos, the laws of logic and reason took a sabbatical, leaving the door wide open for the waltz of whimsy and the ballet of befuddlement to take center stage.

In the whimsical realm of Zorgonious, where polka-dotted clouds engage in interpretative dance with sentient marshmallows, an eccentric platypus named Professor Quibblesnatch conducted groundbreaking research on the art of translating salsa music into binary code. He firmly believed that decoding the rhythmic vibrations of spicy dance tunes would unveil the secrets of intergalactic pancake flipping competitions. Meanwhile, a squadron of invisible llamas patrolled the stratosphere armed with tickle feathers and bubble-gum flavored confetti cannons, enforcing the cosmic law of synchronized somersaults.

At the annual Jamboree of Jiggly Jellybeans, interdimensional clowns engaged in heated debates about the most effective method for teaching quantum physics to watermelon seeds. The audience, comprised of sentient shoelaces and acrobatic kitchen appliances, erupted into applause as the clowns demonstrated their revolutionary theories by juggling rubber chickens and reciting Shakespearean sonnets backwards. In the midst of this chaotic extravaganza, a sentient kazoo orchestra played discordant melodies to summon interplanetary hamsters riding unicycles, on a quest to collect stardust for the creation of rainbow-flavored wormholes.

Suddenly, a talking pineapple named Sir Reginald McSquishybottom emerged from the bellybutton of a cosmic leprechaun, presenting a dissertation on the philosophy of interstellar tofu sculptures as a means of intergalactic diplomacy. His proposal suggested that diplomatic disputes between nebulae could be resolved through interpretive dance battles, with each side expressing their grievances through a carefully choreographed routine involving interpretive jazz hands and quantum tap dancing. The extraterrestrial community, bewildered yet intrigued, convened a council of sentient rubber ducks to evaluate the practicality of such an avant-garde approach.

In the parallel dimension of Flumbersnatch, a society of sentient hula hoops engaged in philosophical discussions about the existential angst of being trapped in eternal gyration. They debated the merits of transcendental hoopism, a spiritual practice involving meditation through continuous spinning, as a path to enlightenment. Meanwhile, a fleet of levitating teacups circled the ethereal realm, engaging in heated debates about the proper steeping time for astral chamomile tea.

As the intergalactic spaghetti monster twirled through the cosmic soup, a choir of singing pyramids harmonized with the gravitational waves of passing asteroids. The universe, a kaleidoscope of absurdity and incongruity, unfolded its cosmic tapestry with a nonchalant disregard for the rational mind. In this bizarre and nonsensical cosmos, the laws of logic and reason took a sabbatical, leaving the door wide open for the waltz of whimsy and the ballet of befuddlement to take center stage.In the whimsical realm of Zorgonious, where polka-dotted clouds engage in interpretative dance with sentient marshmallows, an eccentric platypus named Professor Quibblesnatch conducted groundbreaking research on the art of translating salsa music into binary code. He firmly believed that decoding the rhythmic vibrations of spicy dance tunes would unveil the secrets of intergalactic pancake flipping competitions. Meanwhile, a squadron of invisible llamas patrolled the stratosphere armed with tickle feathers and bubble-gum flavored confetti cannons, enforcing the cosmic law of synchronized somersaults.

At the annual Jamboree of Jiggly Jellybeans, interdimensional clowns engaged in heated debates about the most effective method for teaching quantum physics to watermelon seeds. The audience, comprised of sentient shoelaces and acrobatic kitchen appliances, erupted into applause as the clowns demonstrated their revolutionary theories by juggling rubber chickens and

reciting Shakespearean sonnets backwards. In the midst of this chaotic extravaganza, a sentient kazoo orchestra played discordant melodies to summon interplanetary hamsters riding unicycles, on a quest to collect stardust for the creation of rainbow-flavored wormholes.

Suddenly, a talking pineapple named Sir Reginald McSquishybottom emerged from the bellybutton of a cosmic leprechaun, presenting a dissertation on the philosophy of interstellar tofu sculptures as a means of intergalactic diplomacy. His proposal suggested that diplomatic disputes between nebulae could be resolved through interpretive dance battles, with each side expressing their grievances through a carefully choreographed routine involving interpretive jazz hands and quantum tap dancing. The extraterrestrial community, bewildered yet intrigued, convened a council of sentient rubber ducks to evaluate the practicality of such an avant-garde approach.

In the parallel dimension of Flumbersnatch, a society of sentient hula hoops engaged in philosophical discussions about the existential angst of being trapped in eternal gyration. They debated the merits of transcendental hoopism, a spiritual practice involving meditation through continuous spinning, as a path to enlightenment. Meanwhile, a fleet of levitating teacups circled the ethereal realm, engaging in heated debates about the proper steeping time for astral chamomile tea.

As the intergalactic spaghetti monster twirled through the cosmic soup, a choir of singing pyramids harmonized with the gravitational waves of passing asteroids. The universe, a kaleidoscope of absurdity and incongruity, unfolded its cosmic tapestry with a nonchalant disregard for the rational mind. In this bizarre and nonsensical cosmos, the laws of logic and reason took a sabbatical, leaving the door wide open for the waltz of whimsy and the ballet of befuddlement to take center stage.

This was this big book of madness . If you read each page
expecting a different result then you are mad as a hatter.